NETWORKING PUTINISM

NETWORKING PUTINISM

The Rhetoric of Power
in the Digital Age

Michael S. Gorham

CORNELL UNIVERSITY PRESS   ITHACA AND LONDON

First published 2026 by Cornell University Press

Librarians: A CIP catalog record for this book is available from the Library of Congress.

ISBN 9781501785429 (hardcover)
ISBN 9781501785436 (paperback)
ISBN 9781501785443 (pdf)
ISBN 9781501785412 (epub)

GPSR EU contact: Sam Thornton, Mare Nostrum Group B.V., Mauritskade 21D, 1091 GC, Amsterdam, NL, gpsr@mare-nostrum.co.uk.

For Veronika, Anna, and Jakob

and

in loving memory of William H. Gorham (1933–2015)

Contents

Note on Transliteration and Translation

Throughout this book, I have transliterated Russian according to the Library of Congress system, except where established English spellings of names and place-names exist (e.g., Dmitry Medvedev rather than Dmitrii Medvedev, Alexei Navalny rather than Aleksei Naval'nyi).

All translations are my own unless otherwise stated.

NETWORKING PUTINISM

POLITICAL LANGUAGE AND AUTHORITY IN THE DIGITAL AGE

> **A technology is produced within a culture, and a society is conditioned by its technologies. *Conditioned*, not determined.**
>
> —Pierre Lévy (2001)

On 23 August 2023, exactly two months after his aborted mutinous march on Moscow, the head of the Wagner private military group, Evgeny Prigozhin, met his maker after his private jet careened out of control and crashed into an open field en route from Moscow to St. Petersburg. Although an official cause of the crash was never publicized and has yet to be determined, multiple sources suggest the plane fell due to an onboard explosion, likely the result of an assassination planned by Nikolai Patrushev, head of the National Security Council and loyal confidant of Vladimir Putin (Grove et al. 2023).[1]

Six months later, on 16 February 2024, the politician and opposition leader Alexei Navalny collapsed and lost consciousness after feeling unwell following a walk in the high-security prison where he had been held; he died in the hospital after attempts to revive him failed. Though medical reports attributed the death to either blood clots or "sudden death syndrome," the fact that Navalny had been subjected to 295 days of solitary confinement in paltry conditions made it all but certain that it was Putin and his regime who were responsible for his death (Navalny 2024, 280).

One Internet, Two Murders

In the political cosmos of Putin-era Russia, Prigozhin and Navalny could hardly have featured two more different biographies: Navalny was an eloquent, charismatic,

---

1. Putin, for his part, publicly embraced a theory involving the onboard explosion of a grenade, perhaps with the nefarious involvement of illegal narcotics trafficking (Kagaltynov 2023).

legally trained oppositional politician and corruption fighter from Moscow, who, as an early adopter of social media, had made a name for himself by producing web-based exposés of high-level government corruption. He then leveraged that skill to mobilize citizens in real time to rally against state-sponsored corruption and election fraud. For his efforts, Navalny was poisoned by a deadly nerve agent; convicted of fraud, extremism, and terrorism; and sentenced to nineteen years in a high-security prison.

Prigozhin, by contrast, was a rough-and-tumble ex-con from St. Petersburg, a college drop-out who used his entrepreneurial skills and street smarts to enter Putin's circle of trust. He worked first as caterer to the Kremlin and other state institutions (which earned him the moniker "Putin's chef")[2] and then went on to serve as Putin's go-to "fixer" and master of media manipulation, heading up the infamous "Russian troll factory" and, later, the Patriot Media Group, a conglomerate of web-based news outlets designed to promote pro-Kremlin propaganda. As with many among the power elite, Prigozhin preferred to keep a low public profile throughout most of his career, until Russia's full-scale invasion of Ukraine in February 2022 and Wagner's instrumental role in it brought him out of the woodwork and into the limelight. With the help of a robust media team and a coarse, straight-talking communication style, Prigozhin quickly established a formidable following on the Telegram social networking platform, after joining it in September 2022. "Turbo-patriots" disgruntled with the Russian military brass's clumsy prosecution of the war flocked to his channel to take in his low-register, hi-fidelity videos trumpeting Wagner's feats and frustrations. For *his* efforts—until his August 2023 fatal plane crash—Prigozhin had amassed a personal wealth estimated at $1 billion and received over a dozen medals of honor, including the highest Hero of the Russian Federation award in June 2022 (Plamenev 2022).

Despite their diametrically opposed political profiles, however, Navalny and Prigozhin share striking similarities for the purposes of this study of how new media technologies have influenced and been shaped by political language and authority in contemporary Russia. First, though they were on opposite ends of the political spectrum, neither man would have attained the national and even global notoriety he did were it not for his ability to command a rhetorical presence on digital media. (Neither had much, if any, access to the state-controlled television airwaves.) Second, both played a central role in giving shape to the political language and culture of the Russian internet, though they used quite

---

2. Prigozhin would later claim he never worked for Putin "or anyone," other than while in prison, and that the nickname had been coined by his nemesis, Navalny ("Evgenii Prigozhin v Telegram," 3 February 2023. https://t.me/chvk_wagnerr/2783).

different methods in doing so. Whereas Navalny primarily engaged in debate and investigation, Prigozhin, through the greater part of his career, specialized in disruption and misinformation. Finally, and perhaps most curiously, despite the different treatments they received by the state through the greater part of their careers (one labeled a "terrorist," the other a "hero"), both ultimately fell afoul of that state's supreme authority, primarily due to their ability to harness new media technologies to garner political authority. And both were permanently silenced as a result: One was locked up, the other shot down, each ultimately perishing at the hands of the Putin regime.

In this book, I examine more closely how Navalny, Prigozhin, and dozens of other public political actors and institutions negotiated the emergence of new and dynamic digital communication technologies in order to create, protect, and challenge political authority, looking more specifically at how networked language and communication helped reshape political realities. Given the coincidental confluence of Putin's rise to power with the emergence of the Russian-language internet or "Runet," as it's commonly called, I focus primarily on the rhetorical strategies deployed by the ruling political and cultural elite to secure, solidify, and protect the Putin regime in a volatile communicative environment, and even harness new media technologies to frame, promote, and codify its own authority.

Language and Politics

Observers since the time of the ancient Greeks have remarked on the mutually infused relationship between language and politics. Aristotle's claim that "obviously man is a political animal" has enjoyed wide circulation since the philosopher penned it in his *Nicomachean Ethics*; fewer have noted the claim's direct link to language and speech: "Nature," he continues, "does nothing without some purpose; and she has endowed man alone among the animals with the power of speech" (Chilton 2004, 5).

Sociolinguist John Joseph (2006, 17–18) expresses a similar sentiment about the essentially political nature of language itself, writing that "language is political from top to bottom . . . Every act of language is *potentially* political, in that, even if I do not have conscious political motivations in making a given utterance, it is still capable of positioning me in a particular way vis-à-vis my hearer or reader, who may infer that I had motivations I didn't know I had. They may even be right."

Other scholars focus more specifically on the social and political dynamics underlying the assigning or ascription of power and authority in public discourse.

Pierre Bourdieu (1991, 12–18) describes language cultures in which the confluence of communicative fields and dispositions gives rise to a commonly recognized but "unequally distributed" symbolic power or "linguistic capital" ascribed to manners of speaking and writing among the political and cultural elite. Similarly, Norman Fairclough (1989, 1) argues that language plays a fundamental role in the "production, maintenance, and change of social relations of power . . . and particularly of how language contributes to the domination of some people by others." This idea of the power of public language and domination through language—the inevitable "asymmetries between participants in discourse events, and . . . unequal capacity to control how texts are produced, distributed and consumed"—lies at the foundation of critical discourse analysis (Fairclough 1995, 1–2). Teun van Dijk points out an additional key to understanding the power dynamics of political discourse, arguing that political power is based on control of and authority over scarce resources, resources that are both material and symbolic. Public discourse is among the most powerful of symbolic resources: "Much of political power may safely be operationalized in terms of the means and patterns of access and control of politicians, parties or political movements over public discourse" (van Dijk 1997, 44). Political rhetoric, at least as I understand it in this study, refers to the more concrete execution of this intersection between power and language, as Aaron Hess (2018, 7) puts it, the process of "meaning-making, identification, and persuasion, oftentimes in the context of advocacy, deliberation, argumentation, or aesthetic performance."

Public Debate and Political Communication in Russia

As it turns out, the traditional mechanism for controlling the symbolic resource of public language in Russia has largely been to discourage it altogether. Dmitrii Kalugin (2016, 54) argues that Russia's checkered history of public debate can be traced back to Old Russian didactic literature, in which "the very situation of argument [was] conceived as a negative manifestation of human nature, and [which] . . . taught that verbal confrontations should be avoided." This helped fuel a basic "depoliticization" of language particularly consequential for the emergence of a public sphere in the eighteenth century, as it helped create a situation in which people "refuse[d] to acknowledge that utterance may be a form of political participation," and which resulted in a bifurcated "social contract between authority and society, according to which the one [had] the right to 'act' and the other to 'talk'" (Kalugin 2016, 52–3). This last dynamic is illustrated in the now time-honored tradition of post-Soviet leaders (Boris Yeltsin, Putin,

Dmitry Medvedev, and Moscow Mayor Sergei Sobyanin, to name a few) refusing to engage in political debates during their election campaigns, arguing that they are too busy running the country (or the government or the city) to engage in mere talk.[3] Atnashev et al. (2021, 67) are somewhat more circumspect in their assessment of the viability of public debate in Russia, arguing that it is not so much a matter of the absence and inability to engage in public speech but in the "instability of the power structures founded on deliberative formats." What they call "regimes of tumultuous discussion" can be found (e.g., 1905–17, 1985–89), but limits on public speech still existed, and the episodes "did not result in the successful establishment of mechanisms of publicness in political institutions" (Atnashev et al. 2021, 66–69; cf. Lovell 2015).[4] They argue that Russia has been characterized more by a "soft regime of publicness" in decision-making that does little to take into account the opinions of the general population. Instead, political leaders are more likely to rely on an official or "systemic" public sphere to provide the regime with some semblance of civic legitimacy, a model for public civic behavior (including linguistic), and a safe means of public feedback (*obratnaia sviaz'*) on delicate policy issues (Atnashev et al. 2021).

Focusing more on the "public" side of the equation, Oleg Kharkhordin notes the semantic lacunae in modern Russian language and society for the notion of an active "public" engaged independently in the affairs of society and the state. *Pablik* and *publichnyi* are terms either foreign to Russian ears or linked to awkward images of brothels (*publichnyi dom*). *Obshchestvennik* and *obshchestvennyi*, terms with solid roots in nineteenth-century independent civic activity, have lost much of their legitimacy, in part due to their link to the Soviet-era notion of *obshchestvennost'*, a kind of collectivized notion of "society" smacking of state-approved do-gooders (Kharkhordin 2018, 70–83).[5] Some even argue that the Russian language itself lacks the capacity for a popular political language. The nineteenth-century poet Aleksandr Pushkin noted as much when he wrote that "erudition (*uchennost'*), politics, and philosophy have not yet been articulated in Russian; metaphysical language does not exist at all" (quoted in Khazagerov et al. 2005). Khazagerov et al. (2005) ground similar conclusions in the history of Russian

---

3. In his essay, "Networked Putinism," Strukov (2012, 115) suggests Putin's later absences have as much to do with "his newly obtained status of a media deity who exercises great impact but is rarely visible unless his performance is carefully choreographed and monitored."

4. Although McAuley (2010) argues that the Soviet-era public speaking models and their legacy of hierarchical, authoritarian, and competing bureaucratic structures significantly hampered the articulation of social interests within the new, more democratic, institutions resulting from Gorbachev's reforms and the collapse of the USSR.

5. All three terms share a common root with the Russian word for "society" (*obshchestvo*). *Obshchestvennik* is a common noun denoting a member of society who is civically engaged.

political discourse, where both tsarist and Soviet-era political culture lacked a useable popular political language that wasn't either too lofty (in the tsarist case) or too bureaucratically and ideologically charged (in the Soviet case). It is in part for this reason that, even ten years after the collapse of the Soviet Union, there was a common tendency among Russians in post-Soviet Russia to equate "freedom of speech" with the freedom to curse in public (Gorham 2014). Hence, you wind up with a speech culture antithetical to public debate, and notions of a Russian "public sphere" as "the realm of life in which public opinion is formed" independently of the state become highly questionable.[6]

These factors, together with the emergence of a more-or-less codified and unitary language of the Soviet state in the decades following the Bolshevik revolution (Gorham 2004), led to a discursive landscape dominated by two types of speech, as Vakhtin points out, with neither suitable for compromise or dialogue: "In the *official* variant everything is decided in advance and the communicative model is not at all designed for a real exchange of opinions; in the *private* variant the participants do not even aim to arrive at a common position—they 'have a good talk,' and each of them continues to think exactly as he did before" (Vakhtin 2016, 16).[7]

"Putinism" Rhetorically Defined

Though the term *Putinism* has been around for nearly as long as Putin himself, discussion among political observers over what it is and whether it exists in the first place has really only emerged in recent years. Taylor (2018, 22) argues that "Putinism" is not so much an ideology, in the tradition of Marxism or Communism, but rather a "code"—a combination of ideas, habits, and emotions that have consistently motivated Putin and those in his inner circle over the course of his presidency. The main ideas—statism, anti-Westernism, and anti-liberalism—are the guiding foundation, but these are complemented by "habits," such as control, order, unity, and hypermasculinity, that are more "perceptions" or "attitudes" than beliefs. The main ideas are likewise colored by "emotions," such as resentment and vulnerability. Guriev and Treisman (2022, 76) essentially agree on the lack of a coherent ideology, describing Putin instead as a model "spin dictator" who has

---

6. Edgar and Sedgwick 2002, 90; Chebankova 2013; Vakhtin and Firsov 2016. Gladarev (2011, 167) goes as far as attributing the dearth of public debate in Russia to what he calls "public aphasia," a state in which citizens are unable to speak or listen to citizens of differing opinions, resulting in "communicative stupor."

7. Yurchak (2006) examines how the "last Soviet generation" positioned itself on a variety of levels of communication in relation to (and oftentimes in opposition to) the reigning "authoritarian discourse," even while going through the motions of state-sanctioned public behavior.

instead a "kaleidoscopic mix of images and themes to target multiple audiences at once." In their damning assessment of the Putin regime, Langdon and Tismaneau (2020, 23) end up underscoring the idea of the kaleidoscope by listing a total of ten "core elements" of Putinism: "ultranationalism, Russian exceptionalism, historical revisionism, anti-Westernism, imperialism, militarism, racism, chauvinism, corruption, and kleptocracy." Snegovaya et al. (2023) argue in favor of a more straightforward Putinist ideology that has been relatively stable through his presidency and has taken on steam since Russia's full-scale invasion of Ukraine. But they describe it in a way that echoes many of the features named by other theories of Putinism: "Borrowing heavily from czarist and Soviet themes, as well as other intellectual sources like the twentieth-century radical right, Putinism elevates an idea of imperial-nationalist statism amplified by Russian greatness, exceptionalism, and historical struggle against the West. Notable throughout this period has been the Kremlin's attention to education and memory politics, accompanied by a growing emphasis and reactionary in nature, on what the Kremlin describes as traditional values" (Snegovaya et al. 2023, 2). Suslov (2024) offers the most extended and ambitious consideration of the topic to date and argues that Putinism not only exists as an ideology ("Russia's third official ideology," no less [274]), but may well out last Putin. At the same time, he admits it to being "a work-in-progress with still considerable leeway of possibilities" (277). The central features of the later (post-2012) version, however, resemble many of the aforementioned traits: an "identitarian pseudo-conservatism, which has caused a quick evolution toward anti-Westernism, rabid illiberalism, isolationism, and militarism" (Suslov 2024, 4).

It would be overly formalistic, of course, to claim that speech styles and rhetorical strategies map neatly onto political ideologies or codes. It would not be far-fetched, however, to suggest that, since language serves as one of the primary tools for codifying symbolic authority, it becomes difficult to ignore the importance of a leader's preferred speech registers and styles as important symbolic indicators of his political identity and worldview. As I have shown in a separate discourse analysis of Putin's unscripted public speeches, interviews, and discussion-style performances from his first two presidential terms (Gorham 2012), a handful of distinctive speech profiles clearly stand out. Reexamining these within the context of over a dozen years of evolution and change (for both Putin and Russia), we can divide them into three dominant registers: the technocratic voice of the statist bureaucrat, the low register of the tough-talking strongman, and the high register of the conservative national patriot.

The dominant register in terms of sheer number is that of Putin the statist. It comes, stylistically, in his mastery of the technocratic language of the bureaucratic state and legal system, sometimes referred to as "bureaucratese"—flush with facts and statistics, and marked by complex syntax due to the excessive use of subordinate clauses and deverbal and abstract nouns. Because of its complexity, the language of the statist also tends to be prone to obfuscation. Much of the language of Russian legislation surrounding the internet is steeped in this language, as subsequent chapters show, and in many cases the vague wording conveniently allows the state and its enforcement agencies to apply laws however they deem appropriate and on whomever they deem appropriate.

The statist mentality also manifests itself meta-linguistically in Putin's speech, in phrases and actions that draw direct attention to a primacy of action over words (e.g., "It seems to me you have to judge a person not by what he says about himself, but by what he does" [Putin 2001]). Earlier in his presidency, the efficacy of this rhetorical feature clearly resonated with citizens, judging by characterizations of his appeal by participants in a 2004 focus group: "He [Putin] doesn't toss around words errantly—if he promises to do something, he does it"; "He doesn't waggle his tongue—he does what he says" ("V. Putin" 2004). Echoing the historical assessment by Kalugin and others regarding the privilege of the political elite to obviate public speech and debate altogether, one former Putin-era government official explained, "If you're part of the system, you don't fight with the opposition. You make the system do it for you. . . . For practical reasons, [Putin] kills discussion by not accepting the mere concept of it: When there is no debate, it is impossible to lose a debate. Putin never exchanges views with anybody; he informs" (Fishman 2017).

Less frequent but much more newsworthy are the rhetorically potent moments where Putin shifts out of the statist, technocratic register and into the tough-talking vernacular of the strongman, which arguably has sociolinguistic roots in both prison slang and the language of the security agencies—and, most relevant for Putin, the KGB—and allows a useful breadth of authoritative signaling as a result.[8] His occasional reliance on colloquial, nonstandard speech is arguably the most memorable and thus most potent in shaping Putin's public linguistic profile. Better understood as what Taylor (2018) calls "habits," they quite often reflect a penchant for order and control and are often laced with hypermasculine language and vulgarity. We see it in one of his earliest and most notorious public statements justifying Russian air raids on the Chechen city of Grozny in a September 1999 press conference in Astana, Kazakhstan, when still prime minister to Yeltsin: "We will follow the terrorists everywhere. If we catch them in the shithouse, if you'll pardon the expression, then we'll bump them off in the shithouse once and for all. That's it. The issue is completely closed."[9] Though a small blip on the rhetorical

---

8. I am indebted to Vera Zvereva for pointing out the dual origins of this feature of Putin's rhetoric.

9. "Мы будем преследовать террористов всюду. Если в туалете поймаем, то и в сортире их замочим. Всё. Вопрос закрыт окончательно" (transcribed by the author from Plakuchev [2023]).

radar of his otherwise bland, statist style, the "bump off in the shithouse" (*mochit' v sortire*) phrase played a critical role in framing a public profile of the prime minister as a tough-talking, can-do leader, unafraid of speaking bluntly when the security and stability of the nation were at stake. It likewise served as a discursive permission slip—in the name of stability and order—for behavior that lay outside the bounds of normal rule-based law ("below" it, in the register of the prisoner, or "above" it, in the register of the security elite).

The *mochit' v sortire* declaration became the unofficial slogan of his 2000 presidential election bid (Radzikhovskii 1999), and, once elected, Putin would continue to sprinkle coarse, nonstandard aphorisms into the flow of his unscripted, otherwise bland remarks.[10] In a 2002 press conference in Brussels, for instance, he invoked a different but equally graphic prophylactic procedure in response to a question from a French journalist, who apparently demonstrated excessive sympathy for Islamic radicals: "If you want to convert to Islamic radicalism completely and undergo a circumcision, then I invite you to Moscow. We have a multi-confessional country and specialists in that 'area,' and I'd recommend that you perform the operation in such a way that nothing would ever grow there again."[11] And in a November 2003 remark to the Italian media about Mikhail Khodorkovsky's belated attempt to settle back taxes, Putin euphemistically invoked the image of grabbing oligarchs by the testicles: "So now they've leveled a concrete indictment against him. And he says, 'Well, okay, I agree, let me pay them [taxes].' This kind of trading, this kind of secret deal is impermissible. Everyone must understand once and for all: you've got to obey the law always, and not just when they've grabbed you by the private parts [*za odno mesto*]."[12]

Whether bumping off, castrating, or grabbing someone by the testicles, all actions involve physical violence meted out in hypermasculine fashion to the perceived enemy, internal or external.[13]

Finally, at the other end of the stylistic spectrum, we find a third, loftier style that becomes increasingly prevalent in Putin's speech after his return to power in

---

10. Putin received 53 percent of the vote, compared to 29 percent earned by the Communist Party candidate Genadii Ziuganov.

11. "Если вы хотите совсем уж стать исламским радикалом и пойти на то, чтобы сделать себе обрезание, то я вас приглашаю в Москву. У нас многоконфессиональная страна, у нас есть специалисты и по этому 'вопросу', и я рекомендую сделать эту операцию таким образом, чтобы у вас уже больше ничего не выросло" ("Vyderzhki" 2002).

12. "Вот сейчас ему предъявили конкретное обвинение. Он говорит: "Ну ладно, согласен, давайте сейчас заплачу." Вот такая торговля, такой сговор, он недопустим. Все должны раз и навсегда для себя понять: надо исполнять закон всегда, а не только тогда, когда схватили за одно место" ("Interv'iu" 2003).

13. See Sperling (2015) and Cassiday (2023) for excellent discussions of the intersection of popular culture and politics in what the former calls "hegemonic masculinity" and the latter, "compensatory hypermasculinity."

2012. Particularly when it comes to articulating Russia's special place on the global stage—its status as an alternative "civilization" and a bastion of traditional values— he relies on a language steeped in historical and philosophical terms and references, laced with a hefty dose of national patriotism. The rhetorical profile often goes hand in hand with contrastive discourse about what Russia and Russians are *not*—negative values and geopolitical activities ascribed to its foes and presented as an existential threat to Russian "sovereignty," if not its very existence.[14]

None of these speech profiles and registers is proprietary to Putin, of course, but they do collectively represent the chief strategic quivers in his rhetorical bow. And to a striking degree, we find them resonating in the range of voices that give verbal shape to "networked Putinism." In some cases, such as the more populist language of the strongman, they typify some of the dominant pro-Putin voices coming to his defense online. In other cases, they more aptly typify the meta-discursive rhetoric (talk *about* language) deployed by the "system" to legitimize and legislate greater control of new media technology. Across the case studies in the history of Russian political discourse online examined in the coming chapters, we see manifestations of registers ranging from the course and colloquial to the lofty and patriotic, with the vanilla language of the statist bureaucrat under-girding both. And just as with the polymorphic nature of ideologically based notions of Putinism seen above, Putinist rhetorical styles have varied over time and quite frequently appear in combination with, and even in contradiction to, one another. Indeed, one of the distinctive rhetorical features of Putinism is a cynical willingness to deploy whatever terms (however contradictory or ill-defined) and whatever voices (however cacophonous) are needed to articulate, protect, and foster the authority of the Putin regime online.

Political Communication and New Media Technology

While numerous scholars have warned of the conceptual dangers of technological determinism, there is no question that newer media technologies have had considerable impact on political communication in the public sphere, for better and for worse. On the one hand, they have been widely viewed as a productive medium for the expansion of civil society and democracy. By virtue of their rhizomatic

---

14. At the very outset of the Putin era, sociologist Lev Gudkov (2004) argued that this "negative identity," where national identity is defined primarily in negative opposition to perceived external enemies and internal threats, was a defining feature of post-Soviet society and a core element of Putin's ruling strategy.

structure, the internet, blogosphere, and other social networking platforms carry the potential for breaking through traditional hierarchical models of political communication, enabling citizens and their political representatives to engage in discussion and debate directly, without intermediary (Lévy 2001). Bentivegna has pointed out, for example, that "the creation of an arena made possible by the Internet, where everyone has a voice, together with the possibility of activating direct relations between politicians and citizens, leads to the development of an electronic marketplace" and the "eradication of the gap dividing political life from the daily life of citizens." These new digital arenas thus create greater "equality among members engaged in a discussion" and the "absence of preconceived positions of 'power' in the management of communication" (Bentivegna 2002, 51–52, 53). Particularly in media environments controlled by authoritarian regimes, they create new potential for the creation of "networked public spheres" (Benkler 2006) and what Alexanyan et al. (2012) describe as "an independent alternative to the more tightly controlled offline media and political space" that facilitates the "growing use of digital platforms in social mobilization and civic action." Papacharissi (2013) argues that online social networks create the potential for improving the elitist and nostalgic, classical notion of the public sphere (restricted as it was by gender, race, and class) in the sense that they mark a "retreat to the private sphere" where net-based technologies reside, and from there reengage citizens in the public arena: "Online social networks, such as blogs and YouTube, collectively produced news aggregator sites, networks of online activism, all present popular and new civic habits, reflective of an electorate that is not apathetic, but is merely shifting its attention to different civic landscapes" (Papacharissi 2013, 13, 21).

At the same time, while digitally mediated communication systems bring about new possibilities for networked public spheres, they also expose societies and citizen users to more negative effects.[15] Morozov (2011) warns against assumptions by "cyber-optimists" that "the Internet favors the oppressed rather than the oppressor" (15), reminding readers that the very same technologies were quite capable of "enabling propaganda, censorship, and surveillance, the three main pillars of Orwell-style authoritarian control" (93). For the purposes of this study of language, the potential for the degradation of public political discourse is of particular concern, whether state-generated or otherwise. In part due to the lack of filters they contain, in part due to the broader range of users to whom they give voice, and in part due to the imperfect nature of the communicative

---

15. Here and throughout this book I use the term "mediated" as a simplified synonym for "through media"—similar to, though perhaps less nuanced than the notion of "mediatized" preferred by scholars in media studies. For an in-depth discussion and application of the latter term in the contemporary Russian context, see Hutchings (2022).

platforms themselves, social media are acutely vulnerable to misunderstanding, disinformation, verbal harassment (trolling), hate speech, and worse. How a society contends with such bad online behavior depends not only on the degree of its mastery and control over relevant technologies but also on the political and cultural attitudes and traditions it brings to the technology. Traditional attitudes toward the purity of the Russian language and the sanctity of Orthodox faith, for example, have been invoked to rationalize concrete economic and legislative actions, ranging from the takeover of entire social networking platforms to the fining and incarceration of individual users. At the same time, measures to control speech deemed offensive or dangerous have been sporadically implemented and largely ineffectual, leading to glaring episodes of bureaucratic lawlessness. In some particularly intriguing cases, efforts to restrict or censor have met with resistance from within the state apparatus itself—suggesting there are limits to how much web-based political speech can be tamed, even amid growing calls for a "sovereign internet" beholden to the laws and values of the Russian Federation. In fact, the real notion of limits to constraining these new technologies becomes central to understanding how the Putin government attempts to confront the political and discursive challenges posed by digital media and ensure they remain both pure of pernicious political "viruses" and secure from existential threats from perceived enemies both outside Russia and within.

In this book, I acknowledge and document the profound impact new media have had on public discourse and political rhetoric, in particular, and recognize that the evolution of these technologies is highly influenced by the social, political, and economic conditions of the particular culture in which they emerge. Starr (2004) argues that the shape, emphases, and openness of media are aspects that usually evolve over time and are strongly affected by various traditions, value systems, and other circumstances specific to a particular society, including geography, values, and political goals. To counter tendencies of technological determinism, Baym (2010, 39) suggests that we think more in terms of what she calls the "social construction of technology," a notion that recognizes that "human beings, not machines, are the agents of change." And Morley (2007, 241) notes that "[technological] development follows no natural or preordained course in which the 'intrinsic' capacity of a technology is revealed according to some inner logic, but is always the contingent result of social struggles over the application of technologies, between differentially powerful interests." Toward a better understanding of how this dynamic has played out in Putin's Russia, I trace the rhetorical methods by which authorities have, over the past two decades, helped shape, distort, disrupt, monitor, regulate, commandeer, and otherwise constrain newly emergent and influential digital media. In the process, I document how the Putin regime's somewhat scattershot adaptation to these new media technologies has proven quite adept (if not deft) at reengineering the domain to better fit its ideal image of a systemic public sphere, creating the conditions of a "networked authoritarianism," even if more flawed and porous than the Chinese model to which it has often aspired.[16]

Organization of the Book

I divide the book into eight chapters across four parts. Part 1 examines the early communicative landscape of the nascent Runet and efforts by pro-Putin associates to establish a rhetorical presence therein. Part 2 analyzes two coexisting, democratically oriented models for the Runet as a tool for political transformation. Part 3 explores both institutional and more subversive strategies deployed by pro-state actors for muting the impact of voices of political opposition online. Part 4 discusses how ruling authorities have sought either to rein in and cordon off a space perceived to be a growing threat to their political power or to promote more state-friendly mediated profiles of authority online.

In chapter 1, I look at some of the earliest efforts at web-based political spin by Putin's so-called political technologists from the Foundation for Effective Politics, showing how, from the very start, authorities relied on a hodgepodge of communicative strategies—from positive content production to disinformation—to establish at least some rhetorical presence in the new information sphere. Chapter 2 features case studies of a trio of early Runet influencers with shared origins in a self-proclaimed "counterculture" movement (Konstantin Rykov, Maksim Kononenko, and Egor Kholmogorov), who in different ways enlisted their contrarian pretensions to generate content sympathetic to Putin and his emerging political ideas. Central to the movement was a coarse, irony-laden vernacular called "scumbag language" that came to be negatively associated with the internet, on the one hand, but that, on the other hand, positively echoed the off-color aphorisms sprinkled throughout Putin's own public speech.

---

16. Framing her analysis of Chinese internet policy, MacKinnon (2011) offers the following description of "network authoritarianism": "In the networked authoritarian state, the single ruling party remains in control while a wide range of conversations about the country's problems nonetheless occurs on websites and social-networking services. The government follows this online chatter, and sometimes people are able to use the Internet to call attention to social problems or injustices and even manage to have an impact on government policies. As a result, the average person with Internet or mobile access has a much greater sense of freedom—and may feel that he has the ability to speak and be heard—in ways that were not possible under classic authoritarianism. At the same time, in the networked authoritarian state, there is no guarantee of individual rights and freedoms. Those whom the rulers see as threats are jailed; truly competitive, free, and fair elections are not held; and the courts and the legal system are tools of the ruling party" (quoted in Wijermars 2021b, 16–17).

In chapter 3, I analyze the efforts by Russia's first tech-savvy president, Dmitry Medvedev, to harness new media technologies to bring about what he called "direct internet democracy." I likewise discuss, through analyses of his own online practices and policy debates over creating an "electronic government," the rhetorical and institutional roadblocks to successful realization that stood in his way. Chapter 4 traces the rising star of corruption fighter and politician Navalny and his deft embrace of social media (LiveJournal, Twitter, and YouTube in particular) to fuel his own political ambitions and expose graft and corruption at the highest level of power. Indeed, the combination of Medvedev's limited success and Navalny's outsized impact on both the political language *of* digital media and political attitudes *toward* them dramatically shifted the rhetorical battlefield, compelling advocates of the Putin regime into a more aggressive posture, including reliance on more nefarious forms of web-based communication. Chapter 5 examines the growing ubiquity of online trolling, showing that, while trolling as a rhetorical act long predated the internet and could be understood to play a constructive role in society, in the context of an increasingly disgruntled political climate, it provided state authorities with a potent but cynical one-two punch. On the one hand, trolling equipped the state with an effective tool for disrupting the more antagonistic corners of the information sphere; on the other hand, it provided fodder for those in "official" civil society to provoke "moral panics" about the internet and social media as hotbeds of pernicious, antisocial influences.

In chapter 6, I document efforts by members of the systemic public sphere to portray the internet as a dangerous source of communicative contamination and kindle "moral panics" to justify laws and other prophylactic measures designed to "purify" it of such pernicious content. Chapter 7 features three case studies of more positive models of state-friendly content generation: the online initiatives of a prominent digital media personality (Sergei Minaev), the extravagant Instagram presence of a charismatic regional politician (Ramzan Kadyrov), and the well-funded efforts by a state institution (the Institute for the Development of the Internet) to influence the Runet on the industry level. In the final chapter, I delve into long-standing efforts by the Putin regime to establish its long-sought dream of a "sovereign internet." In addition to exploring the challenges of transferring a notion traditionally reserved for geographical borders to the more amorphous digital sphere, I show how the rhetorical framing used to rationalize the initiative was grounded in two key tenets of Putinism—the belief in Russia as a bulwark of traditional, "civilizational" values and the fear that a "Russophobic" West posed an existential threat to those values and to Russian national security more broadly.

Russia's full-scale invasion of Ukraine in February 2022 marks a logical break in a story devoted to attempts by those in positions of authority in Putin's Russia to come to terms, figuratively and literally, with new media technologies. The book's epilogue uses insights from its core chapters to help make sense of continuities and shifts in digitally networked political discourse since the invasion, with the lion's share of attention devoted to Prigozhin's strikingly effective harnessing of Telegram to nearly overthrow Putin's Ministry of Defense, if not the regime itself.

Any study of the impact of the internet and social media on political rhetoric over a twenty-five-year period has to be selective in what it elects to highlight and underscore. This book does that in three principal ways, hinted at in the book's title. First, it focuses primarily on how the Putin regime and those close to it confronted new media technologies as they emerged and shows that process to be a series of largely ad hoc efforts, at best, to harness them to promote Putin and Putinism, and at worst, to mitigate their negative impact. My focus on Navalny's online rhetoric in chapter 4 marks the main exception to this focus, not because he was representative of *all* oppositional voices but because he was so effective at using social media to promote his ideas and causes that he was able to unleash forces that caused authorities to dramatically recalibrate their approaches to the networked public sphere.

The book is also selective in its demographic scope, aimed mainly at the battle for symbolic authority at the upper ends of rhetorical production—political leaders, public institutions, and prominent public figures and web personalities—and leaving to the side issues of how these rhetorical models impacted and interacted with communication on the grassroots level of online political engagement (with a few exceptions in chapters 4 and 5). While these issues are important and deserving of closer attention, they lay outside the scope of this work.[17]

Finally, while the notion of "new media" can be understood to include a wide range of technologies, I limit my focus here mainly to the impact of the internet and social networks on political communication in Putin's Russia. There is no question that such issues as state surveillance, hacking, online gaming, cybersecurity and warfare, electronic voting, artificial intelligence, and search-engine and tracking algorithms all lend themselves to intriguing rhetorical analyses, some of which have already been conducted.[18] In the interest of time and space, and for the sake of cogency and clarity, I also frequently rely on shorthand sub-

---

17. For studies focusing more on grassroots web-based communication, see Zvereva (2012 and 2020b); Guseinov (2014); Gorham et al. (2014); Koltsova and Bodrunova (2019); Wijermars and Lehtisaari (2020).

18. For issues in Russia-related hacking, spamming, cybersecurity, and surveillance, see Klimburg (2017); Krebs (2014); Morozov (2011); Sanger (2018); Soldatov and Borogan (2015); Watts (2018); Biagioli and Lépinay (2019). For a discussion of the politics of website design and search-engine algorithms, see Daucé (2020); Gritsenko et al. (2021).

stitutes such as "new media" and "digital media," fully aware of the historical and technological relativity of these terms (Chadwick 2013; Hess 2018; Lovell 2015; Peters 2009).

The Russian word *vlast'* carries oversized valence in the Russian language. Capable of reflecting abstract notions of power and authority, as well as the more concrete notion of authorities (i.e., powers that be), it lies at the heart of any study of political language and public persuasion and thus occupies a central place in the title and subject matter of this book. Following a long tradition dating back to Plato and Cicero, through to more recent scholars such as Foucault (1972) and Bourdieu (1991), and, still closer to home, my own published volumes dedicated to Soviet and post-Soviet language culture and politics (Gorham 2004, 2014; Gorham, Lunde, and Paulsen 2014), this book takes as a central premise that language plays a critical role in both legitimizing and subverting political authority. As such, the book builds on seminal foundational studies of Runet's complex and often troubled relationship with authority in Putin's Russia (Deibert et al. 2010; Gorham et al. 2014; Gritsenko et al. 2021; Hutchings 2022; Morozov 2011; Wijermars and Lehtisaari 2020) to provide the first concentrated study of the various ways new media technologies have reshaped public political discourse in Russia and the ways Russian vlast' and the language of Putinism, over two decades of coding, have shaped those technologies. More broadly, it offers insight into methods by which authoritarian-inclined powers have enlisted language to create rhetorical mechanisms that allow them to appropriate newly emergent and powerful digital media for their own needs—be it in the form of legislating, punishing, publicly shaming, inciting moral panic, or participating in content generation and online conversations. While to this day the methods are neither coordinated nor perfected, the stakes of the battle over digitally networked communication have become perilously high—in the most extreme cases, such as the rise and fall of both Prigozhin and Navalny, a matter of life and death.

Part 1

RHETORICAL FOUNDATIONS

POLITICAL TECHNOLOGY GOES DIGITAL

Hysteria is rhetoric, too.

—Gleb Pavlovsky (Proskurin 2001)

For those whose first association of the political Runet include the likes of Navalny and the anti-Putin political opposition, earliest memoirs and histories of the space paint a more nuanced portrait.[1] Upon closer look, we find that the Runet did provide a rich and vibrant space for alternative discourses, but those alternatives assumed a broader range of rhetorical manifestations than previously assumed. From the appearance of the first online sharable content in the late 1990s to the popularization of social media in the middle of the 2000s, early Runet users were largely well educated, trained in universities as engineers, scientists, journalists, and philologists. In January 1990 the public organization Glasnet was created with funding from the San Francisco–based Association for Progressive Communications to promote web-based education and projects for teachers, human rights advocates, environmentalists, and other guarantors of open society—an early sign that the Runet ecology was both progressive in its orientation and benefited from significant Western (and largely American) support (Gorny 2000). That same year saw the creation of the Relkom network by specialists from the Demos cooperative, most of whom were employees at the storied Kurchatov Institute, Russia and the Soviet Union's ground zero for research in nuclear energy (Soldatov and Borogan 2015, 29–30). Designed as a means for enabling digital communication among members, the Relkom network essentially constituted the first technical framework for electronic mail in the Russian language (Gorny 2000).

---

1. Among the most informative sources for early Runet history and culture are Gorny (2009), Kuznetsov (2004), and Schmidt et al. (2006).

It really wasn't until the registration of the .ru domain in 1994 that a publicly accessible web beyond scholarly networks appeared for Russian users. It was in this same year that the first full-fledged online book repository appeared—Maksim Moshkov's Library—an impressive endeavor (despite its disregard for copyright law) emblematic of how the internet functioned largely as an outlet for the learned class (fig. 1.1).

Shortly thereafter, creative initiatives among the literati appeared, such as the literary journal *DeLitZyne* and the first interactive literary project, ROMAN,

Maksim Moshkow's Library

Поиск: [   ] [SEARCH]

[Новые поступления] [Хитпарад] [koi-win-lat-iso-alt-mac] [GuestBook] [Mirrors]

15-Nov-99. 1100Mb. Эта самая известная в русском интернете электронная www-библиотека открыта в 1994 г. Читатели ежедневно пополняют ее новыми файлами. Здесь есть все, а будет – еще больше. Современная и античная художественная литература, фантастика и политика, техдокументация и юмор, история и поэзия, КСП и русский рок, туризм и парашютизм, философия и эзотерика, и т.д. и т.д. и т.п. Награды: Тенета98, POTOP99, 108лучших, GoldSite98, RusClassic, RusAmerica, Гусарский клуб, RusHedgehog, НЖМД

[Как помочь?] [Index] [Help&FAQ;] [Благодарности] [RAMBLER's TOP100] [Cyrillic] [GuesBooks]

Н.Э.Б Библион.Ru Lenta.Ru Vesti.Ru OnLine.lib Н.Г. КонкурсКритиков Referat.Ru Pogoda.Ru Конкурс web-дизайнов
Подписка на "Новости библиотеки" [Ваш email] [txt ∨] [subscribe]

MIRRORS: http://lib.ru/ alkar.net kiev.ua neystadt.org aaanet.ru g2.ru ssau.ru novgorod.net odessa.net
http://moshkow.rsl.ru/koi/   pool-7.ru u-parisi0.fr belabm.by lib.kg nnov.ru primorye.ru r-isp.net
http://www.parkline.ru/Library/koi/ tudelft.nl unibel.by nsk.su kirov.ru bryansk.ru web.am
http://moshkow.relline.ru:5800/koi/ donetsk.ua eunet.lv surgut.ru gss.ru yamal.ru bryansk.ru wsnet.ru
http://kulichki.rambler.ru/moshkow/ nikopol.net ase.ee linkor.ru perm.ru minsk.by kuzbass.ru sonet.to

Объявление: Отдам щенка в хорошие руки

РАЗВЛЕЧЕНИЯ

Авторская песня и русский рок   (484)
Водный туризм. White water kayaking(680)
Альпинизм и горный туризм   (146)
Skydiving. Парашютные фотографии   (188) 21 Oct
Горные лыжи   (54)
Учим английский язык   (49) 9 Nov
Впечатления о заграничной жизни   (146)
Humor   (214)
Кинофильмы, TV, video...   (69)
Rock-n-Roll   (142) 8 Nov
Этикетки для магнитофонных кассет
Бридж, преферанс
Шахматы, шашки
Солюшены компьютерных игр
Разнообразные тексты

ПРОЗА

РУССКАЯ   СОВРЕМЕННАЯ ПРОЗА   (48)
РУССКАЯ   ДОВОЕННАЯ ЛИТЕРАТУРА   (14)

FIGURE 1.1. Screenshot of one of the first Runet websites, "Maksim Moshkow's Library," launched in 1994. Source: "Maksim Moshkow's Library" (28 November 1999), https://web.archive.org/web/19991128203354/http://lib.ru/.

designed by Roman Leibov, Leonid Delitsyn, and Dmitrii Manin. The first general news and information sites appeared in 1995–1996 in the form of *RosBiznesKonsalting*; *Zhurnal.ru*, which involved many of the more prominent figures in the early Runet; and *Vechernii Internet* (the Evening Internet), published by another early Runet pioneer, Anton Nossik.

Even by 2005, Gorny observes, access to the Runet remained "a luxury, 'an acquisition of the elite,'" and, as a result, compared to their counterparts in more technologically advanced countries, early Runet users "evinced a clear preference for political and poetic debate in Usenet groups," rather than "online adventures of the 'dungeons and dragons' kind" (2009, 172–73). But this new media intelligentsia cut across a range of political profiles and engaged in online communication toward a variety of goals—some political, others creative, still others purely commercial. To an extent, this usage reflected an ordinary range of uses one might expect from an educated elite on any medium, new or old; but it also reflected conditions specific to the Russian civic culture of the time—not only the immediate state of instability and disarray that characterized the post-Soviet political and commercial sphere but also more stable, cultural attitudes toward public language and communication (Rohozinski 1999). As Schmidt and Teubener (2006) argue, the early Runet served not so much as an oppositional space as it did an alternative "(counter)public sphere," where viewpoints were shared among a relatively small number of educated intellectuals, regardless of political orientation.

Kompromat as a Literary Genre

Any analysis of the early political landscape of the Russian language internet needs to include Gleb Pavlovsky and his political consulting agency, the Foundation for Effective Politics (FEP).[2] Generationally, the man once referred to as "the Kremlin myth-maker" (Stepanova 2005) was a creature of the old-media world, coming out of the samizdat dissident culture of the 1970s and 1980s, when he was involved in various anti-Soviet protest groups and even arrested and exiled in 1982 for his efforts (Bekbulatova 2018).[3] Pavlovsky cofounded the FEP in 1995 together with the art curator Marat Guelman, and the two quickly established a reputation for their mastery of the art of what in Russian has come to be known

---

2. Earlier compelling accounts of Pavlovsky's forays into online politics appear in Schmidt and Teubener (2006) and Gorny (2009).

3. Although even this chapter of Pavlovsky's biography is shrouded in controversy, due to reports that he received a reduced sentence thanks to a confession of guilt to the KGB and agreement to give testimony against some of his closest dissident allies (Musorgskii 1999).

as "political technology." The term can be likened to political public relations, or "spin doctors," in the West but differs in the degree to which it is also implicitly associated with the more questionable side of political "handling." Political commentators writing in the journal *Ekspert* described the profession as early as 1998: "The activity of political technologists is associated with something dirty, dangerous, and secret. A representative of this profession seems to us a certain demonic individual, for whom the goal (the client's victory) justifies any means" (Gurova and Medovnik 1998).

Critical to the toolbox of the political technologist was not only the ability to spin positive images of one's own client but also the ability to generate negative publicity about his or her opponents, sometimes entirely fictitious. One of the earliest of Pavlovsky's noteworthy productions in this regard was the "Versiia no. 1" (Version no. 1) disinformation campaign he curated on behalf of Boris Yeltsin in 1994, a fully fabricated story claiming that Yeltsin's main political rivals were plotting a coup against him ("Versiia" 1994). The story's rapid spread to mainstream news outlets succeeded in discrediting the targets and largely neutralizing them for the upcoming presidential elections in 1996. It also established something of a cynical benchmark for political technology and Pavlovsky as its lead practitioner: "Up to that point we had glasnost," as one of the authors of the story put it, "but with the appearance of 'Versiia', glasnost turned into kompromat[4] and became an instrument of political management. . . . And Gleb sensed all this quite clearly. He was able to orchestrate the formation of the genre" (quoted in Bekbulatova 2018).

In keeping with his reputation as the Kremlin mythmaker, Pavlovsky consistently lent his activities a veneer of intellectualism, distancing himself from the darker associations of political technology and preferring, instead, the image of a more constructive "historian-fixer" (*istorik-remontnik*) (Titorenko 2006). Guelman even went so far as to publish a critical thesis titled "Kompromat as a literary genre," evoking the similarly named works of the Russian Formalists to articulate their political activities in intellectually palatable terms.[5] "Treading a fine line between suspenseful literature and documentary research," the curator wrote, "kompromat can become a new, entertaining genre—in its most elite variation, of course—since work in that genre requires the author to master new artistic devices and use new, at times completely unique expressive means" (Gel'man 1997). In doing so, Guelman conveniently added, the genre also allowed the author "to go outside of the frame of purely journalistic experiments."

---

4. *Kompromat* is the standard Russian term for "compromising material" generated either from actual sources or from whole cloth to tarnish the reputation of one's political enemy.

5. Cf. "The Ode as an Oratorical Genre" (1929), by Iurii Tynianov.

Pavlovsky likewise invoked the language of poetics to justify his use of damning kompromat against then–Prime Minister Putin's main political foe, Yury Luzhkov, in 1999: "In that situation there was no room for argumentation: you could either spit and whistle from the gallery or spin a noxious yarn. . . . There was a desperation [in what we did], after all, I was bent on victory. And where there is hysteria, there are always histrionics (*isterichnost'*), and, again, the inevitable rhetoricality (*ritorichnost'*). Hysteria is rhetoric, too. . . . All our hysterics and obsession were absolutely literary" (Proskurin 2001).

Pavlovsky viewed the political culture of the late 1990s as particularly ripe for influence by manipulators of public political discourse. In fact, thanks to what he saw as an absence of a new, viable public language coming out of politics directly, the Russian political class depended even more than usual on the mass media to articulate its ideas in a manner compelling enough to legitimize authority—to the extent that its own tongue-tiredness left the political class vulnerable to being metaphorically raped:

> Our current political language is a modified language, first, the perestroika years and, then, of Russian media of the 90s. In other words, it's an extremely impoverished political newspeak. It's extremely impoverished; I call it a "liberal state chancery language." As a result, the powers-that-be [*vlast'*] find themselves in a complicated situation: they can't out-argue the media, which can always tranquilize them and, in their tranquilized state, if you pardon the expression, take advantage of them [*poimet'*]. (Penskaia 2007)[6]

As if the absence of a viable political language weren't enough justification for political technologists such as himself—specialists capable of creating the "dramatic plots" on which public political power was built (Penskaia 2007)—the situation was exacerbated by the fact that the "technical information domination" through "massive informational bombardment" was taking place in an entirely one-sided fashion, on the part of an oligarch-dominated media at the expense of the ruling authority of the state (Pavlovskii 1999). In a 1999 treatise on "the market of information wars," Pavlovsky wrote that "the media as a political intermediary has a material interest in the maximalization of political risk (the higher the risk, the higher the rate of profit on the market of 'political money' or 'currency of influence'). Its task is not to facilitate the communication of political forces, but just the opposite—to confuse, disinform, and hold the situation in the artificially worked up, stressed state of uncertainty" (Pavlovskii 1999).

This attitude largely fueled Putin's efforts early in his presidency to reign in the media empires of oligarchs Vladimir Gusinsky and Boris Berezovsky. But it

---

6. It stands noting that *vlast'*, the object of the rape euphemism here, is a feminine noun in Russian.

also sheds light on the reasons for Pavlovsky and the FEP's hyperactivity in the electronic news and information sphere. In a memo to his then boss, Boris Yeltsin, Pavlovsky explained the volatile potential of the Runet: "The Runet currently serves a function that is not so much one of entertainment as it is of consolidation of leading social forces. The most progressive citizens of Russia have united on the net and, given all its differences, this group (nearly 2 mln. people) can become a volatile—non-conformist—segment of the erectorate [*sic*]" (Davydov 2000a).[7]

Despite his primary affinity with old media and self-recognized inexperience with new media in the early years (Davydov 2000b), Pavlovsky and the FEP were among the first in the political PR realm to demonstrate keen interest in online modes of political communication. Nearly all of the most well-known and frequently read online political and intellectual news sources—*Russkii zhurnal, Gazeta.ru, Vesti.ru, SMI.ru, Lenta.ru, Strana.ru, InoSMI.ru,* and, later, the pro-Kremlin blogging platform *Liberty.ru*—were products of Pavlovsky and the FEP, and they offered consistently positive portraits of Putin and his ideas through the first decade of the twenty-first century. Some (*Strana.ru, SMI.ru, Vesti.ru,* and others), at least until 2002, were financially supported by the Kremlin (Bekbulatova 2018). As early as 1999, Pavlovsky's foundation was widely seen as *the* dominant force among online political movers and shakers; by 2007, journalists were already referring to him as "one of the pioneers of the Russian intellectual and political internet" (Vainer 1999; Penskaia 2007).

Among the earliest and most beloved of Pavlovsky's online projects was *Russkii zhurnal* (*Russian Journal*), which, along with Anton Nossik's *Zhurnal.ru*, offered the first serious analytical online resource for the educated elite. Itself a conversion of the print journal *Pushkin*, the *Russian Journal* more than any of his many online projects reflected Pavlovsky's own intellectual roots and pretensions (Penskaia 2011). True to Pavlovsky's humanities training with the well-known dissident historian Mikhail Gefter (Tselykh 2000), the journal regularly featured reviews, news coverage, and articles dedicated to philosophy, history, and literary criticism. Thanks to the contributions of the aforementioned Leibov and collaborator and Runet pioneer Evgeny Gorny, it likewise featured astute, if idiosyncratic, coverage of Runet-related issues and content.[8] Come election season, however, the publication's links to Pavlovsky's FEP came to the fore, with ample space devoted to politics and political promotion (fig. 1.2). During the peak of

---

7. While his use of "erectorate" (*erektorat*) could simply be a malapropism for "electorate," Pavlovsky as a consummate wordsmith may well have meant it as a derogatory pun denoting that portion of the population that is sufficiently aroused to vote (the word *erektsiia* being a loanword from the English "erection").

8. See, for instance, Leibov's (2000) musings on the difficulty of archiving online correspondences or Gorny's (2000) reflections on resistance toward web-based communication on the part of fellow Russian philologists.

РЖ
РУССКИЙ ЖУРНАЛ
www.russ.ru

Сегодня | Политика | Круг чтения | Культура | Net-культура
Вне рубрик

English version
Последнее обновление
04.06.2001 / 02:01

Новости | Медиакратия | the West & the Rest | Экономические беседы | Полемика | Лекции | Вокруг власти

/ Политика < Вы здесь

{ *Поиск* }

искать:

экс-Пресс новости:
неделя 22
1901 На газовом заводе произошел взрыв резервуара.
1911 Борьба с курением опиума.
1921 Эвакуация японских войск из Сибири.
1931 Польские безработные просят работы в России.
1941 Движение протеста в Северной Ирландии.
1951 Американское вмешательство во внутренние дела Ирана.
1961 Россия строит в Бразилии газосланцевый завод.
1971 Приговор по делу четырех евреев в Риге.
1981 Жалеть розги - портить ребенка.
1991 В Приморье - энергетический голод.

SML.RU Темы дня:
12:40 Саммит СНГ
13:03 Заседание совета директоров "Газпрома".
15:17 Подъем "Курска"
18:01 Региональные выборы
13:13 "Медиа-Мост" и Гусинский

Тема недели: ИМПЕРИЯ
Конфликты внутри любой империи неизбежны, зато интересны. Метрополия борется с провинциями, государство - с экономикой. Интеллектуалы, как обычно, борются сами с собой: преодолевая собственный "классовый интерес", пытаются решить общие вопросы гражданства и национальной идентичности.

Сергей Маркедонов. "Русский вопрос" в России
Пятый пункт: "Кровь" vs "Почва", культ этничности против культа гражданства. Пока за "нациями" сохраняется "право на самоопределение", никто в нашей стране не почувствует себя гражданином. /01.06/

Михаил Денисов. В каком направлении нам нужно менять национальный характер?
Пятый пункт: Традиции vs институты. Архаичные и современные механизмы "единомыслия". В современной России не работают ни те, ни другие. Наверное, это - свобода... /01.06/

Имперский игровой автомат
Колонка редактора. С точки зрения "классового интереса" любой интеллектуал - государственник, лояльный гражданин империи. А в силу своей "природы" - наоборот, анархист. "Справедливое государство" построить невозможно. Будем наслаждаться блеском Империи, примирившись с ее нищетой. /31.05/

Сергей Ильин. Властители Дум
PRоблемы. Тела и лица политических лидеров плохо соответствуют текущим политическим задачам. Священная история повторяется в виде фарса. /30.05/

PR и СМИ

Иван Давыдов. Интерпол, выпуск 50. Цифровое настоящее
Туманная история с сайтами "Мемонета" и второй серией "НТВ-протеста". В чем конкретно виноват Гусинский? По утрам Шамиль Басаев ест своих подчиненных. Рунет - зона вражеской оккупации. Началось голосование жюри на конкурсе президентских сайтов. /01.06/

Анатолий Баташев. Дрязги: Березовский и Доренко выдвигают Любимова в Президенты
А вдруг у них получится?! /01.06/

"Медиакратия". Архив

{ *Подписка* }

Ваш e-mail:

Формат рассылки:
HTML ∨ | Koi8-r ∨

подписаться:

Сегодня в РЖ

Круг чтения
Старый муж, грозный муж...
Голод 35
Век=текст. Выпуск 54: 1954
Все о Поэзии 44
Тот самый дом
Шведская лавка # 31
"Немецкий язык - мой личный военный трофей"
Курицын-weekly от 29 мая 2001

Net-культура
Невод: выпуск 230
НасНет: выпуск 47
Интер(офф)вью 1: спросить Юрия Грымова
Интер(акти)вью 44: спросить Дмитрия Мендрелюка

FIGURE 1.2. Screenshot from 2001 issue of *Russkii zhurnal* (*Russian Journal*), one of the first series news and analysis sites on the Runet. Source: *Russkii zhurnal* (4 June 2001), https://web.archive.org/web/20010603221622/http://www.russ.ru/politics/.

Putin's first election campaign, for instance, the journal published a weekly press review by analyst Andrei Madison under the English-language title "Vladimir Putin Enigmatic," which essentially forecasted the mercurial nature of Putinism as an ideology, arguing that the wide range of criticism of the interim president would ultimately lead to naught, due to their utterly contradictory nature:

> On the one hand, Putin is a statist and Great Power advocate (*derzhavnik*), while on the other hand he is "a modern Russian politician from a Western mold." On the one hand, (as a strong leader) he creates rules, while on the other hand (for the same reason), he breaks them. Correspondingly, if

he considers a liberal economy effective, it will be liberal, whereas if he decides a mobilizational one would be useful, then there's no avoiding a mobilization [economy]. In any case, no matter what, he will act based on Russia's integrity. (Madison 2000)

Despite his claims that he felt "no corporate affinity to the internet community" (Davydov 2000b), Pavlovsky was keenly attracted to the medium. Not only did the creative and highly educated profile of its most active users (many of whom were its main producers) appeal to his intellectual affinities, its growingly outsized impact on "opinion leaders" offered the political consultant unique opportunities to shape political discourse or, as Pavlovsky put it in a memo to then-President Yeltsin, "consolidate leading social forces" (*peredovye obshchestvennye sily*) (Ivanov 2002; Davydov 2000a). Particularly at a time when mainstream television media were dominated by oligarchs growing more critical of the Yeltsin presidency, Pavlovsky saw the Runet as a "cheap technology of resistance" for those who were defenseless against the dominant mainstream media and a mechanism for consumers to "configure their own information bundle" (Pavlovskii et al. 2003; Kuz'mina 2007).

The Pavlovsky and FEP cases bring to light two important points about the political language culture of the early Runet. First, while in many ways it served as an outlet for alternative points of view, the media politics of the day featured a landscape in which those inside the Kremlin perceived themselves to be "outsiders" as well. So, for them, the internet was a critical object of desire in the struggle to shape and dictate public opinion. Second, while the *Russian Journal* reflected Pavlovsky's own intellectual grounding in the humanities, he didn't exactly sport a high-minded, idealistic view of the internet. Nor, for that matter, did he hold idealistic views of its potential as an engine for the promotion of a networked public sphere in Russia, even as he witnessed firsthand (and benefited from) the concerted effort by George Soros and his Open Society Foundation to equip Russian universities and nongovernmental organizations with computer technology to foster democracy and civil society ("You can say that it was Soros who invented the Internet for us" [Iakimets 2001]). Instead, in a 2001 interview Pavlovsky offered a skeptical view of the notion of "civil society" itself, calling it a "fabrication" (*vydumka*); a "sacred cow," which, "like any sacred cow, is suspect"; a concept that effectively justified giving citizens "the right to clandestine penetration into the established political balance and imposing themselves in the capacity of an additional vehicle for sovereignty—its 'upgrade'" (Iakimets 2001). In the cynical political technology calculus of the early-Putinist FEP, the new media were more tools for *shaping* opinions than promoting the open exchange of them, and, at least in the early years of the Runet, the group directed its shaping efforts not so much at the "masses" (who for the most part had not discovered the internet) as they did at the political elite, the so-called decision makers.

Such initiatives were more vividly on display in the political work of Pavlovsky's more tech-savvy mentee, FEP employee Marina Litvinovich.

Internet "Eye of the Sovereign"

In contrast to Pavlovsky, Marina Litvinovich came to the political internet as a young phenom, hired by her mentor at FEP in 1996 at the age of twenty-one, not yet having completed her philosophy degree at Moscow State University. Quickly appointed head of internet operations at the foundation, Litvinovich was integrally involved in various web-based efforts to promote pro-Kremlin parties and candidates and more aggressively suppress the antiestablishment vote. She successfully established an online presence for then Deputy Prime Minister Boris Nemtsov and then helped Nemtsov build a web interface for his new right-of-center Young Russia Party, boosting his status among the politically engaged, web-savvy liberals that he needed to bolster his credentials as a young reformer (Smetanin 2002). Particularly successful was the "For a worthy life" initiative she developed for him, which featured a call for netizens "to engage in that which, for the majority has always been distant: politics. You need to do this to avoid turning into lumpen, to have the chance to return to a worthy and free life" (quoted in Smetanin 2002). As one contemporary observer noted, "the forum on [Nemtsov's] site became one of the most popular places for the discussion of political themes on the Russian internet" (Smetanin 2002).

Litvinovich demonstrated similar creativity in engaging citizens online with her design of the website for another young, (then) liberal-minded politician and former prime minister, Sergei Kirienko (a figure who would later play a central role in the internet policy of the Putin administration). To enter the site, users first had to answer a prompt posted across a splash page: "Should we install a more professional management of the country?" (Smetanin 2002).

At the same time, Litvinovich had her fair share of reality checks on the limitations of the internet as a medium for promoting civic debate. The Internet Parliament that she initiated in 1998—an online forum for civic-minded discussion that might provide a sensible road map for the actual legislative chamber—proved less than desirable for its creators, too frequently devolving into an unruly, undisciplined, and often "frivolous chat" (Smetanin 2002), akin to the "private speech register" of Vakhtin's binary. Even more web-enlightened political leaders such as Kirienko paid little attention to the resource as a result, and the site was removed by FEP after less than a year (Smetanin 2002).

Litvinovich also proved more than adept at using the new medium for the darker arts of political technology, spearheading influence campaigns and negative or "black" PR targeting political opponents (see fig. 1.3). On the eve of the

ЮРИЙ ЛУЖКОВ

Открытки
English
Новости
Биография
Семья
Работа
Москва
Прямая речь
Идеи
Отечество
Друзья
О Лужкове
Фотоальбом
Юмор
Ваше мнение

"Сегодня необходимо открыто
говорить о недостатках
и злоупотреблениях,
которые проявляются
в нашей стране,
только тогда Россию
можно будет называть
демократическим государством".

ЮРИЙ ЛУЖКОВ

www.lujkov.com

Новости

Открытки
Новости
Биография
Семья
Работа
Москва
Прямая речь
Идеи
Отечество
Друзья
О Лужкове
Фотоальбом
Юмор
Ваше мнение
English

Предлагаем вашему вниманию ежедневные новости и комментарии:

28 января
Навигатор: Что сегодня почитать в Интернете?

Сегодня в газетах: Фракция ОВР не смогла извлечь выгоду из парламентского кризиса; Генпрокуратура может отменить незаконные сборы московской мэрии; Юрий Лужков подыскал адвокатов.

27 января
Навигатор: Что сегодня почитать в Интернете?

Сегодня в газетах: "Московская правда" считает депутатов ОВР "народными мстителями"; Не исключено, что Лужков будет летать по Москве на вертолете; В рядах ОВР зреет недовольство собственным лидером.

FIGURE 1.3. Screenshot of homepage and "News" page from "Iurii Luzhkov," the fake site created by the FEP to tarnish Vladimir Putin's main opponents in the 2000 presidential elections. While the homepage features an attractive photo of the mayor and an aspirational quote about Russia's potential as a "democratic state," the next layer of pages ("News," "Biography") host content uniformly critical of Luzhkov. Source: "Iurii Luzhkov" (1 March 2000), https://web.archive.org/web/20000301200338/http://www.lujkov.ru/.

1999 parliamentary elections, for example, she and others at FEP created a fake website of their client's main opponent, Mayor Yury Luzhkov, using a modified spelling (www.lujkov.ru instead of www.luzhkov.ru) but similar design, where they posted a damning but false story about the failed attempted at collusion between Luzhkov and members of the Communist Party. As Litvinovich later openly explained of the intended effect of the disinformation, "Reporting the collapse of the proposed deal was to serve as proof that there was, indeed, a desire to reach a deal" (Dzekholovskii 1999).

With Luzhkov essentially out of the picture and Putin serving as interim president and anointed Yeltsin successor, the presidential election the following spring posed the opposite problem for the pro-Putin political technologists: Rather than facing a formidable opponent, their candidate faced no credible opposition whatsoever. Concerned that the lack of competition would cause citizens to stay home from the polls and threaten falling short of the minimum 50 percent turnout required to certify the election, Litvinovich and her colleagues at FEP decided to engineer an alternative in the form of the "Against all candidates" option that, at the time, appeared on all federal election ballots. To do so, they relied heavily on the internet to make the option appealing enough to get citizens to the polls. The young Litvinovich was again quite open about the rationale behind their political-technological handiwork: "Having run up against the absence of any real competition to Putin from the available pool of politicians, we found such an opponent on the internet, [and] promoted it to society through the central TV stations. It was the candidate Against All, who lived on the 'Kremlin Wall' website" (Agamov 2000).[9]

On the heels of the same election, Litvinovich and the FEP launched the website Putin: The Expert Net Channel (VVP.ru) to bring more of the skeptical intellectual elite on board the Putin train. The posted rationale behind the initiative read like a concept memo from the antihero of Viktor Pelevin's *Generation P*, Vladilen Tatarsky, who used his mastery of media and marketing to promote questionable products and politicians. Excerpts of the Putin blurb included the following:

- The country is being drawn into the tasks of the post-electoral period. These tasks need those who will come to formulate and resolve them. **There is no one**.

---

9. Proving too potent a form of resistence for the growingly protective tastes of its creators, the actual "Against all candidates" line didn't last long, having been legislated out of existence in 2006. The initiative nevertheless anticipated later Putinist methods of ginning up enthusiasm in non-competitive presidential races, such as the recruitment of popular TV star and journalist Ksenia Sobchak to run in 2018, who formally introduced herself on YouTube as the "against all" candidate (Sobchak 2017).

- The Russian expert community is facing the future unwillingly, as a terrifying inevitability for it. The fear paralyzes, limiting the field of discussions to unfruitful (and often self-fulfilling) predictions of impending dictatorship. It must be understood that, by "dictatorship," the experts are imagining the prospects of their own unemployment. They doubt that they will preserve their place in intellectual production, be it in power (*vo vlasti*) or in the opposition. Their fear is not unfounded.
- The new president is encountering a loud, unfriendly choir of skeptics where he actually needs help—although a queue of friends and fathers of victory is forming where he actually needs a purge of the cadres. Victory has been dishonored by the worthlessness of old politicians and threatens to be nullified.
- Pressure is needed from new forces in society to compel the media, expert and political communities to recognize a new set of problems, a new agenda. **A new expert initiative is essential . . .**
- With the aim of stimulating such activity, the site VVP: Expert Net Channel has been commissioned, located at the address "www.vvp.ru." The main content of the project is the use of network capabilities in the interest of professional political discussion. Due to the cave-dweller ignorance of the oligarchy-controlled media, the Runet remains practically the only field for [such discussion].[10]

Aside from its cynicism and self-mocking irony (recruiting a new community of intellectuals by reminding them of their own borderline obsolescence), the concept piece underscores the view illuminated earlier in the profile of Pavlovsky: The internet was not only the natural domain of a new political intelligentsia; it was likewise seen as the last remaining bastion of free expression, due to the "dominance of the cave-dweller ignorance of the oligarchy-controlled media." The internet was depicted as the last best hope for ensuring that the new age in politics would be controlled by a professional class, or expert community, capable of tempering the impending dictatorship they (unjustly) feared coming on. That the project was more an effort at co-optation than of good-faith alliance-building later became clear in public statements by Litvinovich, who described it as an attempt to create a more Kremlin-friendly opposition compared to the Communists, Grigory Yavlinsky, and the fearmongers on NTV (Dugaev and Lur'e 2000).[11]

---

10. Emphasis in the original. "Novaia ekspertnaia initsiativa" 2000.

11. The site, which remained virtually unchanged through the first six months of its existence, featured front-page commentaries with such titles as "Putin will bring everyone back to their senses," "I look forward to the strengthening of the power vertical," and "First and foremost, I expect from Putin a predictable economic policy" (www.vvp.ru).

Discursively, these electoral initiatives employed by Litvinovich and the FEP reflected a rhetorical admixture of high-minded intellectualism and low-minded political persuasion that was at times toxic, at times comical, and, in all likelihood, relatively innocuous. As discussed earlier, the FEP had already launched a series of news-oriented websites, which remained relatively objective until election time, when they tilted blatantly toward FEP clients (which, during these early years, primarily meant the Kremlin). In 2000 they took one step closer to outright propaganda and information war through the formation of *Strana.ru*, with Litvinovich serving as general director and editor in chief. Litvinovich and the site's cofounder Mikhail Rogozhnikov were unabashed in their declaration that the resource would reflect state ideology, justifying the positioning as a much-needed counterbalance to the "emptiness of suspicions and myths" that contaminated the oligarch-controlled mainstream news, thanks to operators who, by privileging ideology over information, had "little more to sell than loyalty or opposition" (Litvinovich and Rogozhnikov 2000; Pavlovskii 2000; Tselykh 2000).

In a separate document published together with the declaration in the same issue, Pavlovsky elaborated on the failings of the press in the 1990s (which he called the "Second Republic") due to control by big money from Gusinsky and Berezovsky and pointed to the internet as the last bastion of free speech and a "direct channel for [the population's] ties to power [*vlast'*] as one of the conditions of popular rule [*narodopravie*]"—a notion that would be expanded on later by President Dmitry Medvedev after the emergence of the social media–fueled web 2.0 (Pavlovskii 2000). Yet another piece in this same inaugural issue of *Strana.ru* painted a dire picture of an imminent "information war against authorities [*vlast'*]" by big-money interests invading the new media sphere—a war that had essentially been "lost" and "conceded without a fight" by authorities ("Vlast', Internet i my" 2000).

Strana.ru would put information first and refuse to sell out to the highest bidder, they claimed, and, in so doing, would bring a "death sentence to the old media market" (Litvinovich and Rogozhnikov 2000). So, while Litvinovich promised the site would "bring the voice of state power into the information sphere" (Antonova 2000) and serve as "the eye of the Sovereign" in the Russian regions (Bardin 2000), all this was done, at least so the spin was spun, to restore the information integrity of a "completely decimated communication space" of an oligarch-dominated postcollapse media in which there was "no freedom of speech, no representation of the political spectrum of society, not even a representation of society itself" (Litvinovich and Rogozhnikov 2000).

Curiously, Litvinovich employed a similar sort of rhetorical jujitsu when rationalizing the need for the site for international purposes—namely, to do battle on more equal terms with the United States in what was no longer a "Cold

War" but a "civilizational war," which would take the form of an "information war," a "war of smart people" (Litvinovich 2001). Anticipating a notion central to the later high-style register of Putinism, she saw the internet as a key tool for the propagation of Russian civilizational values globally.[12]

Critics took the FEP's promotion of the internet as the final frontier for democratic expression with a barrel of salt, pointing out that it was the very FEP that enjoyed a near monopoly over web-based news and information outlets, owning upward of twenty-four different projects at a time when there few other viable resources than this (Morochenko 2000). A commentator for the Berezovsky-owned *Nezavisimaia gazeta* dismissed the *Strana.ru* project as another case of the political technologist "kicking a dead dog" (referring to the intelligentsia) (Makarov 2001).

Be that as it may, the rhetorical stakes were clear for the Kremlin's closest public relations advisers, whose footprint in the early Runet news and information landscape grew exponentially in a matter of years: The internet was a prime battleground for the "information war of smart people." The space may have been sparsely populated, but it featured many of the biggest decision makers among the political and business elite (Ivanov 2003). And the consequences of that war were as substantial for the intelligentsia as they were for the young Putin administration. Controlling this new information sphere was a matter of survival.

In a less gloating, more cautious article published after the elections, Litvinovich acknowledged the existence of black PR along the lines of leaks, rumors, and disinformation but tried to stake out higher ground for the FEP, claiming its goal was "to develop the internet, not contaminate it" ("My khotim razvivat' rossiiskii Internet, a ne zagriazniat' ego" [Litvinovich 2002]). But the tension between competing discourses—"internet as last bastion for democracy and freedom of expression" and "internet as the 'eye of the Sovereign'"—may have been too much. The fact that *Strana.ru* did not last more than two years may be an indication of the difficulty, if not impossibility, of squaring the circle ("Putin otreksia" 2002).

The underlying cynicism, disingenuousness, and even presumptuousness of their attitudes and actions certainly didn't help. In response to a provocative question in a 2000 interview with her own FEP-affiliated *Russian Journal*, Litvinovich rationalized her activity by deferring to fate, morality, and the risks that come with being a professional reality shaper:

---

12. The only difference between Litvinovich's info-warrior rhetoric and the language that would come to dominate late Putinism is the notion that such tactics in some way constituted a "smart war." As seen in chapter 6, a large portion of Putin's media-manipulation projects relied on the exact opposite—the assumption that target users were vulnerable due to their ignorance or naive willingness to entertain vapid and at times aggressive verbal exchange with total strangers on social media.

[INTERVIEWER:] You don't feel uncomfortable at times because it is you who sometimes puts out some sort of trifle, trash, or junk onto the net, for instance, and it flies there over our heads, virtually, and irreversibly and horribly changes the nuo-sphere?

[LITVINOVICH:] My job is to change the nuo-sphere. But I take care that only what is needed flies over us. And what that is—I determine myself, based on the moral law within me and the starry sky above.

The notion of the "nuo-sphere" predates the internet but represents an elemental materialization of knowledge that nicely blends with abstract metaphors of "cybersphere" and "cyberspace." The raison d'être of political technology, in Litvinovich's apt encapsulation, was to manipulate the content and contours of those spheres in which knowledge resided—particularly a new media environment dominated, as the early Runet was, by new media intellectuals. Her justification of the occasional "trash" she and her kind emitted suggested a sort of "ends-justify-the-means" attitude: If it is for an ultimately good cause (combating oligarchs, defending the sovereign, etc.), the moral stars allow for it.

Perhaps with the specter of a return to Communism lurking, contemporary political technologists had little trouble rationalizing their web-based engagement in the rhetorical dark arts. Decades later, however, it has become far clearer that it was precisely this sort of activity that laid the foundation for an information "nuo-sphere" rife with propaganda, misinformation, and slander toward the political opposition, often done in the name of protecting the nation and the "Sovereign" himself from both domestic "foreign agents" and external threats.[13]

The other lesson emerging from the FEP story is that, even in the earliest days of the Runet, more micromanaged, top-down efforts at influencing the polity and political discourse tended to be far more effective at the art of manipulation, contamination, and other forms of dirty politics than they were at promoting democracy, civic engagement, or civil discourse. Through their success and failures, however, their efforts did not go unnoticed. In Litvinovich's case, even well after she had turned from pro-Kremlin PR to oppositional politics herself (as early as the 2004 election cycle, in fact), contemporaries remembered well her role as an FEP operative, and, in the wake of a horrific street-side mugging widely perceived as retribution for her later anti-Putin activism, Litvinovich was mocked

---

13. Navalny (2023) offered a scathing, if controversial, rebuke of this attitude, blaming it for directly enabling the culture of corruption and criminality emblematic of the Putin era.

with emotionally charged monikers such as *piarshchitsa* (woman-PR specialist), "scandalously famous political technologist," and "manipulator of public opinion" to lower her status in the arena of public opinion ("Politekhnologicheskii obman" 2006).[14] And though he turned away from Putin after the events of 2011–2012 and became a regular feature on oppositional media, Pavlovsky was remembered widely for his work facilitating Putin's political legitimation, having come up with such memorable, but cynically infused, slogans as "dictatorship of the law" (*diktatura zakona*), "vertical of power" (*vertikal vlasti*), and "the Putin majority" (*putinskoe bol'shinstvo*) (Bekbulatova 2018). More importantly, after activities such as those outlined here, the Runet acquired a growing reputation as a sphere vulnerable to and rife with political manipulation and contamination—a reputation, as seen in the next chapter, that had as much to do with language as it did with politics.

---

14. Fifteen years later, it should be noted, her reputation as a champion for liberal, democratic causes was largely unquestioned, and her online initiatives—particularly her blog-based news aggregator, Besttoday—highly impactful as an alternative to a growingly state-controlled news environment both off- and online.

PUTIN'S ONLINE ICONOCLASTS

If the story of Pavlovsky, Litvinovich, and the FEP marks something of a maiden discovery of Runet as a space conducive for consolidating the symbolic power of a new president viewed suspiciously by the oligarch-dominated mainstream media, the figures profiled in this chapter remind us that authority in that space was (and is) still largely measured in terms of monetization and entertainment. Not too long after the emergence of an alternative pro-Putin web-based information sphere, there arose something of a concurrent trend in more creative, cultural content.

This chapter profiles three early Runet adopters associated with the so-called counterculturists (*kontrkul'turshchiki*) who positioned themselves as cultural contrarians while demonstrating a willingness, if not eagerness, to promote Putin and causes close to him. I call them "iconoclasts," not due to any attempt on their part to shatter the image of a sacred ruler. Instead, their iconoclasm comes in their ability to recast that image in a manner that brought it greater symbolic capital for audiences that were either wary of political authority (and Putin more specifically) or inclined to disengage at the first hint of political content. Rhetorically, the countercultural orientation of the pro-Putin iconoclasts carried a distinct flavor that couched political orthodoxy in the boundary-pushing vulgarity of the language of the (virtual) streets. At a time when the Russian-language internet witnessed the emergence and spread of web 2.0 social networking platforms and concurrent growth in usership, these individuals offered models of promoting Putin and Putinism for audiences less eager for heady political discussions and more inclined to click on engaging content—be it profanity laden, humorous, or accessibly enlightening. At the same time, they collectively reflect an odd combination of the hypermasculinity emblematic of Putin's speech style, the traditional values-laden ideology prominent in his later speeches, and an entrepreneurial recognition of the wealth, fortune, and fame that could come from their contrarian embrace of this rhetoric.

The Producer: Konstantin Rykov

We musn't fear technologies: we need to turn them into our weapon.

—Konstantin Rykov (quoted in Rezchikov 2009)

Konstantin Rykov might be seen as the personified foundation of web-based counterculture, and in interviews he does not shy away from the questionable label, "father of the Russian internet" (Gamzaeva 2007). Most significant from a rhetorical standpoint was his early embrace of salacious content. If Pavlovsky viewed himself as a bearer of the legacy of the late-Soviet intelligentsia, Rykov, born of a later generation and boasting no claim as a man of letters, viewed the early Runet primarily as an opportunity for profit. And few sectors of the early Runet economy were more profitable than sex and porn. By his own admission, Rykov was involved in a good half dozen porn sites as early as 1998, including Neznakomka.ru, Aramis.ru, Erotoman.ru, Ozornik.ru, Popka.ru, and Persid.ru, resulting in accumulated wealth that would allow him to boast that "[he] makes in a single night as much as Yandex makes in a year" (Mal'gin 2007; "Konstantin Rykov" 2001).[1] In 1998, he joined forces with Yegor Lavrov (a.k.a. "Frank Nero") to create Fuck.ru, an early web 1.0 rendition of a social networking site that prided itself in being "the heart of spirituality and counterculture" ("Nevod, i t.d" 2002). It was this same "art project," as Rykov called it, along with his later brainchild, Udaff.com, that would be at the forefront of generating "scumbag language."

Scumbag Language

Few episodes of the linguistic history of the Runet attracted cries of verbal contamination like the viral spread of what came to be known as scumbag language, or *iazyk padonkov*, in the early and mid-2000s. A twenty-first-century "slap in the face of public taste" (jack_patterson 2006), this Runet-spawned slang was distinguished by what Zvereva and Berdicevskis (2014, 123–24) describe as "a

---

1. Yandex, Russia's highly successful search engine, was established in 1997 by the tech entrepreneur Arkady Volosh and has since grown into a multibillion-dollar company.

deliberately erroneous writing, in which a word's written form imitated its pronunciation, a large amount of clichés, the use of low style and foul words, and the declarative denial of repressive literacy"—all of which could be seen in the "Scumbag Manifesto" published originally on Udaff.com:

МОНЕФЕСТ «ПАДОНКАФФ»

Фсвязи с плановым сакрощением фенонсиравонийа аброзаваннийа и истественной ывалйуцией рускава йазыка призывайу:

1. Фсе правела рускай арфаграфии и громатеки—в Бобруйск
2. Фсе учепники рускава йазыка и лейтеротуры—фтопку.
3. Фсем учетилям рускава йазыка и лейтероторы школ и вузов—выпеть йаду
4. Дольнейжее розвитее рускава йазыка паручить энстетутам НИИ БАЦА и НИИ БЕТ.[2]

["Scumbagg" Monifesto

Wit regard to the planned cats to ejucation financing and the nachural evalushon of the Rashin langwich I heerby deklare:

1. Send awl rulz of Rashin arthografy to Timbuktu.
2. Into the fire wit Awl Rashin langwich and liturachur texbooks
3. Poyzin for awl tichurs af Rashin langwich and liturachur
4. The ferther divelapmint af the Rashin langwich shal be asined to the inthusiasts of Fak'd U. and Skrew'd U.]

In addition to their orthographic play, speakers of "Olbanian," as it also came to be called, produced a host of memorable phrases that, at least for a time, seeped into broader public discourse (e.g., аффтар жжот, пеши исчо, аффтар выпей йаду, превед, кросавчег).[3] The scumbags also reveled in eye-popping profanity and the sort of off-color humor that scholars have associated with a hypermasculinity common among earlier Runet adopters—and of early Putinism (Goriunova 2006). In fact, several of the original "scumbags" (including Rykov and Sergei Minaev, featured in chapter 7) would become some of Putin's most eager and active advocates online.[4]

---

2. Quoted in Zvereva and Berdicevskis (2014, 137–38n5) from jack_patterson (2006).

3. In order of appearance (including alternative orthographic renditions of alternative spelling): "the awther burns" [the author is awesome], "rite moor" [write more], "drink poyzon, awther" [kill yourself, author], "hellow," and "gud-lukin'."

4. Kukulin (2016) argues that their aggressive and cynical embrace of linguistic transgression made for a natural fit with the Putin regime's transgressions in the political and geopolitical realm.

Rank and file guardians of the national tongue nevertheless bemoaned the spoiling of the "great and mighty" Russian language and warned of the oncoming moral degradation that would ensue. One teacher claimed her students "treated [scumbag language] as a norm, as legitimized illiteracy," and wondered if it was "possible for a teacher to resist the all-out fashion for illiteracy within the confines of the school curriculum" (Parfeneva 2009). In his *Primer for Olbanian*, Maksim Krongauz (2013, 123–24) observes that the new generation of digital natives was not only more prone to orthographic errors but also lacked any sense of "shame" toward them. Some online advocates of proper, norm-based speech joined a campaign in 2005–2006 to purge the internet of scumbags, posting banners at their blogs that declared: "I can speak [proper] Russian" and "Write in [proper] Russian: authers [*afftary*] need not disturb" (quoted in Zvereva 2012, 69–71).

Upon closer look, however, in scumbag language, we have more than just a simple case of profanity-laden illiteracy. It turns out that it took some work to master it, and as such, the slang instilled a significant level of in-group pride as a linguistic mark of distinction. As Zvereva (2012, 66) notes, "Those located at the source of Scumbag language, even though underscoring its democratism, also aim to enhance the language's status and point to the distinguishing features of 'real scumbags.'" Krongauz (2013) echoes this idea, arguing that scumbag is best understood as a language ideology consciously embracing *anti-literacy* rather than a marker of web-based *illiteracy*. Rather than wallowing in some sort of orthographic anarchy, would-be users must learn a relatively coherent set of counter rules to employ it "properly" (see also Zvereva 2012, 83–128). It also turns out that the use of Olbanian was a relatively fleeting trend. By the time it went viral online in 2005–2006, the experimental slang had already gone out of favor among its founders and then petered out as a popular trend as well. Like most innovative argots, the loss of novelty spelled its own demise (Zvereva 2012; Zvereva and Berdicevskis 2014). But the fact that it even emerged and spread as it did is a testament to the media on which it spread—conducive for an orally modified written language and the viral spread of trending memes. And even though its ultimate impact on contemporary Russian may have been limited to a few isolated words and phrases, the phenomenon drew enough broader attention during its viral period—a period when many Russians were first coming online—to help foster an impression of the internet as a source of verbal and cultural corruption.

Online News Gets a Tabloid Makeover

When he wasn't engaged in profanity-filled word games on Fuck.ru, Rykov was carving inroads into the arena of online political news and information, heading up a host of Kremlin-backed news and information sites such as *Dni.ru*, *Vzgliad.ru*, and Russia.ru. Here, too, his entrepreneurial roots showed through his willingness to market the sites by running banners at the top of his porn sites and using his infamous reality show, Behind the glass (*Za steklom*), as an additional means of pushing eyes to the general news. As one contemporary explained the logic, the increased traffic at *Dni.ru* generated by the links on the porn sites would be attractive to a broader range of advertisers who didn't want to post ads on those sites directly (Borisov 2002). The site featured a political language and content differing markedly from the intellectual orientation of the Russian Journal, with at least half of the news devoted to leisure and entertainment. Interspersed with juicy tabloid offerings, more serious political topics largely reflected the priorities of the ruling Putin elite. On the international front, the site devoted considerable attention to critiquing the United States invasion of Iraq. National coverage included Putin's battles with oligarch-owned media, rich with uncomplimentary portraits of Gusinsky and Berezovsky as dishonest brokers bent on bringing chaos to Russia's domestic security (Fedotov 2002). Coverage of Putin himself gushed on all fronts, playing up his leadership skills ("Putin is full of decisiveness in dealing with the uncorrected injustices from Russia's error filled entry into capitalism" ["Putin pristrunit" 2002]), touting his status as a man of his word ("The President always keeps his word. . . . And he does so strongly. . . . Word and deed. Silence is golden. Say it like it is [*Skazhet—kak otrezhet*]" ["Zachem podnimali" 2001]), and highlighting Western news coverage of the "cult of personality" taking shape around him, as witnessed by the commissioned girl-group "hit" song, "Someone Like Putin" ("Vybory" 2002).

The integration of political and popular language evident in *Dni.ru* had precedents in the infotainment-oriented print and television media common to those spheres in the 1990s. It also marked a noteworthy turn in web-based media, a popularization—at times, even vulgarization—of political speech that would spread still more virally as more everyday Russians populated the pages and networks of the Runet. If Pavlovsky's projects sought to promote Putin by normalizing him in the language of the intellectual elites, Rykov's engaged in a baser PR blitz for the growing number of commoners inhabiting the Runet. His work did not go unnoticed by media heads closer to the Kremlin, earning him an invitation from then head of the newly state-friendly Channel One, Konstantin Ernst, to run the TV station's newly created internet department in 2002 (Vishnepol'skii 2002).[5] It also got him funding in the run-up to the elections of 2007–2008 to enhance the "For Putin!" website (zaputina.ru) and create Russia.ru, billed as "the

---

5. For evidence of Rykov's self-proclaimed associations with Putin ideologist, Vladislav Surkov, see Kukulin (2016, 251–53).

first Russian internet television station" ("Konstantin Rykov" 2012). It was at this point the Runet counterculturist officially joined the political system, by joining the United Russia ticket of candidates to the State Duma representing Nizhegorodskaia Oblast'. But at least one open-minded (and web-savvy) journalist, Oleg Kashin, was willing to give Rykov his due even then, remarking on the pages of *Nezavisimaia gazeta* "Once a scumbag, always a scumbag ('Padonak' ostaetsia 'padonkom'")—having created the internet TV channel Russia.ru to advertise his party, Rykov to the general amazement of its audience proceeded to upload a videoclip featuring excerpts of the United Russia congress set to the theme song from the blockbuster *Pirates of the Caribbean*. The obvious joke, as it turned out, had a much greater impact on the public than memorized monologues on 'sovereign democracy' or Putin's plan" (Kashin 2007).[6]

The Folklorist: Maksim Kononenko

For the most part, I'm guided by two goals in everything I do—glory and money.

—Maksim Kononenko (Tsvei 2004)

As Rykov, Pavlovsky, and others discovered early on, political branding online had always been something of an uphill struggle, with direct efforts at promoting Putin and Putinism often coming across as forced and ham-handed. One of the earliest examples of success came from the digital pen of the computer programmer Maksim Kononenko in the form of a serialized blog bearing the title "Vladimir Vladimirovich™."[7]

A programmer by training and employee at one of the Runet's oldest IT companies, ParallelGraphics, Kononenko established an online presence early, using the pseudonym *Mr. Parker*, under which he would eventually produce Vladimir Vladimirovich™. Even as he was earning "Programmer of the Year" awards from industry associations (Ivanova 2000), Kononenko had more writerly aspirations,

---

6. For a history and analysis of the emergence of digital television, see Strukov and Zvereva 2014. Morozov (2011, 129–32) offers additional background on Rykov's pro-Kremlin online political engagement, though suggests this was more of a dramatic shift from his earlier activities. Rhetorically and stylistically, I am arguing, there is more continuity than break.

7. The title of the series included the trademark symbol and appeared at the website vladimirvladimirovich.ru, which is no longer available after being removed by Kononenko himself. Subsequent references to the series come from the separately published book containing a selection of approximately 550 of the stories (Kononenko 2005a), with both story and page number included. For an early analysis of the project, see Goriunova (2006, 181–83).

having briefly attended the literary institute and developed more creative online projects, such as the virtual tour of Lenin's tomb and a website for the "Lunar Embassy in Moscow," which sold plots on the moon to deep-pocketed Russian real-estate barons (Travin 2001). Kononenko likewise wrote for online news and information platforms, establishing himself as a well-known music critic and journalist, working with the likes of Nossik and Rykov, and even succeeding the latter as editor in chief of the online *Bourgeois Journal* (Burzhuaznyi zhurnal; and later *Dni.ru*). Although his blogging and online journalism earned him the reputation of a digital graphomaniac (Kvasha 2005), the programmer secured his position at the center of Runet subculture, serving on boards and sharing social circles with the leading creators of Runet content in these early years.[8]

The upward trajectory of Kononenko's Vladimir Vladimirovich™ project, from the side hobby of a full-time journalist when it debuted in October 2002 to the most famous political blog by 2005 ("Rossiia v lirike bloga" 2005), coincided with the meteoric rise in popularity of the web log, or blog, while at once maintaining some semblance of intellectual or writerly pretension. By Mr. Parker's own admission, the near daily blog posts for Vladimir Vladimirovich™ were initially inspired by the absurdist writing of Daniil Kharms (Tsvei 2004). But as the project unfolded, it became more akin generically to a synthesis of the Russian joke, or *anekdot*, and what in Russian folklore is referred to as a "tale from everyday life" (*bytovaia skazka*). The most stable structural feature of the post was its formulaic opening, "Once upon a time [*odnazhdy*], Vladimir Vladimirovich™ Putin," which made clear at once the primary subject of interest and the fact that story was not entirely grounded in reality. This latter feature proved to be the blog's greatest marketing tool, as it essentially gave readers something they desperately sought but could not have: an inside look at their comparatively younger new president as he went about his daily business, both public and private. According to Kononenko, the combination of secrecy surrounding Putin's private life and his "bland" public image created fertile soil for the germination of fictional mythologies of the president—a mythology to which Kononenko saw his project contributing. Although he likened it to "a coloring book in which only the basic outlines are drawn, and every viewer can fill in the rest as they like" ("Arkhiv" 2004),[9] Kononenko's persistent use of the trademark symbol with the

---

8. Indicative of this position was his place on the editorial board of the History of the Internet in Russia project (NetHistory.ru) (Al'ians Media 2003).

9. Curiously, Putin himself was frequently portrayed as an expert at mirroring the gestures and expressions of his interlocutors to win them over, a skill attributed to his KGB training (Gorham 2013, 82–84).

president's first name and patronymic made it clear he saw himself as something of a marketer of a popular Putin brand. Depending on their subject matter, posts varied in tonality from the satirical to the absurd to the sober. Regardless of tone, however, the most successful ones used the succinct format of the blog and informal style of folkloric genres to produce a portrait of Putin that entertained and ultimately impressed.

Outlaws and Androids of the Kremlin

Among the more commented-on features of the blog when it first emerged was the author's attribution of nonstandard slang to the national leader, the most emblematic example of which is the character Vladimir Vladimirovich™'s ubiquitous use of *bratello* (the loose equivalent of "mate" or "bruddah"), a form of address characteristic in criminal argot and used for everyone from his chief of staff to the Lord Almighty. Hardly surprising, given Putin's infamous vow as Yeltsin's prime minister to "bump off" terrorists in their "shithouses," the penchant for salty language struck a popular chord, and Mr. Parker built it into the vignettes at every turn. When viewed in the broader context of the political culture of the early Putin era, Putin's language was entirely appropriate—just the verbal tonic needed to deal with the widespread graft and corruption plaguing Russian society, especially the paragons of graft, the Russian oligarchs (Gorham 2014, 131–38). For example, lamenting as he watches the tycoon Roman Abramovich basking in the glory of the adoring Chelsea soccer fans on television (a team he purchased for £140 million in 2003), Putin castigates the oil baron for living the high life as an English Premier League club owner:

> "You're a bastard, Roma," Vladimir Vladimirovich™ said sadly. "And you're father . . . Arkadii . . ."
> "Listen, mate [*bratello*]," said Vladimir Vladimirovich™. "Why don't you call the tax police. Have 'em pay Roma a visit."
> "What d'ya mean?" asked the Chief of Staff with surprise. "He's on assignment."
> "It's still insulting," answered Vladimir Vladimirovich™. "They're there at the stadium singing 'Kalinka', and we're sitting here in the dirt. That's not the way things are done [*Ne po poniatiiam*]. Have them dig something up on him. Make him share." (Kononenko 2005a, #292, 361)

His willingness to deploy the tax police to rectify the monetary and moral injustices of Abramovich's flaunting his wealth technically takes Putin outside the bounds of the law, but in the outlaw (*vory-v-zakone*) culture of post-Soviet Russia (the language of which generously peppers Putin's own speech) conveys a sense of extrajudicial justice, restoring respect and dignity to a people who remain stuck in the Russian dirt and deserving of a share of the profits.

This outlaw mentality can be seen in Vladimir Vladimirovich™'s treatment of the political rank and file, portrayed throughout the series as subservient automatons—"androids," as they're called in the blog—void of self-awareness and fully willing to do the political bidding of the Kremlin. ("They walk like alien-robots [*roboty-gromozeki*], orderly in lines" [#348, 424].) After the Parliament passes the Putin-initiated law granting the president the authority to appoint regional governors, for example, Mr. Parker portrays Putin and his chief political technologist, Vladislav Surkov, salivating over the opportunity to put a new fleet of automatons into circulation:

> "So they've gone ahead and passed the law. Now we designate governors ourselves."
>
> "It's been a long time coming," said Vladislav Iur'evich. "I have about thirty of them gathering dust in storage. By spring we'll do all fifty of 'em. Atomic battery packs. A psychotronic cannon in the head. Everything that people have."
>
> "Excellent," said Vladimir Vladimirovich™. "Did you make any with female bodies?"
>
> "Of course," said Vladislav Iur'evich. "No sexism here." (#477, 578)

The rare parliamentarian who shows some semblance of ethical independence—opting out of state-funded apartments afforded all members of the legislative branch—is treated like a dangerous aberration, likely the result of a malicious hack (#532, 643–45).

While more oppositional portraits may cast this relationship in the negative light of dictatorial overreach, Mr. Parker's satirical kid gloves suggest the dynamic is either more endemic to those immediately surrounding Putin (as in the example with Surkov above) or deeply engrained in Russian political culture and thus something any conscientious leader should take advantage of—gender parity notwithstanding.

Vladimir Vladimirovich™ perpetuates traditional attitudes regarding civic engagement, public discussion, and debate. At times they are ascribed to Putin himself, such as his lack of concern for notions of "electorate" (*elektorat*) and "voters" (*izbirateli*) (#147, 180), or in his boasting, as he watches the broadcast of 2004 American presidential debates, that he managed to win the presidency without having to debate a single time (#421, 512–13). Elsewhere Mr. Parker's Putin is seen as beholden to his more power-sensitive political handlers, who assure him that "freedom of speech" has never been a thing in Russia (#139, 166–70). If Putin had his way, Mr. Parker assures his readers by recreating such encounters, he would freely engage in conversation with his political adversaries, be it Mikhail Khodorkovsky (#152, 185–86; #358, 434–35; #367, 443–44) or Garry Kasparov (#518, 624–25).

Putin Up Close and Personal

Particularly in the earlier years of the blog, Mr. Parker softens the satirical edge of a leader held hostage by a thicket of corruption and bureaucracy by devoting attention to Putin as a loving husband and devoted family man, either cherishing or pining for the ability to lead an ordinary life. One December 2002 post features an exhausted Putin starting his day with a phone call to his wife Liudmila ("'I'm so tired, darling.' 'I love you,' Vladimir Vladimirovich™'s wife uttered with affection. 'I love you,' answered Vladimir Vladimirovich™, and hung up the phone" [#17, 30]).[10] One month later, Mr. Parker shows the president telling a bedtime story to his daughters and, while the story itself about Stalin's exile from Lenin's mausoleum brings out the quirky side of Putin, his "loving gaze" at the two sleeping girls makes it clear his intentions are pure (39). Days later, the same "loving glance" returns when the Putin family enjoys a quiet moment in a city park at sunset, Putin making a wish on a falling star (which an editor's note suggests may have been the US *Challenger* space shuttle exploding after launch) (42–43).

Still more frequently, the reader finds Vladimir Vladimirovich™ rejoicing in the pleasures of life outside the confining walls of the Kremlin (something the real Putin would never be able to do, even if, as Kononenko implies, he would like nothing more), be it listening to subway music during an imaginary commute home ("Vladimir Vladimirovich™ walked, thinking about how wonderful and sad this world was, and how great and talented was the country that he had been fated to rule" [#32, 36]), sharing shots of vodka with a random man on the commuter rail (*elektrichka*) ride to his suburban Novo-Ogarevo home ("'Well then—to victory,' the man whispered. Vladimir Vladimirovich™ nodded and they quickly drank up" [#192, 242]), or shopping for champagne and chocolate for Liudmila's birthday ("'Dear me, you look so much like Putin!' the girl exclaimed and became even more confused. Vladimir Vladimirovich™ unexpectedly blushed" [#503, 607]).

The imagined intersections of the political and the personal serve the dual function of humanizing Putin and personalizing his power. For all the authority he wields, he is at heart a simple Russian soul serving his fatherland for the greater

---

10. Just over ten years later, Putin and his wife used a television interview following their attendance of a ballet in the Kremlin to announce their separation and divorce.

good. That he does so with great sacrifice and reluctance ("I want a simple family life. I want to be with you." [#295, 366]) only enhances the aura of selfless duty. Mr. Parker reinforces the sacrifice by depicting Putin—largely for comic effect—as being trapped in a spartan existence that forces him at one point to admit to a rediscovered childhood friend that he lives outside of Moscow, has no car, has a cell phone with only one button on it, and doesn't even know how much money he makes (#122, 141–43). Dreams of career change are thwarted by the realization that there's no going back ("Who needs an [intelligence] agent whose face is known worldwide?" [#68, 76]). Advisers talk him out of resignation by appealing to his sense of civic duty to the people of Russia (not to mention the FSB): "Have you gone bonkers mate, or what?!! [*Ty chego, bratello, ofonarel, chto li?!!*] What do you mean, resign? Is that what you were elected to this post for? You gotta work, the country is depending on you! The country and the F-S-B!" (#129, 153). Even when he actively attempts to extract himself from the unwanted pressures of power, fate seems to get in the way—as in the March 2004 post in which his call to the Central Elections Commission informing them of his intention not to run for reelection turns out to miss the deadline by a day (#295, 364–67).

These sustained insights into the imagined private world of the president produce a portrait of a reluctant leader painfully aware of both the solitary nature of the position (there's no one to talk to when you're surrounded by sycophants [#404, 494–95]) and the spartan reality of the post ("President? So what? . . . What do I actually have? The Kremlin? Even that's not mine" [#134, 160]). Vlast' for Mr. Parker's Putin is not a key to unbridled power but a sacrifice for the greater good. Particularly in the later period of the blog, disgruntlement over his star-crossed fate results in outbursts of pathos-laden frustration from the growingly tragic hero, culminating in a "why-me" lament on Orthodox Christmas to the Almighty (whom he addresses with his customary *bratello*), when fed up with the litany of accusations—from his destruction of Yukos and gassing of the children of Beslan to his fostering of corruption and fabrication of war in Chechnya: "What kind of monster am I, huh?!? Say, answer me, mate, what do I have to do with it, if it's your will?!?! Huh?!?!?!" (#398, 486–88).

It is only a matter of months before we receive an answer to Putin's rhetorical question, when, in by far the longest post of the entire series, Mr. Parker strips away all hints of the quirkiness and satire that initially established the blog as a persuasive form of web-based political technology, offering in its place a syrupy, patriotic portrait of Putin reciting the presidential oath of office verbatim as he looks into the detached eye of the recently assassinated Chechen warlord Aslan Maskhadov. If final episodes are taken as important markers of the overall import of a literary production (be it a blog or a book), this one clearly underscores the importance of a self-sacrificing Putin in guaranteeing the security and stability of the Russian Federation, easily overshadowing all his quirks and shortcomings.

From the vantage point of political discourse, however, it is precisely once these weightier historical-philosophical issues take command of the blog that it loses the popular appeal that launched it to stardom in the first place. In its earliest permutations, Vladimir Vladimirovich™ still had that fresh, informal tone typical of its new media platform, as one critic put it, "alive like life, anxious and direct" (Bavil'skii 2005). But as patriotic flag-waving overshadows portraits of the quirky, quiet side of the everyman president, Vladimir Vladimirovich™ becomes less appreciated as an innovative form of online entertainment and more subject to accusations of paid political propaganda.

True to his counterculture roots, however, Kononenko embraced political controversy—particularly when economically expedient—and openly acknowledged, if not promoted, his associations with Kremlin insiders. He confirmed and further stoked rumors that Vladimir Vladimirovich™ had become obligatory reading among presidential administration staff (Vinogradova and Stepovoi 2004) and admitted he had even sold the rights to the blog in the fall of 2003 (on the eve of Putin's reelection campaign) "for a healthy sum" to an unnamed buyer for "the right to control the content," arguing, "I produce a literary product. If someone wants to buy and use it, that's good for me" (MacGregor 2004; Zakharchenko 2003). He acknowledged his political preferences for Putin as "the only adult in the room" (a view that would be reinforced come election time when the Putin team would handpick his political opponents to exclude serious threats) and stated directly that the blog was not designed to cast negative light on authorities but rather to humanize the authorities, to "make them all look like people" (Kononenko 2003; Tsvei 2004).

As his writerly star rose, so too did his open embrace of his pro-Putin partisanship: "All in all, impartiality in politics is disgusting," he declared in a 2005 interview. "It's dishonest and stupid, and generally impossible, since politics is a clash between interests, and if you are standing to the side of those interests, you're not in politics. I'm partial, of course. I'm loyal. What's more, I'll probably be loyal to any state machine" ("Kto kupil" 2005).

Statements such as these, together with more provocative declarations against the mothers who lost children in the terrorist hostage debacle in Beslan ("Stop criticizing Putin and give birth to new children" [Kononenko 2005b]), support of a pro-Putin youth group's public condemnation of the writers Vladimir Sorokin and Viktor Erofeev, and his embrace of the idea of a state-sponsored, English-language propaganda television station, Russia Today, earned Kononenko the labels "guard dog of a bloody regime" and "corrupt beast" (*prodazhnyi tvar'*) from the likes of the oppositional politician Grigory Yavlinsky and independent news editor Aleksandr Ryklin ("Gazetchiki" 2005; "'Vladimir Vladimirovich.ru' zakryl" 2006). In the wake of an onslaught of public attacks on him for these and other critical statements about liberal politicians and causes, Kononenko finally closed access to Vladimir Vladimirovich™ in March 2006, essentially depriving it of the popular oxygen that skyrocketed it to fame as one of the freshest and funniest pieces of political satire on the Runet ("'Vladimir Vladimirovich.ru' zakryl" 2006). And in the political season of 2007, Kononenko earned his reputation as a pro-Putin political operator, when he became active in the creation and propagation of two "spoiler" parties (Free Russia [Svobodnaia Rossiia] and Civic Force [Grazhdanskaia sila]) designed to funnel support away from emerging opposition parties with similar names (Fair Russia [Spravedlivaia Rossiia] and Civic Platform [Grazhdanskii platform]).

   With his foray into "big" politics, Kononenko's alter ego, Mr. Parker, quickly fell off the public radar. In 2008, the host platform LiveJournal suspended his account permanently, due to repeat violations of its terms of agreement: Kononenko's 2008 call for bombing of the United Kingdom followed his earlier 2005 participation in the "Kill Nato-ites" movement ("Moivy ne budet" 2008). Three years later he abandoned the Mr. Parker pseudonym altogether ("Maksim Kononenko" 2011). Fleeting forays into mainstream media (cohosting a political talk show with Pavlovsky in 2005) and literature (with the 2008 publication of *Day of the A-student* [*Den' otlichnika*], a defanged play on Vladimir Sorokin's best-selling anti-Putin dystopian satire, *Day of the Oprichnik* [*Den' oprichnika*]) suggested Kononenko's countercultural bona fides meant little outside the confines of the Runet. One commentator, reacting to his TV debut with Pavlovsky, wrote, "While his charismatic 'Vladimir Vladimirovich™' on the pages of *Gazeta* was truly original, fresh, and witty, the venture on the airwaves of NTV has assumed an extraordinarily vulgar and derivative tone [*poshloe i vtorichnoe zvuchanie*]" (Gureev 2005). In his final years, before his death in May 2024, Kononenko worked as a contributing columnist for the state-funded propaganda outlet RT.com in an era no longer suitable for the satire lite of his most innovative Vladimir Vladimirovich™.

The Orthodox Nationalist: Egor Kholmogorov

> LJ is the ideal place of habitation for a man with deep totalitarian complexes in the psyche.
>
> —Egor Kholmogorov (4 August 2001)

As a devout Orthodox Christian and unabashed lover of Russian history, the focus of my third case study, Egor Kholmogorov, hardly fits the profile of an iconoclast at first glance. Despite his status as a university dropout (quitting the MGU History Department after his first year), Kholmogorov made an early name for himself as a strong proponent of Orthodox teachings and the restoration of Russia's historical military, political, and civilizational might, writing long treatises in defense of all on the pages of such conservative patriotic journals as *Otechestvennye zapiski* (*Notes of the Fatherland*) and *Spetsnaz Rossii* (*Special Ops of Russia*).

What makes him iconoclastic and countercultural in the context of Runet history is not the penchant for vulgarity or criminal argot that helped Rykov and Konenenko garner clicks and views but his ability to articulate and promote his unabashedly religious, conservative, and pro-Russian ideological agenda in a space that, at least in these early years, was occupied by intellectual elites more skeptically inclined toward faiths and other -isms. And he did so in a way that managed to legitimize, even popularize, that discourse as the space grew more populated by the public. Particularly after his 2005 icon-toting appearance at the head of a phalanx of neo-Nazi skinheads, Kholmogorov earned the moniker of "nationalist" in the public eye. Offering a more nuanced but unapologetic articulation of his worldview occupied a significant portion of his social media posts on the topic.

A closer examination of the early years of Kholmogorov's LiveJournal blog, *Holmogor*, reveals a fascinating synthesis of popular, religious, and nationalist discourses that anticipated a potent mix of tradition and patriotism that would serve as the main rhetorical fuel for Putinism after the president's return to the Kremlin in 2012.[11]

Community and Communication on LiveJournal

More than any other event, the appearance of the LiveJournal blogging platform in 2001 marked the arrival of social networking and web 2.0 to the Russian-language internet. While news and information sites offered readers discussion forums before that, LiveJournal allowed users with little tech savvy to publish their own content publicly, follow postings of friends and public figures, and join communities organized around common interests. The platform, which swiftly acquired the uniquely Russian moniker *ZheZhe* (from the acronym of its full

---

11. The following analysis is based primarily on the extant LiveJournal posts at holmogor.livejournal.com, the LiveJournal account of Egor Kholmogorov, between March 2001 and December 2005, with gaps from January 2002 to September 2004, where a crash to the account apparently resulted in the loss of content during this period (see the post from 25 September 2004). In all, 1,595 posts, together with the comments for each, were examined for this analysis. See the bibliography for complete citations.

Russian name, Zhivoi zhurnal), differed in key ways from its American progenitor, as one of the platform's first scholarly studies points out (Gorny 2006). First, as with the Runet environment in general, its user base favored an older and more educated demographic. Second, and largely because of this, the Russian space became a vibrant locus for cultural and political discussion and debate—far more so than its American counterpart, which was dominated by the personal diaries of teenage girls. Finally, the Russian ZheZhe featured a "very high level of connectedness and communicativeness" among users (Gorny 2006, 75). Rosen and Zvereva (2014, 74–75) have likewise observed that the absence of a word limit appealed to a Russian penchant for "graphomania," and, because it attracted some of the more well-known voices in political culture, it became something of a public sphere viewed to be "the best place for voices to be heard and answered."

Given this profile of the platform, one can hardly be surprised that Egor Kholmogorov became one of its early adopters, posting his first message not long after the platform's Russian-language launch in February 2001.[12] Having established the nationalist site Doktrina.ru in 1998 with fellow conservative nationalist Konstantin Krylov, and regularly contributing to the likes of the *Russian Journal*, Credo.ru, and GlobalRus.ru, Kholmogorov had already established himself as a web-friendly journalist and commentator by the time of his first post at *Holmogor* (holmogor.livejournal.com) in March 2001. The blogging platform offered new means of making his views known, growing a community of like-minded conservatives, and amplifying his publications and activities in the offline world.[13]

Though inclined in his print writing to deploy the heady academic language of historians, philosophers, and religious thinkers, Kholmogorov quickly adapted to the more informal rhetorical ecosystem and generic particularities of ZheZhe. In keeping with the diary genre commonly associated with the platform, he devoted considerable space to quotidian issues and events—food cravings and eating experiences (19 April 2001, 10 October 2001), favorite childhood poems (1 August 2001 [a]), travelogues from visits to various Russian cities (10 May 2001), and the public observation of important family dates, such as the seventeenth (!) birthday of his wife (13 April 2005) and the announcement of the birth of their daughter ten days later (!!) (23 April 2005).

---

12. The Tartu scholar and Runet pioneer Roman Leibov made the first Russian-language post to LiveJournal on 1 February (Leibov 2001).

13. Kholmogorov occasionally posted to the alternative, Russia-specific LiveJournal platform at http://lj.rossia.org/users/holmogor/ but only sporadically as a backup or temporary alternative space. (The following analysis takes posts from both locations into account.) He used the LiveJournal as the main platform for original posts well into the 2010s, until Facebook and Twitter emerged as viable competitors for the intelligentsia voice in the mid-2010s.

While refraining from the more egregious nonstandard styles made notorious by Rykov, Kononenko, and other proponents of scumbag language, Kholmogorov infused his diary with some of its more high-frequency terms (e.g., *afftar* [3 June 2005], *zhzhot* [11 March 2005]). He adopted slang specific to the ZheZhe speech community, such as the nickname for "diary" (*lytdybr* [23 November 2004, 7 November 2005]).[14] And he participated in the reproduction of viral trends and memes, contributing his own (albeit unoriginal) rendition of the ironic "thanks-to-Putin-for-that" meme that remained popular well into the protest season of 2011–12 ("Another summer day's flown by, thanks to Putin for that" [18 July 2001; *Vot proletel eshche den' leta, spasibo Putinu za eto*]).[15] Several posts in January 2005 provided Kholmogorov's responses to survey questions widely circulated on LiveJournal at the time—one posing a series of what-if questions ("If I could become 3 different animals, I would become" [6 January]) and another posing six questions regarding sex and sexuality ("Craziest sexual adventure?" [24 January]). Also in keeping with early LiveJournal culture, Kholmogorov actively engaged with his followers in the comment section to his blogs—in many cases, in extended dialogue—reinforcing the idea that the platform was a cutting-edge medium for the exchange of ideas on the important issues of the day.[16]

Beyond these stylistic markers, *Holmogor* displayed a linguistic and thematic eclecticism characteristic of the LiveJournal communicative environment. His effusive posting, sometimes over ten separate posts per day, quite often created curious juxtapositions of informal and formal—as on his very first day of posting, which featured an extended (470-word) discourse on the shortcomings of Russian literature (too "ahistorical" for his tastes) with a four-sentence recipe for a calamari sandwich (1 April 2001 [a] and [b]).

Among the more interesting examples of Kholmogorov's use of the LiveJournal blogging platform to personalize the political was his execution of an autobiographical subgenre that had gone viral among platform users during the winter of 2002–03, called "100 facts about myself" (*100 faktov o sebe*). On the blogs of most LJ users, the "100 facts" appeared in a single post and featured short, pithy statements about themselves, oftentimes juxtaposing "the important with the trivial" (Zvereva 2012, 142–43). After losing his original version of the subgenre in a

---

14. The word *lytdybr* is produced when a user types out the Russian word for "diary" (дневник) on a keyboard with Latin letters instead of Cyrillic.

15. For a more thorough discussion of this trend and its Soviet roots, see Lunde (2016).

16. For a typical early example, see the 1 August 2001 [b] exchange with a follower regarding the history of the death penalty in Russia. In another case, Kholmogorov went so far as to post his personal cell phone number for a follower to call, to follow up on a business matter that had arisen over the course of discussion (23 December 2004).

crash that led to the accidental deletion of content from 2001–03 (25 September 2004), Kholmogorov opted to reproduce the "facts" one at a time (in "serialized form," as he put it [13 December 2004]) over a period from September 2004 to March 2005. A good number of them followed the traditionally trivial side of the subgenre. We learn, for example, that he is actually taller than the physical stats listed in his military conscription data ("Fact #1" [25 September 2004]), that his favorite poet is Osip' Mandel'shtam ("Fact #20" [14 October 2004]), that he is an order freak ("Fact #45" [9 November 2004]), that he loves bread but only white bread ("Fact 79" [19 January 2005]), that his first kiss was an entirely inconsequential affair ("Fact #85" [27 January 2005]), that he rarely breaths through his nose ("Fact #9" [15 February 2005], and that he is "a very lazy person" ("Fact #100" [10 March 2005]). Many others of the "facts," however, venture into more serious topics in a verbose manner uncharacteristic of the subgenre. Fact #14, for example, offers an overview of his political ideology, based on the combined principles of Orthodoxy and monarchy, and on which his identity as a "Russian nationalist" is grounded:

> I am an Orthodox imperialist. This means that I believe it is critical that Empire exists on the earth in the historical beauty of that term. I believe that such an Empire can exist only if it is animated by the religious spirit of an Orthodoxy that preserves the possibility of salvation for people in the bosom of the Orthodox Church and prepares itself for the role of final bastion in the resistance against the Antichrist. I believe that all peoples [*narody*] who want and are able to join can live peacefully and happily in this Empire. Moreover, I know that only one people—the Russian people, to whom I have the joy of belonging—is capable of creating and supporting such an Empire. And nothing will come of it if Russians have it badly in this empire. It is for this reason I am a confirmed Russian nationalist. At the same time, I wish evil to no people whatsoever, except for those who wish evil to my people. (8 October 2004)[17]

Fact #26 insists he hasn't a xenophobic bone in his body and elaborates on the distinction in his thought between race and nationality: "I do not approve of racism and ethnic conflicts. The nationalist conflict, on the other hand, is not just a norm of historical existence, but the engine of history, and here one must hold an active position" (20 October 2004).

---

17. Cf. "Fact #50," in which he outlines his "ideal state structure"—"Orthodox monarchy of the Russian type" (14 November 2004).

Embedded in a blog billed as a personal diary, and integrated as they are among more mundane posts about personal quirks and daily events, the philosophical and ideological commentaries take on a more personalized tone, dampening associations with neo-Nazism and, instead, offering readers (and Kholmogorov himself) what Zvereva (2012, 143), writing of the "100 facts" trend, calls an alternative, "complex, hybrid . . . virtual personality."

The diary format of LiveJournal also allowed Kholmogorov to get beyond such black-and-white labels by offering a more nuanced explanation of his ideological convictions. Clearly aware of the negatively loaded associations of the label *nationalist*, he made concerted efforts over his copious blogging output to soften the term by attaching some sort of modifier (most frequently "new"; see, e.g., 13 November 2004), avoiding it altogether by adopting labels like "Orthodox imperialist" (see above quote from 8 October 2004) or "right conservatism" (11 January 2005), and assuring his followers of the clarity of his conscience—insisting, as seen above, he was far from a xenophobe and claiming he had "never been a classic 'kvas patriot" (8 January 2005).[18] Based on a belief that Orthodoxy and monarchy lay at the foundation of Russian historical identity and that Russia had historically been a majority ethnic-Russian nation, his brand of "new nationalism" insisted on the central place of the Russian people in the formation and sustainment of Russian civilization and made it clear (in contrast to the more "skinhead" brand of nationalism) that it was anathema to fascism and had an open-door policy toward any ethnic group (15 December 2004).

Kholmogorov's regular and studied engagement with Orthodox theology also complicated associations with more clichéd portraits of nationalists as xenophobic skinheads. His May 2005 post on Easter Sunday featured the 4,000-word homily "On Easter" from Bishop Melito of Sardis (1 May 2005 [a]). In a series of posts in October 2005, he offered his own "Letters on Christianity," lengthy treatises stylistically reminiscent of Old Russian church writings, replete with opening humility topoi: "I am not sure that all my objections will seem convincing to you. I do not and cannot have a holy rank, and thus my pronouncements, as a result, cannot be understood as pronouncements from the Church, expressing the position of 'Christianity.' The little that stands behind me is personal experience of church life and some knowledge of the Gospels and the traditions of the Orthodox church. It could be that this is too little for my role as witness to be recognized by you as a witness of Christianity, rather than my own personal position" (18 October 2005).

---

18. Referring to the mead-based drink of ancient Rus', *kvasnoi'* carries a negative connotation akin to referring to patriotism as "jingoistic." That said, Kholmogorov did show some sympathy for the label, quipping in a May 2001 post, "Better a *kvas* patriot than a freshwater one [*Luchshe kvasnoi patriotism, chem presnyi*]" (24 May 2001).

While openly acknowledging his lack of bona fides as a church spokesperson, Kholmogorov shrewdly enlisted his status as LiveJournal member and self-fashioned leader to offer something akin to a digital pastoral letter to the members of his community, in this context, aptly reflected in the more traditional tsarist era of the *obshchina,* or village commune. The Orthodox profile likewise appeared in regular posts with policy-related opinions supporting the mandatory instruction of Orthodoxy in schools (10 November 2005 [a]), as well as announcements of various sorts of speeches and participation in church-sponsored events (such as his lecture on "the political eschatology of Orthodoxy in modern eschatological politics," delivered to a conference of religious leaders [15 November 2005 (a)]).

Keywords of Late Putinism

Kholmogorov's positioning as an online lay pastor and ideologue for new-nationalist ideas gave him more independent footing regarding the nascent Putin presidency, but on several fronts, he showed clear support. Particularly when it came to establishing strong centralized rule, cracking down on corrupt oligarchs, and the display of a new energy and comparatively conservative proclivities, Kholmogorov found much to like—so much so, according to a September 2004 post, that he was instructed by the powers that be to dial back his pro-Kremlin rhetoric ("Tone down your pro-Kremlin position. More criticism and irony," he was apparently told [24 September 2004]). Part of this manufactured distancing likely came from political technologists who saw in Kholmogorov and other more extreme nationalists foils for a more "measured" nationalist profile cut by Putin, a role that would become more accentuated one year later by Kholmogorov's prominent role in the Russian March of November 2005—a widely covered nationalist demonstration in Moscow made notorious for the presence at the march of apparent neo-Nazis caught on camera with raised arms and praise for Hitler.[19] For his own part, Kholmogorov distanced himself from the skinheads, dismissing them as "provocateurs" who needed to be "purged" from the movement (8 November 2005), and insisted that the new nationalism he represented marked a "rebirth of patriotism" rather than a threat (1 November 2005).[20] Even in this period of heightened political tension, however, Kholmogorov largely gave Putin a pass, only mildly chastising him for caving to the paid political technology created in the form of the antifascist youth group Nashi (26 July 2005).

---

19. For his own participation in this controversial demonstration, the young activist Alexei Navalny, the focus of chapter 4, also came under sharp scrutiny by the LiveJournal community.

20. Well before the incident, Kholmogorov argued that such fascists were most effectively combatted from a conservative rather than a liberal position (15 December 2004).

That said, Kholmogorov did not hesitate to take Putin to task when the president came up short on nationalist core principles—many of which Putin would later adopt. In January 2005, for instance, Kholmogorov disapprovingly reposted news of Putin's "promise to annul the Molotov-Ribbentrop pact" (21 January 2005)—an implicit admission of the culpability of Stalin in the outbreak of World War II. Four months later, he chastised the president for playing down the idea that Russia strove to once again attain superpower status (6 May 2005).[21] His support, Kholmogorov explained in a 2005 post, stemmed not from any fealty to current authorities (vlast') but rather his devotion to tradition and national interests:

> We defend not the regime, not the proverbial "power" [vlast'], which in reality at times is reminiscent of a cross between a timid mutt and a jackal. We defend the strategic state interests of Russia, national state tradition, which must not be aborted or self-destructed under any authority [vlast']—be it revolutionary or counterrevolutionary, right or left, liberal or conservative. Being on the side of 'existing power' just because it is [in power], is for idiots, and definitely not for politicians. Being on the side of state traditions and national interests is for the true political elders [*muzh'ia-politiki*] engaged in a certain wisdom. (8 December 2005)

While the activities of the likes of Rykov and Kononenko could at least partially be seen as efforts to monetize power using web-based political and creative technologies, Kholmogorov's online rhetorical production was more firmly rooted in ideas—ideas that, while often marginal and even controversial in the early Putin years, would later come to articulate central tenets of Putinism. To name just a few anticipated in early posts on *Holmogor*: mandating the instruction of patriotism and Orthodoxy in schools (12 July 2005), returning Crimea to Russia ("Realistically, but without pathos. We cannot return Crimea now, but we can with all our might support its autonomy so at least something is left to return later" [5 October 2005]), embracing Stalin for his heroic role in the defeat of Nazi Germany (13 February 2005 [a]; 1 May 2005 [b]) and as a symbol of the "once mighty Russian state" (8 May 2005), and dismissing democracy as an ideology foreign to Russian traditions (15 November 2005 [b]).

If Orthodoxy and monarchy served as the dual pillars of Kholmogorov's new nationalism, they got their historical and geopolitical legitimacy largely from two

---

21. By the beginning of his fourth presidential term, Putin was defending Stalin's decision to sign the nonaggression pact with Hitler ("Putin ob"iasnil . . ." 2019) and had persistently punctuated Russia's global relevance with military and diplomatic incursions into Ukraine, Syria, and elsewhere.

notions that would become even more central to Putinism: civilization and sovereignty. In the first complete, extant year of *Holmogor* alone, the nationalist blogger invoked the two abstract notions a remarkable 102 times. Most of Kholmogorov's writings on the civilizational foundations of the Russian nation appeared outside *Holmogor* in longer speeches, essays, and articles, many of which were dutifully promoted, if not reprinted, in the blog.[22] The last of them received the most attention and amplification in *Holmogor*, including a list of the "7 postulates of the 'Russian Doctrine,'" which anticipated one of the main ideological pretenses of Putinism, involving Russian civilization as an alternative to that of the West:

> **New civilization.** Any cultural construction achieves its peak when the nation [*narod*] creates a new civilization as a combination of ethnic groups, behavior, and material forms united by common meaning and values. Russia is already a civilization for herself, but must become a civilization for others as well, based on a new ethos and new culture. This civilization—a civilization of the North—must replace the West in global domination and is fated to lead our world all the way to its eschatological limit, to the threshold of the final events. (2 December 2005)

References within the blog appeared in a variety of contexts, ranging from the negative consequences of perestroika under Gorbachev ("The nightmarish, opium-induced insanity of my nation [*narod*], which, with its own hands [though by another's instigation], destroyed itself, its own country, its own civilization" [4 October 2004]) to the positive legacy of the "civilizational-political community [*obshchnost'*]" in ancient Rus' (8 February 2005), the growing recognition of the economic benefits of returning to said spiritual roots ("The economy in an Orthodox civilization does not develop willy-nilly, but rather in the service of spirituality" [25 February 2005 (a)]), attempts to "create a new civilization" in the Soviet period (13 February 2005 [b]), and the tendency for Russian civilization to avoid breaks with its past ("Russian civilization strives not to reproduce the past, but rather to not break from it" [21 October 2005]).[23]

---

22. E.g., "Theological-political treatise on national ideology" (30 October 2005), "A certain brief 'anti-Weber' dedicated to the economic ethics of Russian Orthodox civilization" (26 December 2004), "Russia as a 'winter civilization'" (28 January 2005), "Russian Doctrine" (10 November 2005 [b]; 2 December 2005). Unlike Marina Litvinovich, for whom the invocation of "civilizational war" was but one rhetorical arrow in a vast, but cynical PR quiver, Kholmogorov clearly took great stock in the idea. With his emphasis on Russia's civilizational identity, he set himself apart from the more blatantly racist nationalists with whom he rubbed elbows at this stage in his career. See Malinova (2020) for a good discussion of the relationship between nationalism and civilizationalism in Putin's Russia and more broadly.

23. Note also his invocation of the "North" (Sever) as a euphemism for a new Russian civilizational model (e.g., 5 March 2005).

Central to the preservation of Russian civilization, for Kholmogorov, was the protection of Russian sovereignty—another concept that would play a growing ideational role in later Putinism. In the wake of mass Ukrainian protests during the 2004–2005 Orange Revolution, he articulated the stakes in terms of a "catastrophic threat" to and potential "liquidation" of the "sovereign state of Russia as such" (25 January 2005; 20 September 2005) and declared national sovereignty an "absolute value . . . regardless of ideology" (3 March 2005). Echoing the German political philosopher Karl Schmitt, Holmogor likewise linked the importance of national sovereignty to the concept of a strong sovereign, whose status as such gave him sole, dictatorial right to adjudicate in emergency situations (19 March 2005).[24]

Threats to Russia's national sovereignty and civilizational roots invited the personification of their origins, which quite frequently took the form of "enemies" (*vragi*) and "Russophobes"—both terms that figured centrally into the political vocabulary of late Putinism. The invocation of Russophobes and Russophobia (fifty mentions in 2005 alone) were particularly prescient and, in Kholmogorov's usage, tended to be reserved for internal enemies.[25] These ranged in type from best-selling detective writers (Boris Akunin [25 February 2005 (b)]) and liberal politicians erecting "provocative" and "slanderous" monuments suggesting the Russian people came from slave stock (11 June 2005) to a Russian press keen on portraying the Russian March using laughably worn clichés (7 November 2005). Ukraine in this regard constituted something of a gray zone for Kholmogorov, describing it as "an anti-Russian state populated by Russians" (5 October 2005)— the very sort of lexical liminality that Putin would echo in his justification of the 2022 invasion over fifteen years later (Kotliar and Iushkov 2021).

In the case studies of Rykov, Kononenko, and Kholmogorov, we find examples of three early Runet influencers sympathetic to the Putin cause, who commandeered their digital expertise to promote Putin, Putinism, and their own vested interests—be they wealth, fame, or ideological purity. Rykov fashioned himself as a master content producer, finding ways to enlist the discursive and cultural underside of the medium to attract more eyes to political content and make a healthy profit in the process. Kononenko fancied himself a writer, establishing an early model of light political satire that harnessed a meme-driven creative

---

24. Cf. Schmitt 1932. It is noteworthy that as early as 2005, Kholmogorov was flagging the need for a state to exercise its "sovereign" power on the internet, specifically in reaction to LiveJournal's decision to ban anti-NATO voices, who purportedly ran afoul of its user rules (14 June 2005).

25. Foreign foes were most often referred to as "enemies" (*vragi*). The internal orientation of the term "Russophobe" was consistent with its original usage in the writing of the nineteenth-century poet and diplomat, Fedor T'iutchev. For an analysis of invocations of Russophobia by Russian propaganda after the full-scale invasion of Ukraine, see Gorham (2024).

space to generate a more user-friendly profile of Putin for Runet readers and a significant dose of notoriety for himself. More than the first two, Kholmogorov was driven by ideas, a view of national identity and leadership that, however marginal in its early instantiation, came to articulate in the popular language of the LiveJournal diary format a vision of Russia and Putinism that would become increasingly prominent over the ensuing two decades. Different as they were in their orientations, they shared a mastery of their media and a willingness to use them to translate the traditionally bland language of power and authority into a parlance more accessible and engaging to the growing number of citizens, many of them apolitical, populating the networked communities of social media. At its core, though, like the work of Pavlovsky and Litvinovich, theirs was an exercise in creative translation—reframing politics and political discourse in a more engaging manner for everyday users. More transformational efforts at using new technology to redefine how politics was practiced are the central focus in the following chapters devoted to Dmitry Medvedev and Alexei Navalny.

Part 2

RHETORICAL REVOLUTIONS

THE MEDVEDEV ALTERNATIVE

If political power [*sila*] can't learn to make friends with the internet, it will die.

I have no doubt about it.

—Dmitry Medvedev ("Vstrecha" 2009)

For all their efforts at promoting Putin and Putinism, the actors thus far studied operated outside the government proper. With the election of Dmitry Medvedev as president in 2008, the Russian state suddenly had an active internet user as its head with big ideas on how to transform government with it. Medvedev trumpeted his status as an early adopter of new digital media. As deputy prime minister, he hosted an online forum, where he spoke competently on issues ranging from the proto-social network "Fidonet" to the notorious Olbanian (Scumbag) language of the counterculturists discussed in chapter 2 ("Medvedev v internete" 2007). His love for all things digital quickly became one of the defining features of his presidential profile. Well before the start of his "modernization" campaign, Medvedev made it clear he viewed internet proficiency as a basic requirement of the modern politician. As a statement in his biography at the official Kremlin website put it, "Anyone who wants to be a part of modern life simply has to know this technology and use it actively" (Medvedev 2011a). And by "use it actively," Medvedev didn't just mean establishing a pro forma presence online with the help of more web-savvy proxies such as Pavlovsky, Rykov, and the like. As an early adopter himself, he envisioned elected officials diving into the digital deep end personally. But as president of a large state bureaucracy rooted in a political culture that placed primacy over power through actions rather than words, this inclination faced considerable resistance—not only in terms of how politicians chose to present themselves on digital media but also in terms of how much verbal authority would be allocated to the public in a new era of "electronic government." To better understand the rhetorical opportunities and dangers facing authorities at this key juncture of the Putin era and the growth of new media technologies, in this chapter I examine Medvedev's attempts to cajole fellow bureaucrats into establishing an online presence, his own self-presentation on Twitter, and some of the broader e-government initiatives launched during his presidency.

Experiments in "Direct Internet Democracy"

Six months after being elected Russia's third president, Medvedev launched the presidential video blog, where, over the course of his single term in office, he would go on to post 295 videos, many of them produced exclusively for online consumption.[1] His stated rationale for the launch was "to speak about some pressing problems the world is facing today" ("Medvedev" 2009). In later posts he elaborated on the opportunity the internet provided for enabling direct access to citizens: "It is important that this kind of information comes directly from the original source and actually ends up on my desk, or rather in my computer. I can simply see for myself what citizens who visit the site and react to my performances in the blog are writing. . . . It's a kind of direct and very effective channel of information linking the president, on the one hand, and all those who wish and who have computers on their desks, on the other" (Medvedev 2009).

Medvedev took the initiative one step further several months later in January 2010 when he prodded fellow government officials to start their own blogs as a means of improving communication and earning the trust of their constituents, warning that bureaucrats unable to use a computer or the internet could be relieved of their duties (Bilevskaia 2010). In March of that year, he chastised Nizhnii Novgorod governor Valerii Shantsev for not getting with the plan: "Those who can do it are modern managers; those who cannot, with all due respect, are not quite prepared" ("Medvedev potreboval" 2010). In a speech to United Russia activists in May, he boldly predicted the return of an "era of direct democracy" due to the way the internet allowed citizens to engage in the political process (Medvedev 2010). Later that fall at his annual World Political Forum in Iaroslavl', he reiterated the idea with a warning to all footdraggers: Thanks to the internet, "the world is so open that no politician can hide; we are simply obligated to synchronize our watches with the people, with civil society, and first and foremost on such sensitive issues as the level of civic freedoms" (Medvedev 2011b).

The frequency and urgency with which Medvedev discussed the need for government officials to foster an online presence suggested that he took the matter

---

1. Transcripts for all Medvedev video blogs and videos for most are available at http://blog.da-medvedev.ru/.

quite seriously, a seriousness also reflected in his own avid use of social media both personally and professionally. The digital embrace also dovetailed with his central policy agenda of taming rampant state corruption in Russia. In a September 2009 article titled "Go Russia!" he again trumpeted the idea of new technology as a mechanism for bringing about democracy ("for the first time in our history"), this time not only for the new freedom of expression it promised but also for its capacity "to identify and eliminate hotbeds of corruption" (quoted in Biagioli and Lépinay 2019).

For a bureaucracy that had for decades, if not centuries, operated according to the rule that power spoke through actions rather than words, however, Medvedev's new vision of "direct internet democracy" came as a rhetorical shock. Particularly in the Russia of the later years of the first decade of the 2000s, where national television was under the relatively tight control of the state, it was the web 2.0 agora where authoritative political discourse could fast become the object of contestation and ridicule. As Stephen Coleman (2004) aptly observed, the politician blogger represented something of a generic contradiction as a symbolically central authority embracing a medium that was, by definition, decentered and mistrusting of conventional hierarchies: "The problem facing politicians who blog is that they are professionally implicated in the very culture that blogging seeks to transcend. . . . Blogging politicians are always going to be seen as a little bit like those old Communist apparatchiks who had to sit in the front row at rock concerts and pretend to swing to the beat." United Russia member and active blogger Aleksandr Khinshtein put it slightly differently, noting the higher primacy the internet space put on independent political expression: "In order to be popular on the internet, one needs to have a certain freedom of actions. What attracts my Twitter subscribers is a free expression of thought [*svobodnoe myslevyrazhenie*] that is not really cared for by the party leadership" (Tirmaste 2011).

Looking back at the most popular political bloggers of the Medvedev presidency, one finds a few interesting trends.[2] Most striking even among the ostensibly pro-establishment blogs is the degree to which the top officials attempted to distance themselves from some imagined "central" source of political power and

---

2. To identify more prominent government bloggers, I relied in part on the website Goslyudi.ru, which ranked each politician blogger according to the frequency with which they posted (their "talkativeness" [*govorlivost'*]), the degree to which their blogs were referenced (*upominaemost'*), and the number of readers they attracted (*chitaemost'*). All these were combined into a single rating which determined the blogger's overall rank (*svodnyi reiting*). (The Goslyudi website and tracking service is no longer available. Archived pages are available through December 2016 at https://web.archive .org/web/20161210081306/http://www.goslyudi.ru/, where ratings may be obtained as well.) Cross-checking this rating system against that of Yandex's blog ratings shows general correlation in the order of the rank, although given that Yandex's is a ranking of all blogs, the distance between politician bloggers is considerable.

authority. This was easy enough for the likes of former Federation Council Chairman Sergei Mironov, who as head of a competing party had no trouble taking it to United Russia and even Vladimir Putin.[3] His diatribes against United Russia brimmed with colloquialisms and populist invective that drew on the contrast between lofty words and power-hungry actions: "Knowing the 'good traditions' (read: habits!) of the Edinorossy [the common nickname for members of the United Russia (UR) Party], everyone understands that, in words, everything will be attractive: concern about well-being, guarantees, the defense of interests and so forth. But the true picture shows the same thing time and again—UR's desire to cling to power [*uderzhat'sia u vlasti*] at all costs" (Mironov 2011).

The distancing came even easier for another leading political blogger of the time, Ekaterinburg Duma deputy Leonid Volkov, who was an outsider by dint of geography and liberal oppositional leanings.[4] In his blog, Volkov devoted generous attention to civic action and local politics, and could tell a good story. In a March 2011 post, for instance, he used digital media to reflect on firsthand experiences from real-world representative democracy—the campaign trail:

> In all honesty, it's not at all a rosy picture. It took me the entire hour to hand out a batch of twenty newspapers. Many people refuse to talk, and the majority . . . couldn't give a shit [*gluboko pofig*]. You get distressed by it all, of course. . . .
>
> ME: Hello! Permit me to lobby you for a moment! [*Pozvol'te, ia vas poagitiruiu!*]
> YOUNG COUPLE: No!
> ME: Then please take a newspaper.
> YOUNG MAN: All right, but we're still not going to vote!
> ME: But why not? In that case, the Edinoross [candidate] will definitely win.
> YOUNG MAN: He'll win either way, whether or not you vote.
> ME: Pardon me, if you will, but I myself am a city Duma deputy, and not a Edinoross. And I won. Now I'm helping my friend. But if everyone reasons like you, then of course we have no chance.
> GIRL: You mean to say that your friend is against United Russia?
> ME: Absolutely. Here, please look at this, everything is explained here!
> YOUNG MAN: So that's the way it is! Then we'll definitely vote for your friend! (Volkov 2011)

---

3. Mironov launched his LiveJournal blog in November 2007, on the eve of parliamentary elections, "in order to be more accessible to people [and] . . . to the fullest extent . . . use the opportunities of the reverse feedback that blogs provide" (Mironov 2007).

4. Volkov would later become a close associate of Navalny, the focus of chapter 4.

Even more so than Volkov, State Duma deputy (Astrakhan Oblast) and Just Russia Party member Oleg Shein's blog served as a primer for representative democracy and civic action. Shein (2011a) regularly engaged with followers in the comments section, at times even chastising them for their knee-jerk dismissal of all United Russia representatives—arguing at one point that the party included "decent individuals" and that the problem rested, instead, with the corruption that came with monopoly. He also regularly posted photos of meetings with his constituents and local civic groups. Like Volkov, he took advantage of its multimedia capacities and broader audiences to expand his democracy-in-action style beyond the physical walls of the public forum (Shein 2011b).

If figures such as Shein, Volkov, and even Mironov could afford to modulate independence, regional governors, beholden as they were to the president and more diverse constituencies, had to be more cautious about how they shaped their online identity.[5] Their marginal status often appeared in a stubbornly apolitical positioning and regional focus. Astrakhan Oblast Governor Aleksandr Zhilkin, for instance, who consistently rated high in the rankings, focused exclusively on regional issues—local accomplishments, visits, ceremonies, and celebrations, for instance—and regularly sought constituents' opinions on issues of pending import. A post that received one of the largest number of comments for this blog (551) invited feedback on the introduction of fee-based fishing in the region, and promised to share the results with the head of the Federal Fishing Agency at an upcoming meeting (Zhilkin 2011a). Virtually absent from his blog in the heat of the contentious 2011–2012 Duma and presidential election season was any sign of Zhilkin's political leanings, although the headline banner on his official website expressed his support for candidate Putin and implored visitors to do the same.[6]

In addition to distancing himself from national politics, Zhilkin used populist, anti-bureaucrat (*chinovnik*) rhetoric to distance himself from vlast' and endear him to the people (*narod*). In response to one reader's off-topic question in the comments to a September 2011 post, for instance—about public access to a newly constructed bridge in Astrakhan—Zhilkin sided with the reader and obliquely chastised the stupidity and corruptness of local bureaucrats, bemoaning, more generally, "our mentality" (*nash mentalitet*) of finding ways to bilk citizens by taking their money and restricting access (Zhilkin 2011b).

---

5. For a complete list of the twenty-nine governors (out of a total of eighty-three) who had launched blogs by May 2010, see Toepfl (2012, 1440).

6. Aleksandr Zhilkin, http://www.jilkin.ru (accessed 5 February 2013). Toepfl (2012, 1453–54) includes Zhilkin among his category of more active and hands-on "internetchik" governor-bloggers, who were clearly a minority of exceptional cases "in terms of the perceived responsiveness and legitimacy of politics."

For those more in line with the elite, venturing into this space unequipped with the appropriate rhetorical tools posed significant risk and gave rise to a range of strategies for dealing with Medvedev's dictum. One was to outsource the task to PR professionals savvier about political image-making. Kirov Oblast governor and avid blogger Nikita Belykh posted a copy of a proposal he had received from a PR firm that alluded to Medvedev's threat to state representatives and included the price list for its services: 163,000 rubles to set up a LiveJournal blog, 84,000 to maintain it, and 199,900 to promote it to "1000-follower" status (Sal'manov 2010). While one saw cases of official blogs that smacked of canned public relations attempts, these also tended to be less successful as measured by level of attention they received, most likely for the reasons of authenticity alluded to by Khinshtein.[7] Among other traits, low-traffic bureaucrat blogs were erratic in appearance and made little if any attempt to promote two-way communication. The blog for Vladimir Iakushev, governor of Tiumenskaia Oblast, suffered from a dense bureaucratic style, thereby aligning himself stylistically with the very *chinovnik* class vilified in other blogs: "Dear friends, I want to thank you all for the fruitful suggestions that have permitted us to expediently introduce amendments to the Law of Tiumen' Oblast No. 128 concerning the provision of living subsidies to workers of the budgeted sphere of Tiumen'. I hope that these changes allow an even larger number of families of budgeted workers to join the program. I talk about the essence of the introduced amendments in my video commentary."[8]

After the 2011–12 election season and the return of Vladimir Putin to the Kremlin, this more technocratic voice gained in credibility among the political class. As older governors retired or soured on LiveJournal, new ones approved by Putin took a more cautious approach to online self-fashioning—either bypassing independent blogging platforms altogether in lieu of multifunctional official websites or enlisting new technology to bring government closer to the people but in a way, technologically and rhetorically, that avoided the awkward dynamics of the blogosphere as oppositional space. Front and center at Vologda Oblast governor Oleg Kuvshinnikov's main oblast website (Ofitsial'nyi portal), for example, were links to "electronic government services," an "online reception area of the governor," and a "Citizen appeals" feature that allowed users to submit

---

7. They belonged to the category that *Vedomosti* reporter Elena Miazina (2010) called "formalists"—those abiding by the president's directives half-heartedly—and *Novaia gazeta* reporter Pavel Kanygin (2010) called "internet-losers" (*internet-lokhi*).

8. Iakushev 2011. "Дорогие друзья, хочу поблагодарить всех вас за плодотворные предложения, позволившие нам оперативно внести поправки в Закон Тюменской области №128, касающийся предоставления жилищных субсидий работникам бюджетной сферы Тюмени. Надеюсь, эти изменения позволят ещё большему числу семей бюджетников присоединиться к программе. О сути внесенных поправок я рассказываю в своём видеокомментарии."

FIGURE 3.1. Screenshot from "Online Reception Room" of Vologda Oblast governor Oleg Kuvshinnikov ("Onlain priemnaia" 2013).

comments, questions, and complaints to the governor and other regional officials. But there was no space for two-way communication. Citizens engaged in the language of petitioning; the governor (or his staff) relied heavily on the stock language of bureaucracy. The platform allowed the governor to remain within the safe confines of bureaucratic competence, while at the same time showing he was actively listening to the population and swiftly reacting to their ideas and requests—a point that was graphically conveyed by the prominent green "Answer has been prepared" line listed under "status" across from the requests (fig. 3.1). The governor and his staff clearly controlled which requests got publicly posted to the site. Among the topics listed were "Roads of the city of Griazovets," "Payment for electricity in Ustiuzhna," "Social defense," "Mama is dying!," "The forest is our wealth," and "Sports in the village." With few if any exceptions, the language of the responses display a fluent mastery of neutral and emotionless bureaucratic discourse—even in contexts highly charged with emotion: "Based on the information of the Head of the healthcare directorate of the Cherepovets Mayor's office, your mother is in critical condition. The Chief of Staff of City hospital No. 1 has been authorized to prepare documents immediately for referral to a federal clinic."[9]

The Power and Peril of a Tweeter-in-Chief

Hi to everyone! I'm in Twitter and this is my6 [*sic*] first message!

—Dmitry Medvedev (2010) (fig. 3.2)

Medvedev's gadget enthusiasm made him a quick and natural adopter of Twitter when smartphone usage began to surge in the Russian Federation in 2010.[10] Compared to LiveJournal and its diary-based platform that had no word limit and encouraged public comments and discussion, Twitter offered a safer mode of "direct democracy" for officials, confining individual posts (at the time) to 140 characters and transforming "friends" to "followers," with accompanying restrictions on commenting. As with LiveJournal earlier, President Medvedev would be among the first prominent members of the political class to engage on the microblogging platform. And, as a closer examination of his first twelve months of posting shows, for all the advantages the Twitter format offered rhetorically, it also gave rise to episodes that considerably compromised political authority.[11]

As one of the more minimalist forms of social networking, Twitter (now known as X) presented a stark contrast to both the long-form blogging typical of LiveJournal and the traditionally cumbersome communicative style of Russian officialdom. Originally intended for the SMS environment, the forced brevity of the then 140-character limit marked the primary distinguishing feature of the platform—no doubt an appealing one for time-pressed government officials.[12] In fact, its evolutionary link to text messaging accounted for Twitter's other primary

---

9. "Mama umiraet" 2012. "По информации начальника управления здравоохранения мэрии Череповца, Ваша мама находится в тяжелом состоянии. Главному врачу Городской больницы №1 поручено срочно подготовить документы для направления их в федеральную клинику." While not yet in office at the time, Kuvshinnikov is emblematic of Toepfl's (2012, 1450–52) "effective statesmen" profile of the governor-bloggers, who, by virtue of their willingness to listen and respond to constituent needs, had a higher likelihood than those blogging strictly for PR purposes of positively impacting civic perception of the bureaucratic state.

10. Medvedev's first tweet, from 23 June 2010 and represented in figure 3.2, was posted to @MedvedevRussia. I've preserved the original spelling and punctuation here and throughout this analysis.

11. The following analysis is based on the 1,165 tweets posted to @MedvedevRussia (and @KremlinRussia) from the day he first posted, 23 June 2010, to 21 June 2011.

12. Twitter subsequently doubled the limit to 240 characters in 2017.

Дмитрий Медведев ✔
@MedvedevRussia

Всем привет! Я в Твиттере и это мое6 первое сообщение!

Translate post

1:13 PM · Jun 23, 2010

FIGURE 3.2.   President Dmitry Medvedev's first tweet to @MedvedevRussia, replete with typographical errors (which soon went viral, of course) (@MedvedevRussia, 23 June 2010, https://x.com/MedvedevRussia/status /16863556707).

intended function—that of a status report: "What's happening?" (or "*Chto proiskhodit?*" in the Russian-language interface) read the main prompt at the top of a Twitter user's home page at the time Medvedev adopted. Unlike text messaging, however, posts here were open for the entire world to see. It was bidirectional to the extent that followers could reply to tweets, but the platform lacked the back-and-forth design that the LiveJournal comment interface offered, making it more limited as a virtual agora. For the most part, it showed only the author's side of the conversation (although clicking on a specific post would give the reader access to followers' responses). For these reasons, Twitter was vulnerable to the cries described by new-tech skeptics such as Nicholas Carr (2007), who wrote at the time of its appearance, "Twitter is the telegraph of Narcissus. Not only are you the star of the show, but everything that happens to you, no matter how trifling, is a headline, a media event, a stop-the-presses bulletin."

For Medvedev, as for most who transitioned from the long-form style of LiveJournal to Twitter, the space restriction produced a more laconic style and shortcuts in grammar, spelling, and punctuation. Although such shortcuts were less noticeable in his Twitter feeds than many (@KremlinRussia and later @MedvedevRussia), the immediacy and forced brevity of the genre had an enormous impact on the communication style, at times enhancing his image as a decisive head of state and anti-bureaucratic man of the people and at times casting him in a less flattering light as a shallow, distracted, or starstruck neophyte.

On policy matters, the countdown from 140 inspired a blunt, decisive, tough-talking tone, accentuated, in the following examples, by action-oriented verbs:

> Awarded Pacific sailors today for valor in the struggle against piracy. Russia will battle with this threat in the future as well. We will not sit on our hands. (4 July 2010)

Gave orders to the Prosecutor General and MVD[13] to take under special control the case of the attack on the journalist Kashin. The criminals must be found and punished. (6 November 2010)

At times, the brevity bestowed on the posts an aphoristic, monologic quality that defied contestation:

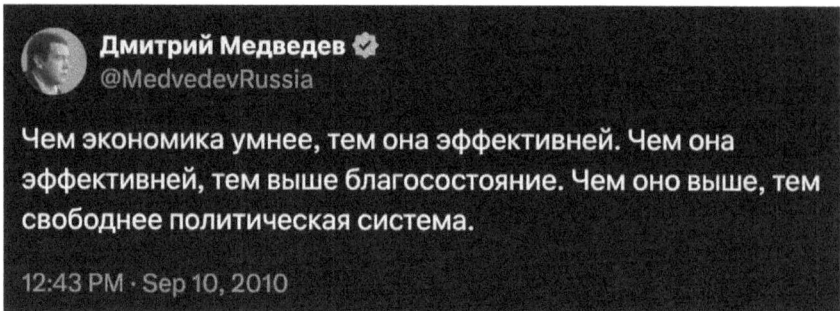

Дмитрий Медведев ✅
@MedvedevRussia

Чем экономика умнее, тем она эффективней. Чем она эффективней, тем выше благосостояние. Чем оно выше, тем свободнее политическая система.

12:43 PM · Sep 10, 2010

The smarter the economy, the more effective it is. The more effective it is, the greater the prosperity. The greater it is, the freer the political system. (10 September 2010)

The awareness of responsibility gives sense to the work and freedom of man. The question of freedom and responsibility is eternal: you can't have one without the other. (10 September 2010)

At times, especially when railing against incompetent or corrupt officials, it cast him in the populist image of a no-nonsense CEO:

Deputies must watch their attendance at parliament sessions. It is simply shameful to look at empty seats. You have to show up for work. (29 June 2010)

The problem of the MVD is an issue of trust, the trust of the people for the police and, no less important, the trust of the employees themselves for their work. (22 July 2010)

And in the occasional tweet Medvedev directly engaged his follower audience, inviting them to provide feedback on draft laws ("Your word here is very important. Today the zakonoproekt2010.ru site is opening where you can read and discuss the draft law" [7 August 2010]) and thanking them for input and

---

13. Ministerstvo vnutrennykh del, or "Ministry of Internal Affairs"—the Russian equivalent to the FBI.

expressing his intent to use it ("To @garipov_radik: I read the tweets I receive. For the proposals, thanks to you and everyone who writes @MedvedevRussia. I'm thinking of using several ideas in my address to the Federal Assembly" [24 November 2010]). In addition to serving a mobilizing function, Twitter allowed Medvedev to publish promptly direct statements on a wide range of important policy issues, often allowing the head of state to model the link between ideas and legislation, words and action.

Beyond adding a dimension to his political technological toolbox, the Twitter feed gave Medvedev and other official microbloggers a more personal image-making device. In this mode he may have been taking greater risks from a PR perspective, but the payoffs were also greater, revealing a more human side of the politician—one with emotions and a biography akin to those of his constituents:

> I visited the graves of my great-grandmother and great-grandfather. Since childhood I've heard much about these places from my grandmother. I was there for the 1st time. As always, for work. (13 July 2010)

> I remember and love my school to this day. I try to visit, though, it's true, not often. The last time I was there was 1.5 years ago. (5 October 2010 [link to photo omitted])

It could give followers a better sense of his passions, be they for photography or soccer:

> I had a little time to take shots of Hanoi last night (31 October 2010 [link to photo omitted])

> Our guys got blown out at soccer. That's bad. And the way they played. . . . (7 September 2010)

Here, even more than in his policy reflections, Medvedev used an informal style to project a more personable image, well removed from the official press-release mode many other national leaders employed in the microblogosphere.

As appealing and effective as this could be in some contexts, however, in others it could make him look preoccupied and terribly trivial. Particularly those involving the global political elite tended to be more narcissistic in nature and collectively projected a less flattering image of the young Russian president as a starstruck newbie:

> It's been a long time since I had a hamburger. Breakfast with Barack Obama at Ray's Hell Burger: . . . . (24 June 2010 [link to photo omitted])

> Angela Merkel admitted that she really loves hamburgers. Even more than Barack Obama and I. (15 July 2010)

Silvio Berlusconi kindly showed me his hometown of Milan. Leonardo's "Last Supper" is a true masterpiece. (24 July 2010 [link to photo omitted])

I talked with @Schwarzenegger not just about investments, but about sports as well (11 October 2010 [link to photo omitted])

Carr's characterization of Twitter as a simulation device for everyday users to prove their usefulness in the world seems applicable to Medvedev's accounts of his rubbing elbows with world leaders: By publishing the tweets and accompanying photos, he was at once attempting to authenticate his status as a coequal.[14] Curiously, it is in this generic subgroup that the only mentions of Vladimir Putin appeared:

Дмитрий Медведев ✓
@MedvedevRussia

Вчера вечером с Владимиром Путиным посмотрели «Брестскую крепость». Неплохое кино о Великой Отечественной войне
http://twitpic.com/3cr473

Translate post

Вчера вечером с Владимиром Путиным посмотрели «Брестскую крепость». Неп...

From twitpic.com

4:19 AM · Dec 4, 2010

Last night Vladimir Putin and I watched *The Brest Fortress*. Not a bad flick about the Great Patriotic War. (4 December 2010)

The attempt to project a familiarity with his mentor seemed particularly awkward, both in his overly formal use of the PM's first and last name, and in the

_____

14. As Carr (2007) put it, "As I walk down the street with thin white cords hanging from my ears, as I look at the display of khakis in the window of the Gap, as I sit in a Starbucks sipping a chai served up by a barista, I can't quite bring myself to believe that I'm real. But if I send out to a theoretical audience of my peers 140 characters of text saying that I'm walking down the street, looking in a shop window, drinking tea, suddenly I become real. I have a voice. I exist, if only as a symbol speaking of symbols to other symbols."

stilted pose that both men assume in the photograph. Other tweets combining the political with the mundane project the image of a distracted leader with a short attention span.

> I'm returning from Turkmenistan. The trip was useful. And this is my first tweet from an airplane. Did it go through? (22 October 2010)

> I left for the summit in Deauville. I'll write about the trip later. I want to say thanks a lot to everyone who is reading me! It's now more than 100,000 people (18 October 2010)

In other instances, he runs into trouble due to the temporal demarcation of the posts. The inclusion of the time and reverse chronological sequencing can create the semblance of a coherent narrative that can make incongruous posts jarring. The most egregious of these, his report on an Elton John concert in the wake of skinhead attacks in downtown Moscow, make Medvedev appear aloof, superficial, and unserious and largely undermine the tough talk and reassurance he offers forty minutes later:

> I was at the Elton John concert. Very serious, quality work—nearly three hours of live music. Photo-iphone.... (12 December 2010 [link to photo omitted])

> [40 minutes later] And the last thing for today. About Manezh (Sq.). Everything is under control—in the country and in Moscow. We'll settle accounts with all those who did harm. Have no doubt. (12 December 2010)

Unfortunately for Medvedev, including the photo in the post also created a forum for comments, many of which came down hard on his mixed-up priorities:

> Dmitrii Nanotol'evich![15] When was the last time you were in Russia, for crying out loud? Get back to reality, most esteemed! They stole under Peter the First, too, but in contrast to your crowd he did a great deed, whereas you are going around to concerts taking snapshots. ("cochegar13")

> Who the hell cares about your snapshots when the country's roof is burning ... WTF? You're president of a superpower ..., but how many years has it been full of disorder and anarchy ... you are a schnook know that 90% of Russians think that way.[16] ("rebellion")

---

15. The wordplay on Medvedev's actual patronymic (Anatolievich) stems from the nickname, *Nano-President*, given to him by the online community as a result of his infatuation with technology of all kinds and his spearheading the development of Skolkovo, a community in suburban Moscow built to become the Russian "Silicon Valley" (with particular concentration on nanotechnology).

16. The sense of misguided presidential priorities goes beyond poorly timed posts to the very act of engaging in Twitter and other high-tech "gadgets" in the first place. As one blogger disparagingly

In addition to exposing his virtual presidential persona to this more blunt, even vulgar, side of "direct internet democracy" (clearly unfiltered feedback that would never be permitted in Putin's televised town-hall simulations), the tweeter-in-chief also left himself exposed to criticism when, after establishing the practice of offering public reflections for mass consumption, he remained conspicuously silent in the wake of more controversial events. He opted not to comment on his decision to fire the powerful Moscow mayor Yury Luzhkov, for instance, among the biggest independent decisions he made as president; nor did he comment in the wake of the December 2010 guilty verdict against Mikhail Khodorkovsky (in both cases, communicative behavior more akin to the traditional top-down attitude toward power and discourse of imperial tsars, Soviet general secretaries, and Putin himself).

Another hazard of the practice, though, was the coexistence of parody accounts who would, in cases like these, fill the void. The self-declared "Official Twitter Account of the President of Ruissa" (*sic*), @KermlinRussia (fig. 3.3), chimed in promptly upon Luzhkov's ouster, alluding to the former mayor's well-known love for beekeeping:

> It was the wrong mayor and he was making some wrong sort of honey.[17] (28 September 2010)

> Today I added @Schwarzenegger to the list of Moscow mayoral candidates. (10 October 2010)

In the wake of the Wiki-leaked telegram in which a US State Department official likened Russia's ruling tandem to popular comic-book action heroes, @KermlinRussia borrowed the photo from its namesake to tweet:

> I watched "Batman and Robin" with Vladimir Putin last night. Not a bad movie, but there's no resemblance in the least. (5 December 2010 [link to photo omitted])

And in the wake of the December 2010 race riots in downtown Moscow:

> We will not tolerate a rise in xenophobia. A person of any nationality can kill another with impunity if he has enough money. (13 December 2010)

> How nice that Russia is a multinational country. You can always find a minority on which to redirect popular vengeance. (16 December 2010)

---

put it, "It looks like a child's dreams come true. The way it was when Deep Purple were brought to Russia. Putin likes to drive [military vehicles] and ride horses, while Dmitry Anatolievich is more into gadgets. I don't blame him, you know, I also like to drive, and I like gadgets, presents, etc. I just feel that it's totally not necessary to become a president for all this" (Asmolov 2010b).

17. "Это был неправильный мэр и он делал какой-то неправильный мед."

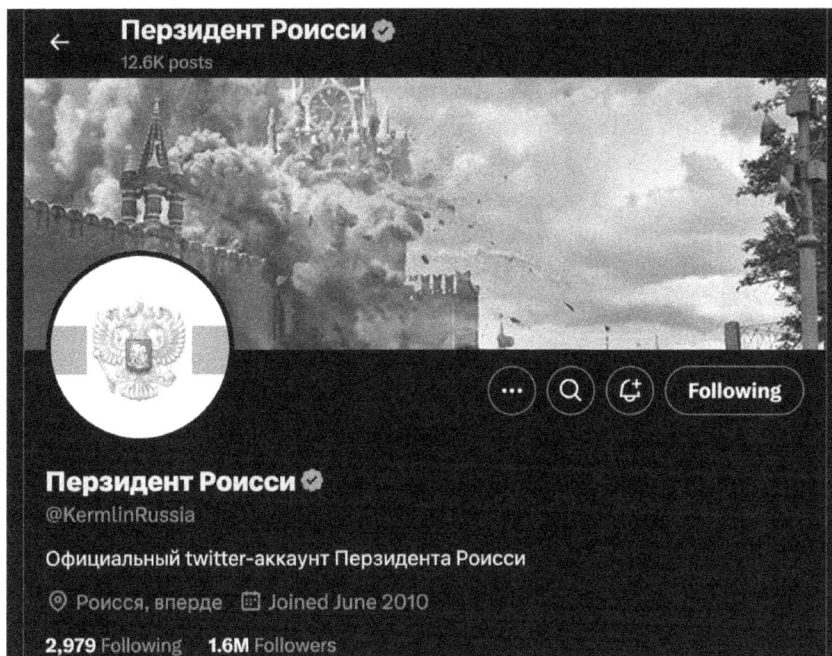

FIGURE 3.3. Account page of spoof Twitter account "Perzident Roissi" (@KermlinRussia). Screenshot of account captured December 2024 and reflects political reality of that time.

One might argue that @KermlinRussia did for Medvedev what Mr. Parker's parodic Vladimir Vladimirovich™ blog did for Putin—serve as a light, humorous means of generating a more sympathetic image of the commander in chief. The anonymous coauthors of @KermlinRussia offered a somewhat similar explanation, though more in terms of projecting the nation's *desired* modus operandi for its leader: "What people really want is for Medvedev himself to be writing it. . . . People still have this hope that our president is actually a witty, discerning, thinking person. Everyone's constantly writing to us that KermlinRussia is just his alter ego, that these are his real thoughts, and that what he writes in the official Twitter is just PR" (Ioffe 2011).

Whatever the reason, @KermlinRussia skyrocketed in popularity and authority, rivaling its source of inspiration in number of followers and Yandex "authority" rating, and being named 2010 "Microblog of the Year" in the annual competition run by Runet industry awards group, ROTOR.[18] The boundaries between

---

18. "Mikroblog goda" 2011. By February 2011, @MedvedevRussia surpassed @KremlinRussia in number of followers, but according to Yandex's more complicated "authority" ranking (which takes into account the number of times a tweet has been retweeted), the parody feed ranked first among Russian accounts, with Medvedev's in the fourth position overall ("Reiting blogov" 2011).

the parody and the original were hazy enough, in fact, that the Kremlin split Medvedev's Twitter account off from @KremlinRussia in November 2010, leaving the latter for more anodyne official posts and giving Medvedev full reign at the newly created @MedvedevRussia. It may simply have been a desire, as Kremlin press secretary Natal'ia Timakova put it, to separate the more official posts from Medvedev's personal observations—thereby giving him greater latitude.[19] But the nominal distance between the blogger-in-chief and the parodic impostor, whether intentionally created or not, also provided Medvedev with a greater buffer from belittlement.

Imagining "Electronic Russia"

If cajoling regional governors into blogging proved a hard sell for Medvedev, promoting new media technologies to make the government apparatus and its services more accessible to citizens was easier, at least in principle. "E-government" initiatives had been embraced by Western countries since the 1990s, and the "Electronic Russia" national project had been adopted early in the first Putin administration. Some early reports suggest primarily economic motivations for the move ("Government sets" 2001; "State mulls" 2001), while others saw it as an effort "to use the computer as a way of bringing vlast' closer to the people, and vice versa" (Smirnov 2001). When then Prime Minister Mikhail Kasianov signed "E-Rossiia" into action as a "Federal target plan" (FTP) in January 2002, his point-person for the project, Tseren Tserenov, talked about putting tax forms online, equipping schools with more computers, and "developing better legislation for the IT sector" ("PM signs" 2002).

It would take nearly two decades of deliberation, legislation, and implementation (however flawed) to resolve the tension between these two models of "electronic government"—one that essentially envisioned a technocratically enhanced reboot of traditional hierarchic relations between state and citizens, and one seeking to transform those relations more substantially with the help of digitally driven mechanisms of access, accountability, and automation. While sections of the plan alluded indirectly to self-government and civic oversight of state institutions, the plan emphasized economics and convenience more than ethics and transparency. Even these more mundane goals were met with skepticism by outside observers due to the low level of tech readiness of most government agencies—what one commentator referred to as "informational feudalism"

---

19. "Medvedev renames" 2010; "Mikroblog Medvedeva" 2010.

(Pravdina 2002). The software security specialist Natal'ia Kasperskaia described her doubt as being "tied more to the general state of the state apparatus [*gosapparat*]" and "its ability to effectively carry out such a complicated and by no means ordinary task" ("Chto mozhet" 2001). Others attributed their skepticism to a political culture in which state bureaucrats viewed themselves not as servants of the people but quite the opposite:

> "E-government" is possible only when the state apparatus recognizes itself as a servant of the population [*sluga naseleniia*], rather than the reverse. (Pravdina 2001)

> The Western view of authorities [*vlast'*] as hired hands [*naemnyi rabotnik*] who are paid by the country's population in the form of tax payments does not work in Russia, due to the geopolitical particularities of the development of the state [*gosudarstvennost'*]. (Boiarinov 2001])

While cutting down on corruption and red tape was not explicitly listed as the goal of the program, it was certainly recognized as an implicit result, however difficult it might be to realize. "The idea of 'electronic government' will most likely meet up with resistance from bureaucrats," Tserenov predicted, "since 'Electronic Russia' means the transparency of the activity of the state apparatus. The majority of bureaucrats use their administrative rent through access to information that is closed off to citizens. They trade with it" ("Chto mozhet" 2001). If anything, another skeptic argued, the "services-without-transparency" model likely to emerge in Russia would likely lead to new technology serving as a greater "mechanism for control by the state over citizens" in the realm of tax collection and crime prevention (Peskov 2002, 37).

Even members of the PRIOR group, who had teamed with Microsoft to develop and sell software for facilitating e-government, recognized the uphill battle such initiatives faced, due to traditional bureaucratic *and* popular views of authority as a top-down hierarchy when it came to decision-making, a state monopoly of action over words. As they observed in a June 2003 press conference,

> In our country, it's customary to think that the role of "individuals making decisions, and therefore taking the responsibility for the results of those decisions" belongs exclusively to the state. . . . For PRIOR, the state apparatus is not the "boss" of society but rather one among the key communities [*soobshchestva*] of development, occupying a clearly delineated niche in the public domain and, together with business, civil society, and the scientific and educational community, shares the responsibility

for the realization of agreed upon decisions. . . . A state isolated from society—that is our past: one would like to believe that our future holds a maximally open authority [vlast'], which allows the participation of the expert community, industry, and citizens in the decision-making process. (Ershova and Khokhlov 2003)

Activity toward realizing these goals remained minimal through the remainder of Putin's first two terms. Though it became law in July 2001, implementation of the FTP remained weak due to the lack of legal and technical infrastructure, as well as cuts to the program's budget (Skripnik and Pichugin 2003; Poshataev 2004; Latkin 2004). Three years into the plan, one public opinion survey indicated that 76 percent of the population had not even heard of e-government and didn't know what it was (Fak 2003). Another observer wrote that, despite the promise of the internet as a game changer in bringing about "cyber-democracy," e-government initiatives had thus far been little more than ineffectual window dressing, designed "mainly for the creation of photo ops for various power structures [*reklamnye obliki otdel'nykh struktur vlasti*]" (Solov'ev 2004, 128).

With the arrival of the technophile Medvedev to the presidency in 2008, the topic of e-government received heightened attention specifically regarding its capacity to decrease government corruption and bring about greater transparency. But Medvedev was the first to bemoan the gap between words and deeds, between the plan and its implementation. At a State Council meeting dedicated to the "implementation of a strategy for the development of an information society in Russia" just two months into his term, the president openly acknowledged the lack of progress of the e-government initiative, which he linked directly to transparency and anticorruption, and attributed it to "computer illiteracy among state and municipal workers" (Latyshev 2008). His frustration over the lack of progress reemerged in the spring of 2009 when he referred to the "sad state" of the initiative, which seemed to be either "non-existent or 'in exile'" (Beluza 2009a). By September, Medvedev was berating ministers for overstating claims about the progress made in its implementation (here, in an exchange with Minister of Education Fursenko): "'So you mean to say that these services are already being provided?' Medvedev asked in amazement. . . . 'What have we put forward? We haven't put forward crap yet [*Ni figa my ne proodvinuli poka*]. So ditch the optimistic picture and speak substantively'" (Shishkunova 2009).

Medvedev's pressure led to modest organizational gains in the fall of 2009, when the Russian Postal Service was chosen as the central provider for e-government services, and a separate Department of Information Technologies and Communication was created to oversee it (Borodulin 2009; Voronin 2009). The initiative received a symbolic boost that season as well, when the Internet Corporation for Assigned Names and Numbers (ICANN) approved the first-ever Cyrillic domain name suffix .рф, prompting Medvedev to claim it would "enable the more active dissemination of electronic government" (Beluza 2009b). Medvedev again linked the initiative to government transparency and his anticorruption campaign, this time in the formal setting of his first annual address to parliament ("Stat' obshchestvom" 2009). In a separate end-of-year meeting with governors, he drew the contrast between words and deeds in a way that made it clear their jobs were on the line: "There have been changes in those places where regional authorities have taken up this issue with interest. But there's been no movement in places where regional authorities think it's some kind of Christmas decoration and that life is hard enough without being asked to come up with some sort of 'electronic government'. . . . Those who aren't working on this issue are simply showing that they are not suited for working under modern conditions" (Granik 2009).[20]

The awkward reality was that Medvedev's allusion to administrative intransigence could have had his prime minister, Vladimir Putin, as its poster child. Though Putin spoke little on the topic at the time, he acted in ways that undermined more ambitious aspects of the plan. Most specifically, Putin sent a piece of draft legislation on electronic government to the Parliament for consideration that led one Kremlin official to come out "categorically against" its passage, due to its "rawness" and a multitude of criticisms that the presidential administration had not been afforded the chance to air. According to the political analyst Rostislav Turovskii, the tension was rooted in a more substantive difference between Putin and Medvedev: "The government [i.e., Putin] understands the realization of this project on a purely technological level. For instance, how to organize document circulation or internet auctions. But this is in no way tied to modernization that understands the development of electronic government in terms of the creation of a feedback mechanism [*obratnaia sviaz'*] for society" (quoted in Bilevskaia 2009).

If Turovskii's claim was accurate, the move amounted to legislative sabotage on the part of Putin's White House that sought to defang the initiative of its corruption-fighting and transparency-oriented dimensions and turn it into a less ambitious, more technocratic plan. And while the Parliament ultimately deferred to Medvedev's Kremlin in this case, the continued troubles surrounding the E-Russia plan ultimately scaled it back to the technocratic form sought by Putin. In fact, separate reporting by the independent newspaper *Novaia gazeta* suggested that the management of the electronic government initiative was itself

---

20. The cause for Medvedev's frustration find corroboration in period testimony by IT consultants close to the development of the Gosuslugi portal (envisioned as a one-stop shopping platform for a variety of state services), who point to uneven, and mostly low, levels of buy-in on the part of both state agencies and regional authorities (Baigarova 2010).

mired in layers of corruption, from how the state funds were managed to the competition for contracts (Revich 2009).

Reporting over the remaining two years of Medvedev's presidency reflected these parallel worlds of e-government. As Medvedev continued to dress down regional governors for their incapacity to navigate online government services (Granik 2010), independent reporters filed reports about the lagging implementation, largely due to mismanagement of funds; complicated systems in need of coordination and oversight; and the watered-down, largely technocratic nature of the project (Rubtsov 2010; Revich and Shiriaev 2010). Medvedev associates met with Western advisers about modernizing Russia through technology, producing such high-minded documents as "A Roadmap for the Construction of an Innovation Economy" and recommending the creation of an outside "shadow" group of advisers answering directly to Medvedev to bypass lingering old-school cadres from the Putin administration who might impede the push to modernize (Vedenskaia 2010). Yet public opinion polling of government bureaucrats showed that "only half of the country's regions had even begun implementing electronic government to date. The rest continued to realize the project in words alone" (Tumanova 2010).

If real power in Russian political culture manifested itself more in the form of action, the bureaucracy's stubborn resistance to Medvedev's tech-based modernization plans represented an act of silent insubordination and confirmation of the limits of Medvedev's own power. The chasm between words and deeds would only widen during the election season of 2011–12, after Putin and Medvedev announced plans to trade positions (in what came to be known as the "castling"), and they and the ruling United Russia Party faced increased scrutiny over mismanagement and corruption thanks to the efforts of web-based investigative reporting by Alexei Navalny. The pressure emanating specifically from the online community was enough to motivate both Medvedev and Putin to up their campaign rhetoric in support of internet-fueled democracy. Medvedev launched an initiative he called "Big government" (Bol'shoe pravitel'stvo), which was pitched as a "prototype of an expanded government," an "'ear' sensitive to good ideas," and a forum for the outgoing president's supporters to share their concerns over trenchant government bureaucracy (Shishkunova 2011; Tropkina 2011). Though separate from electronic government initiatives, the plan reflected Medvedev's inclination to lean on web-based resources, as it was envisioned to be an internet-fueled experiment in "crowdsourcing" public policy. As Medvedev ally Kryshtanovskaia put it in an opinion piece on the pages of *Nezavisimaia gazeta* shortly after the fateful announcement of the Putin-Medvedev castling,

> The concept of "big government" must include a variety of mechanisms: the creation of channels through which the opinion of citizens can be

accumulated, analyzed, and made accessible to those who prepare decisions on the state level. The main instrument here must become the
Internet. Political technology is wiki-politics (or crowdsourcing)—the
collection of opinions and suggestions of people. "Big government"
must include the creation of a management center (let's call it a "public
council" [*obshchestvennyi sovet*]) that would engage in the management
of crowdsourcing, the acquisition of essential and useful information.
The council should become a bridge connecting the people to leadership, a channel for the promotion of constructive ideas, borne among
rank-and-file citizens wherever they live whatever their occupation.
(Kryshtanovskaia 2011)

After a chorus of ambitious, democratically infused proposals that included
holding meetings of the proposed public committee in a space surrounded by
glass walls ("*za* steklom," she wrote, awkwardly invoking the name of Russia's first
and most notorious reality show that featured quite different liaising behind glass
walls), Kryshtanovskaia (2011) closed with an explicitly meta-rhetorical declaration: "The entire stylistics of communication on the part of the authorities with
society [*stilistika obshcheniia vlasti s obshchestvom*] must change: openness, dem-
ocratic-ness, simplicity, [and] a high level of technologism will come to replace
bureaucratic archaism, corruption, and cumbersome luxury."

To implement the plan, the already lame duck Medvedev created and con-
vened the Public Committee of Supporters (elsewhere referred to as the Public
Committee of Supporters of Dmitry Medvedev), which featured a who's who of
the pro-Kremlin (and pro-Medvedev) Runet—including Sergei Minaev (featured
in chapter 7), Marat Guelman (of FEP fame), journalists Margarita Simonyan and
Tina Kandelaki, and members of various pro-Kremlin youth groups linked to
Nashi (Sidibe 2011a; Tropkina 2011; Kashin 2011). But the timing of the announcement, in the heat of a campaign season rife with accusations of corruption and
fraud on the part of Medvedev's United Russia party, and the fact that the body
disappeared from public sight soon after elections had passed, made it clear that
it was either a last-ditch effort to curry favor among a digital elite dismayed over
the return of a less Runet-friendly president, a bureaucratic fig leaf to cover Medvedev's bruised ego, or a combination of both.[21] Invoking the Soviet-era notion
of a top-down engineered civil society, the oppositional journalist Oleg Kashin
(2011) remarked, "After the September castling of Dmitry Medvedev and Vladimir

---

21. Public opinion polling from late December 2011 suggested that only 6 percent of even active
internet users knew about Medvedev's "big government" project; 71 percent knew nothing about it,
and 23 percent had heard vaguely about it (Sergeev 2011).

Putin, the Kremlin has for some reason seen the need again for a loyal society [*ponadobilas' loial'naia obshchestvennost'*]." The plan tellingly faced skepticism from the opposite end of the political spectrum as well—namely, representatives of the top-down engineered Public Chamber (Obshchestvennaia palata) created years earlier by Putin (and featured in chapter 6) to serve as a quasi-independent public sounding board. In a meeting with Putin on the eve of the 2012 presidential elections, a member of the chamber expressed concerns regarding the redundancy and competition posed by Medvedev's "big government" initiative—again, using language laced with new media metaphors:

> Many of us have come out of the Public Chamber that you created . . . And now we hear, "open government", "big government". . . . We wouldn't want to get lost in the shuffle! [*Nam by ne zabludit'sia v etom chastokole!*] Sure, the expert opinion of people, including glamorous ones, is interesting, but the people who represent the real system [*za kotorymi real'naia sistema*] are sitting here! . . . And they're proposing to introduce crowtsourcing [*sic*]! We've been doing this crowtsourcing for a long time now! (quoted in Kolesnikov 2012b).

At least for these public citizens (and their candidate as well), one digitally networked group (from the "real system") was plenty enough "crowt" from which to source ideas from Russia's systemic public sphere.

Nevertheless, facing more forceful public pushback and discontent than they ever had in the wake of the election-rigging scandal of 2011, Putin and his reelection team went the extra mile in their own verbal embrace of new technology as a mechanism for enhanced participatory democracy in a February 2012 policy paper entitled "Democracy and the quality of government."[22] In a section on "new mechanisms of participation," the paper used technology-infused rhetoric to describe a modern world in which, through "friendly, interactive interfaces on the portals . . . of public authority," citizens could discuss and monitor the enactment of plans and programs, all expressed in a language that was, "if not euphonic to the common ear, then at least comprehensible to the addressee of the norms."

The document went on to promote the internet as a mechanism for crowdsourcing draft legislation by giving citizens the opportunity to comment online on bills before the Parliament and even proposed their own draft legislation that would be required for consideration by the Parliament were it to obtain the requisite number of online signatures. In a more convoluted modification of Med-

---

22. "Demokratiia i kachestvo gosudarstva." The piece was published in full in the 6 February issue of *Kommersant* (Putin 2012), whence the following excerpts come.

vedev's terminology, it declared that "internet-democracy must be built into the general flow of the development of institutions of direct referendum democracy." And on the issue of e-government itself, Putin called for greater attention to "the needs and demands of citizens," ensuring open access to the information and activities of state and municipal authorities.

Despite the bold promises of the campaign position paper, Putin's return to the Kremlin in the spring of 2012 sealed the fate of the bolder e-government initiatives linked to transparency, participatory democracy, and anticorruption drives. By summertime, all vestiges of "big government" and "internet democracy" had disappeared, and press reports documented the moribund state of even the most basic, information-oriented aspects of the e-government initiative. One noted the lack of updated information on ministry websites (Rodin 2012); another cited Russia's lagging global status as an electronic government compared even to less developed countries (Shirmanova 2012). While citizens would eventually be able to find a host of government services online in the form of the Gosuslugi platform, most analysts agreed that their ability to have a voice in government decision-making was no better than it had been before the rise of new media technologies. As two independent analyses showed, a combination of mismanaged funds and gaps in administrative, legal, technical, and educational infrastructure caused the projects to fall well short of their original goals and cemented, in the process, the shift in focus from transparency and citizen control to bureaucratic efficiency and technological advancement (Pavliutenkova 2013; Rovinskaia 2014).[23]

Although rhetoric regarding "information democracy" would resurface around future elections (Khamraev 2017), when it came to real power brokering, key processes for deliberation remained behind closed doors, and public information was deliberately obfuscated to make transparent communication as opaque as possible. In one of the more notorious cases involving open bidding for public contracts, technology was even used to *conceal* choice contracts in plain day by digitally manipulating the listings so that only insiders knew how to find them.[24]

On a broader level, of course, Medvedev's more ambitious vision of "direct internet democracy" was doomed by a misplaced belief in the unwavering power

---

23. Gritsenko and Zherebtsov (2021, 46) confirm as much when they observe in their study of Russian e-government that, "the *technocratic* narrative of information technology as a source of increased efficiency for the state has been a prevailing ideology of the ruling elite since 2012 when Medvedev's techno-political modernization agenda was curtailed." For a good analysis of both the shortcomings and the more successful, technocratic initiatives, such as the widely used Gosuslugi services, see Zherebtsov 2019 and Guzik 2023.

24. Navalny and his team drew attention in 2013 to a long-standing trick used by government insiders that involved strategically placing Latin letters in the titles of state contract announcements to make them undiscoverable through searches done in Cyrillic. For details, see "RosPil predlozhil" 2013.

of technology alone to bring about more open, democratic political regimes. As one contemporary of the Medvedev reforms put it in an analysis published on the eve of the 2011 protests of Medvedev, Putin, and the entirety of the ruling "systemic elite,"

> Democracy [*narodovlastie*] and political pluralism begin not with computers: the computer can also be used for strengthening totalitarian structures. . . . Democracy happens when citizens are the decision makers and the bureaucrat is disenfranchised, gradually reduced to a record-keeper. Computer technology makes this possible but does not guarantee it. Guarantees arise—with or without a computer—with the liquidation of the caste-based, oligarchic structure of society, [and] of the current hegemony of the bureaucracy [*chinovnichestvo*] and big business, which have grown together like Siamese twins. (Shubin 2010; cf. Glukhova 2020).

For all the earnestness and sincerity that may have underlay Medvedev's efforts at reform, his status as a systemic insider and presidential placeholder for Vladimir Putin would limit his ability to bring about any substantive reform. In the face of a tradition of state authority in Russia that placed primacy of deed over word and privileged the voice of the powerful over that of rank-and-file citizens, calls for direct, internet-charged democracy and the networking of the ruling elite fell on deaf ears among most of the Russian bureaucracy, and more ambitious plans for electronic government as a foil against corruption shriveled to technocratic upgrades that, if anything, further protected the powers that be. And if his chances in the face of these internal roadblocks weren't enough, outside factors—namely, the rise in political prominence of another tech-savvy but entirely oppositional political reformer—spelled their certain defeat. For in the growingly viral rhetoric of Aleksei Navalny, Medvedev, Putin, and other members of the systemic elite came to see quite viscerally how information and communication technologies could provide volatile fuel for liquidating the "Siamese twins" of trenchant bureaucracy and big, oligarchic-controlled business.

NAVALNY AS MEDIATED OPPOSITION

To remain in authority requires respect for the person or the office. The greatest enemy of authority, therefore, is contempt, and the surest way to undermine it is laughter.

—Hannah Arendt (1969)

My safety valve is Twitter, my favorite social media. I write a lot on there, about everything: here's the breaking news, here's what I think about it, and here are the dumplings I've just eaten. With sour cream.

—Alexei Navalny (2024)

Medvedev's efforts at bringing the government online both rhetorically and institutionally met with resistance for a number of interlocking reasons: (1) The tradition of political communication deemphasized, if not discouraged, public-facing engagement on the part of Russian and Soviet officials, particularly of the less-scripted nature typical of digital media platforms; (2) this lack of experience translated into a certain degree of bureaucratic tongue-tied-ness when it came to public engagement; (3) which in turn led to an increased sense of exposure and vulnerability, particularly in the face of online voices and environments critically oriented to official power and authority. Among the more persuasive of these voices was that of the politician and anticorruption advocate Alexei Navalny. Navalny not only was an early and eager adopter of social media; he also demonstrated a unique affinity for using them to reframe ruling authority critically, to project a compelling political profile of himself, and to create a networked public sphere unparalleled to any others online and capable of challenging authority in the offline world of Russian politics as well. The rhetorical grease throughout was a political language that proved coherent and compelling in a new media environment and broader culture where such speech, if we are to believe the likes of Pushkin and Pavlovsky, was so notoriously elusive.

Navalny was by no means the only significant member of the political opposition, but he stood out for the above-mentioned reasons as one of the most effective and therefore most threatening to Putinism and Putin himself—a claim substantiated by the singularly harsh treatment he received at the hands of that regime up to his death in February 2024. The detailed analysis in this chapter understands Navalny not so much as typical or representative of the largely web-generated political opposition in Russia but as the most successful and potent, from a rhetorical perspective, and as a figure whose political notoriety and impact came almost entirely thanks to the internet and social media. Of course, much of his success had to do with his political message—a potent mix of democratic, populist, and nationalist leanings that resonated with broad swaths of the population.[1] I focus here, however, on how new media helped shape that message. How, rhetorically, did the various social networking platforms Navalny relied on help establish, shape, and grow his political persona? How did he use them to generate such a successful critical portrait of political authority in Russia in the midst of an authoritarian regime keen on controlling the flow of information and channels of communication? I examine Navalny's use of three social networking platforms—LiveJournal, Twitter, and YouTube—to show how they helped shape the messenger and his message regarding authority and corruption and foster networked public spheres that quickly drew the attention and ire of the Putin administration.

LiveJournal and "Blogger Navalny"

When Navalny first began making waves on the national scene in the early to mid-2000s, Russian political leaders and their conduits in state-affiliated media relied on two rhetorical strategies for deflating his authority: they either referred to him derogatorily as "blogger Navalny," or they didn't name him at all. As much as the second strategy was mocked as the "Voldemort" treatment (invoking the main antagonist of J. K. Rowling's *Harry Potter* series), it made sense given what has been said about traditional attitudes toward authority in Russia. If speech took a back seat to actions in the projection of power, publicly naming one's political opponent risked ascribing to that person an unwarranted degree of respect. Instead, Putin reverted to euphemisms that ranged from the neutral "that person" and "that gentleman" (*tot chelovek, etot gospodin*) to more negatively marked nominations, such as "that character" (*etot personazh*, implicitly likening him to a fictitious, storybook character) and even "the Russian edition of Saakashvili" (the former president of Georgia and [in Putin's eyes] inciter of anti-Russian protests and coups).[2]

The pro-Kremlin press could less afford to avoid his name entirely and thus fell back on the first strategy—labeling him with the "blogger" tag (e.g., "According to Mikhail Vinogradov, the blogger Alexei Navalny, who has received wide praise

---

1. For a data-driven analysis of the populist dimension of Navalny's politics, see Glazunova 2020.
2. "Tot samyi" 2017; Khimshiashvili and Kaliukov 2017. For alternative explanations of the phenomenon, see Safonova 2018.

thanks to his investigative articles, may register as a candidate [in the upcoming mayoral elections]" [Sidibe 2011b]). Though the blogosphere had been around a good half decade by 2011, the concept was still foreign to many, and the term itself, an exotic-sounding loanword from English, had something of a superfluous sound to it—to the point where even Navalny himself deplored being called 'blogger Navalny.'"[3] Be that as it may, it does bring up a fundamental question for the purpose of this book: To what extent and in what ways was Navalny's emergence as a key political player shaped by communication via his LiveJournal blog? My analysis of the entire body of his posts from the account's launch in April 2006 until December 2011, when Navalny shifted more full-time to Twitter, reveals a number of notable rhetorical features and trends.[4] Three, in particular, stand out: Navalny's commitment to using the medium to promote small *d* democratic discourse through debate; his mastery of the Russian language and the power of the political metaphor to generate potent (negative) images of ruling authorities (vlast'); and his ability to harness the networking power of LiveJournal to begin building the foundation for an alternative political movement.

Platform for Advocacy and Debate

Though Navalny started his blog as a twenty-nine-year-old member of the Yabloko Party, his early posts were not all about politics. He clearly embraced the same community spirit of LiveJournal that attracted Kholmogorov and others, using the platform, as most users did, for apolitical banter and venting—on everything from the upcoming Eurovision contest to the poor state of Russian dentistry (11 May 2007; 19 February 2007). A closer look at his more overtly political engagement shows that Navalny was fully aware of the platform's potential for shaping and leveraging a fast-emerging networked public sphere to promote civil discourse in the offline world. It's an effort we see Navalny pursuing both as aspiring politician and community advocate. A good portion of the posts from the first two years of his account, for instance, focus on the public debates he organized and moderated as a part the Democratic Alternative movement he created with Maria Gaidar and Sergei Kazakov to get Russian youth more politically engaged ("Politicheskie debaty" 2006). To do that, they staged what they called "DaDebaty!" at local Moscow clubs, luring would-be attenders with head-

---

3. Alexey Navalny (@navalny), "И я НЕНАВИЖУ когда меня называют 'блогер Навальный'." Twitter, 18 January 2011 [7:11 AM], https://x.com/navalny/status/27337323557429248.

4. This analysis considers all 2,501 of Navalny's posts to his LiveJournal blog (*navalny*, https://navalny.livejournal.com/) from his initial adoption of the platform through his peak usage, with the final two years overlapping with his use of Twitter. Henceforth, posts from Navalny's LiveJournal blog come from this same account and are referenced by date only.

Политические дебаты на тему
«ЗА КЕМ ПОЙДЕТ МОЛОДЁЖЬ?»

Где: Клуб на Брестской (http://brestclub.ru)
Когда: 6 июня, во вторник. Начало в 20-00.

Участвуют:
Ксения СОБЧАК против Сергея ШАРГУНОВА

ЗА КЕМ ПОЙДЕТ МОЛОДЕЖЬ?
VS
СЕРГЕЙ ШАРГУНОВ   КСЕНИЯ СОБЧАК
6 ИЮНЯ, ВТОРНИК, В 20-00
КЛУБ НА БРЕСТСКОЙ

Голосование
Вам понравились дебаты
Хатанды против Чадаева
Да   34%
Нет   21%
Я на них не был(а) 45%
Голосовать

Внимание!
Данное голосование не являет собой процентное соотношение проголосовавших зрителей и жюри в зале. Оно носит независимый характер и сделано для возможности последующего статистического сравнения мнений различных аудиторий.

день России

Разместите наш баннер у себя в ЖЖ / на сайте!

КСЕНИЯ СОБЧАК

Код баннера:
```
<a
href="https://web.archive.org/web/20060610152625/http://www.dadebata
m.ru/" target="_top"><img
```

ЖЮЖЮРИ ПОЛИТИЧЕСКИХ ДЕБАТОВ - V
(в алфавитном порядке):

belyh - Никита Белых, лидер партии СПС
drugoi - Рустем Адагамов дизайнер
galerist - Марат Гельман, политтехнолог, галерист
immoralist - Алмат Малатов, писатель, журналист
olgatt - Ольга Гронина, «сетевой гуру»

Вход - свободный. Ка» всегда.

FIGURE 4.1.   Screenshot of ad from "Political Debates" website featuring debate between Sergei Shargunov and Ksenia Sobchak on the topic "Who Will Youth Support?" and list of LiveJournal personalities making up the panel of debate judges (*ZheZhuri*). Source: "Politicheskie Debaty" (2006), Dadebatam.ru, https://web.archive.org/web/20060610152625/http://dadebatam.ru/.

line personalities and plenty of beer (20 November 2006).[5] The list of keynote debaters featured a mix of up-and-coming politicians, political commentators, and rising stars of the ZheZhe community itself, including the likes of Nossik, Kononenko, Kholmogorov, Viktor Shenderovich, Irina Khakamada, Garry Kasparov, Boris Nemtsov, Dmitry Rogozin, Nikita Belykh, Yulia Latynina, and Ksenia Sobchak (fig. 4.1). The debate topics were also selected to provoke spirited dis-

---

5. Characteristic of Navalny the wordsmith, the event title ("Dadebaty!") featured a double entendre that referred to both the name of his political group, Democratic Alternative, and the phrase "Yes to debates!"

cussion: in September 2006, for instance, Nemtsov and Rogozin sparred on the topic "Russia-Georgia: Where are the purges?" (16 September 2006). A February 2007 debate featured Sergei Minaev and Konstantin Krylov on "Russian Nationalism: Is it the death or the salvation of Russia?" (5 February 2007).

Navalny's persistent efforts to gin up active involvement among the ZheZhe community suggests that he saw in these online communities unrealized potential for political action in the unmediated public sphere (e.g., 11, 12, and 25 May 2006). He and fellow organizers even tapped prominent LiveJournal personalities to serve on the "LJury" (*ZheZhuri*) for the debates. As Navalny himself put it in an interview at the time: "LJ is the sort of crowd [*tuskovka*] where there are enough young politicians, and journalists, and just plain old folks who find it interesting to come to a debate. There are some who think this is a problem. Maybe it is. We try to get beyond the bounds of LJ by hanging flyers at universities, but if we don't manage to do that, that's not a terrible problem" (Bobrova 2006).

Early signs suggested he had a winning formula. Mainstream media coverage of the debates grew, brimming with reports of packed audiences and rowdy repartees ("Viewers hung like grapes from the balcony, sitting two-to-a-chair and literally stepping on one another's toes" [Poliak 2006a]). Another review, titled "ZheZhe Conquers Space," noted there was nowhere to sit a half-hour before the start of the debate and remarked that the event also seemed to serve the purpose of allowing members of the virtual ZheZhe community to emerge from their digital lairs and commune with one another in three dimensions: "The audience, filled with familiar faces from userpics, seemed like home [*rodnym*], with friendly greetings sprinkled about and smiles of recognition radiating. Everyone was definitely feeling good—almost as good as being at home in front of your favorite computer with a user-scroll [*iuzer-lenta*] on the monitor" (Poliak 2006b).

The series drew the attention of like-minded groups in other cities around Russia, and in February 2007, Navalny was even invited to bring the initiative onto the air at the TVTs television network under the title "Fight Club" (Boitsovskii klub). The experiment was short-lived, though, canceled after two episodes for somewhat ambiguous reasons that Navalny ascribed to politics.[6]

A similar fate notably came to the "DaDebaty!" series later that year at a debate between Maria Gaidar and Sergei Markov dedicated to the provocative theme "Putin's Plan or Putin's Clan?" Before the event began, a group of hooligans

---

6. It was not, in any case, due to poor ratings (the second televised debate having earned TVTs its highest ratings for the day on which it aired). Navalny added cryptically, "I'm aware only of conspiracy theories about the reasons for cancelation. But they are so flattering for my political ego that I won't talk about them, as you'll say that I made them up myself" (9 April 2007).

began heckling the organizers, prompting Navalny to pull out a trauma gun and shoot one of the intruders in the stomach—and thereby putting an end to the event. Though the link was never formally established, Navalny assumed it the work of the United Russia Party and the presidential administration, writing, "I know perfectly well that our debates have caused heartburn in various directorates of domestic politics there, because we invite whom we want and, because of that, 'amplify the wrong individuals' and 'create the wrong trends'" (1 November 2007). Some from the mass print media latched onto the scandalous event as evidence of the hooligan underpinnings of Navalny style democracy: "Seeing as 'in the best of democratic traditions' the debates took place over a mug of beer, everything ended poorly—a collective drunken brawl, gunshots from a trauma gun, and the arrival of a squadron of police" ("Debosh debaty" 2007). Whatever the cause, the event served as an apt metaphor for the spotty history of debate culture in contemporary Russia (and the ruling elite's fear of it) and effectively brought an end to Navalny's early experiment in melding the political energy of LiveJournal into the bars and clubs of urban Russia. But by his own admission, the experience taught him a critical lesson: "I saw how much could be achieved without money and without the 'protection' of the Kremlin, indeed, in spite of the Kremlin. What I needed was a group of supporters to work with me, and I found that group through the internet" (Navalny 2024, 192).[7]

In addition to amplifying Navalny's interest in promoting civic debate, the LiveJournal account highlights his offline commitment to community advocacy. The early blog entries teem with references to his work as cochair of the so-called Committee for the Defense of Muscovites, helping local residents stand up to special interests with ties to the mayor's office—be it to defend a local sports complex from the construction of housing for the FSB (13 May 2006) or prevent their own relocation from prime real estate in the center of Moscow to the outer regions of the city (9 June 2006). This sort of grassroots work with central and regional community leaders exemplified the sort of civic action that Kharkhordin (2018) refers to as "republicanism"—initiatives that engaged local citizens in a way that only basic problems of local infrastructure could and, as such, sparked in them a degree of political activism otherwise unseen. They also illustrate how Navalny's online activity largely served an amplifying function for his offline work. Much as the official monikers would claim otherwise, he was far more than just a "blogger."

---

7. For his own account of the debates and likely state-sanctioned disruption of them, see Navalny 2024, 190–92.

Reframing Vlast'

While the LJ blog served largely as a means of leveraging his offline efforts to promote civil society and republicanism, Navalny devoted substantial attention to national politics. And in these early posts, we hear a tone that would come to be associated with the rhetorical style of the mature Navalny—rife with sarcasm and irony directed at the corruption and incompetence of political authority but at the same time laced with a wry jocularity that at once appealed to the LOLs-oriented environment of the online community and deflated the symbolic authority of Putinism.

As noted earlier, the word *vlast'* does double duty in Russian, referring to both the abstract notions of "power" and "authority" and the more concrete "authorities," or "those in power." As such, it was a core concept in Navalny's constellation of figurative political speech, appearing in its various morphological forms 433 times across the 2,501 posts he made over the period studied. When Navalny used the term in reference to Putin, Putin's associates, and the power they wielded, he did so in one of three related semantic clusters. The first and main cluster portrayed vlast' in Putin's Russia as criminal and corrupt, featuring authorities at all levels engaged in various nefarious power grabs: stealing elections, embezzling

авальный

инальная битва между добром и нейтралитетом

о subject)

Ω navalny
September 27th, 2007

27 сентябрь, 2007
Заявление

Ответим на смену правительства и операцию «Преемник» вооружением населения!

Политические события в очередной раз демонстрируют нам, что властную элиту России не интересует ничего, кроме жалкой возни, в которой одни жулики сменяют других. Это уже даже борьба не бульдогов под ковром, а свиней у нефтяного корыта.

FIGURE 4.2. Screenshot from beginning of Navalny LiveJournal post calling power elites "crooks" and ascribing their motives to pure self-interest. Source: "Navalny," Navalny.livejournal.com (27 September 2007), https://web.archive .org/web/20120208055543/https://navalny.livejournal.com/163552.html.

budgets, abusing suspect perks, or blatantly manipulating the law to protect their positions of power. For example:

> The power elites of Russia aren't interested in anything except pathetic maneuvering where one set of crooks replaces another. (27 September 2007) (fig. 4.2)

> We won't grieve too much, but this whole "Skolkovo" thing is an obvious swindle. Just one problem: when translated from power-vertical speak into Russian [*s vertikalevlastnogo na russkii*], the key phrase "all financial flows will merge" simply means "we'll steal twice as much." (10 May 2011)

The second cluster spoke to the authoritarian nature of power under Putin, in which political ideology was but a pretense; repressive machinery was engaged at the slightest impulse; civil rights and political opposition were mutually exclusive; and political beatings, murders, and provocations were the coin of the realm:

> You can suck up to power [*oblizyvat' vlast'*] with all the intensity you want, but they'll still find the slightest of excuses to unleash the repressive machine. The machine will work. (30 December 2008)

> The logic of power says that from the moment you go out to any mass event, you completely lose all of your civic rights. (26 November 2007)

The combination of corruption and authoritarianism fed into the third semantic cluster coloring Navalny's use of *vlast'*—the underlying impotence or illegitimacy of the regime, particularly in its ability or desire to address the real needs of the population. The corruption-plagued aloofness manifested itself in various forms of sensory deprivation (especially muteness and deafness), as well as a level of incompetence or inaction that essentially rendered it useless, if not nonexistent:

> All the while, the authorities keep humbly quiet [*vlast' skromno umalchivaiut*]. (27 November 2006)

> To solve the problem, the authorities took the path of silence [*vlast' poshla po puti zamalchivaniia*]. (7 June 2007)

> Come to the demonstration! We'll force the authorities to hear us [*Zastavim vlast' nas uslyshat (sic)*]. (19 May 2009)

> A stunning example of how there is no authority in the country [*vlasti v strane net*], and what is called "authority" has lost all meaning for the population. (6 July 2011)

Quite often, the semantic fields were closely intertwined, illegitimacy being a result of excess corruption and repression (as well as public willingness to look the other way): "The absence of an adequate reaction of society to the unprecedented level of corruption, official lies, the ubiquitous bribery and thievery, bureaucratic mayhem and the cynical attitude of authorities [vlast'] to the people has allowed this self-indulgent, torn-from-society handful of people and usurpers of state power [vlast'] to go on far too long" (25 June 2007).

In the aftermath of the contested 2011 parliamentary elections that led to widespread protest, Navalny turned to physiognomic allusions to liken falsified election results to a Botox treatment that had gone wrong (clearly alluding to widespread rumors of Putin having undergone facial enhancement treatment over the preceding year [e.g., Beshlei and Mostovshchikov 2011]): "The paltry 49% [of the vote]—is the same sort of botoxed physiognomy of power [vlast']. It's obvious and unpleasant that there's something artificial about it" (12 May 2007).

Not only did the volume and repetition of these semantic clusters help lay the groundwork for more viral labeling campaigns commonly associated with Navalny's rise to prominence, as witnessed in the graphic images of the overly Botoxed mug, Navalny had a deft touch for generating memorable labels in a medium that lent itself to the propagation of memes. His use of humor acknowledged the importance of the entertainment factor in attracting views, likes, and shares, while at the same time recasting Putin and Putinism in a less threatening, more pathetic light. Such attempts at rhetorical branding appeared quite self-consciously in the blog, as in Navalny's invocation of the phrase "Bloody Regime" (*Krovavyi Rezhim*) in reference to Putin's rule—used in various permutations thirty-seven times over the period examined, all appearing in upper case letters and a number even featuring the trademark symbol ("Bloody Regime™" [2 February 2008]).[8]

The notion of criminality was most frequently reinforced through the association of vlast' with various permutations of the notion of *zhulik* (crook), which appeared a total of 542 times (including 31 mentions of *kremlezhulik* [Kremlcrook] and *kremlevskii zhulik* [Kremlin crook] alone), though, in this case, not exclusively in reference to Putin and his associates. In one dazzling display of morphological creativity—devoted to a profile of Putin-era crookedness—Navalny generated four different forms of the notion in a single sentence: "The Putin-style crooks [*zhul'e*] are more cynical crooks [*zhul'e*], but still operating in secret.

---

8. See also "Кровавая Гебня (тм)" ("Bloody [K]GB-ists™") (14 March 2007); "русский фашизм (тм)" ("Russian fascism™") (31 October 2006); "Полицейское Государство (тм)" ("Police State™") (24 April 2006). See Borenstein (2022) for an excellent discussion of the power of internet memes in contemporary Russia culture—among other reasons, for the alternative irony-laden critique of power they often bring to bear.

[Crooks] fully cognizant of their own crook-like nature [*zhulikovatost'*] and therefore hiding from us in the Swiss town of Zug. It's not much better, but better than the messianic type of crook, who operates openly and claims the moral right to engage in crookedness [*zhul'nichat'*]" (12 May 2008).[9]

Most infamously and consequentially, however, was Navalny's deployment of the "crookedness" attribution in the phrase "Party of Crooks and Thieves" (*Partiia zhulikov i vorov*) to the United Russia Party in the months leading up to the most contested election season of 2011 and 2012. While United Russia went on to win a majority of seats in parliament (with substantial help from election fraud), the party's national reputation dropped precipitously over the time span, just as Navalny's meme went viral well beyond the bounds of the online political opposition.[10]

Networking the Public Sphere

A commitment to the networked foundation of social media stands out as a third noteworthy feature of Navalny's early use of LiveJournal. It appeared in his heavy use of hyperlinks to his own past comments, to those of fellow LJ users, and to outside sources on topics of relevance.

It appeared in his own level of engagement in the comments section of his posts, which averaged a mere 11 comments per post during the first year of the blog but ballooned to 839 by 2011 (without the number of posts notably changing) (table 4.1). Communication in the comments resembled the discourse of

TABLE 4.1.   Level of engagement in the comments section of navalny.livejournal.com from 2006 to 2011

YEAR	NO. OF POSTS	AVERAGE COMMENTS PER POST
2006	290	11
2007	418	19
2008	586	23
2009	268	64
2010	479	456
2011	454	839
Total	**2,501**	**255**

Note: Navalny's first post appeared on 19 April 2006.

---

9. Elsewhere in Navalny's posts from this period we find *zhul'nichan'e* (one mention), *zhul'nicheskii* (eight mentions), and *zhul'nichestvo* (nine mentions).

10. For a more detailed account of this rhetorical branding, see Gorham (2014, 177–82).

the tight-knit community or *tusovka* of the early LiveJournal, offering Navalny a mix of encouragement, jocular jabs, and concrete advice (e.g., "I can help find people interested in American oil companies.")—and, more often than not, with Navalny himself answering back:

Playlife
tigra_playlife
September 11 2008, 15:17:36 UTC

главное, фотокарточка на позитиве, моментально понятно, на чьей стороне автор)))

REPLY LIKE

Re: Playlife
navalny
September 12 2008, 07:01:11 UTC

это существенная часть моей кампании: даже те, кто меня не любит всё равно на моей стороне, потому что быть на стороне этих упырей невозможно

> tigra_playlife: the important thing is that the photo is positive. it's immediate clear whose side the author is on)))

> navalny: this is an essential part of my campaign: even those who don't like me are nevertheless on my side, since it's impossible to be on the side of those vampires

уважуха
youngmeteor
September 11 2008, 15:17:07 UTC

Кстати, я могу помочь найти людей которые инвестируют в американские нефтяные компании - они могут поделиться комментариями относительно уровня раскрытия информации и защиты миноритариев... может кому будет интересно с научно-популярной точки зрения

REPLY LIKE

Re: уважуха
navalny
September 12 2008, 07:00:13 UTC   COLLAPSE

ну да, было бы отлично
REPLY LIKE

> youngmeteor: By the way, I can find people who are interested in American oil companies—they can share opinions relating to the level of disclosure and protection of minority shareholders . . . maybe it'll be interesting from a popular scientific point of view.

> navalny: yes, that would be great

And it appeared in his explicit acknowledgment of social media as a networking tool, to the point where he talked about a "network culture" and "networked organization" in his first platform statement for the "national-democratic" NAROD movement he launched in 2006 with a handful of other "new nationalist" fellow travelers (including Zakhar' Prilepin): "Only a **network culture** [*setevaia kul'tura*] that unifies representatives of the vast majority of parties and ideological movements can be successful in the fight against the regime. **As one of the cornerstones and foundations for a future successful opposition, we propose our networked organization** [*setevaia organizatsiia*]—**The National Russian Liberation Movement 'NAROD'**" (6 December 2007).[11]

The vision stayed with Navalny at least until 2011, when, less than a week before Dmitry Medvedev nominated Putin to return to the presidency, Navalny expanded on the idea of a "cloud democracy" that would feature "100 thousand anonymous citizens, debating, discussing, and then voting for one resolution or another, [thereby] generating that very 'popular will.'" Reflecting on a linked article by Leonid Volkov (mentioned in chapter 3) and Fedor Krasheninnikov, he writes,

> They describe a system of "cloud democracy," which Russia needs more than anything else now. In the context of the total illegitimacy of power, it's just what we need: 100 thousand identified citizens [*neanonimnye grazhdane*], arguing, discussing, and then voting for one or another outcome, generating that very "people's will." The real political power of their decision[s] would be higher than the power of the decision of random idiots who accidently and temporarily sit in the Kremlin. Of course, there is the non-trivial task of making sure the circle of participants extends beyond the bounds of the traditional clique [*mezhdusoboichik*] of LJ and political activists of a common orientation. In other words, it must not be a system for putinists/anti-putinists, Westernizers/Slavophiles, etc.
>
> It is a means of discussing and making decisions for everyone. Such a thing is possible. It seemed like a utopia ten years ago, but now the iron steed of the entornet [*zheleznyi kon' entornet*], user verification programs and digitization have come to replace the peasant horse of presidiums and meetings of party activists. (19 September 2011)

This idea of everyday citizens breaking out of their walled gardens to engage in free and open debate—regardless of the whim of whatever "random idiot" ended up in the Kremlin—went well beyond Medvedev's vision of "direct internet democracy," although both recognized the potential of the internet as a democratizing force. But these ideal visions, as it turns out, represented a high-water mark in the discourse on language and politics online in Putin's Russia. Largely

---

11. Emphasis in the original. Navalny lists himself along with Prilepin as "Co-Chairs" of the group in a post from 29 June 2007.

thanks to the political opposition's success at harnessing new media to mobilize hundreds of thousands against corruption and elections violations by those in power—as well as the emergence of newer technologies that lent themselves more to bite-sized, meme-driven statements than to the thoughtful exchange of opinions among thousands of debating citizens—political rhetoric both on and about digital media grew far more contentious, and digital gardens, ever more exposed to authoritarian censorship.

Twitter: From Friends to Followers

We already saw in chapter 3 how the shift in platform from LiveJournal to Twitter affected political communication. While the microblogging platform proved more efficient for the busy bureaucratic blogger, it fell short of LiveJournal in its capacity to promote two-way exchange and debate. As noted earlier, this was not such a bad thing for the elected officials who adopted blogging reluctantly, as it offered a convenient limit to the energy required and offered a modicum of insulation from the unrulier voices of the contrarian Runet. How did the shift in platform focus effect those political voices on the outside of the system looking in?

"What's Happening?"

As was the case with LiveJournal, Navalny was a relatively early adopter of Twitter, launching his account at the end of 2009.[12] His first tweets reflected the curiosity of a digital native, comfortable with the informal, colloquial speech register promoted by the SMS-like interface but not without some confusion over both the function and the terminology. They also displayed a self-deprecatory sense of humor that at once underscored his political ambition:

Alexey Navalny ✓ @navalny · Jan 16, 2010   · · ·
не понимаю я, чё с этим твиттером делать..

💬 10   ⇄ 26   ♡ 86   ⬆

i don't get what to do with this twitter thing.

---

12. The following analysis is based on the 6,270 tweets Navalny posted over the first two years of his presence on the platform, from January 2010 to December 2011, to his account @navalny (https://twitter.com/navalny).

Alexey Navalny ✔ @navalny · Jan 18, 2010

пытаюсь разобраться в твиттере. ужасно заболела голова. надеюсь это пройдет, иначе революция отменяется

💬 1   ⟲ 11   ♡ 20   ⬆

i'm trying to figure out twitter. i have a terrible headache. hope it passes, otherwise we'll have to cancel the revolution

The curiosity extended to his discovery of the hashtag function, leading him to conjecture that, for Russians, the most popular tag would be a four-letter word commonly written across fences (punch line: "Always trending." [13 July 2011]). Still in jocular exploratory mode several posts later, he tests the hashtag's linguistic limits:

Alexey Navalny ✔ @navalny · Jul 13, 2011

Тест #какойинтереснодлиннымможетбытьрусскийхэштэг

💬 6   ⟲ 9   ♡ 2   ⬆

Test #Iwonderhowlongarussianhashtagcanbe

Soon enough, he was joining in viral episodes of hashtag politics himself—including the very same Putin-celebrating, couplet-composing competition joined by Kholmogorov in chapter 2:

Alexey Navalny ✔ @navalny · Oct 7, 2011

Проснулся, а весь твиттер завален #спасибопутинузаэто чё происходит-то?

💬 48   ⟲ 17   ♡   ⬆

Alexey Navalny ✔ @navalny · Oct 7, 2011

Ща я тоже что-нибудь сочиню

💬 25   ⟲ 3   ♡   ⬆

Alexey Navalny ✔ @navalny · Oct 7, 2011

Ничего другого не придумывается: Рамзан купил кабриолетто, #спасибопутинузаэто

💬 36   ⟲ 89   ♡ 7   ⬆

I woke up and all Twitter was inundated with #thankstoputinforthat. What's going on?

Hang on, I'll compose something myself

Can't think of anything better: Ramzan bought a Cabriolet, #thanksto putinforthat

[Ramzan kupil kabrioletto, #spasibo Putinu za eto][13]

As seen in the informal and impromptu nature of these last examples (*che, shcha*), Twitter promoted more oral, colloquial, and spontaneous communication and rewarded the quick-witted wordsmith. The mobility of the platform, easily accessible from smartphones, made it easier for Navalny to share snapshots from his home, injecting a level of affability and intimacy that helped shape a more three-dimensional profile of the emerging public figure. This included mundane portraits of him as a family man: watching TV with his wife ("My wife is watching *shkola*, and I'm watching with her. cool show [*krutoi serial*]" [13 May 2010]); eating her food, with too much ketchup, to her dismay ("My wife made a breakfast of pasta with calamari and some sort of fennel. I covered it all with ketchup. So she said I was a sucker [*loshar*]" [14 May 2010]); taking the family fishing on his birthday ("We decided to go to a vacation house as a whole family for my birthday. I'm teaching the blonds [*blondinchegi*][14] how to fish" [4 June 2011]); and playing "train robbers" with his son before bed, in lieu of boring state politics (Okay, I'm sick of this ER [the acronym for United Russia], I'm going to play train robbers with Zakhar. He refuses to go to bed without it" [27 November 2011]). At times, he engages followers more actively in his family life, such as a July 2011 series of tweets in which he solicits recommendations for the best rooftop dining in Moscow:

> experts of Moscow institutions, I need help [*ai nid khelp*]. My wife asked me to find a "nice restaurant with a good view," while I'm online. Are there any in Msk? (10 July 2011)

His personal posts capture moments of everyday joy (here, with the weather):

> How nice it is outside. Makes you wanna ditch the car and walk to work [*Priam khot' brosai mashinu i peshkom s raboty idi*]. I adore this kind of weather (1 June 2011)

---

13. "Ramzan" here refers to the leader of the Chechen Republic (featured in chapter 7), who was notorious for an opulent lifestyle presumed to have come largely from the region's generous federal budget.

14. The word Navalny uses here, *blondinchegi*, was a popular neologism originating in the Scumbag language discussed in chapter 2.

Frustration (here, with the traffic):

> I'm tired of the office and really want to go home. But Yandex-traffic says that, instead of home, I'll wind up in HELL. (21 December 2010)

And his infatuation with stars and trends in popular culture:

> lady gaga has twitter it seems, i want to follow, anyone know what she goes by here? Thanks (27 April 2010)

> How about that. She has more followers than Obama. But then she sings better, it's true (27 April 2010)

Sometimes, they illuminate weaknesses that make him seem more relatable and human, such as his succumbing to watching vacuous reality TV after a failed attempt at reading James Joyce:

> ok, since *Ulysses* doesn't want me to read it, I'll watch *Home-2*[15] (12 November 2011)

Since in Twitter the language of the sound bite replaces the expository prose afforded by traditional blogging, it places greater emphasis on word choice, intonation, and register to engage followers. When humor is involved, as is often the case on Navalny's feed, timing is also key. In the following observation that has Navalny critiquing new technology for not appreciating the Russian common man's affinity for chewing sunflower seeds, he takes care to split the post into a setup–punch line form, akin to a traditional Russian *anekdot*:

Alexey Navalny ✔ @navalny · Apr 27, 2010   · · ·
Пишу 'мужики с семками', а чекспеллер исправляет на 'мужики с самками'. Не понимает чекспеллер России..

♡   ↻ 2   ♡ 1   ↥

I type "guys with seeds" and spell checker changes it to "guys with females." Spell checker clearly does not understand Russia.

Alexey Navalny ✔ @navalny · Jun 9, 2011   · · ·
Тапочки в поезде всегда ставят меня в тупик. Где правый, где левый?
http://lockerz.com/s/109007531

♡ 4   ↻ 7   ♡   ↥

---

15. Loosely modeled on *Big Brother*, *Dom-2* was one of the first and longest-running reality TV shows to air in Russia, launched in 2004.

The slippers they give you on trains always confuse me. Where's the right and where's the left? (link to photo omitted)

In a series of tweets surrounding his ten thousandth post, Navalny uses both timing (this time, across consecutive tweets) and a contrast between high and low speech registers for comedic effect (here, again, shared in a stream-of-consciousness style, and at the expense of the country's ruling tandem):

Alexey Navalny ● @navalny · Sep 28, 2011
Блин, зачем я увидел, что это 9999-й твит? Теперь придется придумывать специальный торжественный твит номер 10 000

💬 23   ↻ 4   ♡ 2   ↥

Alexey Navalny ● @navalny · Sep 28, 2011
Это юбилейный и торжественный 10 000-й твит. Он направлен на установление демократии и верховенства закона в России.

💬 16   ↻ 52   ♡ 4   ↥

Alexey Navalny ● @navalny · Sep 28, 2011
Это твит 10 001 : Путин-шмутин

💬 7   ↻ 17   ♡ 2   ↥

Alexey Navalny ● @navalny · Sep 28, 2011
Это твит 10 002: Медведев-шмедведев

💬 13   ↻ 11   ♡ 2   ↥

Rats, why did I notice that this was my 9999th tweet? Now I have to think up a special ceremonial tweet number 10,000

This is my solemn, anniversary 10,000th tweet. It is dedicated to the establishment of democracy and supremacy of the law in Russia.

This is tweet 10,001: Putin-shmootin

This is tweet 10,002: Medvedev-shmedvedev

In some cases, he uses humor to soften the edge on his political views. Soon after posting a promotional link to an interview with national radio on his controversial anti-immigration slogan, "Stop Feeding the Caucasus!," Navalny follows up with a post indicating the views have concrete negative consequences at home as well:

> [I had] an interesting conversation on Ekho about "Stop feeding the Caucasus." Thanks to @Varfolomeev and @Dobrokhotov there's a video—the text is coming soon. (link to video omitted) (22 October 2011)[16]

> I got home, hungry, only [to hear from the wife]: Stop feeding you [*Khvatit tebia kormit'*]. (22 October 2011)

Stand-Up Microblogging as Political Action

Turning to his more explicitly political tweeting, we see many of the same formal features at play: creativity, brevity, spatiotemporal immediacy, and a sense of humor often laden with irony, at times at his own expense. Just as he did in his personal life, Navalny took advantage of Twitter's mobility by using it for on-the-spot reporting from various battlegrounds against corporate and state corruption. We are with him, for instance, as he does battle with state-run companies in court and at shareholder meetings—here, mocking the alien discourse of corporate governance and celebrating his team's minor victories:

Alexey Navalny ✔ @navalny · Sep 11, 2011   ···
Корпорэйт говернанс бубубу, литигейшн бубубу, стейкхолдерз райтс бубубу.

💬 11   🔁 7   ♡ 2   ⬆

> Corporate governance, bla, bla, bla, litigation, bla, bla, bla, stakeholders' rights, bla, bla, bla.

> Ololo! We won against Transneft' in the "ninth." The court dismissed their appeal. (21 April 2011)

We follow his entertaining live tweeting of United Russia's party congress (part of a twelve-tweet string):

---

16. Navalny is referring to the influential independent radio station Ekho Moskvy (Echo of Moscow), its deputy editor Vladimir Varfolomeev, and the journalist and oppositional activist Roman Dobrokhotov. "*Khvatit kormit' Kavkaz!*" was the organizing theme of a nationalist demonstration that Navalny attended and spoke at on 22 October 2011. His appearance at the rally and endorsement of the slogan would soon become a political liability, cited both by members of the democratic opposition and by supporters of the Putin regime as cause to question his viability and legitimacy as a political candidate. For background, see Malover'ian (2011) and Volkova (2021).

Damn, I've missed the UR congress! Has it finished? (27 November 2011)

Ooooo. It's still on. The magical Gryzlov is sharpening his moustache [*Volshebnyi Gryzlov toropshchit usiki*]. (27 November 2011)

I hope many people watch this broadcast. I can't think of better agitation against the PCT. All in all, it's HELL (27 November 2011)[17]

And later we follow him as he organizes and participates in postelection demonstrations that lead to his arrest and arraignment (at which point wife Yulia takes over the tweeting):

I'm sitting with the boys [*patsany*] in the paddy wagon. They all say hi. (link to photo omitted) (5 December 2011)

Here's a group picture from the "north izmailovo" police department (5 December 2011)

Hi! I'm Yulia, Aleksei's wife. If any news about his arrest and whereabouts appears, I will inform you. (6 December 2011)

Navalny's Twitter feed displays the thought process of a conscious verbal craftsman, regularly drawing attention to the curious turn of phrase or the memetic potential of the bon mot. In reaction to coverage of the annual summer retreat of pro-Putin youth groups in Seliger, for example, he questions the appropriateness of various monikers for the group.

Alexey Navalny ✔ @navalny · Jul 3, 2011   · · ·
Интересно, а что такое 'инновационная молодежь'?

    ♡ 49   ⟲ 7   ♡ 2   ↥

Alexey Navalny ✔ @navalny · Jul 3, 2011   · · ·
Replying to @Memfis1962
@Memfis1962 мммммм.. Я считал, что этих надо называть 'начинающие жулики' :)

    ♡ 2   ⟲   ♡   ↥

I wonder what 'innovative youth' are? (3 July 2011)

hmmmm. I was thinking that you should call them 'novice crooks':) (3 July 2011)

---

17. "PCT" – "Party of Crooks and Thieves." With this spelling of "hell," Navalny is invoking another common meme of scumbag language.

Elsewhere, it's clear he's thinking in terms of viral memes, when suggesting members of the opposition embrace a phrase originally used as criticism of them:

Alexey Navalny ✔ @navalny · Sep 22, 2010
Мне кажется это может стать отличными мемом. 'поступить невежливо и нетактично'

💬   🔁 1   ♡ 2   ⬆️

Alexey Navalny ✔ @navalny · Sep 22, 2010
А давайте поступим с ним невежливо и нетактично

💬   🔁   ♡   ⬆️

It seems to me this could become a great meme. "act rudely and tactlessly"

Let's act rudely and tactlessly with them

To the point where he openly advocates for the spread of what he deems worthy political neologisms, here, the verb *s'edinorosit'* ("embezzle like a United Russia member"):

Alexey Navalny ✔ @navalny · May 16, 2011   •••
Гениально RT @partofegor: @navalny тут поступило предложение продвинуть выражение «съединоросить», как замена устаревшего «скомуниздить»

Genius proposal to spread the expression "*s'edinorosit'*" as a replacement of the outdated "kommunizdit'" ["embezzle like a Communist Party member"]

Though humor and language play seem to have come naturally to Navalny, he clearly recognized them as potent political strategies for online communication—particularly when it comes to fighting a regime that relies largely on threats and fear to tame its public. As he put it in one 2010 interview, "I try to demonstrate that fighting the regime is fun" (Asmolov 2010a). Navalny's biting humor can be seen in the multiple posts devoted to the ruling elite, Putin and Medvedev in particular. While the leaders of vlast' were regular targets in his LiveJournal blog, the more sound bite level communication of Twitter reoriented his rhetorical focus on more easily consumable portraits of power, be it in the caustic setup-punchline form seen above:

> So how is Medvedev going to prove he's cooler [*krucho*] than Putin? (24 December 2010)

> It'd be really cool if Medvedev were to come out before the people in an Elvis wig and costume. Putin would turn green with envy. Then it would be clear who The King was (24 December 2010)

Alexey Navalny ✔ @navalny · Sep 24, 2011
Путин - президент. Медведев - премьер. Ура, товарищи

💬 72   ↻ 225   ♡ 8   ↑

Alexey Navalny ✔ @navalny · Sep 24, 2011
На смену Айподу приходит Андроид

💬 24   ↻ 106   ♡ 5   ↑

Putin is president. Medvedev is Premier. Hooray, comrades

The iPod has been replaced by the Android[18]

Or in the form of a more traditional Russian anecdote:

Alexey Navalny ✔ @navalny · Jul 4, 2011
- Самый популярный торт в Москве сейчас "Медведев".
- Да? А Что это за торт?
- Как "Наполеон", но только без яиц.

💬 42   ↻ 442   ♡ 80   ↑

- The most popular cake in Moscow is now the "Medvedev."

- Oh? What kind of cake is it?

- Like a "Napoleon," only without eggs.[19]

---

18. In this short punch line, Navalny invokes Medvedev's well-known infatuation with new, Western technology (Apple products) and Kononenko's memorable meme for Putin-affiliated bureaucrats ("androids") from Vladimir Vladimirovich™.

19. "Eggs" (*iaitsa*) is the colloquial Russian term for "testicles."

Metaphors linked to crime and corruption, familiar from the previous discussion of his framing of power on LiveJournal, made frequent appearances in Navalny's Twitter feed, as well. After the "party of crooks and thieves" was first coined in the winter of 2011, morphological variants of *zhulik* featured in seventy-six of Navalny's tweets and *vor* in fifty-two. The fact that United Russia representatives took Navalny to court over the slanderous phrase did not help their cause:

> United Russia is taking me to court: They in all seriousness are assuring that they are not crooks and thieves. That's humor for you. (link to photo omitted) (15 February 2011)

In fact, shortly thereafter, Navalny launched an online contest for best United Russia recruiting jingle to incorporate the meme and then reposted some of his favorite entries:

Alexey Navalny ✔ @navalny · Feb 22, 2011   · · ·
#er гениально! RT @merzlyavchik: @navalny Пристрой родню в Совет в директоров! Вступай в Партию Жуликов и Воров!

♡   ⬡ 12   ♡ 1   ⬆

Alexey Navalny ✔ @navalny · Feb 22, 2011   · · ·
#er RT @SergioSazonov: @navalny Хочешь яхту в сто метро'в - Welcome в партию жуликов и воров!

♡   ⬡ 3   ♡ 1   ⬆

> brilliant! [retweeted tweet]: Make your offspring corporate trustees! Join the Party of Crooks and Thieves! (22 February 2011)

> Want a yacht to sail the seas—Welcome to the party of crooks and thieves! (22 February 2011)

From Community to Movement

As for its potential as a networked public sphere, Twitter, by way of comparison to LiveJournal, shifted the communicative model from a distributed to a decentralized network. We see vestiges of the tight-knit community atmosphere of LiveJournal at least early on in Twitter, as Navalny continues to "follow" and spar with the likes of not only well-known opposition members such as Oleg

Kashin, Aleksandr Pliushchev, and Lev Gudkov, but also prominent web-savvy Putin apologists such as Kononenko, Rykov, Minaev, and Ilya Varlaamov, and even members of the presidential administration, such as Arkadii Dvorkovich.

As committed to debating political foes as Navalny is, however, Twitter turned out to be an imperfect medium for such small *d* democratic exchange. Even when not reduced to one-liner jabs, efforts at sustained dialogue tended to get lost in the chronological clutter of the Twitter feed. One day in late August 2010, for example, Navalny entered an intriguing Twitter "conversation" with the television personality and Putin apologist Vladimir Solov'ev about the nature of power in Russia and the prospects of the opposition movement. When spliced together into consecutive lines, the exchange makes some sense, but it loses nearly all discursive coherence otherwise, given that the thirty-nine-tweet exchange transpires across eight hours and is embedded on each tweeter's account in a swamp of subsequent posts that have nothing to do with the "conversation" at hand.

The different communication model was reflected in the very nomenclature used by the platforms themselves: what in LiveJournal were "friends" became "followers" in Twitter. Navalny stumbled over the difference at first, when noting the number of followers he had attracted shortly after joining Twitter:

Alexey Navalny ✔ @navalny · Jan 18, 2010   · · ·
ОО! Сколько народу меня зафрендило, то есть это.. зафоловило. Привет, чуваки

   ♡   ⟲ 4   ♡ 4   ↑

Ooo! So many people have friended me—that is, . . . followed. Hey dudes

Over time, though, he grew accustomed to the relationship and even became somewhat fixated on the growth of his "following":

> oh! by the way, I have become a 5000-follower [account] on twitter. Hey dudes! (19 October 2010)

> Oh! I got my 30 thousandth follower yesterday. Anyone know where I can get 30 thousand rifles? There's a certain fun thing I want to try out (23 March 2011)

Rather than the semblance of a smaller and more intimate community, Twitter afforded Navalny the means of networking a political movement, with all the transactional and mobilizational communication that entailed. In fact, quantitatively, this may be what Navalny did most on Twitter—seek help, share information, or link to items posted by third parties. It became a critical means of organizing collective action, be it online:

> let's toss Medvedev tweets about Rosoboronpostavka.[20] I'll write something now, and you retweet, please (1 February 2011)

Or offline:

> reminder that at 1900 there will be a demonstration at Chistye Prudy.[21] Come. And you should also have time to send 5 sms's to your friends and call on them to join you (5 December 2011)
>
> 24 December. Sakharov Prospect (22 December 2011)[22]

Critical to the growth of a political movement, of course, is giving it a face, associating it with appealing protagonists. Beyond the compelling glimpses into his private life discussed earlier, Navalny devoted considerable attention to more overt forms of self-promotion, such as providing updates about his various anti-corruption cases and activity in the political sphere and reposting links to press coverage of him and his activities.

> The death of Magnitsky—Navalny talked to the American congress about corruption in Russia (link omitted) (10 November 2010)
>
> Alexei Navalny: when Putin goes—Radio Liberty (link omitted) (8 April 2011)

Clearly aware of the conventional wisdom that says that "all publicity is good publicity," Navalny links to negative coverage as well, though usually with some sort of ironic framing:

> One more confirmation of the fact that I am a Kremlin project.[23] The interview came out in AiF (link omitted) (11 May 2011)
>
> Navalny underwent training in the USA for leaders of developing countries, including a course on "how to organization a revolution and seize power" (30 December 2011)

---

20. Rosoboronpostavka is the federal agency responsible for military procurement.

21. A historical neighborhood in the center of Moscow.

22. As Navalny noted in his memoirs, "No one in the Kremlin realized that the internet mirrored real life: you could post a message asking for leaflets to be distributed, and people would go to an actual street and actually hand them out. Rather than a backwater, it was infrastructure" (Navalny 2024, 193).

23. Particularly after Navalny's rise in prominence as a political public figure in 2011–12, rumors that he was actually receiving his material from sources inside the Kremlin became common currency among his critics.

What we see over his first few years on Twitter, then, is the emergence of a mechanism for shaping a compelling online profile; generating critical, meme-friendly portraits of power; and building a networked public sphere of opposition-minded citizens that, while limited in its ability to promote small *d* democratic discourse, enabled him to expand a movement embracing those principles, even to the point of effecting change in the offline political world. The movement and its face would acquire even greater national notoriety as "blogger" Navalny morphed into "broadcaster" Navalny, after his wholesale embrace of YouTube.

YouTube as Oppositional Broadcasting

Creature of social media that Navalny was, his interaction with YouTube began early and evolved substantially over time. One has to go back to some of his earliest LiveJournal posts to find his very first experimentations with the medium, relatively short and primitive clips that assumed the form of political ads or public service announcements, more than anything else. In his September 2007 LiveJournal announcement of his "arrival to YouTube," Navalny clearly saw the platform as an alternative to the broadcast television from which he and other members of the so-called nonsystemic opposition had been blacklisted.

The clip itself, a promotional video for the legalization of handguns produced by his NAROD group, offers a curious testimony of both early Navalny and early YouTube ("Agitatsionnyi" 2007) (fig. 4.3). Replete with undulating green screen and video graphics on par with twentieth-century low-budget horror films, it shows its

А мы пошли на YouTube

Видеороликов, которые мы сделали специально для Ютюба, ещё нет, но "Акция" про них уже написала.
"В российской действительности добавляется полная невозможность пробиться на ТВ,– утверждает Алексей Навальный – Она не пускают нас в телек – наплевать на них. Аудитория Рунета – десятки миллионов человек. Если ролик сделан интересно и затрагивает актуальную тему, то его посмотрят десятки и, может быть, сотни тысяч человек"

Первый ролик - движение НАРОД за легализацию короткоствольного огнестрельного оружия - скоро выложу.

FIGURE 4.3.   Screenshot of one of Navalny's first YouTube videos (posted to his LiveJournal account), featuring political ad promoting the right to carry a handgun. The caption reads, in part, "They don't let us near the telly—to hell with them. The Runet audience has tens of millions of people. If a video is interesting and touches on an important topic, then tens, maybe even millions, of people will watch it" (10 September 2007).

technological age. But the focus and style are textbook Navalny. Politically, the younger Navalny proudly flaunts his nationalist and populist leanings, labeling himself as a "certified nationalist" in the title frame. Rhetorically, he opts not for fire and brimstone but deadpan humor, as he uses a pistol to fight off Chechen rebels transformed into a giant, menacing cockroach.[24]

Campaign Platform

The platform became a frequent tool for Navalny's political work starting with his Moscow mayoral campaign in the summer of 2013. The first thirty-five videos uploaded to what would become his main account (Алексей Навалный [@NavalnyRu]) mainly featured short clips linked to the campaign—content familiar to Western-style elections but relatively new to the Russian context.[25] They included DIY instructions on how to assemble a pop-up campaign booth designed for mobile agitation across the city's public spaces (the infamous "Navalny cube" ["Kub" 2013]); promotional ads imploring viewers to "Change Russia, by beginning with Moscow!" ("Izmeni Rossiiu" 2013); short endorsements by well-known Muscovites ("Viktor Shenderovich" 2013); excerpts from stump speeches by Navalny himself ("Vstrecha" 2013); and montage testimonies by everyday locals on-site at Navalny events, praising the candidate's "fantastic speech," his ability to "answer hard questions," and his willingness to "meet directly with the people" ("Moskvichi" 2013).

The broadcasting function of YouTube stood out particularly in four episodes of what his campaign called "Navalny circles" (*Krugi Naval'nogo*), meetings between the candidate and groups of citizens, each dedicated to a single issue: migration and nationality, education, the legal system, and health care ("Krugi" 2013). Everything from the set design and professional lighting to the dynamic camera work and well-groomed participants gave them the feel of a "made-for-television" production (fig. 4.4). As if to drive home that message, Navalny's team included wide-angle views of the set that showed the camera and its operator at work. As importantly, the "circle" videos projected the image of an articulate, affable, and engaged candidate and provided voters with a more nuanced view of his politics—particularly his controversial anti-immigration positions. Rather

---

24. Though no longer available in the blog post, the political ad may be viewed on YouTube ("Agitatsionnyi" 2007). For a more explicit video statement promoting his "certified" brand of nationalism, see "Stan' natsionalistom!" 2007. Navalny writes about his early allegiances to Russian nationalist movements in his memoirs (Navalny 2024, 184–88).

25. This second account (https://www.youtube.com/@NavalnyRu) featured Navalny's name in Cyrillic letters (Алексей Навальный), in contrast to the earliest account (https://www.youtube .com/@navalny), which appeared in English transcription (Aleksey Navalny). Video posts referenced henceforth come from the more prolific, second account.

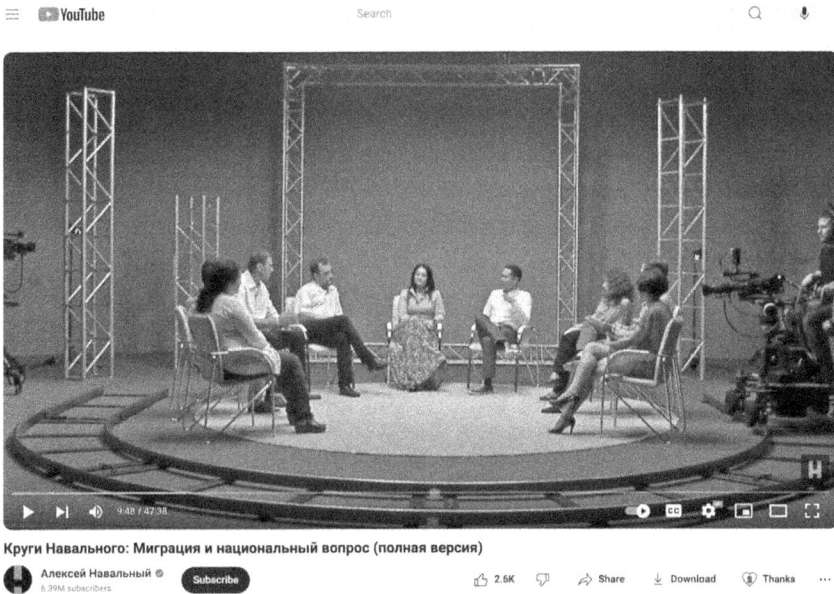

FIGURE 4.4. Screenshot from "Navalny circles: The migration and nationality issue" ("Krugi Naval'nogo" 2013).

than divisive, headline-grabbing slogans like "Stop feeding the Caucasus!," viewers heard Navalny staking out the economic argument for prioritizing local hiring and listening carefully to the alternative views of his interlocutors.

Although he ultimately lost, Navalny managed to win 27 percent of the vote in an election where his opponent, incumbent Mayor Sergei Sobyanin, enjoyed overwhelming advantages in resources and media access ("Itogi" 2013). His surprisingly good showing testified not only to the appeal of his message but to his ability to use social media to foster a viable, alternative public sphere—enough so that Navalny's name was never allowed on a ballot after that.[26]

Anti-Corruption Foundation

True to his earliest LiveJournal roots, Navalny used the platform to stage political debates with prominent political figures, such as Igor' Girkin (a.k.a. Strel'kov) ("Debaty Live" 2017) and Ksenia Sobchak ("Debaty Naval'nogo" 2018). He used it to launch his "smart voting" campaign, an electoral strategy designed to coor-

---

26. Navalny offered an entertaining history of his organization's inability to register as a party in a brief video from August 2018 ("Putin otvetil" 2018).

dinate voters' discontent by encouraging them to vote for whichever candidate in their district had the best chance of defeating the candidate from United Russia—regardless of party ("Kak nam pobedit'" 2018). The Kremlin was concerned enough by the web-based effort that it shut down Navalny's smart-voting informational website months before the 2019 parliamentary elections were scheduled to take place ("Roskomnadzor" 2018).

In terms of both quantity and notoriety, however, Navalny and his team at the Anti-Corruption Foundation (*Fond bor'by s korruptsiei*, or FBK) enlisted YouTube most successfully when it came to broadcasting investigations into the corruption of the Putin regime and those close to it. The genre had become a staple of Navalny's LiveJournal account dating back to the fall of 2013, when the FBK posted the results of extended investigations into the suspiciously extravagant properties and wealth of the head of the Russian Railroad, Vladimir Yakunin (8 October 2013), and the development of contiguous estates outside of Moscow by five government leaders and United Russia party members, including the then deputy director of the presidential administration, Viacheslav Volodin (27 November 2013). Though heavy on text and flow charts, even in the LiveJournal environment the investigations assumed a strongly multimedia format, combining aerial photography, which allowed for full appreciation of the size of the estates, with financial and tax documents available from the public record that clearly showed the degree to which the government officials were living a lifestyle far beyond their declared means. And it still gave ample opportunity for Navalny's mocking, meme-driven humor to show, as in his highlighting of Yakunin's specially constructed fur coat storage chamber (which Navalny nicknamed the *shubokhranilishche* ["fur coat storage chamber"])—a special, climate-controlled room in his estate designed to store his wife's fur coat collection. Once coined, the comical neologism became an irony-infused shorthand for the railway magnate's graft-fed opulence in all subsequent posts about Yakunin and his ilk:

> Vladimir Ivanovich himself strolls in solitude around his *shubokhranil'ishcha,* leafing through the common history textbook and thinking about the Fatherland and patriotic education. (8 October 2013)

> And it's precisely in order to break up this band of thieves [*vor'ie*] with their *shubokhranilischi* that each of us must engage in politics. (8 October 2013)

The switch over to YouTube allowed Navalny to synthesize the expository format of LiveJournal with the slogan-oriented, sound-bite register of Twitter to

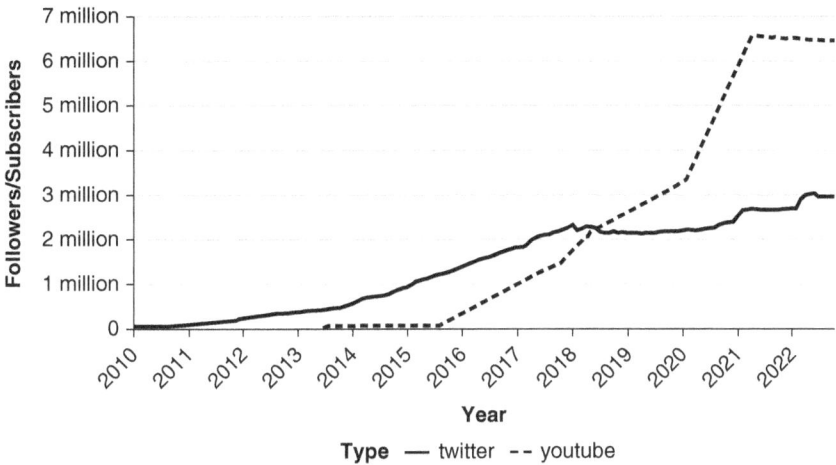

FIGURE 4.5. Trends in Navalny's Twitter followers and YouTube subscribers.

produce a more visual, fluid, television-style journalistic reporting, all on a platform whose increasingly popular, open-access delivery system afforded Navalny and his team a viewing audience and subscribership that dwarfed the "friend" and "follower" groups of LiveJournal and Twitter (fig. 4.5).[27]

The platform became the central distribution point for high-profile exposés starting in 2016, when over a two-year period Navalny and his team launched videos exposing the ill-begotten riches of Space Agency chief Rogozin, Finance Minister Igor' Shuvalov, Putin's daughter Ekaterina Tikhonova, his son-in-law Kirill Shamalov, and numerous members of the business elite, including the oil and gas oligarchs, Igor' Sechin and Aleksei Miller, the media mogul Alisher Usmanov, and Putin's dark-arts fixer Evgeny Prigozhin.[28]

Anatomy of a YouTube Exposé

It was a March 2017 investigation into then Prime Minister Medvedev's secret real estate empire that broke all previous viewership records on the Navalny site,

27. According to Bodrunova et al. (2021), YouTube had become the third most popular website beginning in 2017, with a monthly reach of 26 percent of the Russian population, putting it on par with state-controlled television.

28. In the order listed, "Georgii Alburov" 2016; "Sobaki" 2016; "Kto finansiruet" 2016; "Kak Vladimir Putin" 2016; "Putinskii chinovnik" 2017; "Tim Kuk" 2017; "Oligarkh" 2016; "Povar Putina" 2016. Navalny and the FBK team produced a total of 116 investigations before his death in February 2024.

garnering over 7 million views in the first week and 25 million views in the first three months after posting. The extended fifty-minute length of the video, titled "Don't call him 'Dimon'" (2 March 2017), allowed Navalny and his team at FBK to outline seven different case studies of Medvedev's largess, including a mansion in the tony Moscow suburb of Rublevka, a dacha in the mountains, a family estate and agribusiness in Kursk, vineyards on the Black Sea, a historic palace on the bank of the Neva in Petersburg, and an offshore shell company that funneled funds to finance two megayachts and a vineyard and chateau in Tuscany. It also allowed them time to document how they came to establish Medvedev's ownership of the empire, relying on a familiar array of public documents, private accounting records, and photos and posts from Medvedev's own social media accounts that provided corroborating evidence for the cases. Although all these elements had factored into his LiveJournal-based investigative reporting, YouTube provided a means of synthesizing them into an engaging story, delivered by a more formally dressed Navalny seated in a studio featuring a bookcase backdrop speckled with memes linked to Medvedev's riches (fig. 4.6).

High-quality audio, video, and editing foregrounded Navalny's skills as a public communicator—here, not in the limited context of a 140-character tweet or thirty-second campaign ad but rather in a broadcast hybrid of a prosecutor's court case and an irony-laden remake of *Lifestyles of the Rich and Famous.*

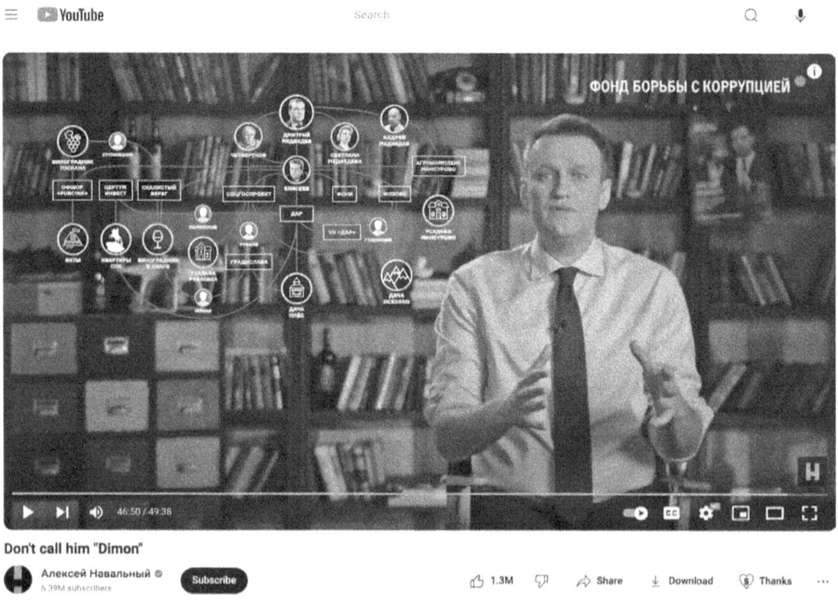

FIGURE 4.6. Screenshot of broadcasting set for Navalny's YouTube expose of Medvedev's wealth ("Don't call him 'Dimon'" 2017).

The deft synthesis of humor and hard-hitting exposé produced a ridicule-laden condemnation of the corruption and cynical hypocrisy of the Putin-era elite in general and Medvedev in particular, who had made the crackdown on state corruption one of the primary issues of his presidential term.

Rhetorically, Navalny deploys a variety of voices to engage his audience and to make the complex case of corruption and graft against Medvedev more viewer-friendly. The documentary itself is broken into "chapters," most bearing titles resembling that of a fable or folktale ("Chapter 2: How oligarch Usmanov gifted Medvedev a Rublevka palace"; "Chapter 3: How Medvedev built himself a secret dacha in the mountains") and even accompanied by faintly folkloric musical themes. In his role as fabulist and storyteller, Navalny repeatedly engages his viewers directly, be it by drawing them in with a provocative hook ("Let me tell you an amusing story of how we discovered Medvedev's empire with the help of some regular online purchases"); anticipating their questions ("I'm sure by now you've warmed up to asking, 'Where does this money come from?' 'Who is sponsoring this feast?' and 'How does this actually work'"); noting their likely reactions ("'What a stylish entrance hall,' I hear you saying. It's not an entrance hall, guys. This stairway is located *inside the apartment!*"); or inviting them on guided tours of the properties in question, largely thanks to aerial drone technology first adopted by Navalny's team at FBK to supplement his LiveJournal exposés ("I suspect you can't wait to see Medvedev's Rublevka estate. I can't refuse you this pleasure: let's have a look!").

Navalny maintains his affable tone as much as he can when delving into the complicated legal and financial machinations undergirding Medvedev's corrupt schemes, making them more accessible through the generous use of flowcharts and graphics (fig. 4.6) and balancing them with lighter humor and appeals to the voyeuristic side of his viewing audience, curious (and envious) about how the megarich live. And when it comes to specific portraits of his main protagonist, Navalny opts for ironic humor and derision, deployed ruthlessly to underscore both the ridiculousness of the man ("He's a smartphone gadget enthusiast, a ridiculous simpleton, who falls asleep during important events"; "Proof that the real owner of this residence is this remarkable skier in a pom-pom hat can be found in his Instagram and his love of romantic winter photos" [fig. 4.7]) and the extravagance of his corrupt ways ("But swanky houses and churches aren't enough for a real nobleman estate"; "Also there is the stucco work with angels, gryphons and Greek caryatids. There's even a special accommodation for the servants with its own entrance").

A favorite rhetorical strategy involves using Medvedev's own words against him to underscore the hypocrisy of his behavior. Given the centrality of fighting corruption to his agenda, Medvedev provided ample material toward this

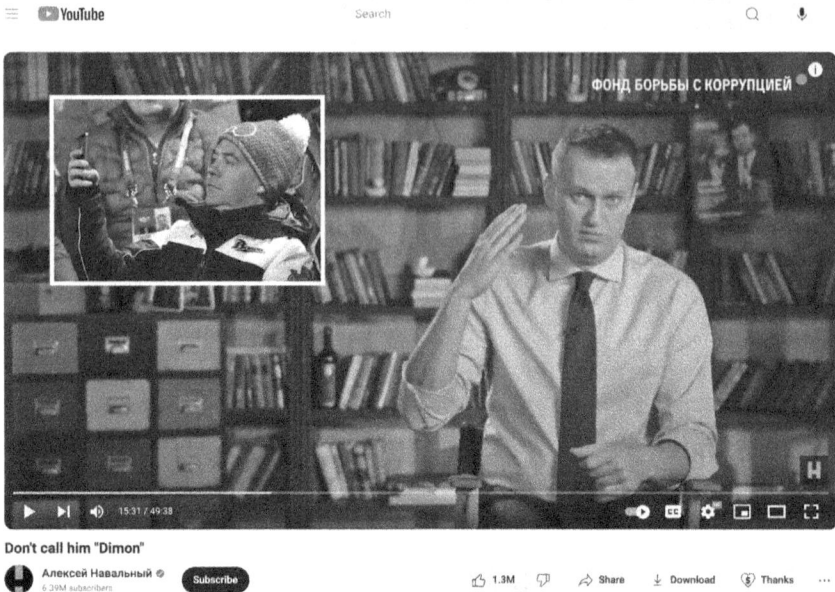

FIGURE 4.7. A key Navalny strategy: trial by public ridicule, with meme-friendly rubber ducks in the background ("Don't call him 'Dimon'" 2017).

end, caught on video and dexterously spliced into Navalny's narrative ("Corruption should not just be illegal; it must become indecent [*neprilichnyi*]"; "We have declared war on corruption. And we know who our enemy is").[29]

Despite the comical dimension, Navalny and his team are careful to drive home the fact that, in a normal, law-based society, Medvedev's dealings would be immediately subject to legal proceedings, in all likelihood ending with a conviction ("And here we come to the description of the real felony"; "The episode of the illegal gift of a country estate valued at five billion rubles is enough to send both Usmanov and Medvedev to the felon's dock"; "In the wonderful Russia of the future [*prekrasnaia Rossiia budushchego*] we could condemn a prime minister for blatant lobbying activities in favor of an industry in which he has a personal financial interest. In the wonderful Russia of the future, with its rule of law, he would be sacked along with his minister of agriculture"). To remind viewers of the stakes involved, Navalny takes care to assign dollar amounts to each of Medvedev's schemes and underscore the extent to which he is only a small—

---

29. Another viral Medvedev meme used repeatedly through the documentary involved his televised response to an elderly woman in Crimea's plea for timely pension payments, which over time became reduced to "There's no money, so hold tight (*Deneg net, a vy derzhites'*)" ("Medvedev—pensioneram" 2016).

albeit prominent—part of a larger epidemic of cynicism and state corruption fostered throughout the Putin era ("These secret palaces are guarded by the state secret service, so basically the secret is kept only from you and me—the people of Russia—at whose expense all of this is being built. But within the corridors of power itself everyone knows everything perfectly well").

The most viral of the memetic components of Medvedev's estates emerged from an earlier video dedicated to his mountain dacha on the bank of the Volga River in the village of Plyos. The residence featured a ski slope, multiple sports arenas, servants' quarters, a historical palace built in 1775, and a man-made pond, including what Navalny labeled a special "duck house" (*dom utochki*) that had been constructed on the pond—an ornate wooden structure perched conveniently for all of the premier's web-footed friends to visit ("Sekretnaia dacha" 2016) (fig. 4.8). If the "Dimon" video served as catalyst for public protests of state corruption in the winter and spring of 2017, the rubber duck served as their mascot—an internet meme potent enough to bridge the gap between the virtual and the real world (fig. 4.9).

The combined impact of the documentary and Navalny's ability to use social networks to mobilize led to nationwide demonstrations, the likes of which had not been seen since the election-related protests of 2011–12, and a precipitous

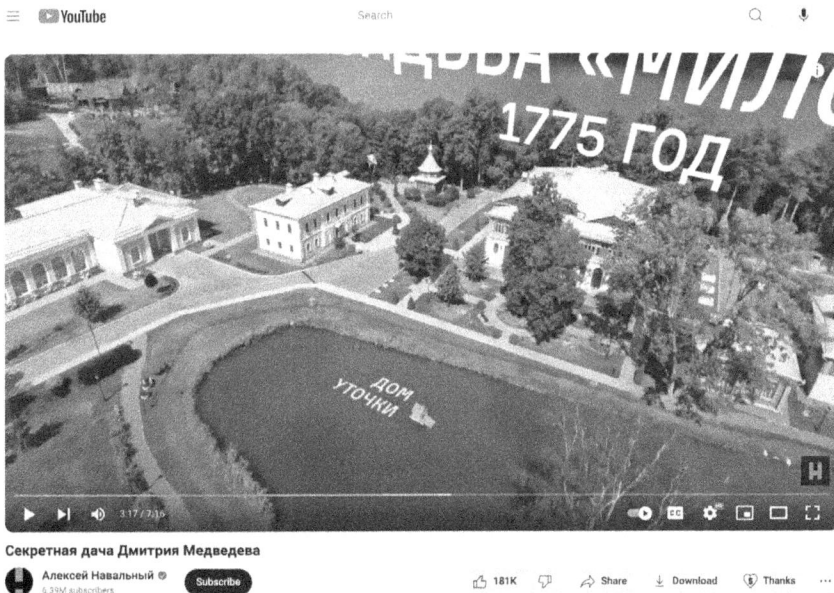

FIGURE 4.8. Aerial shot of infamous "duck house" at Medvedev's country estate on the Volga River ("Sekretnaia dacha" 2016).

FIGURE 4.9. Demonstrators at anticorruption meeting. Photograph by Nikolay Vinokurov / Alamy Stock Photo.

decline in the approval ratings of the prime minister himself.[30] Official reaction to the documentary and ensuing protests was mixed. Some acknowledged the population's intolerance for corruption among officialdom and called for further investigation and accountability (Baimukhametov 2017; Muzipova 2017; Ziuganov 2017). Others dismissed Navalny as a self-interested politician seeking to foment a "colored revolution" in Russia and called for measures to protect the school-aged population from his pernicious influence.[31] A couple of brave souls from the elite, Usmanov and the head of the Russian National Guard, Viktor Zolotov, confronted Navalny on his own digital turf, posting their own videos denigrating him as a shrill, self-serving, PR-seeking "liar" and "scoundrel," who was all talk and no action, a "rotten-to-the-core," "immoral," "oppositional pug who thinks he's an elephant," "spitting, barking, and yapping," trying to "nab

---

30. Protests took place in ninety-seven towns and cities across Russia, with the total estimate of protesters ranging from thirty-two thousand to ninety-eight thousand ("26 marta v tsifrakh i sloganakh" 2017; "Skol'ko liudei" 2017). In analytical terms advocated by Tufekci (2017) when assessing outcomes, Navalny's use of social media demonstrated clear "narrative capacity" to influence power and even noteworthy "disruptive capacity," given the precipitous decline in Medvedev's standing from that time on (see Taranov and Cherkasov 2017). His impact has been less notable on the institutional level.

31. Kholmogorov 2017. For a good discussion of the reasons for Navalny's success on mobilizing younger citizens, see Gorbachev 2017.

someone by the pants" (Usmanov 2017a and 2017b; Zolotov 2018). Beyond dispute, though, was the degree to which Navalny and his FBK colleagues had been able to harness YouTube as an alternative broadcast medium in a system where television remained completely controlled by the state. Combined with the community-building potential of LiveJournal and Twitter's capacity for adding depth to both his profile and the movement, YouTube brought Navalny and his brand of user-friendly populism the star power and viewing audiences that in some cases far surpassed television broadcasting—an audience, moreover, that helped lay the groundwork for a network of volunteers and campaign offices across eighty regions of Russia.[32]

Aside from posting dueling "response" and "rebuttal" videos, as Navalny enthusiastically did with Usmanov and Zolotov, YouTube made it less conducive to the sort of back-and-forth exchange one sees on LiveJournal or even Twitter. As broadcaster, Navalny was more personality and movement leader, limited in his capacity to interact with an online community beyond unidirectional pleas and invocations (on his part) and "likes," comments, and "shares," on the part of his viewers. The medium could still function as a networked public sphere; it simply became more of a decentralized than a distributed network, in which communication stemmed from a single organizational center rather than spread across a diverse group of nodes.[33] Arguably, it was precisely the combination of the broadcasting feel and the cross-platform sharing capacity that made the YouTube-charged version of Navalny most threatening to authorities.[34] It is not by accident, then, that it was around this time that various corners of the Putin state accelerated their efforts to build, legislate, and articulate controls over web-based modes of communication in an effort not only to curb its potential as an oppositional political tool but to harness it for more "productive," state-friendly uses. It is this first impulse to thwart, deflect, and distort online voices of dissent that is the focus of the next two chapters.

---

32. Though for the purposes of this discussion of rhetorical strategies I have focused largely on contrasts across platforms, it should be noted that Navalny used them contemporaneously and often in a complementary fashion.

33. As Burgess and Green (2018, 81) point out, YouTube was not really designed as a community-building tool like other social networking platforms. It is more about the videos than the communities or users. At the same time, it is designed to be used and shared across platforms and "has never functioned as a closed system, from the beginning providing tools to embed content on other websites like blogs." Dolbaum et al. (2018) show that, even with the vast network of volunteers and eighty regional offices Navalny was able to establish in the aftermath of the "Dimon" protests, his operation retained "a high degree of centralization."

34. Strukov (2012) likens this "new style of politics," featuring a degree of authenticity and immediacy afforded by new media platforms, to the opposition-oriented media of perestroika-era broadcasting.

Part 3

RHETORICAL DISRUPTIONS

THE RHETORIC OF TROLLING

Search engines and social networks are becoming the finest and most powerful instruments of manipulation. Due to its inertia the state has been slow in mastering them, but when it does a lot of interesting things will happen.

—Vladislav Surkov (Leskov and Sadchikov 2010)

For all their differences, Medvedev and Navalny shared one thing in common: Each optimistically saw the internet and social media as a vehicle for positive transformation, a communication sphere capable of shaking up corrupt, trenchant bureaucracies and ushering in a system of authority that was somehow more accountable. There's no question that Medvedev's vision of a blogging bureaucracy and e-government was more incremental, building in some assurances of transparency and automation that would make the system more efficient and, therefore, more sustainable. Navalny used new digital technologies to bring about a more radical form of transparency that left little room for sustainability, at least as far as the Putin regime was concerned. In fact, it is fair to wager that Navalny's relative success in realizing his vision, at least rhetorically, served as something of a death knell for any more incremental change built into Medvedev's. The "nano-president," as he was derisively called, faced headwinds even without Navalny's concurrent crusade to oust, not overhaul, Putinism, operating in a political culture that privileged a form of authority based in the power of actions over words, where those in command had little incentive to engage discursively with citizens. But the rise of Navalny—so tethered as it was to new media technologies—served to saturate the digital communicative sphere with such an aura of insurrection and dissent that it became a space fraught with risk for all but the most web-savvy members of the ruling elite. The following two chapters examine some of the main rhetorical strategies authorities and their online emissaries adopted in coming to terms with this highly contested space, attempting at least to disrupt its potency as a tool for revolution and at best to harness it for their own political interests. The first of these features the quintessentially internet-linked rhetoric of trolling.

What *Is* Trolling?

Trolling is at once rhetoric and rhetorical—an act of public speech and a figure of speech characterizing a manner of verbal engagement. At least in its original figurative use, it is a discursive act associated with online communication. Semantically the term is quite malleable; it carries a range of potential connotations ranging, for instance, from mocking, harassment, insult, and boorishly bad behavior to disruption, distraction, and insolent disregard—all the way to "speaking truth to power." The range of meanings with which trolling was used and framed by the mainstream Russian media during the rise of social networks aptly reflected, first, the tensions underlying public communication and the rhetoric of power in the digital age; second, the dysfunctional state of political discourse in Russia at the time; and finally, the degree to which new media technologies were implicated as a main cause for verbal degradation of all kinds.[1]

Depending on whom you ask, the term comes either from Norse mythology or fishing, but in each case the etymology involves random attacks on innocent targets or passersby—be they unsuspecting bridge crossers or fish. Beyond these more literal definitions, the term *trolling* enters the lexicon in the murkier realm of figurative language, where it almost immediately takes on layers of alternative meaning. In its primary figurative usage, it refers to a type of communication on social networks and other online discussion platforms aimed at disrupting the natural flow of communication and provoking a negative, emotional response from targets—often by posting offensive or utterly off-topic comments.

Stricter definitions of trolling in its "purest" sense identify its main motivation as "lulz" (a.k.a. "LOLs")—the web-based equivalent of doing something for a laugh, "just for kicks." Earliest trolls often self-identified as such and did so proudly. But the term quickly evolved into a catchword for all sorts of online bad behavior, to the point where, as the troll scholar Whitney Phillips put it, trolling became a behav-

---

1. It is perhaps appropriate to offer two trolling-related caveats before proceeding. First, as a part of a larger discourse analysis about perceptions of and attitudes toward new media technologies, my focus here is as much on public discussions and statements about trolling and its impact on public language as it is on the language and discourse strategies of trolling itself. Second, despite my focus on "moral panic" and my occasional defense, if not celebration, of trolling, I fully recognize that the internet and social media do abet certain types of communication that promote deviant behavior, some of which can be detrimental to the mental health and well-being of users, young or otherwise.

ioral category that essentially existed "in the eye of the beholder" (Phillips 2013). This was no less true in the Russian context, where, outside the relatively narrow circles of digitally savvy purists, "trolling" in its everyday manifestations came to be associated with a variety of forms of verbal aggression, including *provokatsiia* (provocation), *izdevatel'stvo* (mockery), *travlia* (hounding, persecution), *oskorblenie* (insult), and *khamstvo* (boorishness). It was also commonly assumed that trollish provocations were largely a result of the anonymity that web-based social networking afforded. Because trolls could remain anonymous and dislocated from their targets, they remained "deindividuated," making it easier to violate the norms of social interaction. But this, too, is was overblown assumption according to Phillips (2015, 8), who argued provocatively that, while exaggerated, trolling essentially projected the attitudes and norms of the society in which it took place: "Rather than functioning as a counterpoint to 'correct' online behavior, trolls are in many ways the grimacing poster children for the socially networked world."

Other scholars of trolling have found reasons to come to its defense as well—or at least be more accepting of it. As early as 2000, Jon Katz viewed trolling, flaming, and other forms of uncivil online discourse as the proverbial "canary in the coal mine"—an indication of the level of freedom of the internet (Katz 2000). Gabriella Coleman (2012, 101, 111) wrote that trolls, like hackers, shared "a rich aesthetic tradition of spectacle and transgression" and characterized them as anti-PC warriors in an era when political correctness had gotten out of control. She likened trolls to "tricksters," who, as provocateurs and saboteurs, "help to renew the world, in fact, to renew culture, insofar as their mythological force work to 'disturb the established categories of truth and property and, by so doing, open the road to possible new worlds'" (Coleman 2012, 115). Phillips (2015, 126) quotes the online *Encyclopedia Dramatica*, which identifies Socrates as the first troll, as evidenced by the line attributed to him in Plato's *Apology*: "I am that gadfly which God has attached to the state, and all day long and in all places am always fastening upon you, arousing and persuading and reproaching you."[2]

Particularities of National Trolling

Some affinities to these Western "apologies" for trolling can be found in the Russian cultural context. In response to a question regarding the need to regulate

---

2. As the preceding and subsequent discussions show, trolling as a rhetorical phenomenon both predated digital media and enjoyed something of a "revival" in the offline world as a subsequent result of them.

online trolling, internet ombudsman Dmitrii Marinichev echoed Phillips, noting that "there's little that differentiates trolling from everyday life. If we punish boorishness and such things in real life, then we should somehow put an end to it here [online] as well. But this is a people problem, not an internet problem" (Kazakov 2015). Trolling-like features factor into what Lipovetsky (2011, 21) calls the "trickster" in Soviet and post-Soviet culture, "the living and breathing allegory of language who incessantly fuses destruction and creation . . . , who destabilizes meanings and discovers ambivalence within established beliefs and categories, and who transgresses taboos and playfully reveals their linguistic nature."[3] Anti-PC tendencies have been evident in the cultural policies of Putin at least since his second term as president (as is seen more in chapters 6 and 8). And the rich tradition of the Russian intelligentsia brings up obvious parallels to Socrates's gadfly.

The importance of this last association to Russian trolling and internet culture can be seen in the semantic distinction made in Russian between *tonkii* and *tolstyi* trolling, literally translated as "thin" and "thick" but better understood as "nuanced" versus "crude" trolling. Maksim Kornev (2014) makes the case that, while the "crude" troll "conducts itself openly aggressively and rudely, and plays the role of a barefaced provocateur," its "nuanced" counterpart "is distinguished by a keen wit, resourcefulness, lively mind and often high IQ," and "crafts a complex system, anticipates the reactions of its victims, [and] actively launches information and psychological attacks. The 'nuanced troll' is a master of communication and provocation." He goes on to describe "trolling for the sake of trolling" as "a sign of quality and a confirmation of mastery for professional communicators" and even likens them to the "'sanitary engineers' of the forest" in the "ecosystem of the internet," who "identify vulnerable communities or groups of people, controversial themes [and] often point out substantive problems that evoke bitter arguments or painful reactions" (Kornev 2014).

With references to astuteness, ingenuity, quality, mastery, communicative control, style, masking, and elites, these defenders of "nuanced" ("thin") trolling reflect a perspective on public discourse and dispute akin to the broader logocentric disposition of the Russian intelligentsia and its self-proclaimed prerogative over language.[4] It is not surprising to find, à la Socrates, a moral or ethical

---

3. For a discussion of a contemporary, geopolitical form of Russian tricksterism, or what he calls "state pranking," see Budnitsky (2024).

4. It is noteworthy that the intelligentsia has exercised this same sort of cultural capital over another dubious linguistic domain—the proper use of Russian *mat* (Gorham 2014, 81–83). Zvereva (2020c, 119) focuses more on trolling as a literary genre and suggests that part of the differentiation between "thick" and "thin" trolling came from a desire by more established online users to distinguish their online verbal art from the coarser behavior of digital neophytes.

dimension associated with trolling as well, a degree of power and authority less commonly associated with the commoner's "crude" trolling.[5]

These more elitist readings of the mastery required of the thin troll square with the demographic and cultural evolution of the Runet in its early years, which, for a good decade or so, was primarily the purview of a more educated class of techies and intellectuals that prompted the likes of Litvinovich (2001) to imagine digitally fueled "information wars . . . of smart people." But the fact is, trolling broke into common parlance only with the popularization of social networks over the second half of the first decade of the twenty-first century and thus coincided chronologically with what Runet elites might have called the "vulgarization" of the internet. Popular views of everyday trolling were more of the plebeian, "thick" sort, and it was these that were more likely to contribute to the spread of "moral panics" about online communication that proved symbolically detrimental for web-based political discourse.

Everyday Trolling, Verbal Pollution, and Moral Panic

To trace the range of perceptions of and attitudes toward trolling in the mainstream Russia media, I examined over three thousand mentions of the term across fifteen periodicals from the central print media appearing between 1995 and May 2019.[6] Earlier mentions tended to portray trolls as relatively innocuous in their disruptive activities, likening them to petty hooligans seeking to entertain themselves at the expense of unknowing novices through the provocation of conflict—as in the following, relatively neutral, description from a 2012 article in *Rossiiskaia gazeta*: "The original meaning of the word 'trolling' came from spoon fishing, but, with the formation of internet communities, trolling grew into hooligan entertainment, where people appeared on the hook, instead of fish. The goal of trolling is to incite conflict among internet users by means of posting provocative messages on different sites. . . . People 'swallow the bait,' and the

---

5. The troll, here, becomes akin to the *holy fool*, with all the historical gravity and rhetorical and political power ascribed to that figure in Russian culture. Cf. Epshtein (2012), who notes the "befitting incongruity" of the holy fool's saintliness and his filth, rough speech, obscenities, and disgraceful behavior, given the importance of the "apophatic tradition" to Russian spirituality.

6. In alphabetical order (with number of mentions of "trolls" or "trolling" in parentheses), the main titles include *Ekspert* (27), *Izvestiia* (344), *Kommersant* (92), *Komsomol'skaia Pravda* (177), *Moskovskii komsomolets* (144), *Nezavisimaia gazeta* (144), *Novaia gazeta* (137), *Ogonek* (24), *RBK* (43), *Rossiiskaia gazeta* (501), *Russkii reporter* (47), *Sobesednik* (16), *Sovetskaia Rossiia* (18), *The New Times* (75), *Vecherniaia Moskva* (692).

troll nonchalantly laughs at them. In English, such laughter is indicated by the abbreviation LOL" (Kozlova 2012).

More problematic invocations associated trolling with the various forms of verbal aggression mentioned earlier—mockery, insult, and boorishness:

> The fact of mockery and insults on social networks (trolling as it is called by internet users) may now be confirmed by a notary, which allows for the initiation of a court trial. (Alekseevskikh 2016)

> Elderly people (who prefer LiveJournal or Facebook) are traumatized by internet-boorishness (*internet-khamstvo*), so-called trolling. (Raevskaia 2013)

These more negative descriptions of trolling often involved associations with soiling, pollution, and other kinds of figurative contamination. One advice column recommended legal action when trolls "literally covered a person with dirt online" (Kulikov 2017). A *Literaturnaia gazeta* reporter accused those who criticized his paper's reporting as trolls "specially trained to litter the internet," who "deftly distort discussion space with insults and spittle [*plevki*]" and whose "single emotional tool [was] boorishness" (Makarov 2013).

Not infrequently, however, trolling came to be associated with far graver ills, behavioral malfeasances that tended to transmit a sense of a community or society spiraling out of control. *Rossiiskaia gazeta* sounded alarm bells relatively early in a May 2011 article called "Tender Networks" ("Laskovye seti") that warned in its lede, "Electronic swindlers are stealing money and corrupting children with pornography" (Avdeev 2011). The author directly equated trolling with harassment (*travlia*) but made it clear that this was but the first step in a string of online calamities that culminated in blackmail and information war: "Often a fraudster becomes aware of a teenager's personal data, which then leads to so-called 'trolling,' otherwise known as harassment. On the internet, in forums, in discussions, in wiki-projects, they plant provocative messages for their own personal entertainment and, at the same time, for the creation of conflicts between participants. That's necessary to establish the circle of friends, teachers, and parents of the teenager to later send the provocative photographs that they've received. In short, the criminals can then blackmail the teenagers, demand that they transfer money to an indicated account to bring an end to this information war" (Avdeev 2011).

A major general from the cyber police force, "Directorate K," included trolling in the same semantic string as extremism, cybercrime, prostitution, and blackmail, to demonstrate the threat social networks posed to "the foundations of society" (*ustoi obshchestva*): "Extremist groups organize and agitate on social networks. They collect money for criminal groups and coordinate their actions.

There are those who get to know minors and entice them into prostitution. Some engage in trolling, that is, harassment, posting provocative messages to create conflicts among users, or for blackmail. Many fraudsters also populate social networks" (Falaleev 2011).

Implicit in the reference to "provocative photographs" were broader concerns, when it came to the corruption of Russian youth, with pornography and pedophilia. It seems a large rhetorical leap from trolling to pornography (and then, again, to pedophilia), but the associative links were actually quite common in the public framing of trolling, as in a 2011 report that discussed "the high likelihood of stumbling across material of an erotic and pornographic nature, [and thereby] becoming the victim of pedophiles or trolls (people who anonymously and harshly abuse [others] online)" (Mostovshchikov 2011).

The most extreme invocations went as far as associating trolling with suicide, particularly among vulnerable youth. An article from *Vecherniaia Moskva*, for example, referred to trolls as "provocateurs who intentionally push[ed] desperate youth to take the final fatal step" (Filatova 2013). In a similar vein, Natal'ia Kasperskaia made the associative link between trolling and both suicide and terrorism: "Trolling and psychological terror are also present. It's girls who most often fall prey here. And in a number of cases it has led to suicide" (Shadrina 2014).

The worry that trolling could be the cause of teen suicides received further substantiation in May 2016, when *Novaia gazeta* published a feature titled "Death Groups" ("Gruppy smerti") on the purported social-network-based provocation of teen users to participate in online "games" that challenge them to perform increasingly risky tasks, culminating in suicide (Mursaleva 2016). The front-page story set off widespread fears and a wave of media coverage that lasted through 2017, and, while no teen suicides were confirmed as a direct result of the game, the mere association and blanket coverage heightened the rhetorical impact of the link between trolling and suicide.[7]

The "Death Groups" scare is a particularly apt case of what the sociologist Stanley Cohen has called a "moral panic," an overblown, media-stoked mass anxiety over a perceived threat to the moral fabric of that society.[8] But to a certain extent, the internet and social media have consistently been the objects of moral panics, largely due to their perceived pernicious impact on youth—their most high-volume users (and the political future of Russia). For Cohen (1972/2002, xliv), moral

---

7. Cf. "However, as experts relate, notaries are often consulted not only to document proof of trolling, but also, for example, to establish the harassment [*travlia*] of a child on the internet or the discovery of a 'death group' encouraging teens to suicide" (Kulikov 2018).

8. For a conversation on the origins and real threat of the "death groups," as well as the role of the internet and new media in bringing them about, see Lialenkova (2017).

panics are, at their core, "condensed political struggles to control the means of cultural reproduction," a connection that becomes equally clear in the contemporary Russian context, where such discourse on trolling and other forms of communicative bad behavior online emanates more often than not from the ruling elite with a political or economic interest in reining in the internet's potential to generate "networked public spheres" beyond the control of the state.[9]

Trolling for Vlast'

We've thus far seen how perceptions of trolling on the everyday level evolved well beyond the narrow original meaning of disruption and provocation for the sake of "lulz" to become something far more sinister. As it assumed a place in the vernacular, trolling became a metaphor for a broader sense of society-threatening communicative and moral degradation indelibly linked to the rise of the internet and social media. When we shift our focus to the field of political language, where it just as quickly became common parlance at all ranges of the political spectrum, we find that trolling retains its connection to notions of disruption and provocation and maintains a basically negative connotation. The main difference is that the figurative signification shifts away from issues of social contagion to issues of political authority and legitimacy, and trolling itself becomes an openly recognized tool (however subversive) aimed at delegitimizing power.

Industrialized Trolling at the Internet Research Agency

Deliberate political trolling by pro-Putin groups first drew public attention with the 2012 leak of emails between then Nashi press secretary Kristina Potupchik and head of the Federal Agency for Youth Affairs (Rosmolodezh'), Vasilii Iakemenko. It was clear from these early correspondences that their trolling was aimed to disrupt, but the motivations had nothing to do with "lulz": Instead, they aimed to make the networked public sphere as inhospitable as possible for the political opposition. As Iakemenko put it in a directive quoted by multiple sources at the

---

9. The line between moral panics and well-established threats to the social fabric are sometimes fine but distinguishable nevertheless. Fears arising from the "blue whale" scare were proven unfounded, as later acknowledged by youth organizer and pro-Kremlin web PR specialist Kristina Potupchik (Loshak 2019). And writing off public outcries to "moral panics" does not deny the existence of serious threats to user well-being in web-based communication. Nor are social-media related moral panics unique to Russian culture. For an example of the phenomenon in the American context, see Herrman (2017), and compare this to the more nuanced and substantive treatment of the adverse effect of social media in books like Jonathan Haidt's *The Anxious Generation* (2024) and the discussion surrounding it.

time: "Every member of the opposition must be put under constant pressure, from unrelenting trolling on all social networks to spamming their personal mobiles with requests to call back or deposit money" (Tropkina and Novikova 2011; Ermolin 2011). Or, as one of the bullet points in a Nashi strategy document put it, "In the network of commentators we will increase the number of commenters, hang out to dry [*vyiavliat'*] enemies who conduct targeted work against us and Putin, and troll them, creating the sort of environment in the comment section that will force publications to close their comment services entirely" (Pyrma 2012).

Two years after these leaked aspirations, this trolling-as-rhetorical-contamination strategy assumed industrial dimensions in the form of the Internet Research Agency (Agentstvo internet issledovanii), funded by the Kremlin through Evgeny Prigozhin's shady Concord Catering Company (Soshnikov 2015). Run out of offices in the Petersburg suburb of Ol'gino, what came to be known as the "troll factory" had an operating budget in the spring of 2014 of between 30 and 33 million rubles ($610,000) per month, the lion's share of which ostensibly went toward the employment of upward of four hundred workers to help spread pro-Kremlin opinions online. Day-to-day operations fell to a pair of brothers, Denis and Igor' Osadchii, who also had ties to Gazprom and other Petersburg-based government initiatives ("Vskrytaia novaia 'fabrika trollei'" 2014; Nikulin 2014).[10]

The degree to which those working at the agency were doing so out of political conviction is questionable. The posted job advertisement's promise of flexible hours and contract arrangements (working above or under the table), decent pay, and the opportunity to acquire new skills may have been the real draw: *"Wanted: Internet operators! Work in a chic office in OL'GINO!!!! (metro Staraia derevnia), salary 25,960/month. Description: placement of commentaries on targeted internet sites, writing of thematic posts, blogs, social networks. Screen-based accounting. Work hours determined individually.... Remuneration on a weekly basis, 1180 per shift (from 8:00 to 16:00, 10:30 to 18:30, 14:00 to 22:00). WEEKLY PAYMENTS AND FREE MEALS!!! Employment available officially, or by arrangement (as preferred). Training possible!)"*[11]

One former employee confirmed that, while there were some "fanatics" who really believed in the ideology underlying the information they posted, the majority of youth working there mainly did it for the money and were themselves apo-

---

10. As Zvereva (2020b, 230) points out, the troll factory was but one of a variety of state-sponsored efforts to establish a "grey zone" where "the right to express the state authorities' point of view was delegated to third parties: bloggers (users who regularly publish materials on their pages on internet platforms), trolls (users who aim at communicative provocation in order to infuriate other users, to provoke anger and rage or frustration and anxiety) and hackers (skilled computer experts using their knowledge to break into computer systems and gain unauthorized access to data, from unknown users to well-known characters and celebrities of Runet)."

11. Garmazhapova (2013). Emphasis and italics original.

litical and generally ignorant about politics (Rain Sounds 2015). Given the source of such testimony (an *ex*-employee), one must treat it with some care; in fact, other evidence suggests a certain degree of patriotism motivating the pro-Kremlin trolls. Korotkov (2014), for instance, quotes the LiveJournal post of a proud employee of the Ol'gino Trolls, who writes, "Trolls write poorly, do they? Some yes, but the Ol'gino Trolls don't. They don't just write any old way: they are PATRIOTS of their country and some of them are even proud to be called 'trolls from Ol'gino'. Better to be a Troll (with a capital 'T') and love your country than anonymously curse authorities and hate the country where you were born and live."

Employee motivation aside, the pay structure and work hours reveal a highly regimented, top-down corporate structure. Ex-troll "Marat" characterized the work environment as "repressive," where employees were discouraged from talking to each other, forbidden from going outside during the shifts (which last twelve hours), and were fined for showing up to work minutes late (Rain Sounds 2015). According to another employee, "Attrition is huge. . . . You go into the cafeteria and wonder, 'Who are all these people . . . ? Students, former radio announcers, invalids, members of informal organizations, skinheads, housewives, girls who look like lesbians, even couples'" (Soshnikov 2015).

Essentially, the agency featured a corporate culture akin to a factory or telemarking company, where efficiency, volume, and productivity were at a premium. And this was not all that surprising, given the high-volume nature of its verbal subversion. (According to Garmozhapova [2013], salaries were paid out only to those meeting a one-hundred post-per-day minimum threshold.) The focus on volume, in fact, suggests the activity taking place at the agency was something more nuanced than trolling, which was explicitly discouraged by managers: "It's not worth entering into a polemic, because people on the other end want to gab, where for you it's a workday" (Garmazhapova 2013). Rhetorically, it might be more akin to what's sometimes known as "astroturfing" (artificially covering the information sphere with the desired [mis]information) but which company literature most frequently referred to as *raskrutka* ("promotion"). The emphasis on quantity and scope more closely resembles basic marketing strategies rather than trolling, though strategies still designed to disrupt and delegitimize. As the agency manager Aleksei Soskovets put it, "We operate on the 'Yandex-Market' principle: beneath each item there are commentaries of people who say this is a great telephone, this is a bad telephone" (Garmazhapova 2013).[12]

---

12. At least one eye-witness account—from former Prigozhin employee and black-PR specialist Andrei Mikhailov—suggests that the focus on volume had an adverse impact on efficacy. In a 2018 interview, Mikhailov told *Novaia gazeta* that he had a team of ten "professionals" under his management at the time whose output "overtrumped" (*perekryvali*) that of the novice trolls (Korotkov 2018).

The Operating Manual

Certainly, if one looks at the concept script for video narratives attributed to Igor' Osadchii, first about the United States and then about the Russian occupation of Crimea, one finds justification for others' claims that their language production was largely dependent on cliché, stereotype, and viewer manipulation:

> Scenario 2: America, maximally dirty frames, harsh and somber music, homeless people, homos, fat people, prostitutes, drug addicts, unhappy clerks tormented by debt, the well-fed power elite by contrast, text with statistical data and numbers. Final message Americandream?
>
> Scenario 5: Crimea, unification, patriotic sound, images—people in crimea walking with Russian flags, mass street marches with shouts about the unification with Russsia, images—signing the agreement over the incorporation of crimea, applause, joy happiness of people in crimea, at the apogee of the musical score (to goosebumps). Mr. Putin like a strongman peaceful, worthy, magnificent. looks into the distance. Final slogan.[13]

But if one looks at the outfit for what it was—a cross between a campaign headquarters and internet-sales marketing department—then the clichéd, repetitive nature of the content should not come as a great surprise. In fact, if we are to trust the documents leaked by Soshnikov (2015), factory directors provided employees with a variety of "how to" documents, called "Technical Assignments" (*tekhnicheskie zadachi*, or simply *TZ*), containing the talking points of the day—documents that read more like conceptual overviews for marketing campaigns than ideological treatises (and not unlike those likely generated by Pavlovsky and Litvinovich in the days of the Foundation for Effective Politics).

Perhaps more interesting than the repetitive or clichéd nature of the assignments was the willingness on the part of their authors to embrace a world of multiple realities, even self-contradictory narratives. One ex-troll described how this phenomenon transpired in the aftermath of the assassination of former deputy prime minister and opposition leader Boris Nemtsov, in February 2015. First, they were instructed to "hint that it was the U.S. who murdered him." "Then, the next TZ comes in, and now we are hinting that there is a Ukrainian trail!" (Rara 2015). Or, as the troll Igor' Mangushev explained, "There were a wide range of assignments, beginning with the Navalny campaign, where we wrote both for him and against him. Working for the same client" (Korotkov 2014).

---

13. "Patriotizm" 2014. The remaining examples cited in this section come from this same source. Spelling and punctuation are original, unless otherwise noted.

Also noteworthy is the attention devoted to helping budding trolls master the language of the social media battlefield (blogs, twitter feeds, discussion forums). In addition to thematic instructions, employees received glossaries of words and phrases commonly used in the blogosphere and social networks. The preface to the vocabulary list reads like an instructional guide for nonnative speakers wishing to operate in the local language of some foreign land: "The guarantee for successful conspiracy in an argument with oppositional commentators or bloggers is literate speech, working with the traditional slang of whatever site the employee is working on."

The list of terms seems a bit random; some are current but many others are either marginal or outdated. Among them:

алсо (*also*)	also
бот (*bot*)	bot
белоленточный (*belolentochnyi*)	white ribboner
Баттхерт (*battkhert*)	butt-hurt
ватник (*vatnik*)	wadhead, philistine
GTFO	Get The F*** Out
контент (*kontent*)	content
копипаста (*kopipasta*)	copy-paste
капча (*kapcha*)	capture
КГ/АМ (*KG [kreatiff govno]/AM [afftar mudak]*)	creative [work] is shit/author is an asshole
LOL	
линк (*link*)	link
мем (*mem*)	meme
оффтопик (*offtopik*)	off-topic
пруф (*pruf*)	proof
тролль (*troll'*)	troll
фотожаба (*fotozhaba*)	photoshopped image
чсф (*chsf [chuvstvo sobstvennoi vazhnosti]*)	feeling of self-importance

The definitions themselves vary from neutral interpretations ("The goal of a troll is to produce arguments over topics that knowingly insult his interlocutor") to commentaries bearing more marked interpretations on the nature and behavior of the online opposition:

For a successful ideological victory over **"white-ribboners"** it's worth using the entire arsenal of internet slang, accompanying the text with memes.[14]

WADHEAD [*vatnik*] (pl. wads)—a very popular term of derision in our time used by **oppositionists** to refer to the pro-Russian patriot. . . . As a rule, oppositionally oriented internet users (in the absence of arguments or with the goal of intentional provocation) call a wadhead anyone who disagrees with them. In such a case, it's worth using in reply the less censorial version of the term, "white-ribboner."

Efforts to master the target medium extended beyond basic vocabulary. A document titled "Comments for kingpins" ("Kommentarii patsanov") offered employees over 180 example posts on high-priority topics ranging from "Ukraine" to "the USA." Stylistically and pragmatically the models stand out for their effort to project a personalized view, in the following examples, through the use of deixis:

Bad news **again**. Ukraine is **now** sinking into a pit dug for them by an illegitimate government.

Well **there's** news for you. Ukraine **as usual**. I think that as long Ukraine has **this** ruling elite, nothing is going to change for the better, and **it'll** only be worse. [Emphasis added]

Or through the inclusion of self-referential and other dialogic markers signaling subjectivity of the opinions and thereby imbuing them with a greater sense of accessibility or authenticity:

News. Ukraine. **It's all mixed up in my head**. When will this good-for-nothing war end?!

As someone with relatives in Kiev, **I** often watch the news of Ukraine and **really suffer**

Watching recent events in the world, **I'm somehow calmed** when I look at Putin. Say what you will, our RF president is a real leader.

I'm completely satisfied with Putin's policies. Everything is done for people, and that's really nice. **It makes me feel remembered!** [Emphasis mine]

---

14. "White-ribboners" (*belolentochniki*) refers to members of the political opposition, for whom the white ribbon became a symbol during the election-fraud protests of 2011–12.

The perspective quite often expanded from the first-person singular to plural to project the image of a broader, like-minded community of people who shared the ideas expressed:

> What great news! Putin never forgets **our** domestic politics and that can't help but make you happy!

> With a leader like **our** RF president, **we** have nothing to worry about. He's a real alpha [*Eto nastoiashchii vozhak*] who won't allow his country to fall apart!

This sort of striving for authenticity and engagement extended to instructions regarding the recommended ratio of political to nonpolitical posts in blogs. According to the guidelines for maintaining fake blogs, employees were encouraged not to post too many politically oriented comments at a time:

> 4. For every account, the adding of information no less than about three times a day (photographs, status reports, interesting reports without political overtones) is essential

> 5. For 30% of politicized accounts adding information every day is essential, approximately 10% of it—politicized information.

The desire for authenticity extended likewise to the level of dramaturgy, as in the technique where a trio of trolls would "travel" around regional websites visiting forums and comments sections "staging" a dialectical discussion in which one of them would assume the role of the "enemy," another would play the pro-Kremlin patriot, and a third, after "listening" to what the two had to say, would express his or her newfound conviction as to the sensibility of the Putin way (Rain Sounds 2015).

These stylistic and pragmatic strategies of *raskrutka* (promotion) would be ideal communicative methods if not for the underlying fact that the agency trolls were essentially engaging in the *simulation* of civic discourse and exchange. Whether their motivations were pecuniary or patriotic, they were reaching out not so much, if at all, to persuade or be persuaded but rather to push a particular agenda, spin a proscribed narrative, or sell a product.

In a sense, this practice of civic simulation was right in line with similar strategies on other levels of public politics in Russia. At least from the perspective of Western-style democracy, the Russian court system, the electoral system, the Parliament, the Public Chamber, television talk shows, and the nightly news all appeared to be institutions simulating public communication founded on democratic, civic values. At the same time, the variability of the narratives put forth for public consumption suggests that, at least in connection to matters where the powers that be may have been particularly vulnerable, such as the Nemtsov murder or Ukraine, the goal was not so much to promote a single, coherent image, idea, or ideology but rather to convey a general sense of relativity or conditionality to *all* information transmitted online (cf. Pomerantsev and Weiss 2014). Rather than reflecting some truer reality, the Kremlin trolls sought to make the mirror as crooked and confusing as possible so that "reality" depended largely on the standpoint of the viewer, and nothing could be taken for settled truth.[15]

Provocateur or Politically Unhinged?

Especially after the outing of the Internet Research Agency, state-affiliated trolling of all stripes became an easy target for critics, who used it as a means of questioning the legitimacy and authority of the language of power. Some simply dismissed them with the socially damning epithet *neadekvatnyi* (literally, "inadequate," but in the sense of "inappropriate" or even "maladaptive" or "unhinged"), for example, "One should enter dialogue, of course—although there are trolls, I don't react to them. A lot of trolls from *Molodaia gvardiia*—maladaptive people."[16]

Others, such as opposition politician Gennadii Gudkov, framed it as a sign of the political elite's fear of the opposition and of the free exchange of opinion: "The authorities [vlast'] are afraid of the alternative points of view that are freely expressed on the internet, and are trying to neutralize them using all means necessary" (Akhmirova 2012). His characterization of the "brigades" of trolls as being *paid* "for the crap that they put on the web" further undercut their legitimacy by questioning their sincerity and allegiance to the cause (Akhmirova 2012). The oppositional commentator Yulia Latynina (2019) used the same mercenary motivations of the trolls to cast doubt on their loyalty and their effectiveness in shaping public opinion online: "All those Russian talking points [*metodichki*] about hybrid war are full of fantasies about how the internet can be manipulated and exaggerated impressions about the power of trolls. It's no wonder: after all, the talking points are written by the trolls themselves, who are thinking only about how to squeeze more money out of their masters." Even the Kremlin sympathizer Sergei Markov agreed that troll-based support had minimal impact in promoting pro-state causes, particularly in contrast to true believers with "firm political

---

15. As Kurowska and Reshetnikov (2018, 346) argue, this strategy of what they call "neutrolization" had the added effect of "neutralizing civil society attempts to cast the regime as a societal security threat."

16. Barabanov 2011. *Molodaia gvardia* ("Young Guard"), in this context, refers to the youth branch of the pro-Putin political party, United Russia.

views": "For the development of the country and to ensure a Kiev Maidan doesn't repeat itself, it's important not to convene imitators and public trolls, but to create public coalitions that will attract people with firm political views."[17]

Indicative of the protean rhetorical power of the term, trolling quickly and frequently appeared in a secondary figurative sense to describe communicative acts that had nothing to do with the internet. When we look at trolling ascribed to pro-state elements on this level, we find a new layer of associations relating more to insolence and conceit than fear and weakness. Navalny used trolling as a synonym for "brazen insolence and boorishness" in his comment on the Astrakhan governor's public acknowledgment in 2012 of having used state funds to acquire three German cars totaling 70 million rubles ("Sometimes it seems like they're just trolling us all. How else do you explain the brazen insolence and boorishness" ["Naval'nyi zapodozril" 2012]). A consumer rights advocate characterized the "foreign agent" law passed by the Parliament in 2013 as an act of trolling, remarking, "It's just a blatant challenge to civil society. There's no other way to describe it but trolling civil society on the part of authority [vlast']."[18] *Izvestiia* commentator Vadim Levental' (2013) dismissed as "trolling" new legislation by the Russian parliament that further restricted web-based content in the name of "protecting children" (a law to be examined more closely in the following chapter). And a *New Times* reporter used the trolling metaphor to explain why so many Muscovites voted for Navalny in the 2013: "There's a lot they don't like—an ageing president and his calcified power vertical, a bad healthcare system, 'Orthodox homophobia': the authorities [vlast'] are trolling the population" (Beshlei 2013).

In a 2013 article called "Trolls at Twilight," Aleksandr Morozov elaborated on this "vlast'-trolling-society" motif, claiming that trials such as those against Khodorkovsky and Pussy Riot went well beyond "postmodernist fun" to mark a level of absurdity that represented a "new post-Soviet doublethink," sweeping discursive gestures that symbolized the lawless and often random imposition of violence on the part of authorities against a helpless population—almost with the express purpose of witnessing and celebrating that power: "In answer to the question 'Why are the authorities doing this?' you hear more and more frequently, 'Putin is trolling.' The absurdity is reaching such high temperatures that the only answer can be an absurd one: 'The authorities are teasing us' [*Vlast' draznit*]. They

---

17. Markov 2015. For insight into the business sensibilities of a professional troll, see Merkacheva (2013).

18. Kamyshev 2013. One of the interlocutors of this published discussion called for answering such trolling on the part of the state "adequately, and in a coordinated, unified manner—with the formation of public opinion."

have no other goal except provoking the impotent reaction of society and taking delight in the spectacle of that impotence" (Morozov 2013).

This idea of trolling as a cynical Putinist celebration of power over the population's helplessness echoes Lipovetsky's (2011, 50) observation about the importance of "the performance of power's transcendental status" in cynical cultures, such as those that characterized Stalinism, and what Kukulin (2017, 223) described as the transgressive language of "messianic cynicism," a "new model for social communication" that he argues emerged over the second half of the Putin era. Whether a Soviet redux or more novel form of messianism, the range of symbolic associations outlined here points to both a heavy figurative load borne by a rhetorical trope that received new life and meaning thanks to new media technologies. So protean was the metaphor, in fact, that it came to be invoked equally adeptly in reference not only to those in power but to those in opposition to power as well.

Trolling Vlast'

When we turn the tables and look at framing strategies for critics of *oppositional* trolling, we find a somewhat different dynamic, though one no less damning. They still call into question legitimacy and authority but tend to underscore the fact that, in contrast to vlast', the opposition has very little *other* than language to rely on to demonstrate its political will—a dynamic that resembles Kalugin's "social contract between authority and society" I referred to in the introduction. With vlast' as the sole agent of deeds, trolling discourse attributed to members of the opposition tends to be framed in terms of "all talk and no action" or "empty rhetoric."

The rhetorical impotence of the opposition is signaled in the discourse by derogatory characterizations of speech itself, such as in the 2012 *Izvestiia* commentary that likened oppositional trolling to "yelling from the rostrums" (*kriki s trubun*) and "gloomy grumbling 'in the kitchens'" (*ugriumoe burchanie 'na kukhniakh'*) (Il'nitskii 2012), or the *Rossiiskaia gazeta* editorial that dismissed opposition demonstrations as useless trollish substitutes for real political action ("Truly unruly psychos, who are ready to storm the Kremlin rather than simply troll the internet, do not exist in Russia" ["Zavinchivanie" 2012]).

Unsurprisingly, trolling has been commonly ascribed to the on- and offline activities of Navalny, as one of the more prominent and effective oppositional leaders. In August 2013, the political commentator Leonid Radzikhovskii (2013) dismissed Navalny's mayoral campaign as a "bluff" and the "mere trolling of the authorities" (*lish' trolling vlasti*). Once the elections were over, he rejected

Navalny's status as a politician and, in a mix of metaphors, likened him to a snail ("crawling once again into the internet and trolling moronically") and a "balloon man" (*chelovek-vozdushnyi shar*), full of little more than rhetorical gas when he didn't have a campaign to run (Kuznetsova 2013).

This "troll, not politician," formula became a common rhetorical tactic for demeaning Navalny's status as public figure and quelling his political ambitions. The justification, when provided, usually had something to do with the limitations of his rabble-rousing. During the same mayoral election cycle, for instance, the columnist Dmitrii Lekukh (2013) used the contrast to describe Navalny as a "breaker," not a builder: "No matter how much his benefactors from the 'liberal wing of the government' of the Russian Federation would want it, Navalny is not a politician. He's an internet meme, a troll who's come out onto the square, an instrument 'calibrated' [*zatochennyi*] for only strictly defined actions—'turning' something 'upside down' without 'admitting' anything, 'breaking,' not 'building.'"

Whether they refer to Navalny's actual online presence or his broader involvement in the political public sphere, the troll-lined frame created by his critics carried common markers: His activities went little beyond the empty populist rhetoric of a "breaker," "soiler" (*zagazhivaiushchii*), "hypocrite," vindictive self-promoter, and paid political hack (Galimova 2017; Danilov 2016; Kiselev 2014; Zubov 2017; Prosvirova and Sokolov 2014). Even his countless court appearances as defendant were framed as attempts to "monetize his activity as an internet troll by means of the Russian court system" (Ukhov 2017).

The examples involving Navalny seen thus far have been uniformly derogatory, denying him even the dubious discursive status of "politician." But other voices acknowledged his function as the "gadfly" invoked by Plato's Socrates and deeply embedded in the tradition of the Russian intelligentsia. In some cases, such as the observation of the writer Eduard Bagirov (himself a product of the "countercultural" strain of Runet intelligentsia), the acknowledgment was grudging, though ultimately damning: "When in his blog he would shake out the underwear of some corporate crooks—by order of other corporate crooks, as it later turned out—it was at least interesting, and precisely this is how he achieved wide popularity on the internet. And trolling the party of power—that's a sacred affair loved by us all. As for digging up dirt for pay (*zakazukha*)? That's the normal stuff of a popular Russian blogger" (Bagirov 2013).

In other cases, the ascription of trollishness to Navalny was far more complimentary. In a 2012 interview, the former FEP founder Gleb Pavlovsky described Navalny as a "highly talented troll," invoking the Russian formalist Iurii Tynianov and the Decembrists in a manner that made it clear the political analyst was placing the opposition figure squarely in the intelligentsia tradition of the "thin" troll, or gadfly: "Navalny engages in a highly talented trolling. He trolls authority in a quality way, always alighting on concrete personalities. He is strong in this regard. It's just what Tynianov said about the Decembrist Lunin: 'He would taunt the bear with a stick'" (Morozov et al. 2012).[19] Perhaps somewhat self-servingly, Pavlovsky extended the bear-teasing analogy to acknowledge how important mastery of communication was in the modern era—and how tentative power was in the absence of such mastery: "Using modern communication, Navalny taunts the bear, who doesn't know how to use communication. This exposes the symbolic fragility of the Putin system and its symbolic nature in general. The capital of this system, in essence, is real only as symbolic capital, and as such may easily be over-valued" (Morozov et al. 2012).

Whatever one thinks of Pavlovsky's legacy for the political culture of the Putin era, his remarks here are quite perceptive and shed light on the underlying tension embedded in this rhetorical battle over trolling, its relationship to broader issues of political communication in Russia after Putin's return to the presidency, and the role of the internet and social media in shaping that political language. On the one hand, pro-Putin interests held considerable authority over dictating the political terms of engagement—a power that came not by virtue of their natural eloquence or ability to formulate and defend an argument but by their institutional, political, and economic control over channels of communication and the flow of information. In fact, as Pavlovsky noted, the "bear's" mastery of public political discourse was quite frail. Particularly with the growth of the Runet as an alternative medium for networked public spheres and consummate gadflies such as Navalny who deftly mastered communication in them, that frailty became even more exposed. Recalling Kornev's ecological metaphor of the troll's function, one could argue that Navalny and his ilk served a "sanitizing" function of the political ecosystem.

That members of vlast' recognized this potential is evident in a variety of ways. We see it in Putin's stubborn refusal to pronounce Navalny's name in public and, ultimately, his effort to shut up Navalny entirely by relegating him to solitary confinement and eventual death. We see it in the ill-advised attempts by members of the ruling elite to confront Navalny on his own turf, by calling him out in their own amateurish YouTube videos (as seen with Usmanov and Zolotov in the preceding chapter). And we see it in the steady flow of speech-related regulation that was put into law since 2010, to which we turn more immediately in chapter 6.[20]

---

19. Navalny himself used the stick-poking metaphor to describe the small but nevertheless incremental impact of grassroots oppositional activity on vlast' (for example, "Ushakhidi po ukhabam" 2010).

20. It is precisely the year 2010 that Kukulin (2017) identifies as the start of the "messianic cynicism," referred to above, a public discourse originating from the ruling political elite and marked by the same sort of provocation and khamstvo embodied by trolling as discussed here.

All these initiatives can be understood as efforts to use the legislative and judicial levers of power to curtail unwanted trolling in its broader political gadfly sense of challenging political authority and engaging it in serious public debate. As a result—likely more intentional than not—debate culture, as Viktor Toporov put it in a 2013 opinion piece in *Izvestiia*, became degraded into a troll culture of the decidedly thick, boorish sort: "If the goal of polemic—be it scholarly, political, or legal—is to prove oneself right and, correspondingly, the incorrectness of one's opponent, then the goal of trolling is to provoke one's opponent into poorly thought out, emotionally unchecked, and, ultimately, plain-and-simply false and (most importantly) self-incriminating words and actions. Trolling the would-be enemy, you don't compel him, along the lines of the memorable Perestroika slogan, 'Boris, you're wrong!'—No, you brazenly and forcefully tell him, 'Boris, you're a bastard,' and the goal of these insults is to get him to become unhinged and conduct himself exactly like a bastard" (Toporov 2013).[21] Toporov's use of the trolling metaphor, as I've tried to demonstrate, is not accidental. While the term began as a humorous figure for a narrow form of online provocation, it quickly spread into the vernacular as a symbol for broader manifestations of verbal aggression and corruption, in both politics and everyday life. Its digital origins helped fuel a moral panic that cast the internet as a rhetorical garbage dump responsible for everything from relatively mild forms of insult to pedophilia and suicide—a set of figurative associations that proved useful for those affiliated with *vlast'*, who recognized digital media and the trolls and gadflies that populated them as threats to their political authority as well. And while, rhetorically, their symbolic authority may have been frail, particularly in the wake of the protests of 2011–2012, authorities still had at their full disposal the power of the state regulatory system to temper the impact of the vocal opposition. To rationalize the slew of censorial actions in the realm of online communication that would follow, they relied heavily on a pair of complementary metalinguistic clusters—one centered around issues of "purification," the other around the notion of "civilization."

---

21. Toporov's use of the phrase "Boris, you're wrong!" invokes one of the more memorable rhetorical moments of the Gorbachev era, when conservative Communist Party and Politburo member, Egor Ligachev, used a more indirect version of it during a televised speech at the Nineteenth Party Congress in June 1988 to object to fellow Politburo member Boris Yeltsin's more radical interpretation of Gorbachev's policy of perestroika.

DIGITAL PROPHYLAXIS

Cheap, sensationalist publications created by non-virtual members of the systemic public sphere [*obshchestvennost'*] have the false impression that the Net is a meeting place for child molesters, hackers and international terrorists. They can spoil the blood, mood, and appetite of any netizen.

—Anton Nossik (1997a)

There's no dearth of irony in the fact that, just as the troll became the poster child for all that was wrong with the internet from some official corners, pro-state actors elsewhere were cynically institutionalizing trolling as a means of disrupting the oppositional political voices that were gaining traction thanks to networked communities. But the fact of the matter is, it did not take long for early adopters of online communication in Russia to bemoan the perceived verbal degradation of the new information sphere. Anton Nossik, perhaps the best known of them, contemplated this awkward truth as early as 1997. On one level, he blamed scandal-driven, capitalist motivations of journalists, who exaggerated the worst aspects of new media to sell copy, and the blogging community itself for falling prey to the same dynamic: "Our respected reader awaits scandal from us. Scandal increases for all of us traffic, popularity, visits, linkability, citation index, profits from advertising" (Nossik 1997a). On another level, he blamed what he called the "profanization of the Web" on the growth of the user base to include "lamers [*lamera*], the clueless, AOLers and other foul publics, who turned the elite Net of the bygone days into a bazaar of cheap, entertaining consumer goods [*shirpotreb*]" (Nossik 1997b).

Egor Kholmogorov reflected on the rising vitriol on the part of his adversaries in a 2004 post and even acknowledged in a roundabout way his own complicity in their coarsening ("I'm ashamed of my enemies, because since they are my enemies, it means I am somehow guilty of their brutalization [*oskotinivanie*]").

A year later he remarked on the negative effect of the internet on his own communicative skills, changing him from a "very communicative guy . . . with a mass of friends" to a "manifest sociopath" with sapped energy (Kholmogorov 2004; Kholmogorov 2005). In a 2007 interview, Gleb Pavlovsky noted the blogosphere's civility problems, attributing it to what he called a "culture of triumphant boorishness, an energy of authorized hate," an "anonymous demos" that "introduced the element of attack on the user," and an "ignorance" that "challenged expert opinion" (Kuz'mina 2007). Even Konstantin Rykov, producer of some of the more rhetorically dubious online content in the early stages of the Runet, later warned of the internet's ability to "infect people with a reactive psychosis" and of the "YouTube-ization" of consciousness (Rykov 2010a, 2010b). Indeed, the very trendy argot of the scumbags that Rykov had been instrumental in perpetuating created easy fodder for language purists, who would cite it as Exhibit Number One of how the internet was spoiling the Russian language and, by association, Russian civilization.

Yet while there is no doubt the medium had always lent itself to negative critiques that at times ballooned into all-out moral panics, the number and intensity of attacks on the new media from key government or pseudo-government institutions grew demonstrably precisely when it became clear that they were the primary venues for rising *political* opposition, personified most vividly and potently in the web-fueled political success of Navalny. Growing perception of the internet as a virus-ridden space teeming with trolls, boors, hate speech, and vulgarity coincided with the largely web-dependent spread of oppositional discourse, as exemplified by the meteoric rise of Navalny, the FBK, and their critiques of the corruption of vlast'. The following discussion explores some of the more official, public-facing leaders and institutions that helped articulate the demonization of new media technologies in Russia, providing rhetorical justification for the flood of laws regulating public political speech, particularly in the months and years following Putin's return to the Kremlin in 2012. Underlying many of their attempts to discredit online oppositional discourse was a shift in rhetorical framing: the digital spaces that once promised new opportunities for civic engagement were now ground zero for the preservation of national and civilizational purity.

Purging Runet of Boors and Pedophiles

Given the lofty status of the Russian language as an icon of national identity, moral panics about linguistic contamination often served as the first line of preservationist protest. Well after the peak of the scumbag craze and the spread of online trolling, Orthodox Metropolitan Kliment, speaking at a meeting of the Public Chamber's Committee for the Preservation of Cultural and Spiritual Heritage, lamented the "alarming" state of Russian online culture: "Users of the Internet network [*set' Internet*] write it just as they hear it, copying oral speech, shortening words, changing their meaning, and intentionally distorting Russian orthography. And this language of communication, just as the culture of communication in general, will become more and more primary for young people" ("Vystuplenie Metropolita" 2009). Duma Deputy Elena Mizulina made a similar point at a roundtable on vulgarity on the internet, remarking that "one shouldn't be surprised that young people flood their real life with all the aggression and obscene language that they learn online" (Nabatov 2013).[1] Sociologists provided academic backing for such sentiments, producing reports describing the detrimental impact of the internet on the "mentality" of Russian youth (Laboratoriia Kryshtanovskaia 2013).

Such concerns over the incivility of discourse in social media were not the sole purview of purist-minded church leaders and legislators, however. In a 2010 LiveJournal discussion sparked by a fashion blogger's desperate question "Why is there so much hatred in the Russian blogosphere?" (blondycandy 2010), scores of everyday users chimed in with responses, many blaming the anonymous nature of many internet exchanges:

> дык все просто. зависть и невоспитанность. ну и чувство безнаказанности в сети. при личной встрече вряд-ли кто-то осмелится высказаться (alien_stone)

> [it's all just wild. envy and immaturity. and a sense of impunity online. in a face-to-face meeting it's doubtful someone would have the nerve to express themselves that way]

> вот вот -- раз инет, меня никто не знает и не узнает, и буду я делать что хочу (the_madqueen)

> [that's it—since it's the web, no one knows or recognizes me, and I'll do what I want]

More tellingly in this discussion, however, is the fact that most of theories posted in response to the blogger's question rested on the idea that such verbal

---

1. "Не стоит удивляться, что молодые люди в реальную жизнь выливают всю агрессивность, нецензурную брань, которым научились в сети."

aggression was not unique to internet communication but rather an accurate barometer of the level of boorishness, or *khamstvo*, in Russian everyday life—either due to some Soviet legacy or simply a distinctive feature, or "mentality," of Russianness:

> А злости полно вокруг у нас и в обыденной жизни.Продавцы— хамят на пустом месте . В автобусе—водитель орет и т д . Кругом негатив.Общество такое—депрессивно-злое.

> [why there's plenty of anger around us in everyday life.Salespeople are boorish at the drop of a hat . The bus driver yells in the bus etc. It's negativity all around.That's the way society is—depressively evil.]

> стадность и неприятие индивидуальности. плюс- совковая мораль и лавочные гены

> [it's a herd mentality and refusal to accept individuality. plus—a Soviet-style ethic and shopkeeper's genes]

> Гадость, конечно, это чужое г.но, которое всплывает в хорошем блоге или дневнике—но такова наша действительность—Мы не уважаем себя, мы не уважаем других.

> [It's vile, of course, it's someone else's sh*t that pops up on a good blog or diary—but this is our reality—We don't respect ourselves, we don't respect others.]

> это наша общая национальная черта

> [it's our common national trait]

> Это не только в рунете, это российский менталитет такой. На улицах, в транспорте, в коллективах, повсюду склоки, травля, грязь и мерзость.

> [It's not just the Runet, it's the way the Russian mentality is. On the streets, public transportation, in collectives, everywhere there's squabbling, harassment, filth, and abomination.]

Even if these assumptions about national character are debatable, they are indicative of a commonly held impression that khamstvo was endemic in Russia and certainly predated the internet boom. In fact, as early as 1906, writer and critic Dmitrii Merezhkovskii addressed the problem in an essay titled "The Impending Boor" ("Griadushchii kham"). A search of khamstvo-related articles in the Russian press over the first decade and a half of the Putin era produces hundreds of examples of public laments over boorish public behavior by everyone from bureaucrats and law enforcement officials to shopkeepers, drivers, and public transport users. In a 2010 poll, citizens listed it as the most annoying feature of everyday life in Russia, and many of these acknowledged that, "unfortunately, it was an indelible part of Russian reality" (Mikhailova 2010). Sokolov (2016) quoted an unnamed poll listing it as the third most annoying feature of civil servants, behind indifference to the population and red tape. In a more historical and philosophical essay on the topic, the philologist Aleksandr Floria (2010) argued that the "triumph of boorishness" (*torzhestvo khamstva*) in contemporary Russia was a result mainly of "the absence of a unifying goal [or] inspiring idea in society." Alternatively, Besedin (2019) suggested that "boorishness in the Soviet Union or in Russia was always in part both a way of thinking and a reaction borne either out of a totality of power [*polnota vlasti*] or, on the other hand, out of desperation or fear. And it had long ago become natural and even organic."

More likely true was the assessment of Rogovskii (2006) and others, who argued that, while not the root cause of language aggression, the internet by virtue of its *pervasiveness* helped spread the already existing "virus" more rapidly and broadly than it might have in the pre-internet days. Looking at similar issues in the United States, Baron (2008) argues that web-based communication did not so much *change* the rules of discursive engagement as act as an *intensifier* of offline verbal practices. This intensification may have been even more acute, because, dating at least back to the mid-nineteenth century, the bar for language standards in Russia had always been set higher. As Paulsen (2009, 66–80) explains, speakers and writers have always been measured against what in Russian is called *literaturnyi iazyk* (literary language)—as defined by the masters of the mostly nineteenth-century literary canon—rather than simply *standartnyi*, or "standard language," as it's more commonly referred to in other language cultures. The "speech culture" (*kul'tura rechi*) movement that dominated Soviet language pedagogy from the late-Stalinist era on embraced this linguistic ideology of *literaturnost'* (loosely translated as "literariness") and further imbued it with the moral overtones of *kul'turnost'* ("cultured-ness")—the idea that one needed to conduct oneself in a *civilized* manner in both writing and speech (Gorham 2014). So while it was much easier in the modern wired world to weigh in on and even influence the contours of public language, regardless of obedience to norms, metalinguistic awareness of Turgenev's time-honored "great and mighty" (*velikii i moguchii*) Russian language still carried clout, making the norm gap all the more noticeable.

While bad grammar and khamstvo no doubt irked many Runet users, it was legislation ostensibly designed to protect Russian children that presented the first serious legislative challenge to web-based communication. The 2010 law On the Protection of Children from Information Harmful to Their Health and Development (Federal'nyi zakon No. 436-FZ 2010) authorized the creation of a unified registry of websites, which quickly came to be referred to as the "blacklist," containing information deemed to promote child pornography, drug use, or suicide.[2] Although a worthy cause in principle, the law was loosely written to allow not just for the removal of pages and sites in violation but for the closure of entire hosting platforms such as YouTube, LiveJournal, and Facebook—even if the text in violation had been posted by a provocateur in the comment section of a single post (Dobrokhotov et al. 2012). When legislators then proposed adding obscene language, or *mat*, to the mix, the deputy minister of communications openly admitted that they weren't quite sure "what to block and what not to block, what [was] life and health threatening, and what [was] not" (Zykov 2013a). Critics promptly accused the Parliament of "technical censorship" poorly concealed "under the flag of concerns for public morality as understood from a conservative, patriarchal, [and] religious point of view" (Nikiforenko 2013). In the face of such complaints of state censorship, which was forbidden by the Russian constitution, defenders of the law were quick to fall back on issues of morality to rationalize their actions. The law's Duma cosponsor Mizulina notoriously dismissed critics as belonging to "certain circles that can be associated with the pedophile lobby" ("Glava komiteta" 2012; Dobrokhotov et al. 2012).

Be it the very language of the law or the extralegal rationale for its implementation, symbolic language of contamination and prophylaxis figured centrally into policy decisions regarding the web-based public sphere. As early as 2010, Putin notoriously dismissed the internet as being comprised of 50 percent pornography, and during the 2012 presidential elections, his campaign adviser Stanislav Govorukhin declared it a "garbage dump" (*pomoika*) controlled by the US State Department ("Stenograficheskii otchet" 2010; "Govorukhin" 2012). State-run television (perhaps feeling the growing competition for advertising dollars from the internet) echoed these perceptions, featuring debates about the internet framed as a choice between "freedom" and "licentiousness" (*vsedozvolennost'*) in which the latter impression would inevitably dominate ("Politika smotret'" 2013).

---

2. Federal Law No. 436-FZ went into effect beginning September 2012. Mechanics for the creation, maintenance, and enforcement of the registry of "dangerous" sites were authorized weeks before the law went into effect ("Polnaia istoriia" 2024). For a detailed discussion of the operation and limitations of the registry, see Sivetc (2020).

Civilizing Civic Unruliness

After the widespread protests in the wake of the 2011–12 election season, official discourse and legislation largely did away with the moralistic pretense of defending children and the purity of the national tongue, targeting more directly digitally borne political combativeness. As with the On the Protection of Children law, legislators sprinkled new laws restricting political communication both on- and offline across a variety of different areas of the criminal code (Gusev 2012), creating a foundation of legal jeopardy against oppositional speech that the political analyst Andrei Kolesnikov (2012) called a "quadrangle . . . that covered all possible uncensored thought, expressions, and actions."[3] In addition to the On Protection of Children law, these included a June 2012 law that authorized Russian police to arrest and fine citizens who "violate[d] the order of proper conduct at public rallies," including web-based dissemination of information about unlawful demonstrations (Federal'nyi zakon No. 65-FZ 2012); a July 2012 amendment to article 128.1 of the criminal code recriminalizing slander (reversing the decision by Medvedev from less than a year prior to decriminalize it) ("Zakon o klevete" 2012); and a July 2012 law labeling NGO's "foreign agents" if they received foreign funding and engaged in political activities (Federal'nyi zakon No. 121-FZ 2012).[4] Add to these the 2013 Law on Punishment for the Defamation of Religious Feelings (otherwise known as the "antiblasphemy law"), a legislative response to the Pussy Riot scandal in February 2012 ("Prezident podpisal" 2013; Federal'nyi zakon No. 136-FZ 2013), and you're left with a situation in which "any criticism of power [vlast'] in the public sphere and the internet [was] now easily transferrable to the legal-criminal sphere" (Kolesnikov 2012a).

For some, however, the rash of laws aimed at taming public speech signaled underlying weakness on the part of the Kremlin and the ruling party despite its resounding electoral victory. As the political observer Mikhail Fishman (2012) put it, "The speed with which legislators have been tightening the screws should theoretically show that the regime is strong and has no fear. But in reality it's just the opposite, and the image of the ruling authorities [vlast'] is suffering: if everything's alright, then what's all the rush? Especially since public opinion understands perfectly well that all these laws are only needed to shut the mouths of the disgruntled [*zatknut' nedovol'nym rty*]." Fishman (2012) went on to characterize

---

3. For a more detailed overview of internet-related legislation and regulation, see Lonkila et al. (2020), who argue that 2012 marked a turning point commencing what they refer to as the state's attempted "occupation" of the Runet.

4. Later that fall, the United Russia Party promised a more ambitious, internet-specific raft of laws, but that initiative proved too ambitious (Dorokhov 2012; Zykov 2013d).

the initiative as "second-rate journalism disguised as legislative norm," essentially echoing the Kolesnikov notion that legal integrity was taking a back seat to political expediency. The very vagueness of the laws' wording, in this regard, must be understood as a feature rather than a bug, which enabled authorities to use the law and court system to quiet or silence altogether political opposition.[5]

The next set of speech-oriented legislation, targeting "extremism," offers a good case in point. Sponsored by Duma deputy and ex-FSB officer Andrei Lugovoi, Federal Law 398-FZ authorized the extrajudicial blockage of any networks, online or otherwise, deemed to be promoting "information containing calls for mass disorder, the implementation of extremist activity, [and] participation in mass (public) events conducted in violation of established order" (Federal'nyi zakon No. 398-FZ 2013). In practice, authorities used the law almost immediately after it went into effect in February 2014 to shut down Navalny's LiveJournal blog and three leading online independent (and largely oppositional) news outlets—*Grani.ru*, Gasparov.ru, and *Ezhednevnyi zhurnal* ("Polnaia istoriia" 2024). Merely citing "'calls for unlawful acts' and extremism" (Rozhkova et al. 2014), in none of the last three cases did the office of the general prosecutor, who under the law was given the power of a judge, indicate which pages of the resources were in violation of the antiextremism law (Epifanova 2014).[6] Another "antiterrorism" package of laws proposed in January 2014 set limits on anonymous online payments and donations and required internet providers and site owners to store for up to six months all information about and posts by users of their resources (Rothrock 2014). And the so-called law on bloggers passed later that spring extended rules meant for media outlets to bloggers with more than three thousand followers, thereby holding them responsible for inaccurate, defamatory, or obscene content in both posts and comments (Federal'nyi zakon No. 97-FZ 2014).

While the Duma tightened screws on civic discourse in the legislative realm, Putin from the start of his third term spoke with increasing frequency and a heightened linguistic register about language as a bulwark of national identity and cornerstone of Russian civilization. This civilizational turn by Putin and other members of the ruling elite effectively sought to shift the focus from "civic" to "civilized" society, placing greater importance on traditional, conservative val-

---

5. Lonkila et al. (2020) document the growth of internet regulation from 2008 and 2017, as well as more specific cases of the laws' selective application toward members of the political opposition. Gabdulhakov (2020) argues that the "opaque conditions for understanding what is allowed and what is not in online self-expression" reflect a "throwback to authoritarianism" and promote competition among various practitioners of citizen-based vigilantism.

6. In the case of Navalny's blog, prosecutors cited violations of conditions of Navalny's parole that prevented him from posting on social networks (Epifanova 2014).

ues and the need for normative verbal behavior rather than citizens' rights to free speech.[7] In his 2013 speech at the inauguration of Sergei Sobyanin as Moscow mayor, for example, Putin drew a direct contrast between "destructive actions and civic confrontation [*grazhdanskoe protivostoianie*]" and "civilized [*tsivilizovannye*] democratic procedures."[8] Although he did, on occasion, invoke the notion of "civil society" (*grazhdanskoe obshchestvo*), Putin was as likely to use the modifier "civic" with such headwords as "responsibility" (*otvetstvennost'*) or "solidarity":

> It is precisely in civic responsibility, in patriotism, that I see a basis for the consolidation of our politics. (Putin 2012b)

> Authority must not be an isolated caste. Only then is a sturdy moral foundation built for the creation, for the confirmation of order and freedom, morality and civic solidarity [*grazhdanskaia solidarnost'*], truth and fairness, for a nationally oriented consciousness. (Putin 2012a)

The discourse of civilized speech, then, was offered up as an alternative, more anodyne model of communication—including that which was electronically mediated—to the more aggressive and contentious discourse of civic exchange.

In this same 2012 address to the Russian parliament, where Putin devoted considerable attention to the need for Russia to forge a new national identity, he places language at the foundation of what he calls a "state-civilization" (*gosudarstvo-tsivilizatsiia*): "For centuries Russia has developed as a multinational state—that's how it was in the beginning—a state-civilization, held together by the Russian people, the Russian language, and Russian culture, which are native for all of us and unify us, preventing us from dissolving into this polymorphic [*mnogoobraznyi*] world" (Putin 2012b).[9] Rather than notions of free speech or

---

7. Though often conflated in English, "civic" and "civilized" are more distinct in Russian—*tsivilizovannyi* as opposed to *grazhdanskii*. Daucé (2017) makes a similar point in her discussion of "the civility of oppression" in authoritarian societies and Putin's Russia in particular. For an in depth analysis of the history of "civilizationalism" in Russia and its re-emergence in Putin's political world view, see Mjør and Turoma (2020). While they rightly focus on the broader philosophical and religious dimensions of the concept, my focus here is on its rhetorical implications.

8. "Люди увидели, что в нашей стране вообще и в таких крупных мегаполисах, как Москва, власть формируется не с помощью деструктивных акций или гражданского противостояния, а с помощью цивилизованных демократических процедур" ("Vladimir Putin" 2013).

9. Cf. One year later Putin attributed the same civilizational idea to Russian philosopher Konstantin Leont'ev and added the "Russian Orthodox Church" to the list of pillars of national identity: "Russia, as the philosopher Konstatin Leont'ev expressively put it, has always developed as a 'blossoming complexity' [*tsvetushchaia slozhnost'*], as a state-civilization, bonded together by the Russian people [*narod*], Russian language, Russian culture, the Russian Orthodox Church, and the other traditional religions of Russia" ("Zasedanie" 2013).

freedom of expression, it was the institutions of traditional language (*literaturnyi iazyk*) and culture that ensured the self-determination and uniqueness (*samobyt-nost'*) of citizens and made them proper "patriots" (Putin 2012b). Govorukhin echoed this idea in an opinion piece on the need to promote national culture at a time when Russia stood at a "civilizational crossroads" (*tsivilizatsionnaia raz-vilka*): "No one can dissuade me of the fact that the foundation of Russian national identity is Russian culture, which is multinational in its form, and humanistic in its content. And its foundation, without doubt, is the Russian language. Not only for fellow citizens, but for the entire world, it is first and foremost the language of Tolstoy and Dostoevsky, Chekhov and Bulgakov" (Govorukhin 2013).

Particularly in the context of this discourse on language as a foundation for Russian civilization, it should come as no surprise that, viewed as a profanity-filled garbage dump infested with pedophiles and pornographers, the internet played the role of the barbarian—particularly given Putin's requirement that "civilized discourse" must abide by the rule of law (especially as he had rewritten it): "Civilized [*tsivilizovannyi*] dialogue is only possible with those political forces who promote, justify, and formulate their demands in a civilized way, advocating them within the framework of the law" (Putin 2012b).

"Cyber Patrols" to the Rescue

In this light, the appearance of the nongovernmental organization Safe Inter-net League (Liga bezopasnogo interneta) made perfect sense. With legions of volunteer *kiberdruzhinniki*, or "cyber patrols," it warned of "external enemies" in justifying its efforts to create a "clean internet" (*chistyi internet*) by hunting down and reporting websites containing dangerous content. The group's name held dual historical significance, both evoking traditions central to Putin's civili-zational turn. The oldest referent harkened back to the personal armies, or *dru-zhiny*, of the princes of ancient Rus', formed to help them consolidate power and enforce control over large swaths of territory. The notion was resurrected in the Soviet era in the creation of volunteer civic organizations (*Dobrovol'nye narodnye druzhiny*), which aided security agencies in the maintenance of public order.[10] The new Putin-era *druzhinniki* essentially merged the traditions by presenting authorities with a loyal civil corps of volunteers who would keep watch over the wide swath of digital territory that remained largely untethered by state security

---

10. I am grateful to Oleg Budnitskii for providing historical context on the *druzhina* and *dru-zhinniki*.

agencies on their own. Over the first two years of operation, the Safe Internet League recruited more than twenty thousand volunteer *druzhinniki* across Russia and internationally to root out pernicious content (Zykov 2013b). In October 2012, they struck an agreement with the governor of the Kostroma Oblast' to connect new users by default to a prepackaged "clean internet" option—a so-called white list of sites preapproved by the league and other government officials ("Liga" 2013). As the league's executive director Denis Davydov explained, "If someone want[ed] to look at pornography, scenes of violence and cruelty, then he need only request that the "clean internet" be turned off and approve warnings that he would henceforth assumes all risks" (Zykov 2013c).[11] In addition to the implied *pure-impure* binary, the overlying nomenclature of the organization invoked notions of "order" and "defense" deeply rooted in traditional Russian (and Soviet) history. As an early version of their website explained,

> In ancient Rus', the *druzhina* fulfilled the function of ensuring internal order and defended the state against external enemies. Only the most skillful and competent warriors would belong to the *druzhina*. In the times of the USSR [*Vo vremena SSSR*] the *druzhinniki* would help the militia secure law and order.
>
> The Cyber-*druzhina* is a voluntary association that operates online. It unites volunteers who are prepared to keep a close watch [*otslezhivat'*] on lawlessness on the internet and report about it to law enforcement agencies. Members of the Cyber-*druzhinniki* are people who are not indifferent about the fate of the country's next generation. ("Kiberdruzhina" n.d.)

Invoking the dual historical images of medieval princely retinues and Soviet-era snitches, the cyber *druzhina* played to nostalgic, patriotic, and authoritarian tendencies that had grown more pronounced in the Putin administration since his return to the presidency. As it turned out, like many pro-state NGOs of the Putin era, this ostensibly "nongovernmental organization" had quite close ties to the Kremlin. It was the brainchild of two members of the ruling elite in particular—the presidential adviser and former minister of communications Igor' Shchegolev, who was also chair of its board of directors, and Konstantin Malofeev, who at the time was the largest minority shareholder of the state-owned telecommunications firm Rostelecom. The project was further underwritten by the Saint Basil the Great Charitable Foundation, an organization close

---

11. After substantial protest, the "clean internet" was offered only as an option rather than the default setting to users when the service went live in January 2013 (Sochnev and Kolomiichuk 2013).

the Russian Orthodox Church, and had an annual budget of $40 million (Earle 2013). Critics understandably viewed the project as a state-sponsored Trojan horse, an example of what former Finance Minister Aleksei Kudrin derisively termed "imitative mechanisms, quasi-NGO's" (Tagaeva 2013). As the web consultant Arseny Bobrovsky (a.k.a. "KermlinRussia") put it, "The declaration of war against child pornography and pedophilia [was] an effective means of getting 100 percent public support and a high level of trust for the projects of the League, so that society [would] regard any of its actions with the maximum degree of uncriticalness" (KermlinRussia 2013).[12]

Between its inception in 2010 and 2024, the league claimed to have conducted 12,000 information security tutorials online, recruited hundreds of cyber patrols across Russia, and blocked over 180,000 sites deemed to contain "dangerous content" ("O lige" 2025). Davydov ceded the executive director position in 2018 to Ekaterina Mizulina (daughter of the internet-slaying Duma Deputy Elena Mizulina) to pursue what likely turned out to be more lucrative work in cryptocurrency (Arenina 2021). The younger Mizulina, for her own part, established herself as a prominent (and glamorous) public spokesperson for a Runet purified of pernicious content—most prominently in the roundtable circuits of Putin's Public Chamber.[13]

Public Chamber as a Civilized Civil Society

The institutional structure of the Safe Internet League as an "imitative mechanism" has time-honored roots in a Russia that, as Kharkhordin (2018) argues, has traditionally lacked a true "public sphere" (and corresponding "public language") for the exchange of opinion on matters separate from the state. Instead, both tsarist Russia and the Soviet Union relied more on the artificial formation of what might be called a "systemic public sphere" in the voice of the multiple quasi-NGOs that assume the role of Soviet-style obshchestvennost' and function as "an army of supporters of government policies who are not, strictly speaking, part of officialdom, [but who] may get paid or receive other non-monetary perks, or they may just get a small portion of power in

12. For more on the overlapping political and financial interests in internet censorship, see "Tsenzor" (2013). A second problem, of course, lay in the duplicitousness of such discourse, given the Kremlin's own willingness to propagate its own web-based boorishness in the form of paid anti-oppositional trolling (see Grigor'evna and Chuviliaev 2012; Garmazhapova 2013).

13. For the first in a series of NavalnyLive YouTube investigations into the extravagant lifestyle and wealth of the younger Mizulina, see "Kiberstukachestvo" 2022).

exchange for advocating state policies, both informally and socially" (Khark-hordin 2018, 84).

The most formalized and prominent of these forums for Putin-era obshchest-vennost' was the Public Chamber created by Putin in 2005 for the express pur-pose of becoming "a platform for the congruence of positions regarding state policies, on the basis of which are formed highly democratic instruments for cooperation between obshchestvennost' and the state" (quoted in Kharkhordin 2018, 84).[14] As stated by the chamber itself, it was created to "bring about the interaction of citizens with organs of government power [vlast'] and local self-government in order to respond to the needs of citizens, defend their rights and freedoms in the formation and realization of state policy, and provide a means of public control [*obshchestvennyi kontrol'*] over the activity of the organs of power [vlast']" ("O Palate" n.d.). As a prominent embodiment of obshchest-vennost', authorized by vlast' to serve as a pseudo-public, pseudo-independent conduit between the authorities and the citizenry, the Public Chamber and the discussions, policies, and events emanating from it can be seen as an important articulation of an official public view of internet and social media technologies.[15] Indeed, a comprehensive analysis of internet-related discussions from the body's founding in 2005 it to be a pseudo-civic group very much concerned, especially since 2012, with civilizational matters.[16] And with close ties to the legislative halls of power (members of the Parliament often appeared at chamber roundtables), it served as a convenient government-sanctioned institution for Kremlin-friendly public debate, where key actors engaged in Runet-related issues could promote their lines of argument and transform them into publicly vetted and approved legislation.

Early Advocacy of Direct Internet Democracy

Despite the oversized presence of the state in the original formation and makeup of the body (40 of the 168 members are appointed directly by the president and

14. For an analysis of civil society in Putin's Russia and the role of the Public Chamber as a benign "simulacrum," see Greene 2014.

15. A conduit, albeit, whose decisions are nonbinding (Chebankova 2013, 110). As Richter (2009) observes in his in-depth study of the body, "the Public Chamber not only 'represents' society in terms of being its advocate, but also serves as a representation, or model, of what that society is supposed to look like."

16. The following analysis is based on the examination of webpages, videos, and documents relating to Public Chamber activity between 2005 and 2022 on issues relating to the internet and social media, the majority of which were identified through keyword searches at the chamber's web-sites (www.oprf.ru and www.old.oprf.ru).

another 85 come from regional chambers), one could still find, in the early years of the chamber, advocates of the internet as a positive tool of engagement on the part of authorities, in the spirit of Medvedev-era e-government initiatives and "direct internet democracy." In a 2006 meeting on the development of an "information society," for example, chamber member Elena D'iakova spoke of the need to create "electronic citizens" as a means overcoming the "information gap" that has appeared in society ("V Rossii" 2006). The 2008 meeting billed as the chamber's first dedicated solely to matters relating to the internet reflected a range of sentiments. On one end of the spectrum, Mikhail Fedotov and Pavel Astakhov advocated for a more hands-off approach, with the former dismissing the notion of a "sovereign internet" as incompatible with the global web and the latter invoking newly elected President Medvedev's declaration that "the authorities [vlast'] must be loyal to internet users so long as they are not committing crimes." On the other end, members warned of the digital specter of terrorism, threats to teens, and child pornography and called urgently for regulation that would forbid "the realization of terrorist activity or the justification of terrorism, the distribution of extremist materials, as well as material propagandizing pornography, cults of violence, or cruelty," and irradicate the internet as a "sphere of licentiousness, impunity, and arbitrariness [*proizvol*]" ("Zakonodatel'noe regulirovanie" 2008). Two years into Medvedev's presidency, the pro-internet momentum had grown, with television personality Tina Kandelaki echoing Medvedev's justification for "direct internet democracy" in her observation that new media could be a "useful instrument for authorities [vlast'] to 'monitor' issues of importance to citizens" and act on them in a timely fashion ("Ne tak strashen" 2010). Vladimir Mamontov even lamented how little the chamber knew about the "parallel civil society" online and how "people completely trusted each other there, while here [in the chamber] we are in search of trust" ("Sozertsatel'noe" 2010).

The Prophylactic Turn

With the 2011 "castling" from Medvedev back to Putin, shifts in internet-related rhetoric out of the chamber echoed those outlined in chapter 3: although e-government initiatives quietly chugged along, talk of "direct internet democracy" waned precipitously starting in 2012. From that point on, the chamber largely assumed the role of an impatient and outraged public, demanding that authorities take measures to protect the nation and citizenry from the slew of web-borne threats enumerated above. Initially, the threats were domestic and came in the form of profane speech, pedophilia, terrorist or extremist activity, and the promotion of drugs, crime, or suicide. Children and youth dominated as the perceived targets and victims. Countering the activities of the online scumbag, criminal, huckster, terrorist, extremist, or pedophile usually entailed some form of cleansing, purification, or prophylaxis—be it in the form of monitoring, restrictions, blacklisting, or rapid response. This discourse was laced with alarmist language designed to stoke the sort of moral panic seen in some of the more extreme reactions to trolls and trolling. In a 2016 discussion of web-based threats to the safety of youth, for instance ("How not to lose youth in the dangerous webs of the internet"), chamber member Sultan Khamzaev hit on a plethora of ills, including "alcohol and drug use" and "pornography, terrorism, and extremism," all of which should concern "socially oriented NGOs" ("Kak ne poteriat'" 2016). In the wake of a 2017 school-shooting incident in the Moscow region of Ivanteievka, chamber member Dmitrii Nosov blamed the internet without any evidence, arguing that a space so pernicious as to occupy their children "constantly" and promote "death groups" and the "poison of narcotics" most likely "pushed" the shooter to act: "We in the Public Chamber have been trumpeting about this! Together with the parent community we must solve this problem— either by restricting access to the internet, or by controlling it constantly in those online communities where kids frequent, [and monitoring] whom they interact with" ("Uchenik" 2017).

By 2017, the chamber had established its own monitoring center, called Security 2.0 (Bezopasnost' 2.0), which according to the chair of the Committee on Traditional Values, Elena Sutormina, was designed to "engage in the exposure of dangerous content on the internet, in different social networks" in a manner flexible enough to account for the troubling fact that "terrorists [were] constantly perfecting methods of recruitment, and had adjusted their tactics for social networks" ("Bezopasnost'" 2017). Several months later, shortly after the Security 2.0 center's launch, Sutormina warned of the need for further monitoring, given the capacity of unnamed "technologists" to use social networks to conduct "psychological workovers" on youth: "It's important not to miss . . . the fully intentional attempts by unknown technologists, who specialize in psychological workovers, to somehow comprehensively and massively influence youth, spreading content that provokes deviant and criminal behavior" ("Sotsseti" 2018).

Metaphors of digital hygiene and contamination took on double meaning during the Coronavirus pandemic, particularly in connection to the rise in false web-based information, or what in Russia had come to be called *feik-nius* ("fake news"). At an expanded meeting of the "working group for the protection of rights of internet users, [and] the development and facilitation of internet security," the blogger Iuliia Vitiazeva spoke of the need for "information hygiene" in an age where especially younger users approached online content with "clip thinking" (*klipovoe myshlenie*) instead of "critical thinking": "Just like we teach children to wash their hands before meals, cross the street in the proper place, we need to engage in teaching information hygiene, so that they understand or at least try to understand where the truth is and where there are lies, and get a sense as to when they are being manipulated. So that they stop being simply consumers of information and try to apprehend it, because we have clip thinking; critical thinking is altogether absent. No one tries to find the truth today; people don't even read the headlines" ("Volna feikov" 2020).

Aleksandr Mal'kevich, a media personality who had emerged as one of the Putin regime's most prominent propagandists on matters relating to the internet, invoked the notion of an "infodemic" that spread "faster than any virus" to describe false information online regarding the Coronavirus pandemic and attributed it to unnamed "provocateurs . . . located outside the boundaries of the country" ("Sokhraniaite spokoistvie" 2020). And in response to questionable web-based information regarding the national referendum on proposed changes to the Russian constitution (designed to ensure Putin an avenue for running for president for a fifth and sixth term), he accused the "so-called media—foreign agents" of producing a "wave of false information (and) flurry of fakes" and indicated that it would be a constant threat to the Russian body politic that would require "collective immunity on society's part: Information virus is with us now always. Our goal is to work out rules of information hygiene, precautionary measures, to live with this virus and develop a collective immunity to it for society" ("Nasha zadacha" 2020).[17]

Navalny as Pied Political Piper

To be clear, the laundry list of threats had some grounding in reality, in Russia just as any in other modern society. What qualifies reactions to them as "moral panic" is the degree to which they were exaggerated, linked specifically to the internet as the source cause, and served as justification for bringing about more draconian laws that were used for broader, politically motivated purposes.[18] A good example of this sort of rhetorical overreach can be seen in statements from Public Chamber members in the aftermath of the public protests of January and April 2021 inspired by the FBK's publication of an hour-long exposé of

---

17. Asmolov (2020) shows how state-generated fake news can actually shield political authority from criticism during crisis situations by deflecting popular attention from the "vertical" axis of political power to the "horizontal" axis of digital communication systems and their propensity to promulgate false information and narratives.

18. And to a certain extent, this tendency is not unique to Russia. Malcomson (2016, 153) also points out how discourses of moral panic—what he calls "the 'Four Horsemen of the Infocalypse: terrorists, pedophiles, drug dealers, and money launderers'"—are often questionably invoked in attempts to rationalize sovereignization of the internet.

Putin's ill-begotten wealth in "Putin's Palace," and Navalny's own return to Russia from Germany, where he had been recovering from an attempted assassination (from nerve-agent poisoning). The events brought to the streets people in cities across Russia in numbers that hadn't been seen since the 2011–12 election cycle, many of whom cited Navalny and his fate as their main inspiration (Ivanov and Mukhometshina 2021; Erpyleva and Zhuravlev 2021). While official sources downplayed the turnout in public, the high level of concern on the part of vlast' was clear from the onslaught of rhetorical and legal attacks that followed. State-affiliated media accused Navalny of "political pedophilia," claiming (inaccurately) that the rallies had been attended predominantly by minors whom Navalny and his team had lured out through manipulative use of TikTok, the popular Russian social media platform VK, Facebook, Twitter, Instagram, and YouTube.[19] And on 16 April Moscow prosecutors petitioned to classify the FBK as an "extremist organization"—the court approval of which ultimately led to a ban of its operations, the seizure of its assets, and the liquidation of the enterprise.

It's of little surprise, then, that those tasked with articulating the interests of "civic society" dug into the issue in subsequent months. As early as 3 February, the Public Chamber's Committee on Demography, the Protection of Children, and Traditional Family Values held a hearing dedicated to "preventing minors from being drawn into illegal activities through social media" ("Rebenok" 2021), at which several of the usual suspects spoke out. Ekaterina Mizulina warned that "every second teenager in Russia is being subjected to actively destructive effects on social media" and complained of the "double standards" and "blatantly manipulative behavior" of the major social networking platforms when it came to enforcing Russia's laws against participation in unsanctioned demonstrations. Sergei Rybal'chenko reported that the chamber had already recommended that Roskomnadzor either banish said platforms from the Runet or severely restrict access to them if they continued to permit the "distribution of illegal content urging children to participate." Although the committee's final recommendations included concrete measures, such as requiring special age-specific SIM cards in the smartphones of minors and "information security" courses in the school curriculum, much of the committee's final report consisted of platitudes of an authoritarian nanny state, including references to the "systemic maturation of minors" and the "formation of the successful, socially active individual demanded by modern society" ("Rekomendatsii" 2021).

---

19. Mirumian 2021; "Vozbuzhdeno" 2021; Ivanov and Mukhometshina 2021; Starikova 2021. Subsequent sociological studies determined that minors made up only between 1.1 and 5.7 percent of total protesters (no significant change from previous rallies), with the majority (42.7–47.7 percent) consisting of citizens between the ages of 25 and 39 (Zotova 2021).

Later that year, the same committee hosted a four-hour roundtable on "the protection of children from internet content bringing harm to their psychological, physical, spiritual, and moral health" ("Zashchita detei" 2021). According to the chamber's own coverage of the event, the issue was framed as a matter of "demographic security," given the internet's growing influence on younger generations as an "agent of raising and socializing children and youth," particularly in the face of a "tendency for parents to gradually recede from the raising of children." And while much of the conversation mirrored global discussion on the adverse effects of the internet on young minds, roundtable participant and State Duma Deputy Inga Iumasheva made it clear that national security was at risk, due to the threat of pernicious domestic political forces ("In essence, destructive content is a part of a policy aimed at destroying our country from within") and the internet must be viewed first and foremost from this perspective ("Mashina-mama" 2021).

Word for word, the Runet may not have been the best place to find traditional models of cultural norms and civilized communication (though they certainly were there, if sought out). But as long as "civilized" was used as a code word for "normative" or "traditional" as defined by central authorities rather than "tolerant" and "cognizant of diversity" as it is commonly understood in cultures where the notion of "civil society" was developed (Hall 2013, 22–26), the "uncivilized" communicative environment of Runet would be one of the main reasons for that domain's potency as a space for civic opposition and exchange.

Soon after the dramatic political events of 2011–12, the main strategy for containing oppositional discourse became to frame its primary digital medium as a breeding ground for forces that would threaten the moral and national foundations of Russia, forces that lay outside the bounds of normative behavior: foul-mouthed blasphemers, slanderers, drug addicts, pedophiles, and foreign agents. There's little question that the *perception* of degradation and pollution on the structural and communicative levels of digital media helped foster a broader image of the internet as a garbage dump foul with anarchy and licentiousness. This perception, in turn, made the Runet vulnerable to symbolic associations with all sorts of taboo or otherwise socially unacceptable behavior, ranging from cursing to treason, with slander, blasphemy, extremism, and pedophilia somewhere along that spectrum, and thus provided rhetorical justification for further regulation, reining in, and (as we'll see in chapter 8) repatriation. Particularly in contrast to the lofty norms of the traditional literary language, electronically mediated communication tended to reflect the more vulgar verbal realities of everyday life. The countercultural, nonhierarchical, and uncensored traditions of the Runet certainly did and do expose the medium to such associations; but as I've tried to show here, these features were, more often than not, either amplifications of existing discursive ills offline (in the case of boorishness) or (in the case of scumbag language) medium-specific features that showed little real sign of contaminating speech culture at large, and no sign of political partisanship. It could also be said that, on a broader level, the various forms of rhetorical purification—be it the punitive bureaucratic language of new legislation, the moralistic language of the Orthodox Church, the civilizing language of the systemic public sphere, or the belligerent language of the self-proclaimed cyber patrols—themselves constituted a very real and arguably more pernicious form of verbal aggression.[20]

One might also question the real impact of these efforts by various corners of obshchestvennost' to portray the internet and social media as the bugaboo of all social and political ills of contemporary Russia. At some point, the sheer volume of output in the form of policy papers, press conferences, and more concrete prophylactic initiatives—all supported by generous media coverage—begins to impact popular perception. Aside from the benefit their activities brought to their own private and corporate interests (which in many cases may have been the prime motivation), the efforts of the *obshchestvenniki* did provide a valuable rhetorical layer of public legitimacy to the policies already under consideration and adoption by the central government. But the causal relationship between the managed voices of public concern and the policies is quite clear: the latter drove the former, not the other way around. Nearly all the voices and initiatives examined here were essentially reactionary in nature—an effort to purify and cleanse the body politic and networked public sphere of pernicious voices of viral contamination and inoculate them from further "infodemics." More creative and proactive articulations of Putinism provide the focus of chapter 7.

---

20. As Rogovskii (2006, 63) put it, "Morality as an attribute of Authority [vlast'] (state, spiritual-religious) too often becomes the most specious form of motivation for violence, has acted as a goal justifying violent means, that is, in its socially significant manifestations itself has become infected with the very same 'virus' of violence." See also Potsar 2013.

Part 4

RHETORICAL RESTORATIONS

MEDIATING VOICES OF AUTHORITY

Making positive content is hard, and popular positive is even harder: it's much easier working with negative content.

—Aleksei Goreslavskii ("Finalistov" 2022)

At first glance, it would seem the main protagonists of the preceding chapters should have been mortal enemies. To the likes of Mizulina, Mal'kevich, and the Safe Internet League, the internet trolls represented all that was wrong and pernicious about the internet and social media, a vile virus to be sanitized and exterminated at all costs. The purity and moral integrity of Russian society depended on it. From a rhetorical perspective, however, they shared a common strategic goal—to compromise the growing authority of the opposition-oriented networked public sphere. They even worked toward that goal in a somewhat complementary fashion. The trolls generated disruptive speech with the aim of so polluting the space that it no longer functioned as a viable forum for civic discussion and debate; the purists created associative links between that digital swamp and broader social ills, however exaggerated, that helped provide civic cover for the generation of civilization-preserving laws. The three case studies in this chapter profile online initiatives that sought not to disrupt or shame, but to generate more positive and state-friendly content that was at once supportive of the ruling authority and compelling for Runet users.[1] Stylistically, they run the gamut from low to high, brash to polished, with a colorful dose of plain-talking authoritarian charisma in between.[2]

---

1. Gunitsky (2015, 50) draws the contrast in terms of a shift between "contestation" to "co-optation."

2. In the interest of time and space, I limit this discussion to three case studies of relatively prominent pro-state figures and institutions. For additional examples of leading bloggers, trolls, and other more grassroots pro-Kremlin content producers, see Gunitsky (2015) and Zvereva (2020b, 242), who describes the pro-Kremlin communicative space as a "grey zone of communication . . . in which the right to express the state authorities' point of view is assumed by different 'volunteers'—pro-Kremlin authors writing in blogs and social media, paid propagandists and amateur supporters, trolls and 'soldiers' in the information war."

Sergei Minaev and Scumbag Patriotism

When Kremlin media handlers were looking for figures to produce content that might distract attention from the likes of Navalny online and better establish a political voice more closely inflected with Putin-friendly tonalities, Sergei Minaev stood out as a uniquely qualified candidate. An early adopter of Runet and self-fashioned "creative," Minaev rubbed virtual elbows with Rykov, Kononenko, and other "scumbags" linked to udaff.com and fak.ru, and like them found early wealth and fame from his countercultural transgressions.[3] Beyond his status as a native-speaking scumbag, Minaev was among the LiveJournal blogging elite as that platform was coming of age (through his account @amigo_95) and in 2006 gained celebrity status with the success of his best-selling novels *Dukhless* ("Soul-less"; 2006) and *Media Sapiens* (2007). The popularity of the books was not shared by those in the literary establishment, who widely panned them for their extensive (and gratuitous) use of Russian obscenity (*mat*) and for being riddled with basic grammar and spelling errors.[4] That their subject matter cast the "creative class" and oppositional movement in negative light did little to help Minaev's reputation among the liberal-leaning literary intelligentsia.[5]

But it did likely draw the attention of Kremlin media handlers. His success as a popular fiction writer willing to use playful invective and wry cynicism to poke holes in the credibility of the opposition helped launch Minaev's debut on broadcast television in the form of a prime time talk show, *Chestnyi ponedel'nik* (*Honest Monday*), launched in 2009 on the television station NTV and financed, in its final year, to the tune of 15 million rubles as part of an effort to promote "socially significant" content (Akhmadieva 2013). As with his internet and literary production, the show combined brash rhetoric with generally pro-Putin sentiments in a way that attracted Kremlin handlers as much as they repelled more critical sectors of the population. Writing on the project shortly after its debut, the *Novaia gazeta* columnist Slava Taroshchina (2009) described Minaev and his project as a harbinger of what she called "trash patriotism" and "trash TV,"

---

3. As Kukulin (2016) explains, this involved complementary linguistic and political (pro-Putin) "transgressions."

4. As one critic put it, "There's so much of our beloved mat in the book that one starts to get a little nauseated. Minaev knows by heart all the words relating to the lower half humankind, and uses them like a bum, for connecting words" (Kopylova 2007).

5. The second novel, *Media Sapiens*, featured a delusional, drug-induced political spin doctor who staged bogus, anti-Kremlin demonstrations. The topic prompted Russian writer Dmitry Bykov (2007) to write, "He has taken up the very anti-orange project that no one else from among talented writers has managed to promote." A *Kommersant* critic writing about Minaev's literary production used a formulation that brought the two perspectives together into a single phrase, describing his first book as "the apotheosis and quintessence of readers' taste in Russia today" (Chuprinina 2007).

which featured a style that was "everything low, excessive, pushing boundaries, parasitizing the worst clichés, bad taste, banality [*poshlost'*], and primitiveness." In short, just the sort of substandard norm breaking that brought Putin rhetorical notoriety a decade earlier. So it should be of little surprise that, as Putin was sarcastically writing off election protesters as vapid Kipling-esque "banderlogs" sporting white ribbons that looked like "condoms" (Makutina 2011), Minaev was working overtime on the set of his online talk show, *Minaev LIVE*, to generate content not only countercultural in form but counter-oppositional in content.

Minaev LIVE debuted in May 2011 just as the 2011–12 election season was getting underway.[6] Its launch may well have been due to the fact that Minaev had always considered himself a creature of the internet, but the show would also offer Putin's political handlers an additional voice in the medium that had become so politically problematic for the leader of the "Party of Crooks and Thieves."[7] Though like *Honest Monday* the project featured a talk-show format including prominent guests from the political and social sphere, *Minaev LIVE* differed from Minaev's broadcast television programming in subtle but important ways. First, it offered viewers a more intimate setting. While *Honest Monday* took place in a brightly lit studio with a live audience, and guests and hosts standing on a raised platform, *Minaev LIVE* was aired in a smaller, dimly lit studio, with host and guest sitting in comfortable high-back chairs separated by a table and an open bottle of Dewars whiskey—a setting not too far off from the imagined setting of its online streaming audience.[8]

Although a handful of visitors populated a balcony that remained largely out of site, Minaev and guests oriented themselves more immediately to the large video screens projecting screenshots and live internet footage strategically placed to be visible to viewers as well. Virtual audience members, in turn, would call into the program via Skype and wait patiently, images lining the bottom of the screen, until Minaev worked them and their questions into the conversation (fig. 7.1).

A second difference appeared in the show's lineup of guests and topics. While, like the broadcast show, *Minaev LIVE* featured a healthy dose of politicians, jour-

---

6. The following analysis is based on viewings of twenty-four episodes of *Minaev LIVE* spread evenly across a one-year period between its debut on 26 May 2011 and Putin's third presidential inauguration on 7 May 2012. Episodes were usually one to one and a half hours in length, with longer exceptions during live coverage of various public rallies and demonstrations.

7. In an interview on 02TV, Minaev declared outright: "I grew up out of the Internet. I did a lot of writing on the Internet. I cut my teeth in the mess of social networks [*v setevykh srachakh*]. Everything that is now happening on the net was done by the counter-culturists. The Internet is our everything" (oberkovich 2007).

8. The Dewars product placement not only helped strike a contrast to conventional broadcasting interviews, but it also flowed naturally from Minaev's main line of work as a wine and spirits distributor.

MnaevLive - 01.11.2011 Ксения Собчак

FIGURE 7.1.   Screenshot of set of YouTube talk show *Minaev LIVE*, featuring a Sergei Minaev interview with the television celebrity and then political opposition sympathizer Kseniia Sobchak. Source: *Minaev LIVE* (1 November 2011), https://www.youtube.com/watch?v=_ytArasMrNE&ab.

nalists, and other figures from the political public sphere, the YouTube-based guest list leaned heavily on stars and topics linked to Runet culture, as well. The two worlds converged in the very first episode, in which Minaev spoke at length with the film director and arch traditionalist Nikita Mikhalkov, billed as "the most talked about personality on the Runet over the past month." Minaev offered his guest the chance to elaborate on his recent open letter to Putin and Medvedev calling for them to "bring order" to the culturally degenerate mass media (and internet in particular) and then gave him a chance to defend himself from accusations that he used a personal vehicle equipped with a blue emergency siren—a viral symbol at the time of the privileged power elite (*Minaev LIVE*, 26 May 2011[9]). Later that summer, Minaev hosted a pair of "top bloggers" famous on the Runet for their "+100500" series of comical YouTube shorts, where they discussed the newly emerging microblogging platform, Twitter, and its impact on Runet content (Minaev: "140 characters is a killer of creativity") (25 August 2011). While the dialogue would be a hard slog for those uninitiated to Runet shoptalk, the jocular banter about monetizing Twitter and the perils of meeting

---

9. All subsequent references to episodes of *Minaev LIVE* will refer to the date of the broadcast only. See the reference list for complete bibliographic citation.

online followers in the offline world was enough to attract 18,000 streamers by the closing minutes of the program.

A third, less subtle difference was the communicative style of *Minaev LIVE*, which featured a register less formal in tone than Minaev's television program and sprinkled with obscenities that would never be permitted on the broadcast airwaves. On several occasions, Minaev had to give guests assurance when they cautiously inquired whether the "colorful lexicon" was permitted on the show, as he did with Margarita Simonyan, head of the state propaganda channel, RT, in his conversation with her (10 April 2012).[10] In a more extreme case, an hour into his interview with the journalist Oleg Kashin, Minaev welcomed a Skype call from the notorious pro-Putin tabloid publisher Aram Gabrelianov, who proceeded to light up the conversation with a flurry of invective, scolding Kashin for wasting his journalistic talent by sucking up to the likes of Navalny and Nemtsov.

> Габрелянов: Во-вторых, просто, я Олегу уже говорил. Я тебе честно скажу. Проблема его в чем? Я хочу вопрос ему задать. Ты же меня для этого позвал?
>
> Минаев: Конечно. Не, не вопрос.
>
> Г: Я хочу спросить у Олега, когда он вернется в свою профессию и будет писать репортажи, как в русской жизни про сахарный завод и перестанет быть спецпропагандистом.
>
> Кашин: Арам Ашотович, я Вам сегодня уже говорил: "Прогоним Вашего Путина, и тогда будем писать заметки про сахарный завод.
>
> Г: Я уже десять раз говорил, пописай в сторонке. Опять ты меня заводишь. И твоему Навальному говорил, и всем, блядь. Хуй вам, а не власть. Но опять ты меня заводишь, блядь. Сейчас я опять начну суетиться, блядь.
>
> М: Арам, продолжай, пожалуйста. То, что ты говоришь, очень важно для всех.
>
> Г: Потому что ну действительно бесит меня. Папа вас любит, а вы его бесите, еб твою мать. Ну действительно, блин.
>
> М: Да, я знаю, что ты видишь всю нашу хуйню.
>
> Г: Реально. Да, я вижу. Он действительно талантливый парень. . . . Он стал бы иконой русской журналистики. А он превратился, хуй его знает, в жалкое подобие, блядь, Геббельса. Да какой там Геббельс! Он превратился, блядь, в рекламную хуйню, блядь,

---

10. See Strukov (2016) for a discussion of Simonyan's influential role as a representative of what he calls the "second-tier agency" on which Putin has relied for the promotion of conservative and patriotic values.

при всех этих, блядь, Немцовых, Навальных. Нахуя ему это нужно? Вот я не понимаю, честно. Вот я не понимаю, Олег, нахуя тебе это нужно. Ты же талантливый человек, блядь. Они два слова связать не могут. Вот это мой вопрос. (2 February 2012)[11]

[GABRELIANOV: I've already told Oleg, I'll be honest with you, you know what his problem is? I'd like to ask him a question—that's what you asked me here for, right?

MINAEV: Of course.

G.: I want to ask Oleg when he is going to return to his profession and write reports like [the ones he wrote] about Russian life, about the sugar factory, and stop being a special propagandist.

KASHIN: Aram Ashotich, I've also told you that once we get rid of your Putin, I'll start writing about the sugar factory. . . .

G.: I've said it ten times before. Mind your own business [lit. "You're pissing off target"]. Here you go, winding me up again. You, your Navalny, everyone, can just go fuck off. Fuck you, not the authorities [vlast']. But you're fucking winding me up again. Now I'm going to start making a fucking fuss again.

M.: Aram, please continue. What you're saying is very important for everyone.

G.: Because it really drives me crazy. Your daddy loves you, and you're driving him crazy, goddam it. Really, what the hell?

M.: Right, I know you see all our shit.

G.: For real, I see it. He's really a talented guy. . . . He would have become an icon of Russian journalism. But he's become fuck knows what—a pathetic imitation of fucking Goebbels. He's no Goebbels! He's turned into a fucking advertising shit for all those Nemtsovs and Navalnys, for fuck's sake. What the fuck does he need that for? Honestly, I don't understand him. I just don't understand, Oleg, why the fuck do you need that? You're a talented fucking man. They can't string two words together. That's my question.]

Gabrelianov's flood of Russian obscenities elicits from his interlocutors (including Kashin) appreciative smiles that soon turn into boisterous laughter. But Minaev's obvious glee comes not just from the editor's mastery of mat: he is clearly thrilled that it so effectively authenticates Gabrelianov's main message—that Kashin has sacrificed his journalistic talent at the altar of oppositional

---

11. I am grateful to Oleg and Liza Budnitskii for their expertise transcribing this obscenity-laden passage.

politics and engaged in hypocritical behavior that recasts a desired public image of high-minded moral rectitude into one laced with base opportunism. That Minaev takes obvious pleasure in both the message and the language in which it is delivered is emblematic of his and his program's political orientation. Himself a product of the Scumbag counterculture corners of the Runet, Minaev would be the last to launch lofty lectures about the need to rally around the president to preserve stability and avoid chaos. Instead, he relies on a variety of less direct rhetorical strategies to poke holes in what he perceives to be overly self-righteous political positions represented by Kashin, Navalny, and other members of the nonsystemic opposition. At times, such as with Gabrelianov above, he leans on friends and associates to do the rhetorical heavy lifting. We see this same strategy at work in his interviews with the Runet pioneer (and Navalny supporter) Anton Nossik, where Minaev calls in his comrade-in-scumbag-arms Konstantin Rykov to play the role of attack dog (14 February 2012).

As the political season heats up, the show's content itself gets more political, but the slate of guests remains diverse, and Minaev's rhetorical approach remains subtle—skeptical of the political opposition, but cognizant of the corrupt and clumsy shenanigans of the "system" at the center of its attacks. November and December 2011 feature visits from the controversial television host and opposition sympathizer Ksenia Sobchak (1 November 2011) and the nationalist Runet old timer Egor Kholmogorov (15 December 2011).[12] Minaev presses both on their political views and probes their vulnerabilities: Why did Sobchak insist on "boorishly" trolling Rosmolodezh' leader Vasilii Iakemenko in an expensive Moscow restaurant, and where is her evidence that he had ever been accused of pedophilia? Why did Kholomgorov think the Russian nationalist movement was so poorly represented and organized online? Conversations are quick moving, with ample criticism in all directions, but when push comes to shove, Minaev assumes a more pragmatic position—calling a spade a spade: Sobchak is at times a boor; Kholmogorov, a racist; both have views worthy of treating seriously; and (most critically) neither presents a viable alternative to Putin and Putinism. "What would happen," he asks Kholmogorov, "if Putin suddenly flew off to Mars and was out of the picture?" The question, Kholmogorov's silence in response suggested, was itself rhetorical.

This "If not Putin, who?" retort would be a common rhetorical strategy of the pro-Kremlin media during the 2011–12 demonstration season, one Minaev would frequently revive during the run-up to the presidential elections—though critically tempered for a web-based audience that skewed skeptical, if not cyni-

---

12. Sobchak brought the show just under 68,000 viewers at its peak, while Kholmogorov attracted 45,500.

cal. In a 26 January discussion with the political analyst Nikolai Zlobin, he allows his guest to elaborate on Putin's multiple weaknesses: he rules intuitively and single-handedly by means of "manual control" (*ruchnoe pravlenie*) rather than using logic or the governmental system there to support him; the population is tired of him and he doesn't seem to care. When it comes to discussing alternatives, however, Minaev and his guests summarily dismiss the candidacies of Vladimir Zhirinovsky and Mikhail Prokhorov; they contemplate the weak presidency that would emerge if Putin bowed out and the most likely replacement, Communist Party candidate Gennadii Ziuganov, were elected; and they avoid discussing altogether the possibility of a "nonsystemic" oppositional figure (such as Navalny) coming to power, given that none has been allowed to appear on the ballot.

Acknowledging the discontent of the protesters ("many of whom are acquaintances"), Minaev allowed many Runet-savvy viewers, who numbered just shy of 63,000 at the peak of the broadcast, something of a permission structure to continue supporting the status quo, as imperfect as it was. His live coverage of mass protests in Moscow on 10 December, 4 February, and 23 February served a similar function. On the 4 February broadcast, featuring coverage of competing demonstrations—anti-Putin protests at Bolotnaia Square and pro-Putin demonstrations organized by the state in another central Moscow location—Minaev and guests discuss crowd size, organization, and messaging. Minaev offers a modicum of objectivity in his commentary, with ample complements and airtime to the opposition, especially in contrast to the over choreographed, even strained feel of the pro-Kremlin staging. Minaev brings in two guest commentators: Mikhail Dvorkovich, a former Kremlin event planner, and Pavel Piatnitskii, a journalist, lawyer, and member of the youth arm of Zhirinovsky's Liberal Democratic Party of Russia. As their critical commentary suggested, both men shared Minaev's ostensibly open-minded attitude toward the protests, as well as his underlying loyalty to the Putin system. All three criticized the pro-Putin event for the high number of participants who were likely paid to attend and the offputting rhetoric of "enemies" by some of the speakers. And they expressed open wonder at the large number of orderly demonstrators at Bolotnaia. But in filling the nearly three hours of live coverage devoted to the events, they also managed to cover a wide range of conspiracy theories surrounding the opposition and their demonstration—from rumors of illicit funding by the US State Department to the mounds of compromising material the FSB had thus far gathered on Navalny (information, they insisted, that would cause his supporters to "turn on him in a minute.") The extended discussion of the ubiquity of FSB surveillance no doubt also served as a gentle disincentive for viewers, who numbered 88,000 by halfway through the coverage, from getting too far out of line.

Whether or not *Minaev LIVE* was bankrolled by the Kremlin, given Minaev's personal and professional biography, it would not be too far-fetched to assume he was quite at home engaging in political straight talk over a bottle of whiskey with a who's-who list of political, cultural, and Runet influencers in a manner that was at once clearly grounded in an affinity to Putin and Putinism and pliant enough to allow those more opposition-adjacent viewers to feel like their alternative views were being both heard and voiced. Rather than the "trash patriotism" that Taroshchina and her ilk dismissively labeled Minaev's television endeavors, the internet project featured a more subtle "scumbag patriotism" that at least established a competitive presence for extended pro-Putin rhetoric in the online talk and information sphere and at most provided viewers a more politically palatable permission slip for accepting, if not actively supporting, six more years of the status quo.

Ramzan Kadyrov and Authoritarian Instagram

If in Minaev's YouTube broadcasts we see an effort to essentially "translate" a more pro-Putin discourse into a language more organic to early Runet culture and its users, the Instagram posting of Ramzan Kadyrov, longtime head of the volatile Chechen Republic in the North Caucasus, suggests an entirely different strategy for modeling the language of power: enlisting the multimedia potential of the platform to project an appealing portrait of the authoritarian leader directly. Absent the presence of Putin himself on social media, Kadyrov's active use of Instagram from 2013 up until the time the platform blocked his account in December 2017, offered one of the more compelling examples of how an authoritarian leader could broadcast his message and promote his brand to his most ardent followers and more conventional users alike ("Kak Kadyrova" 2017).

While he may have been new to social media when first opening his account, Kadyrov's authoritarian track record had by then become well established. Putin appointed him president of the republic in 2007, three years after the assassination of Kadyrov's father and former president, Akhmat, and proceeded to pour billions into rebuilding the region after years of fractious war with the Russian military and look the other way as Kadyrov used an iron fist to ensure control in the region.[13] By 2016 Kadyrov controlled a local army of close to 30,000 troops—"Kadyrovites" (*kadyrovtsy*) as they're known—sworn in loyalty

---

13. Between 2007 and 2015, the Russian Federation invested an estimated 464 billion rubles in subsidies to Chechnya and accounted for an estimated 80 percent of the Chechen regional budget (Iashin 2016).

to Putin (and, implicitly, to Kadyrov himself) and battle ready, be it for duty in Syria, Ukraine, or wherever the commanders in chief dictate (Iashin 2016). In addition to being accused of torture and linked to a series of high-profile political assassinations, he has effectively muzzled all significant independent media in Chechnya, regularly appears on Chechen television publicly shaming citizens who have run afoul of his values system, and labels members of the Russian opposition "jackals," "satanists," and "enemies of the people." At the same time, like over 90 percent of Chechens, Kadyrov is a devout Muslim; his father, in addition to being president, was also a mufti, and both father and son promoted a moderate brand of Sufism.

When first adopting the Instagram platform, Kadyrov pointed to its democratic potential when explaining its allure: "It's actually a very useful thing. I now have the opportunity to monitor public opinion in real time" (Elder 2013). A closer qualitative examination of four months of posts to @Kadyrov_95 in 2015 and 2016 shows concerted effort to project a combination of leadership traits that brake roughly along Max Weber's (1921/1978) tripartite delineation of authority.[14] We see the legal-rational leader, meeting with ministers and presiding over cabinet meetings; we see the traditional leader bestowing pearls of Muslim wisdom; and we see the charismatic leader calling upon his followers to ignore, if not condemn, the written law when it compromises a higher set of unwritten rules. Weber himself recognized that these ideal types were by no means mutually exclusive, and in the case of Kadyrov, they were quite complementary: the medium itself contributed to their successful fusion. He cut a charismatic profile, as was widely acknowledged in the popular press, but did so largely by harnessing new media technologies to channel the image of an action-oriented leader and values firmly rooted in traditional authority. In this case, that authority came from a curious amalgam of piety and bellicosity.[15] In terms of thematic content, four dominant profiles of the leader emerge from the posts examined: Kadyrov as executive (37 percent), Kadyrov as faithful Muslim (19 percent), Kadyrov as family man (16 percent), and Kadyrov as sportsman (16 percent).[16]

---

14. The core data for this study comes from four months of posts—June–July 2015 and April–May 2016—at @Kadyrov_95. During that time, Kadyrov posted 755 times for an average of 6.2 posts per day, all of which were examined in their entirety by the author for purposes of this analysis.

15. Rodina and Dligach (2019) offer a different perspective on the impact of Kadyrov's Instagram activity, arguing that it is a combination of the personal and the political that generates a sense of "authenticity" underlying his populist self-presentation (which they also suggest, in passing, is charismatic).

16. Cf. Rodina and Dligach (2019), whose topic modeling of just over three years of posts was based on twenty-five topics.

Executive Authority

Posts featuring Kadyrov in an executive capacity accounted for 37 percent of the total. Some featured the traditional one-on-one, across-the-table encounters commonly used at the federal level to mark the executive's status as one who was both informed and demanding of accountability (fig. 7.2).[17] Of the various meeting genres, Kadyrov tended to prefer the larger committee format to the one-on-one meeting, possibly underscoring his head-of-state status (fig. 7.3).[18] In either case, the accompanying text to these posts featured a mastery of the language of the competent, forward-thinking executive: "The time has come to work in a new way, look twenty years ahead, and think about how to attract investments capable of ensuring a leading role for Chechnya among the more economically developed regions of Russia."[19]

FIGURE 7.2.   Screenshot of Kadyrov meeting with Chechen mufti Salakh Mezhiev.

17. 10 June 2015, https://instagram.com/p/3wWTQciRsy. Unless otherwise noted, all references refer to Kadyrov's official Instagram account, @kadyrov_95. Due to the aforementioned closure of the account in 2017 by Instagram, none of the links to individual pages work at the time of this writing. Screenshots were collected by the author over the course of the autumn of 2016.

18. 21 July 2015, https://instagram.com/p/5aVNFfCRku.

19. Given Kadyrov's notoriously poor mastery of Russian, there is little doubt that these posts were drafted by members of his media team.

Instagram   Q Search

kadyrov_95   **FOLLOWING**

16.5k likes   12w

kadyrov_95 Ассаламу алайкум. Сегодня вечером провёл совещание с руководителями министерств и ведомств. Я всегда говорил и сейчас повторяю, что наше правительство состоит из профессионалов, способных грамотно и оперативно решать самые сложные задачи развития экономики и социальной сферы. Однако, потенциал используется не в полной мере. Я высказал целый ряд критических замечаний в адрес министров здравоохранения, труда, занятости и социального развития, образования и науки, физической культуры и спорта, а также культуры. Сегодня республика вступила в совершенно новую стадию своего развития. Пришло время работать по-новому, заглядывать на 15-20 лет вперед, думать, как привлечь инвестиции, способные обеспечить ведущую роль Чечни среди наиболее

♡   Add a comment…   ● ● ●

FIGURE 7.3.   Screenshot of Kadyrov chairing meeting of heads of Chechen Republic ministries.

Far more common in Kadyrov's visual repertoire was the genre of the site visit, which more readily promoted the image of an executive who got things done. In most cases, the underlying narrative involved Kadyrov taking a direct hand in the transformation of Chechnya from a war-torn region to a twenty-first-century development miracle. He doled out instructions at the site of a world-class Olympic facility (fig. 7.4).[20] He received an on-site update on the construction of an international special-forces training center (fig. 7.5).[21] He took his Mercedes SUV for a test drive on the track of a new speedway on the outskirts of the Chechen capital Grozny (fig. 7.6)[22] and oversaw the construction of numerous roads, schools, mosques, and public parks.

Although reproduced here in still format, nearly all posts featured short, looping video clips—fitting for Kadyrov's world, which was seldom static and quite often over-the-top dynamic. If most dignitaries elected to travel to outlying regions in the comfort of their chauffeur-driven vehicles, for instance, Kadyrov was as inclined to mount his Harley to make an impromptu inspec-

20. 25 July 2015, https://instagram.com/p/5kWEDECRps.
21. 9 June 2015, https://instagram.com/p/3uGlG3CRkZ/.
22. 23 June 2016, https://instagram.com/p/4Smz44CRuA.

kadyrov_95   FOLLOWING

16.2k likes   11w

kadyrov_95 Дорогие друзья! Чеченская Республика постепенно выходит на ведущие позиции по подготовке спортсменов мирового уровня. Чемпионов мира и Европы уже не сосчитать. Но задача ставится воспитать чемпионов и призёров олимпиад. Для этого мы создаём прекрасные условия. В субботу я ознакомился с ходом строительства многофункционального спортивного зала. Он находится в Гудермесе. В настоящее время работы вступили в завершающую стадию. Зал рассчитан на тренировочные сборы спортсменов на завершающей стадии подготовки к чемпионатам, олимпиадам, престижным кубкам. Причём они будут изолированы от внешнего мира, проживать рядом в специальных домах. По нашим наблюдениям выездные сборы не всегда дают должного результата.

Add a comment...

FIGURE 7.4.   Screenshot of Kadyrov visit to Olympic training facility (video).

kadyrov_95   FOLLOWING

16.4k likes   17w

kadyrov_95 Мы быстрыми темпами ведем строительство Международного учебного центра сил специального назначения. Сегодня я в очередной раз посетил объект и остался доволен увиденным. Пояснения давал помощник Главы ЧР Даниил Мартынов. На площади около 300 га, где ранее была заболоченная территория, одновременно возводятся стрелковый комплекс, тактический город, дайвинг-центр, здание для теоретической подготовки, аэродинамический комплекс и многое другое. Темпы работ и качество хорошие. Также будет оборудован зал с большим макетом горно-лесистой местности. Здесь будет находиться пульт оперативной связи со всеми правоохранительными структурами Чечни. Финансируется полет путем привлечения инвестиций. #Кадыров #Россия #Чечня #Спецназ

Add a comment...

FIGURE 7.5.   Screenshot of Kadyrov site visit at special operations training facility construction site (video).

Instagram   Search

kadyrov_95   FOLLOWING

20.7k likes   15w

kadyrov_95 Дорогие друзья! Скажу по
секрету, что я взял отпуск. Но мой
отпуск отличается от остального
времени тем, что работать приходится
еще больше. Сегодня я проверил, как
обстоят дела на строящемся в
Заводском районе Грозного автодроме.
Это большой инвестиционный проект.
Автодром строится на месте заводских
развалин. Надо отметить, что размах
впечатляет. На территории почти 60
гектаров расположились картодром,
автокросс, сафари с прямой и
кольцевой трассами. Всего пять трасс,
отвечающих лучшим мировым
стандартам. Комплекс не имеет
аналогов в России. Убедился, что
картодром практически готов, а все
остальные объекты в стадии
завершения работ. Куратор стройки
первый вице-премьер правительства
Иса Тумхаджиев сообщил, что в августе

Add a comment...

FIGURE 7.6.   Screenshot of Kadyrov test drive of new racing speedway (video).

tion tour (fig. 7.7).[23] (Like his mentor in the Kremlin, Kadyrov is an honorary member of the patriotic biking gang Night Wolves—leader of the local Chechen chapter, in fact ["Ramzan Kadyrov stal" 2015].) While most elected officials deemed the hard hat and shovel sufficient for a photo op at a groundbreaking ceremony, Kadyrov preferred to get behind the controls of the heavy machinery himself. ("Glory to Allah," he notes, "the machinery turned out to be responsive" [fig. 7.8].)[24]

In one July 2015 post, Kadyrov channeled his inner Putin in a different executive manner when he dressed down a local official for littered streets and forced him to take broom in hand to "take part in the manual labor."[25] Not even Putin, though, would exercise his executive accountability practices in the boxing ring, as Kadyrov did in April 2013 when displeased with the Chechen minister of sport for the dilapidated appearance of his ministry building: "As promised, I conducted an instructional conversation in the ring with

---

23. 27 June 2015, https://instagram.com/p/4csUFYCRtF/.

24. 11 July 2015, https://instagram.com/p/5AXUEqCRrC/.

25. 24 July 2015, https://instagram.com/p/5iFFbUiRrG/. The incident was reminiscent of Putin's own famous dressing-down of oligarch Oleg Deripaska in a televised meeting during the then-prime minister's visit to Pikalyovo, Russia, where factories idled by the metals tycoon had led to worker protests (Zagoruyko 2009).

FIGURE 7.7. Screenshot of Kadyrov motorcycle outing to outskirts of Chechen capital, Grozny (video).

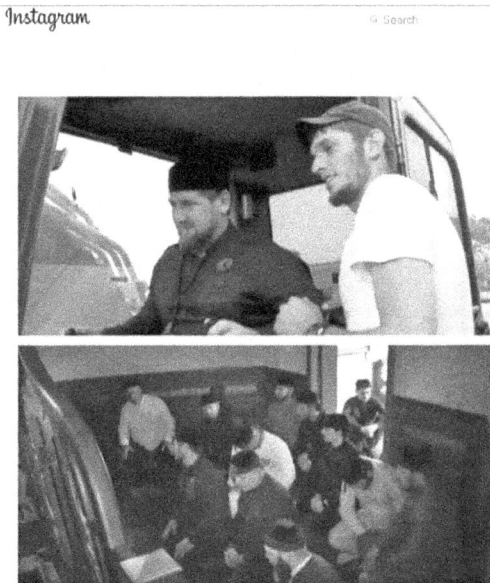

FIGURE 7.8. Screenshot of Kadyrov at the controls of a construction excavator (video).

the Minister of Physical Education and Sports. Over the course of our dialogue (or rather, sparring), I gently and unobtrusively—with a hook from the right and the left—explained to him . . . that he needed to use his head on the job" (quoted in Ponamareva 2013).

In a certain sense, this sort of bravado can be seen as a charismatic gesture, flaunting convention to mete out a self-styled form of punishment. But on another level, the hypermasculine disciplinary behavior flows directly from a strong strain of traditional authority that dominates the cultural and religious dimensions of Kadyrov's Instagram world, and models an action-oriented and masculine code characteristic of Putinism.

Traditional Authority: Sport, Faith, and Masculinity

The prominence of this traditional strain also explains the initially perplexing consistency with which Kadyrov devoted attention to two seemingly contradictory preoccupations: fighting and prayer. Sports themes were featured in 119, or 16 percent, of the posts. Particularly central was Kadyrov's passion for boxing and mixed martial arts, which manifested itself on a variety of levels.

He was the founder of the Akhmat Fight Club, named after his father, which trained Chechnya's leading pugilists in a world-class facility in Grozny

FIGURE 7.9. Screenshot of announcement of MMA fight hosted by league named after Kadyrov's father.

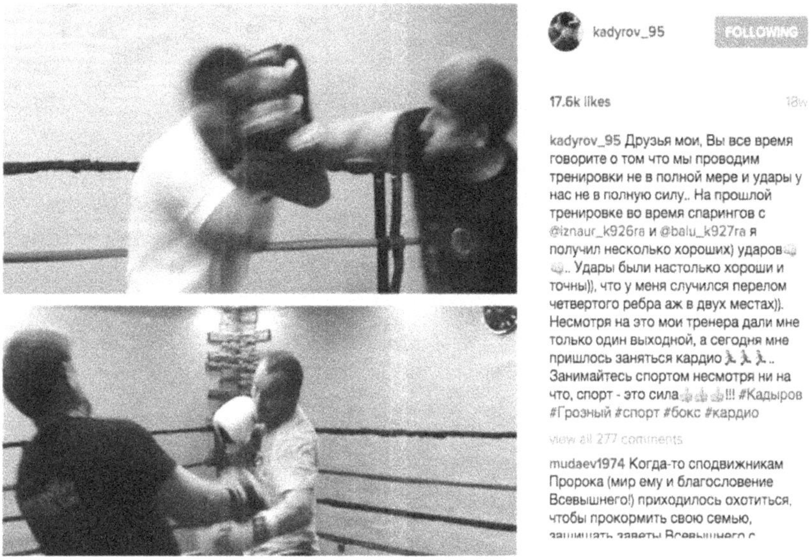

kadyrov_95   FOLLOWING

17.6k likes   18w

kadyrov_95 Друзья мои, Вы все время
говорите о том что мы проводим
тренировки не в полной мере и удары у
нас не в полную силу.. На прошлой
тренировке во время спарингов с
@iznaur_k926ra и @balu_k927ra я
получил несколько хороших) ударов
.. Удары были настолько хороши и
точны)), что у меня случился перелом
четвертого ребра аж в двух местах)).
Несмотря на это мои тренера дали мне
только один выходной, а сегодня мне
пришлось заняться кардио .. .. ..
Занимайтесь спортом несмотря ни на
что, спорт - это сила.. .. .. !!! #Кадыров
#Грозный #спорт #бокс #кардио

view all 277 comments

mudaev1974 Когда-то сподвижникам
Пророка (мир ему и благословение
Всевышнего!) приходилось охотиться,
чтобы прокормить свою семью,
защищать заветы Всевышнего с

FIGURE 7.10. Screenshot of Kadyrov in boxing ring taking serious blows from his sparring partner (video).

(fig. 7.9).[26] He regularly hosted fighters from around the world and was Chechnya's biggest cheerleader when one of its own was competing on the international stage.[27] As seen with the sports minister, Kadyrov himself got in the ring regularly and, at least according to one post, was not doing it solely for show (fig. 7.10). "So good and precise were the blows," he noted, "that I fractured my fourth rib, in two places even. Despite this my trainer only gave me one day off, and today I had to do cardio. Do sports no matter what—sport is strength!!!"[28]

Kadyrov realized his inner sportsman and warrior in other ways as well: in late-night soccer matches ("It's the game of real men, beautiful and noble"[29]); at folk festivals celebrating traditional expressions of male prowess;[30] by dressing in traditional costume, as in this dzhigit outfit he sported in a photo with his minister of property and land relations (fig. 7.11);[31] or the suit of armor he donned for a full-scale palace celebration of Chechen culture.[32]

26. 26 July 2015, https://instagram.com/p/5mPYzyCRhy.
27. n.d., https://instagram.com/p/5pbhXFiRrq/.
28. 6 June 2015, https://instagram.com/p/3mqHn-CRrK.
29. 30 January 2014, https://instagram.com/p/4XvBleiRsH.
30. 14 June 2015, https://instagram.com/p/36txyXiRrr.
31. 31 May 2015, https://instagram.com/p/3XCd0XCRo2.
32. n.d., https://www.instagram.com/p/BKqHtn3hFx8/.

FIGURE 7.11. Screenshot of Kadyrov with Chechen minister of property and land relations, dressed in traditional dzhigit garb.

His fidelity to traditional Chechen values echoed from his comments to that post, appropriately calibrated in a loftier register:

> Dear Friends! Religion, traditions, customs, language, culture, and history are the basis, the foundation for the strength and durability of each nation. In losing these, a nation ceases to be a unified nation, capable of preserving itself.... Recognizing this, I have, from the very beginning set the goal of bringing about the revival [*vozrozhdenie*] and preservation of truly popular [*narodnye*] traditions, language and culture, and inculcating respect and love for them by the younger generation and all inhabitants.... The Caucasus is the bulwark [*oplot*] of our Great Russia! And the Chechen nation, as one of the largest indigenous nations of Russia, played and plays an important role in the defense of the Fatherland—Russia![33]

With few exceptions, these exhibitions of tribal strength featured the male members of the clan, as in the evening feast Kadyrov hosted for the boys from the

---

33. cf. his reference to the movie *The Magic Crown*, in which Kadyrov himself played a leading part: "The film shows how beautifully our ancestors lived, how respectfully they treated one another, how splendidly they took in guests, loved to labor, and raised true warriors, brave youths" ("Ramzan Kadyrov sygral" 2015).

Akhmat Fight Club, featuring the Chechen bard Sharpudi Izmailov singing his hit single "Male Friendship Is Like a Rock" ("Muzhskaia druzhba kak skala").[34] This also explains the attention he devoted to his three sons, Akhmat, Eli, and Adam, who regularly figured into their father's training sessions, and participate in martial arts demonstrations of their own.[35] In a February 2017 post, Kadyrov threaded themes of fighting, family, masculinity, and heritage in an elegy to the clenched fist:

> DEAR SON! We have preserved the heritage of our ancestors like a price-less pearl of unflagging Wisdom, passing it along from generation to gen-eration. For us, carriers of the ancient fighting spirit of watchtowers, an open-handed slap to the face was absolutely unacceptable in any fight, even of an everyday kind. The mountain dweller deprived of his Honor by a slap could not return It even with the fatal blow of a sharpened sword. A strong FIST is at times handier than a sword. This I tell you for your edification. Now, clench your fists, dear son . . . Look at them closely. You must be proud of THEM, if THEY are adorned with callouses. Remem-ber! These are expressive markings of hard work in training, they are elo-quent symbols of your masculine "I." . . . If you do not plan to use THEM to wipe away tears, then they are a noble and the most reliable weapon for the defense of your Honor, Dignity, Family and People.[36]

It is only natural that boys who trained on the mat by day would transition to more modern warfare by night, as seen in this post of a surprise nighttime battle-readiness test (which they passed) (fig. 7.12).[37]

It's only natural, in Kadyrov's charismatic world, that a national leader inclined to seek the limelight and realize his warrior ways should agree to take the lead role in a more contemporary action-adventure film called "Whoever doesn't get it, will" (*Kto ne ponial, tot poimet*), the announcement and trailer for which appeared in a May 2015 post (fig. 7.13).[38]

This image of himself as a warrior had deep roots in Kadyrov's public self-fashioning, dating back at least to a 2004 interview by Anna Politkovskaya, in

34. 12 June 2015, https://instagram.com/p/32XmUAiRmI.

35. 31 May 2015, https://instagram.com/p/3XfMPGiRgC.

36. February 2017, https://www.instagram.com/p/BQWVn3bgWLb/?hl=en. Seven years later, a sixteen-year-old Adam would earn global notoriety for taking his father's advice to heart, when, in a Telegram message posted by his father, he was shown ruthlessly beating a man who had been arrested for setting fire to the Koran (Istomin 2023). For an in depth investigation into the power and wealth amassed by Kadyrov and the role his children play in taking over as his health fails, see "Vozvrashchenie" 2025.

37. 28 September 2015, https://instagram.com/p/8MRXOzCRnDWdBZeVPJiIFYOKZzmbfVjfx 76cU0/?taken-by=kadyrov_95.

38. 25 May 2015, https://instagram.com/p/3G06hziRmd/.

FIGURE 7.12. Screenshot of Kadyrov boys out on a nocturnal military training exercise (video).

FIGURE 7.13. Screenshot from trailer to action film starring Kadyrov (video).

which, when asked what sort of activity he most liked engaging in, he answered, "Fighting. I am a warrior" (Politkovskaia 2004).

Kadyrov's Instagram persona took on complementary traditional hues in the posts featuring female members of his family. His wife, whom he referred to by the more formal first name and patronymic—Medni Musaevna—was praised for her piety, childrearing skills, and love of gardening; his daughters, for their studies, their help around the house, and their knowledge of the Koran.[39] Nearly every

---

39. n.d., https://instagram.com/p/3hCmJ3CRp_; n.d., https://instagram.com/p/5FrOeXiRo7/. If independent reporting is accurate, Kadyrov's traditional family values did not include monogamy, given that, at the time this writing, he was reported to have at least fourteen children by at least four women, including his wife (Badanin and Maglov 2024).

female family member's birthday was marked with a Kadyrov-sized bouquet of flowers.[40] Depictions of these family bonds sometimes doubled as a means of underscoring the patrilineal order of Chechen politics—as in a reposted post by Kadyrov's brother explaining the reverence held by his sons for Uncle Ramzan: "The boys attentively listen to the guidance and advice of their dear UNCLE and follow them strictly. After all, his word for them is law."[41]

Equally as central to Kadyrov's public image as sportsman, warrior, and family man was the image of the faithful Muslim. Again, it might at first seem contradictory, if not for the common ground they shared as bulwarks of traditional authority. In fact, this religious face constituted the second largest number—30 percent—of the posts from the period examined. The very byline of his account ("Love the Prophet, say your prayers!") spoke to the devotional dimension. Visually, followers witnessed, on a nearly daily basis, Kadyrov at prayer (fig. 7.14).

Perched among fellow worshippers, reciting prayers, prayer beads between fingers, he clearly looked to muftis and imams as spiritual authorities and dutifully transmitted their messages to his own followers. In one post he wrote, "In his sermon Imam Aslan Abdulaev talked about how slander and malicious gossip are great sins. He reminded us that Islam sharply condemns slander and gossip,

FIGURE 7.14.   Screenshot of Kadyrov at morning prayer session (video).

40. 4 July 2015, https://instagram.com/p/4uPj_WiRkY/.

41. 26 June 2015, https://instagram.com/p/4agAPDiRiW. This patrilineal order, in fact, has presented Kadyrov with a succession challenge, according to independent reporting, given that superior administrative acumen has been displayed mainly by his eldest daughter, Aishat ("Vozvrashchenie" 2025).

suspiciousness, since these sins lead to enmity between people, [and] destroy society from within."[42]

At times, however, the sermon seemed to come directly from Kadyrov himself (who was, in fact, the son of a mufti), as in a June 2015 post where he wrote,

> Peace be with you! Religious leaders in their sermons often talk about how he who contemplates evil and committing sin must choose a place where he won't be noticed by Allah. In so doing, they remind us that there is no place in the world that will remain a secret for even the smallest misdeed or sin. In the holy Koran it is said, 'do you not know that Allah is aware both of that which is in the heavens and that which is on earth?' There can be no secret conversation among three, where He is not a fourth; or among five where he is not a sixth. . . . Verily [*voistine*], Allah knows about everything.[43]

The medium in any case positioned Kadyrov as a religious focal point, either the purveyor or the central recipient of spiritual truths.[44] While the very act of posting images of oneself at prayer may on the surface come across as self-promotional, Kadyrov may also have been using the multimedia capabilities of Instagram to promote a more moderate and popular strain of Islam (Fuller and Doukaev 2007). The regular overlaying of musical audio tracks to the prayer clips certainly suggests as much. And how else might one explain the bizarre post of Kadyrov out on a bike ride with Mufti Salakh-Khadzhi Mezhiev (fig. 7.15)?[45]

More overt commentary against the Islamic State and like-minded radical organizations in the context of religious posts made the point more directly: Chechnya and Kadyrov were solidly grounded in the Muslim faith, one in which there was no place for "Wahabbists":

> This is an exclusively virulent evil. It must be pulled out by its core, roots and all. . . . I once again declare [*snova zaiavliaiu*] that there is no place for them in Chechnya, nor will there be. . . . May the almighty Allah set these wayward ones on a path of truth![46]

Charismatic Authority: Kadyrov Above the Law

In fact, when we consider the more controversial episodes that brought Kadyrov squarely into the public eye, they often involved this sort of declaration, echoing

---

42. 5 June 2015, https://instagram.com/p/3i9bR7iRjo/.
43. 5 June 2015, http://grammio.com/en/kadyrov_95/3iph6MCRrC/.
44. 3 July 2015, https://instagram.com/p/4swBiNiRu5/.
45. 24 June 2015, https://instagram.com/p/4UQDKuiRgq.
46. 7 July 2015, https://instagram.com/p/41L580iRlu.

FIGURE 7.15.   Screenshot of Kadyrov riding bikes with Mufti Mezhiev (video).

the classic Weberian discursive marker of charismatic authority, "It is written . . . , but I say to you" (Weber 1978, 243). And we frequently find him bucking legal-rational institutions out of fidelity to either traditional or clan authority. It was not by accident that it was this mode of charismatic authority to which Kadyrov turned in some of his more controversial moments in the national limelight. He thus defended his Chechen associate Zaur Dadaev, who had come under suspicion for the assassination of the former deputy prime minister and then oppositional leader Boris Nemtsov: "I knew Zaur as a true patriot of Russia . . . one of the most fearless and brave service men of the division. I'm firmly convinced that he is sincerely devoted to Russia, and was ready to give up his life for his Motherland."[47] He likewise invoked charismatic authority when, days later, he posted a clip of himself taking target practice with his gold-plated pistol at a "virtual shooting range" (with video footage of real "human targets").[48] And he appealed to it when, in response to an April 2015 incident in which neighboring Stavropol' police gunned down a Chechen national on Chechen territory, Kadyrov gave orders on state television to his own internal forces to open fire on any

---

47. 3 August 2015), https://instagram.com/p/z-dKqICRuaRoyxHemuCiZHnIftKEAVo5P09_Y0/.

48. 3 September 2015, https://instagram.com/p/0BQp8CCRmzoT780qszNm_qqVeC5hPVHG6lMn00.

federal security officers operating on Chechen soil without advance notification: "I officially declare to you that, if on your territory without your knowledge there appears a Muscovite, a Stavropolian—it doesn't matter, you are to shoot to kill. We must be reckoned with" ("Glava Chechni" 2015).

Beyond these charismatic declarations, there was a more rational, medium-related reason behind Kadyrov's phenomenal Instagram success. For starters, the camera angles, constant flow of fresh footage, audio tracks, and clean editing all suggested a considerable amount of professional work invested in the endeavor by a team of media specialists around Kadyrov (who was nearly always the main protagonist and subject of his own posts). He understood the medium in another, more important sense, as well: People spent time on the internet far more for the purposes of entertainment than politics. Kadyrov, whose charismatic and at times idiosyncratic personality predated his foray into Russian social networks, gave plenty of cause for people to follow him and like his posts. And a closer, more sustained look at Kadyrov's Instagram shows there to be a relatively coherent effort at self-fashioning and messaging that went beyond self-promotion and glitz.

As with his mentor in the Kremlin, Kadyrov received most press coverage when he was at his most brazen or exotic—posing with wild animals, calling out enemies with colorful language and thinly veiled threats, and bucking expectations as to what constitutes proper decorum for a head of state. But the Kadyrov of Instagram was at root a devout believer and consummate warrior, unafraid of meting out punishment that at times spilled over into clan justice, and it was from these largely traditional roots—recast through the multimedia capabilities of modern technology—that the charismatic figure was forged. It was a fusion, moreover, perfectly suited not only for a postwar Chechnya but for a post-Crimea Russia keen on reestablishing its own imperial might and civilizational values.

It should be of little surprise, then, that Putin has given Kadyrov relatively free rein—not just as a mini-Putin, but also a self-described "foot-soldier" (of Putin) and effective leader, able to enlist modern-day technologies (both digital and political) to project an image and message that not only ensured stability in Russia's most fragile region but promoted patriotism, traditional spiritual and civilizational values, and staunch loyalty to Putin as well—traits that would come to drive Putin's own rhetoric with increasing intensity over the second decade of his rule.

Institute for "Positive Content"

For all their differences, Minaev and Kadyrov represented highly personalized models of authoritarian discourse on the Runet—the former through his reputation as budding writer and internet bad boy, the latter through his bona fides as a traditional, charismatic leader. Certainly, they helped generate positive spin for Putin-style authoritarianism among the online community, but their contributions were limited if not in number of posts and views (in Minaev's case), then in the coordination of their messaging (Kadyrov was largely a solo operator who generated enthusiasm for his *own* charismatic authority first and foremost). The subject of this third case study allows us to look at what happens when Kremlin operatives try to establish a more direct and sustained control over Runet policy and content on the institutional level. The vehicle for doing so was the Institute for the Development of the Internet (Institute razvitiia interneta, henceforth IDI), created in 2015, and its evolution from a largely regulatory body to a generously budgeted overseer of what came to be called "positive content." An analysis of its structure, activities, and output offers insight into Kremlin efforts at influencing digital content beyond its more familiar levers of disruption and regulation.

Industry Liaison or "Spoiled Institute"?

In many ways, the history of the IDI mirrored the trajectory of state and state-affiliated institutes grappling with a new information sphere that largely lay beyond the control of authorities. The impetus for the institute's creation came initially from Viacheslav Volodin, then first deputy chief of staff of the presidential administration. Its "charter members" had close ties to the state apparatus as well.[49] As for its mission, press coverage of the institute's launch in 2015 indicated that the internet had developed to such an extent that it was high time a structure be created that "modeled a more effective dialogue between representatives of internet business and the state" (Bogdanov 2015). The "dialogue," it was made clear, was to acknowledge the fact that "the Runet, to a large extent, had become a national interest for the state."[50] Nonetheless, the IDI, its members, and Putin himself described the group in its publicity as an "expert organization," the voice of the business and IT community, and a communicative intermediary: "We help the dialogue between industry, the state, and society," as they stated on the home page of their website ("IRI" n.d.).

---

49. In addition to the Russian Ministry of Science and Higher Education, the oversight board included representatives from the Foundation for the Development of Internet Initiatives (FRII) (itself a brainchild of Vladimir Putin [Bogdanov 2015]), the Russian Association of Electronic Communication (RAEK), the telecommunications giant MKS, and ROTsIT (a "regional public organization" for internet technology).

50. Leonid Levin, one of the appointed codirectors (and himself a Duma deputy and chair of the Duma's Committee on Information Policy), further identified the goal of the institute as "bringing about the 'digital sovereignty' of the country" (Bogdanov 2015).

Early signs of tension within the institute brought to bear the conflicting priorities: While industry leaders prioritized reducing burdensome legislation and red tape and enlisting the state's support in their competition with foreign competitors, the state stressed security and national sovereignty. Under the pretense of greater inside access, Putin himself suggested the head of the IDI be designated "presidential adviser" and brought directly into the Kremlin, explaining that it was "essential for them to have 'one of their own inside' state structures" (Nagornykh and Rozhkov 2015). More critical observers at the time interpreted the appointment as the latest manifestation of Putin's "hybrid regime," an attempt to "create new mediating structures that would submit to the logic of the 'spoiled institute.'" On the one hand, such a mediator must pretend to consider the opinions of society and convey the positions of concrete social groups to power structures [*vlastnye struktury*]. On the other hand, he must serve as a cover for unpopular decisions made by those authorities" (Komin 2016). In short, the essential goal appeared to be to create a systemic public sphere for the internet business community that would, when necessary, carry water for the Kremlin.

The adviser duties fell first to the programmer and tech entrepreneur German Klimenko, who fulfilled the "spoiling" function to script, promptly calling for a complete overhaul to the "road maps" that had been in the works for months, to ensure they were more in line with the views of the government (Rusiaeva et al. 2015). Over the course of his two-and-a-half-year tenure, Klimenko would go on to advocate for isolating the Russian sector of the internet, outlawing internet anonymity, and shutting down recalcitrant social networking platforms, to name just a few of the controversial issues he embraced as the Kremlin's "industry spokesperson" (Samokhin 2016; Borodina and Kashevarova 2015; Turovskii 2018; "German Klimenko" 2016). As for the promised "insider" access to the president? This privilege proved more elusive, as reports on the eve of his ouster in May 2018 suggested Klimenko had only met with Putin once during his term (Ivanov et al. 2018). In purely practical terms, however, the perpetual redrawing of "road maps" confirms more recent critical accounts of the IDI, which suggest it was heavy on the optics of state engagement in the internet but light on concrete results. As one industry player put it, "I was always left with the feeling that it was a sort of imitation of frenzied activity that had little practical sense" (quoted in Reiter et al. 2023). Essentially, early advocates of the IDI were card-carrying members of obshchestvennost' with an official spokesperson as a budgeted state worker, happy to toe the party line in exchange for social status and financial security. The degree to which they actually represented, let alone influenced, policy or public opinion remained questionable.

Promoting Virtual Patriotism

The institute received a new lease on life when, in 2016, Sergei Kirienko assumed Volodin's position as first deputy chief of the presidential administration and brought in Aleksei Goreslavskii to curate the internet portfolio. Officially a "deputy director of the management of public projects," Goreslavskii brought to the position a distinguished track record as online disruptor of the political opposition and implementer of pro-Putin media. His web-based media presence dated back to a stint as editor in chief of the online journal *Vzgliad*, rubbing virtual elbows with scumbag entrepreneurs Rykov and Kononenko. Goreslavskii made an even more pronounced name for himself in the Runet media sphere when he was tapped to take over the highly respected (and independent) news website *Lenta.ru* after the forced removal of its founder and editor in chief, Galina Timchenko, and bringing it more in line with state outlets.[51] He then served as a senior manager at the Kremlin-friendly search engine, Rambler. In short, by the time he arrived at the IDI, Goreslavskii was well established as a "system" player well versed in the quickly evolving industry of web-based news, information, and communication.

Once revived, the institute established a remarkably wide footprint on internet-related matters in the halls of power. More notably, it assumed a more nuanced approach to dealings with the Runet, with a stronger emphasis (at least publicly) on shaping it with a combination of objectively useful tools and services and promoting content that, if not serving the direct ideological interests of the state, then at least not did not fly in the face of those interests. Some initiatives seemed a direct respond to concrete public needs, such as the proposal to come up with uniform standards for disabled users or the effort to authorize ordering and receiving prescription medicine online (Krivoshapko et al. 2019; Pichugina 2019). Others harkened to Medvedev-era efforts to bring regional bureaucrats online. In early 2019, for example, the institute was "improving the digital literacy of bureaucrats in the regions" by helping them navigate the world of social networks, maintain Facebook and Instagram, and even establish anonymous Telegram accounts (Antonova 2019). In contrast to Medvedev-era initiatives, however, this iteration of official digitalization demonstrated a more sober set of expectations, regarding not only the capabilities of the bureaucrats but also their obligations to the networked public. Instructions on "the proper creation of official communities of regions on social networks" viewed the internet less as a tool for engaging one's constituents than a means of fabricating more sympathetic

---

51. Timchenko and many of her associates would go on to found the widely respected Meduza news agency, based in Riga, Latvia.

publics. "Experts" from the institute warned officials that web-based ills such as cybercrime and fake news would increasingly threaten citizens' (and particularly children's) security in coming years, if measures weren't taken (Lemutkina 2019), and provided government agencies with lists of domestic apps, vetted by its experts, capable of replacing foreign products that legislators sought to supplant in the large-scale "import replacement" effort (Tishina and Lebedeva 2019).

With a new charge and replenished coffers, the institute burst back into the limelight of content generation in November 2019, when it was selected by Ros-molodezh' to serve as the coordination center for "the production of socially sig-nificant content for youth"—content aimed at strengthening their "civic identity and spiritual and moral values" [*grazhdanskaia identichnost' i dukhovno-nravst-vennye tsennosti*]. Authorities allocated 2.4 billion rubles for the project, a consid-erable sum comparable to the amount of state funding for the film industry for the same period, and forced oligarchs close to the Kremlin to match funds (Reiter et al. 2023; Parfent'eva and Astafurova 2019). Beyond the need for "socially sig-nificant" content, few restrictions were placed on either themes or media used. According to one source close to the Kremlin at the time, "It could be anything at all—video, audio, web series, podcasts, social media projects, educational pro-grams. Themes could also vary, beginning with national projects [*natsproekty*] and ending with the celebration of next year's 75th anniversary of Victory [Day]. But the decision would be made by the oversight committee. The main thing is for the state to be able to talk to youth on topical issues in a language comprehen-sible to them" (Galimova 2019).

Despite the publicized state funding and the fact that Kirienko himself would serve as chair of the initiative's oversight committee, the Kremlin operative insisted, "This was not a state order for the production of internet content, where some bureaucrats determine what they want and send out corresponding requi-sitions. We are counting on the fact that the support will also be directed to the development of projects by market leaders. One of the goals of the state here is to support domestic players [and] create conditions for competitiveness for them" (Parfent'eva and Astafurova 2019).

The generous ruble amount of the initiative was augmented by vocal support from prominent cultural leaders, such as the blockbuster film director Timur Bek-mambetov, who welcomed the program as a long-needed "civilizing" of a digital sphere, particularly for young users, which "had no norms [or] rules of behavior" and created "an enormous amount of fear and stress" (quoted in "Milliardy" 2019). The state initiative, Bekmambetov continued, "should set the goal of helping Rus-sian users, including youth, reflect on their lives in the new digital space and make sense of the new reality, with the help of stories such as the great masterpieces of literature that are accessible to everyone" (quoted in "Milliardy" 2019).

That same summer, in July 2021, the IDI announced another competition, this one with 3 billion rubles earmarked, for developing web-based youth content as a part of the "digital culture" federal project.[52] Another 7 billion went toward the development of spiritual and moral digital content for youth ("Chinovniki" 2021). As with previous initiatives, Kirienko served as head of the oversight board, whose responsibility it was to select the two hundred awards by the end of the calendar year ("Chinovniki" 2021). Reactions in the press were skeptical, seeing the initiative as just another opportunity for elites to skim funds from state coffers. In an op-ed piece titled "Virtual Patriotism," Dmitrii Popov argued that, so long as the Russian elite was fixated on money and showed no patriotic inclinations themselves (choosing to vacation abroad, when given the chance), their institutions couldn't possibly generate positive, patriotic models for the next generation: "They could blow a hundred million on them, rather than ten: a patriotism and reality that are virtual will beget just the same—virtuality" (Popov 2021).

Goreslavskii himself acknowledged the difficulty of the task of making content that was both popular and "positive" (presumably from the perspective of the state), noting in a February 2022 interview, "Making positive content [*pozitivnyi kontent*] is hard, and popular *pozitiv* is even harder: it's much easier working with *negativ* [negative content]" (Finalistov 2022). The video game developer Viacheslav Makarov concurred when discussing how the funding might be realized in that lucrative but Western-dominated sector, suggesting that the bar for patriotic content might need to be set considerably lower: "It is acceptable for the foundation to finance games in which the setting . . . is connected to Russia and there are no harsh attacks against the state: 'It would be a lot worse if they were to demand the game be turned into to a political agitation tool, since the market generally ignores projects in which the ideological component takes priority over the quality of the design'" (Korolev 2022).

The Reiter et al. (2023) investigation offers detailed insight into just how the mounds of state money were doled out by the institute to a wide range of projects, some of which had no perceivable "positive content" to speak of, others of which even flew in the face of official state ideology. But rather than fostering "the conditions for competitiveness," as had been the stated rationale for the broadly cast net, the process more closely resembled a network of system players feathering one another's pockets with rubles from the state budget.

The report of winning projects for the first "National Content" competition shows an eclectic mix of content deemed "positive."[53] Although the institute provided submitters with a two-page directive outlining the four "thematic lines"

---

52. The support came despite reservations from Putin confidante and security council chair Nikolai Patrushev about the mismanagement of funds ("3 mlrd rublei" 2021).

53. The following discussion is based on winning proposals from the August–November 2021 submission cycle.

submitters were to address—"Heroes of our days and causes for pride," "Quality changes to life in Russia as a steady trend," "Stable development of the country," and "The defense of national interests and social [*obshchestvennye*] values"—winning proposals suggested at least some degree of flexibility in the types of projects that ultimately received support.[54] At the same time, certain themes and trends do emerge from a closer look at over two-thirds of the 367 proposals funded for the three media categories distinguished ("audiovisual content," "content for social media/messengers," and "special internet projects").[55]

Pushing the boundaries of what might be considered positive, a few proposals made little attempt to hide their anti-Western, blatantly propagandistic orientation—"Problems of the First World" featured negative exposés of the United States, and "Beautiful Russia bla-bla-bla" (*Prekrasnaia Rossiia bu-bu-bu*), sponsored by state-owned RT, featured a web-based talk show dedicated to cultural excesses in the West.[56] A slightly larger group featured lectures on Russian history—some long and decidedly low-tech, such as "Russia's Special Status" (*Osobennaia stat' Rossii* 2021), others more savvy to the shorter attention spans and need for visuals of their online viewing audience, such as "History Notebook" (*Tetradka po istorii* 2022). The creators of "Sleigh Petersburg" (*SANKI Peterburg*, a play on the city name, Sankt Peterburg) opted for a niche theme—popular games enjoyed by Petersburgers through Russian history—and used puppets to bring that history to life (*SANKI Peterburg* 2021).

A far greater portion of the winning projects featured some sort of celebration of the exceptional or inspirational nature of Russia and Russians. Those focusing on the country frequently highlighted the ecological or ethnographic uniqueness of the regions, such as profiles of the subarctic city of Arkhangelsk, "Wealth of Siberia," "The Image of the Russian Village," "Heritage of the Don," and "Russia's Places of Strength" (*Mesta sily Rossii*).[57] Those focusing on the population usually provided portraits of exceptional people—not only notable figures through Russian history, such as "Made in Russia" (a history of Russian inventors and inventions) and "Nobel Laureates of Russia and the USSR" ("Nobelevskie" 2021) but also models of contemporary achievement and exceptionalism: "New society" (a miniseries of environmental discovery and invention, with strong youth presence ["Novoe obshchestvo" 2022]); "Young geniuses, or 'Lefties' [*levshi*] of our

54. A complete list of the proposed "themes and directions" may be viewed by following the appropriate links at "Otbor kontenta" (2021).

55. A complete list of contest winners may be viewed by following the appropriate links at "Arkhiv konkursov" (n.d.).

56. The name of the latter is an ironic reference to the "beautiful Russia of the future" phrase made famous by Navalny during his later political campaigns.

57. *Arkhangl'sk* 2021.

time"; "The Feats [*podvigi*] of Ordinary People" (a podcast five to ten minutes in length telling about real-life episodes of brave feats of courage by average citizens ["Podkast 'podvigi'" 2021]). Underlying most of these was a message that Russians and Russian youth in particular (1) had much to be proud of, (2) had an enormous capacity to create, invent, and change the world for the better, and (3) were actively engaged in such creation, invention, and change. Some among the winners even made an attempt to recognize and address serious challenges young people may be facing in uncertain times, with initiatives bearing titles such as "You're not alone," "I understand you," and "I'm nearby" (*Ia riadom*).

All in all, the institute contest promoted a form of youth engagement grounded in the tradition of obshchestvennost', and more Putin-friendly modes of public expression that privileged national pride and self-betterment over public protest. Rather than turning out to decry corrupt leaders and their ill-gotten wealth, groups such as the nostalgia-tinged "*Timurovtsy* of the 21st century"[58] or the more future-facing outreach activities of the youth group Inspirers (Vdokhnoviteli) invited youth to engage in state-sponsored volunteerism in the interests of the motherland and, in the process, feel good about themselves, join a cohort of healthy, attractive, positive (always smiling) peers, and possibly gain access to opportunities, connections, and career paths that would ensure security and success (*Vdokhnoviteli* n.d.) (fig. 7.16). "Join a large community," implored the website of the Inspirers, "where you can level up [*prokachat'sia*], find like-minded people, and make yourself heard." Rife with industry leaders and happy young faces, the organization's promotional video encouraged would-be members, "Inspiration is already inside of you; now we are together!"

Without access to the ruble amounts granted to specific projects, it is difficult to assess the return on investment these projects produced for the state. Judging by engagement-related data available at their websites and account pages, they covered a broad range of impacts, with some projects producing quite limited content for a small number of viewers (less than a dozen for the "Special Status" history lectures) and others generating a larger, more sustained level of content for a viewer- and followership that numbered in the thousands, and remained active to the time of this writing. From the perspective of public political discourse, however, the initiative is emblematic of how this key player in Putin's systemic public sphere attempted a more nuanced approach to regulating the often-unruly voice of the Runet public. While it continued to have a hand in more aggressive forms of content and domain regulation, as I explore further in

---

58. *Timurovtsy* 2021. The *timurovtsy* were grassroots youth volunteer groups, inspired by a story by the Soviet writer Arkadii Gaidar ("Timur and his team" 1940) that emerged during World War II to engage in local volunteer work and even military partisan activity.

FIGURE 7.16. "You, too, can inspire!" the homepage to the Inspirers' website assures young visitors. Source: Vdokhnoviteli, https://xn–b1aaffobumib0c5a.xn –p1ai/ (accessed 18 December 2024).

chapter 8, the IDI understood that, much as some of its older overseers would have liked, the internet was not a public space that could be entirely closed off or regulated into total submission. A more sustainable approach involved the production of compelling narratives of national pride, public belonging and engagement, and personal happiness and success—narratives that promised all of this through younger citizens' buying into a less politicized and more uplifting systemic public sphere.[59]

Even if the positive content initiative was based on a system prone to financial skimming and slanted toward pro-state ideology, the more hands-off, decentralized approach carried greater promise for having a positive impact on younger users—certainly more than the motivationally suspect and fundamentally restrictive initiatives of the likes of the Safe Internet League. Because it allowed more breathing room for authentic and interesting content that placed as high a priority (if not higher) on affect as it did on ideologically useful content, it more closely approximated the models of digital content generation that had proven more successful in Russia and beyond. And judging from the size of the budget (much to Patrushev's dismay), it's clear the presidential administration recognized that moral-panic-based, regulatory discourses dominating the systemic public sphere

---

59. In this sense, the IDI's approach is more akin to what Zvereva (2020b) calls the pro-Kremlin media sphere's "soft power" approach to online political communication.

carried both limitations and dangers—limitations that state-friendly voices and initiatives would be ignored altogether and dangers that overly strict regulation would lead to pushback by an otherwise apathetic (and proportionally large) swath of the networked citizenry. If Minaev made Putinism more palatable by giving its foes voice and running it through a critical filter (however regulated), and Kadyrov made it charismatically cool while reinforcing traditional, devout, patriotic, and masculine values, the later initiatives of the IDI sought to remove Putin and Putinism from the rhetorical frame explicitly, replacing them with more appealing associations with national pride, beauty, and everyday heroism, laced with a healthy dose of human decency. The degree to which this sort of positive patriotism remained virtual is difficult to gauge. But particularly since the models of positive authority profiled here are neither exhaustive nor mutually exclusive, they suggest a recognition on the part of vlast', whether grudging or strategic, that the Runet geography remained diverse, often out of direct control, and therefore necessitated a modicum of creativity and flexibility in content generation. That said, efforts at securing greater control persisted, in part, in the name of "sovereignty"—the focus of chapter 8.

DICTATING INTERNET SOVEREIGNTY

> **What exactly is a unipolar world? No matter how you embellish it, in the end it means just one thing in practice: a single power center, a single center of decision-making. It's a world with one master, one sovereign. And in the end it's fatal not only for those located within the framework of the system, but also for the sovereign himself, because it destroys him from the inside.**
>
> —Vladimir Putin (2007)

> **The gates of hell are locked from the inside.**
>
> —Igor' Tsukanov (2014)

Putin's 2007 speech at the global security summit in Munich, Germany had little if nothing to do with the World Wide Web, but the notion of "internet sovereignty" would become increasingly central in his articulation of internet policy over the course of his presidency. The notion proved critical largely thanks to the dual orientations it has commonly implied.[1] From an external, geopolitical perspective, the notion of sovereignty allowed Russia to lay claim to authority and control over digital space directly affecting its population and territory vis-à-vis Western, mainly American, organizations and corporations that were largely responsible for the emergence and growth of new media technologies. At the same time, from an internal, domestic perspective, the discourse of "internal sovereignty" provided a rhetorical framework for legitimizing regulation and control over the use of the internet and social media in a manner that strengthened the power and authority of the sovereign himself—a need that, by the beginning of Putin's third term, had assumed a scope and degree of urgency that far surpassed Litvinovich's 2000 vision of a digital "eye of the Sovereign."

Yet three tensions consistently complicated attempts to translate this promise of authority from rhetoric into practice. The first and most obvious had to do with

---

1. Political theory has long distinguished, in fact, between "internal" and "external" sovereignty. As the following discussion shows, the Putinist articulation of "internet sovereignty" relies on both but presumes a "sovereign" more of the sort envisioned by Thomas Hobbes and, later, Carl Schmitt— a sole authority and absolute leader who symbolically represents the nation and state and, as final arbiter of the law, stands above it (Philpot 2003).

the structural design and evolution of the communication systems themselves. From the start, the internet was by design rhizomatic, decentralized in structure, meant to seamlessly function across national boundaries to create a web that was truly worldwide. Second, it was largely the product of Western and specifically American design, in its earliest rendition linked to the Department of Defense but soon transferred into the hands of a nongovernmental organization, the International Corporation for Assigned Names and Numbers (ICANN), whose mission was to coordinate operation and stakeholder interests globally. Finally, even for digital spheres that lay well within the control of domestic authorities, user-generated content and behavior proved persistently difficult to regulate. In the following discussion, I examine how narratives regarding the notion of a "sovereign internet" came to assume increasing symbolic authority in public debates about Russia's new media technologies, how the above-mentioned tensions manifested themselves in those debates and subsequent attempts at implementation, and how language about defending Russia's national digital borders often served as a rationalization for further enhancing the stability and power of the Putin regime itself.[2]

Regathering Sovereign Lands, Physical and Digital

We saw in chapter 6 how the earliest expressions of alarm over the detrimental impact of the internet often zeroed in on language and the desire to protect Russia's youngest citizens from internal forces of digitally mediated internal forces of linguistic perversion and cultural contamination. Urgent pleas from industry insiders, clerics, and members of the systemic public sphere warned of immanent demographic calamities involving rampant vulgarity, violence, pedophilia, and suicide if the nation did not contain these web-borne diseases. Their efforts facilitated the swift passage of the law "On the Protection of Children," the creation of blacklists and volunteer cyber patrols, and the proposal of a "clean internet" consisting of preapproved, state-friendly content. The tumultuous political events of 2011–12 subsequently led to a second wave of laws, these aimed not so much at protecting citizens as at muting public speech considered detrimental to the authority of the regime. By the end of 2013, a citizen posting, reposting, or even liking commentary deemed politically inappropriate risked being labeled "slan-

---

2. As Chander and Sun (2022) document in their study of sovereign internet policy across a broad range of countries, the push toward some sort of digital sovereignty, or "data sovereignty," has become a global trend. As they point out, however, there are key differences in the targets and motivations of different states' initiatives, which the following discussion is designed to unpack for the Russian case. Cf. Drake et al. (2016). For a good early overview of the pros and cons of internet sovereignty in the global arena, see Zittrain and Palfrey (2008).

derer," "blasphemer," "foreign agent," "extremist," or "terrorist" and subjected to the substantial fines or prison sentences that went along with them (Van der Vet 2020).

When in February 2014 Putin saw fit to use political unrest in Ukraine as a pretense for "regathering" lands he believed rightly belonged to Russia by sending Russian troops to occupy portions of eastern Ukraine, discussions of internet security shifted focus yet again, this time from internal threats to external threats to Russian sovereignty writ large. Although warnings of various "fifth columns" within the country persisted, the reality of kinetic conflict in eastern Ukraine raised the more urgent specter of "hybrid," "information," and "culture wars" with Russia's external enemies. In a meeting about the writing of history with young historians earlier the same month, for example, Putin alluded to outside attempts to "recode" Russian society: "We see that attempts to re-encode society are being made in many countries, including recoding society in our country, and this cannot but be connected to the rewriting of history, dressing it to fit someone's geopolitical interests" (Putin 2014).

The discourse of national purity and border sovereignty likewise converged in comments by the Safe Internet League's Denis Davydov during a televised, prime-time debate over the internet's threat to society, where he likened the virtual space to polluted, shark-infested waters: "Let's go back to the source. Who built the Internet? It was the Americans who created it. Imagine a pool, just a pool, that we all swim in. This pool belongs to the Americans and they let either crocodiles in, or sharks, or they dump sewage there. And we ask, 'What can we do? It's our society that's that way, see, it's a sewer, there's scum there.' Maybe that's why it's worth building our own pool next to it, that would be connected to the American pool, from which only clear water would flow" ("Vremia pokazhet" 2014).

On the Information War Front

The new, post-annexation wave of laws reflected a wartime mentality that saw the Runet as space over which Russia should have sovereign rights but which was vulnerable to foreign and enemy manipulation at a time when Russia was in the midst of an increasingly acrimonious "information war." A term that in the 1990s and first decade of the 2000s had been used sparingly and primarily to describe battles between warring oligarchs through their media empires, "information war" had become geopolitically marked by the 2010s.[3] First in reference

---

3. By way of example of the earlier usage: "In 1997 a controlling package of the holding's stocks were sold at auction, an act which gave rise to an 'information war' between the two oligarch groups [*gruppirovki*]" (Veletminskii 2005). The term dates back to American Cold War military policy (Hutchings et al. 2024, 30) and, nowadays, is invoked loosely by both sides concerning revived tensions between Russia and the West. Hutchings et al. (2024) argues that the overuse of the term by Western governments in reference to Russian state propaganda has actually acted to turbocharge the impact of RT in particular as a "populist pariah" among counterhegemonic audiences on the alt-right and alt-left.

to the Georgian media in 2008, then the Ukrainian media in 2014, and most recently the Western media of the sanctions era, the notion with few exceptions signified acts of media-based aggression (often in the form of mis- or disinformation) brought upon Russia by a foreign adversary—as in the following warning appearing on the pages of the official government newspaper, *Rossiiskaia gazeta*, in 2016: "When our enemies [*nedrugi*] are coming down hard on us with fierce anti-Russian campaigns or information wars, they are seeking not only to weaken our international positions, but also to bring chaos upon the consciousness of Russians [and] undermine the spirit and unity of the people" (Mironov 2016).

The metaphor was key in framing the 2014 law "On Personal Data" that required all companies doing business on the Runet to store user data on servers located inside the Russian Federation (Sivkova 2014; Federal'nyi zakon No. 242-FZ 2014). United Russia deputy Evgenii Fedorov defended the data localization measure by declaring the internet "a direct weapon of 'orange' intervention" and labeling foreign internet companies "fifth-columnists" who used data about Russians stored on foreign soil against them. LDPR deputy and cosponsor Iaroslav Nilov justified it by pointing to a "global information war" that was currently in its "aggressive phase," thus making internet regulation critical to Russia's national security interests (Sivkova 2014).

For his own part, Putin by spring 2014 had shifted his own framing of the internet bogey monster from pornography to American spies, declaring the internet "a specialty project of the CIA" (Putin 2014) and ordering government agencies to conduct joint exercises designed to test the vulnerability of Runet to external attack. In the fluent but mind-numbing language of the bureaucracy, the Ministry of Communications announced the results of exercises designed to test Runet integrity and vulnerabilities in the event of external attack:

> В ходе учений была проведена общая оценка состояния защищенности и стабильности функционирования национального сегмента сети, степень критичности его связанности с глобальной инфраструктурой, оценены потенциальные уязвимости, определен уровень готовности к совместной работе отраслевых организаций, операторов связи и ситуационных центров федеральных органов исполнительной власти в случае негативного целенаправленного воздействия. ("Minkomsviaz'" 2014)

> ["During the exercise an overall assessment of the state of security and stability of operation of the national segment of the network, of the degree of criticality of its connection to the global infrastructure was carried out; potential vulnerabilities were assessed; [and] the level of

readiness for joint work among industry organizations, communications providers, and situational centers of federal organs of the executive branch was determined in the event of a negative targeted incident."]

As a result of these training exercises, the issue of internet sovereignty and, more specifically, closing the Russian-language internet off from the global internet topped the agenda of an October 2014 Russian Federation Security Council meeting. Putin warned that, although the information age had brought considerable benefits, Russia's adversaries were trying to "use their dominant position in the global information space to achieve their military-political goals, as well as their economic ones," and that their hard- and soft-power activities had grave implications "for the country's military preparedness, for the stable development of the economy and social sphere, for the defense of Russia's sovereignty in the broadest sense of the word" ("Zasedanie" 2014).[4] At the same time, while he insisted that the state was "obligated to defend its citizens," Putin took care to deny the possibility of "putting the web under total control [or] nationalizing the internet [*ogosudarstvlivat' internet*]" ("Zasedanie" 2014). Presidential aid and former communications minister Igor' Shchegolov qualified the nod to independence in a slightly different fashion: "We are for the openness, honesty, and transparency of relations, including on the Internet. But unfortunately, they are trying to isolate us from the outside" (Annenkov 2014).

The mere mention of isolation and internet nationalization (lit. "state-ification"), however, together with timely launches of mega web projects such as the state-run Sputnik search engine and proposals for a Russia-only intranet nicknamed "Cheburashka," were enough to give pause to proponents (and investors) of open and diverse web options coming out of Russia.[5] As one skeptical commentator put it, "With every new legislative initiative concerning the substitution of something foreign—produce, servers, software, drilling platforms, foreign presence in the media—you start to believe less and less that talk of an autonomous internet was initiated 'just in case.' All the more so since it seems there are no cases of blocking internet access by one country or another from the outside. As the Christian writer Clive Staples Lewis wrote, 'The gates of hell are locked from the inside'" (Tsukanov 2014).

---

4. Nocetti (2015) argues that much of Russia's policy on the internet from this time reflected a combination of projection and security. For a rationalization of sovereign internet grounded specifically in the seventeenth-century Westphalian notion of sovereignty, see Zinov'eva (2013).

5. The intranet proposal came from Federation Council member Maksim Kavdzharadze and marked the first such proposal for a closed system from either house of parliament. Kavdzharadze proposed naming the system "Cheburashka," after a beloved fictional Russian cartoon character. While no concrete plan materialized from the section, subsequent efforts at sovereignization were frequently referred to mockingly by opponents using the cartoon character's name. ("V Sovete" 2014).

The increased importance of internet sovereignty when one compares two Putin-era iterations of the "Doctrine of Information Security of the Russian Federation"—the first in 2000 and the second in 2016. The first, which came out in Putin's first year in office at a time when social networks were nonexistent and internet usage was generally low, barely mentions the notion of sovereignty. When it does, it places it on equal footing with "the constitutional rights and freedoms of . . . citizens" and "the development of equal and mutually beneficial international collaboration" ("Doktrina" 2000). The 2016 doctrine, by contrast, mentions "sovereignty" on nine separate occasions and mostly in the context of something that is vulnerable to "undermining" (*podryv suvereniteta*, which appears four times), in need of protection (*zashchita suvereniteta*, which appears three times), or the object of harm (*nanesenie ushcherba suverenitetu*) ("Doktrina" 2016). In the 2021 equivalent policy statement, mentions of sovereignty increase to eighteen, including references to informational, cultural, economic, and financial sovereignty ("Ukaz" 2021). And while the notion of information war is missing from all three, the 2016 version invokes "information threat [*ugroza*]" a total of twenty-one times (compared to zero mentions in 2000), and the 2021 document features an entire section devoted to "information security."

Nationalizing the Transnational

Once digital media technologies became a central concern of national security and sovereignty, the need to secure the very architecture of the Runet became paramount.[6] Not long after Putin's CIA claim, the newspaper *Kommersant* reported on a plan involving a tiered system of internet access that would limit the reach of local and regional networks and provide access to global networks and services only at the highest, national level, where traffic could be better monitored and controlled (Novyi et al. 2014). In March 2015, Minister of Communications Nikolai Nikiforov delivered what was widely billed as a "speech on the 'sovereignty' of the Russian internet," in which he laid the groundwork for many of the legislative and structural initiatives that subsequently followed (Magai 2015). He proposed bringing under state control four key companies responsible for some aspect of the Runet framework, including those controlling Russia's internet exchange points (where major internet providers exchange traffic) and the coor-

---

6. It should be recalled that new media technologies posed security concerns from the very onset. As early as 1998, the government required the installation of the System of Operative Search Measures (SORM), designed as "'a system of technical means for providing investigative procedures on electronic networks'"—the official description of the eavesdropping mechanism as quoted in Soldatov and Borogan (2015, 66).

dination center responsible for the administration of top-level domains on the Runet.[7] He proposed forbidding commercial companies from using communication lines that crossed national borders. He proposed creating a domestic backup system of existing root servers, all of which were located outside the Russian Federation, either in Western Europe or the United States. And he proposed creating a complete backup copy of the systems critical to operating Runet without interruption. A year later, in December 2016, Nikiforov submitted draft amendments to the law "On Communications" ("O sviazi") proposing the creation of internet exchange points on Russian soil, controlled by Russia and through which internet service providers would be required to route their Russia-based clients. The goal, according to a report on the policy as announced by the ministry, was to reduce the amount of Runet traffic traveling outside Russian boundaries from 99 percent (the estimated figure in 2014) down to 1 percent by the year 2020 (Kantyshev and Golitsyna 2016). The presidential internet adviser Klimenko justified the move as a means of preserving the integrity of Runet: it was "important that electronic mail, telegraph, telephones and social networks in Russia continue to work. Critical infrastructure, including a copy of the domain zone, must be located on our territory, so no one can turn it off" (Bondarev 2017).[8]

Despite Putin's April 2017 assurances to participants in a media forum sponsored by the All-Russian People's Front (ONF) that restrictions on the internet were sufficient "for now," the steady flow of bills and initiatives promoting internet sovereignty continued with the emergence of multiple initiatives aimed at weaning Russian users off their dependence on foreign technology ("Vladimir Putin" 2017). One followed up on the Personal Data Storage law by creating a registry of software secured and approved by the FSB, with a stipulation that all software and mobile apps seeking inclusion would need to be compatible with a new, state-certified operating system (Sailfish, later rebranded as "Aurora"), in addition to American-made systems such as iOS and Android (Belokopytova 2017). Another involved the creation of a "closed internet" for official state use (called RSNet) and the development of a secure, Russian-designed messaging service for the same purpose (Zykov 2017). A third initiative would prohibit all anonymous use of social networking and messaging services in general, which, according to Klimenko, was "the most serious [remaining] problem with the internet" (Sedov and Boletskaia 2016; Zykov 2016).

---

7. Officially known as the "Coordination Center for the Russian Domain of the Internet," the center was created as a nonprofit entity in 2001 and over the course of the 2010s came under increasing control by the state.

8. Critics argue that this very centralization of traffic would make Runet *more*, not less, vulnerable to attacks, offering an easier target than the more dispersed and redundant setup that currently exists (Kantyshev and Ser'gina 2017).

The general shift from monitoring content to more ambitious attempts at sovereignization could also be seen in Russian initiatives in the international arena. Here, tellingly, the language used to rationalize the move shifted from the semantic terrain of national security to that of international precedent, democratic rights, and free-market values. In a 2014 interview, Shchegolev justified Russia's growing push toward internet sovereignty by noting that "the concept of digital sovereignty [was] more frequently cropping up in the official documents of many countries," going on to cite France in particular (Annenkov 2014). "As a democratic state," he remarked, "we observe freedom of the press [and] the right of citizens to receive and distribute information" (Annenkov 2014). And like Western European governments, he pointed disparagingly to the monopolistic tendencies of US corporate titans Google, Facebook, and Twitter when threatening to throttle traffic to them for their failure to comply with Russian law (Annenkov 2014).

Addressing the oversight issue at an October 2014 meeting of the International Telecommunications Union in Seoul, Nikiforov called for the establishment of "international norms and rules," declaring that, "on the platform of the UN, we must propose an evolution of relations on the internet, in which states return to themselves their sovereignty" ("Glava Minkomsviazi" 2014). Six months later, a cooperative agreement between Russia and China on cybersecurity echoed the same norm-based justification for internet sovereignty, demanding (in convoluted bureaucratese) that "state sovereignty and the international norms and principles that emanate from state sovereignty extend to the behavior of states in the framework of activity tied to the use of information and communication technologies, and the jurisdiction of states over the information infrastructure on their territory" ("O podpisanii" 2015).[9]

The Debate over "Suvernet"

Five years after the seemingly quixotic call for a digital Cheburashka, the "Sovereign Internet" law (Federal'nyi zakon No. 90-FZ 2019) marked the first comprehensive legislation to apply territorial notions of sovereignty to the very concrete, architectural design of the internet. Passed in May 2019 for implementation in November of that same year (and more formally referred to as the "law on a stable internet" [*ustoichevyi internet*]), the law called for the construction of an inde-

---

9. Safe Internet League director Davydov was more direct in his characterization of the import of the agreement, calling it the "first nail in the coffin of American hegemony . . . over the management of the internet" ("Suverennyi internet" 2016).

pendent infrastructure that would allow full functionality of the Russian segment of the internet if internet operators were unable to access root servers situated beyond Russia's borders.[10]

The "Suvernet," as it came to be referred informally (a neologistic compound of the Russian phrase *suverennyi* [sovereign] *internet*), was justified by top leaders as a means of ensuring "functional security," "stability," and "integrity," primarily against outside threats. They frequently identified the United States as the main risk, given its proclivity for violating international law. Kremlin spokesperson Dmitry Peskov pointed to illegal American sanctions on China, Iran, and Russia as a rationale for the Suvernet ("V Kremle" 2019). His counterpart at the Ministry of Foreign Affairs, Maria Zakharova, justified it on Facebook by pointing to US attempts to overthrow the elected government in Venezuela (Zakharova 2020). Duma deputy Andrei Lugovoi berated his foot-dragging colleagues during parliamentary debate of the bill, exclaiming, "This isn't kindergarten! All of the websites in Syria have been turned off by the United States" ("Russian Internet" 2019). Security Council secretary Patrushev likewise framed the law as a defensive measure, warning that Russia might be overthrown by cyberattacks thanks to a US national cybersecurity strategy that embraced the principle of "preserving peace through strength" ("Sekretar' Sovbez" 2019).[11]

At the same time, in the June 2019 edition of his annual "Direct Line with Vladimir Putin," the president assured a blogger that the law was designed to protect Runet from outside attempts at compromise and declared elsewhere that "a free internet and sovereign internet [were] not mutually contradictory concepts" ("Vladimiru Putinu" 2019; "Putin: Rossiia" 2019). Shortly after the bill's signing, Duma deputy Leonid Levin, chair of the Information and Technology Subcommittee, framed the "four principles" of the bill strictly in terms of citizens' rights and freedoms: (1) "defending citizens' right to use the internet freely"; (2) providing high-speed internet (operating entirely on Russian soil) that works better than global internet; (3) doing all this at no extra cost to Russian citizens; (4) with no impediment to access to information (Lysenko 2019).

When we look beyond the carefully modulated language of seasoned politicians to interest groups from the systemic public sphere, we find that justifications for the Suvernet became something of a rhetorical catch-all for solving all sorts of internet-related ills and grievances. Voices from obshchestvennost'

---

10. For background and analysis of the plan, see Kotov 2019; Polovinko 2019; Kolomychenko 2019a; Soldatov 2019.

11. Specialists consulted in both 2014, when the topic was first raised, and 2019 expressed doubt about both the possibility and the desire of international foes such as the United States to initiate some central "kill switch" that would be able to cut off Russia entirely from the World Wide Web (Rubin and Luganskaia 2014; Dobrynin 2019; Latynina 2019).

chimed in with more urgent calls for vigilance due to web-borne threats to the moral fabric and national security of the nation. In August 2020, one defender of Runet integrity, Aleksandr Mal'kevich, hosted a two-hour forum devoted to "Western techo-giants as a threat to the digital sovereignty of the state." In addition to regulars such as Ekaterina Mizulina, Mal'kevich invited Putin loyalist Konstantin Malofeev to make the case that Google was financed by the CIA and the Pentagon; its founder, Sergei Brin (a Russian ex-patriot), was a well-known Russophobe; and that, given Google's vast state subsidies, its Russian competitors would not have a chance to survive without the sovereignization of the Runet ("Zapadnye tekhnogiganty" 2020). As Russia's relations with the West continued to deteriorate, advocates of internet sovereignty became more focused on fostering the development of alternative platforms to the Russophobic monopolists Google, Facebook, and YouTube. As Duma deputy Sergei Vostretov put it in an April 2020 press conference after YouTube blocked the central channel of the Prigozhin-led Federal News Agency (FAN), "We must not dance to the tune of the USA. We need to create our own platforms, so that any citizen can express his opinion" ("Vostretsov" 2020).[12] After what advocates deemed wholesale unprovoked censorship of state-affiliated Russian news websites by social media giants in the United States, Mal'kevich argued it was critical to force them to abide by the laws of the Russian Federation and for Russia to create alternative online platforms that could take their place, and that "only the Chinese approach [*kitaiskii variant*] would save [Russia]" (Gurov 2020; Mal'kevich 2020). If Russia were to "show strength" like China did with its internet policy, it would reduce the likelihood that internet monopolies would "declare information war on resources defending the positions of Russia in the world" (Mal'kevich 2020).

Discourse on external threats notwithstanding, the Suvernet law must be seen as one of a number of mechanisms designed to tame the Russian-language internet from threatening internal forces as well. With Russia entering a fresh election season in 2018–19 and Putin's popularity flagging due to his decision to raise the retirement age, members of the ruling elite had plenty of reason to temper public criticism, most of which emerged through web-based networked public spheres. Two other laws, passed by the legislature just prior to the sovereign internet law, aided the effort at containing public pushback to power. The first came veiled in the deadening rhetoric of the bureaucracy, calling for "the limitation of access to information, rudely expressed, which insults human dignity and public morality, [or demonstrates] a clear disrespect for society, the state, official state symbols of the Russian Federation, the constitution of the Russian Federation, or

---

12. For details on the origins, operations, and financing of FAN and its parent company, the Patriot media group, see Kovalenko 2019; Zvereva 2020a.

organs realizing state authority [vlast'] in the Russian Federation" (Federal'nyi zakon No. 30-FZ 2019).[13] It quickly came to be known by the simpler but still euphemistic "law on the disrespect for authority" (*zakon o neuvazhenii k vlasti*), and the most important of the "state symbols" was the president himself. While the law sometimes targeted those posting rudely worded criticism toward local officials, be they local judges, FSB agents, or police officers ("Zachem v Rossii" 2021), it was far more often applied in the case of citizens posting "unflattering comments about Vladimir Putin," who accounted for three-quarters of convictions brought over the first year of the law's enforcement and 1.2 million rubles in fines ("V Rossii" 2020). The second law essentially addressed the issue of "fake news" online, barring the propagation of "false information of public import that is distributed in the form of accurate information [and] the risk of mass violation of public order and (or) public security" (Federal'nyi zakon No. 31-FZ 2019). But like "disrespect" in the first law, the notion of "false information" (let alone "fake news") remained undefined, left to the interpretive whims of law enforcement and the judiciary.[14] Aimed more at restricting verbal production in the domestic (and mainly digitally networked) public sphere, both laws had everything to do with protecting the power and authority of vlast', and very little to do with the integrity of sovereign borders. As one observer put it, "They are in practical terms aimed at the further walling off of Russian authorities from any sort of criticism" (Krashennikov 2019).

From Sovereign Dreams to Wake-Up Calls

Beyond the evident slippage in discourse between external and internal sovereignty, the sovereign internet project also suffered from a significant gap between *metaphors* of internet sovereignty and the actual *mechanics* required to pull it off. The gap consisted of confounding technical, economic, and political factors. Structurally, there was little in the way of demarcated territory or borders over which internet sovereignty could be exercised—at least none corresponding to national political boundaries. Bratton (2015, 6) argues that traditional Westphalian (geography-based) notions of sovereignty become "obsolete and brittle" due to the internet's multilayered, "stacked" architecture. Mueller and Badiei (2017,

---

13. "...ограничение доступа к информации, выражающей в неприличной форме, которая оскорбляет человеческое достоинство и общественную нравственность, явное неуважение к обществу, государству, официальным государственным символам Российской Федерации, Конституции Российской Федерации или органам, осуществляющим государственную власть в Российской Федерации."

14. Although in some cases, the vagueness worked in favor of the accused ("Sto nedrugov" 2020).

437) point out that country code top-level domains such as .ru, .su, and .рф are purely semantic in nature, arguing that internet routing protocols "recognize network operators, not nations." Indeed, it was only in the Suvernet law, as suggested by Korolev (2020), that these domains were declared to make up the Russian "national domain zone." Couture and Toupin (2019, 2308–9) describe sovereignty as it regards the internet as a "discourse" or "speech act" invoked as a "specific form of legitimization," particularly in situations where authority is contested or weak.[15]

Be this as it may, the Suvernet law was quite specific in the territorial nature of its architectural intent. It gave the state (specifically Roskomnadzor and the FSB) sole authority over the monitoring and flow of information, by restricting authorized nodes of transmission (internet exchange points), limiting them to Russian soil, and requiring internet service providers to install equipment on them, both at the borders and within the country, that allowed for traffic monitoring and the blocking of illegal content (Kolomychenko 2019a, "Eks-glava" 2019; "Roskomnadzor trebuet" 2020). The law referred to the equipment as "technical means for combatting threats" (*tekhnicheskie sredstva protivodeistviia ugrozam*), or TSPUs, an amorphous but official-sounding term that led skeptics to wonder if the drafters had any idea what they were talking about.[16] It further required the creation of a Russia-based and Russian-controlled Domain Name System, a national DNS that citizens and state organs would be obliged to use starting January 2021 (Kolomychenko 2019a; "Eks-glava" 2019).

Even if the proposed measures were viable from a technical standpoint, critics argued, the negative repercussions would substantially undermine the efficacy of the system. Not only would the introduction of monitoring boxes at all exchange nodes risk degrading the flow of information ("It's like closing your airspace," one expert observed [Khrennikov and Kravchenko 2019]); the reduction in the number of internet providers that would likely result would potentially decrease the system's stability and economic competitiveness (Gavrichenkov 2021). Potentially the initiative could fail on both grounds at once: not preventing outside disruption as promised and making the Runet weaker and more vulnerable internally.[17] Nevertheless, early expert analyses of the system's functioning suggested that the TSPU-based system eased the state's ability to compromise the functionality of targeted sites, apps, and platforms deemed threatening—be it blocking Navalny's

---

15. For a sense of the legal ambiguities surrounding notions of internet sovereignty, see Svantesson (2017) and Shaw (2017).

16. The device is manufactured by a daughter company of the state-owned Rostelecom ("Giprosviaz" 2020).

17. For a summary of the variables at play here, see "'Suverenizatsiia Runeta'" 2021.

smart-voting app in the run-up to the 2018 elections or throttling access to the Twitter platform in 2021 ("Zakon o 'suverennom internete'" 2021).[18] But here, as with other past episodes, the process has unfolded in a cat-and-mouse manner, and, exacerbated by the specter of widely available satellite service, Suvernet may quickly become obsolete (Mel'nik 2019).

Beyond the technological unknowns it brought into play, sovereignty-related legislation gave rise to economic concerns among industry leaders. As early as 2014, hastily written data storage laws requiring tech companies to store users' account information on Russian soil left them confused over what needed to be stored by whom and how much the initiative would cost ("Kakie biznesy" 2014). Representatives from the industry-leading search engine Yandex complained that "the need to comply with applicable Russian laws and regulations could hamper [their] ability to offer services that compete effectively with those of [their] foreign competitors and may adversely affect [their] business, financial condition and results of operations" ("'Iandeks' predupredil" 2014). All but one of the major mobile internet providers opposed the law when first proposed, out of concern for the millions of rubles they would need to spend on acquiring and installing the additional servers and monitoring equipment demanded by it (Korolev 2019).[19]

Businesses were not the only ones to complain about the added costs required to implement sovereignty-related legislation. Even the Ministry of Economic Development in 2018 complained about the financial and technological burdens required by the "Iarovaia Law" that required internet companies to physically store sixth months of user data (Iastrebova 2018). Others involved in the cutting-edge development of new technologies linked to "smart city" projects and the Internet of Things feared a Suvernet-burdened system would be too slow to handle the new technologies required to realize their visions (Tishina 2019). Internet Ombudsman Dmitrii Marinichev acknowledged that the state had it within its capacity to realize the control mechanisms promised by the Suvernet law but warned of the "catastrophic" long-term impact on the telecom industry due to state monopoly and lack of competition ("Internet-ombudsmen" 2019).

That very lack of competition, according to others, was the main point of the bill. The centralization of traffic monitoring and flow led to the creation of big

---

18. Access to the Navalny app was removed using article 282.2 of the criminal code, due to the Anti-Corruption Foundation's status as an "extremist organization" ("Roskomnadzor ob"iasnil" 2021). The temporary compromising of the functionality of Twitter was ostensibly punishment for the platform's failure to remove "more than three thousand items" that had been banned dating back to 2017 ("Roskomnadzor: Zamedlenie" 2021).

19. For more in-depth coverage of the negative economic impact of the law for the telecom industry, see "'Suverennyi internet' negativno" 2019.

winners, such as state-affiliated giants Rostelecom and Mail.ru Group: the former being one the central nodes of operation for the new system and provider of key hardware; the latter being, like Yandex, the beneficiary of less competition and a smoother path to providing a viable alternative to YouTube (Korolev 2019; Torop 2019). This led multiple critics to conclude the law was little more than a money grab by state and near-state authorities (Dik 2019; Kharitonov 2019). As the commentator Aleksandr Isavnin put it, regarding funding for the Suvernet project and its parliamentary sponsors, "It appears that some money has been found that someone wants to spend on technical devices, on the organization of a center for the management of the network, on conducting exercises. We understand full well that neither Bokov, nor Lugovoi, nor Klishis [all three members of the Parliament—MSG] are the real authors of the laws, judging by how they bungled even the debate. Someone is trying to get to that money by selling the idea of patriotism, sovereign internet, reliable internet, [and] answering the threats of the Americans" (Dobrynin 2019).[20]

Basic politics provided a final check on the exuberance of the political elite to better contain the national boundaries of the Runet. It was one thing (and not a very big one) to alienate already antagonistically inclined members of the "non-systemic" opposition but quite another to risk antagonizing the growing share of population that had come to depend on access to foreign-based services and a relatively open and free internet. Perhaps the most graphic example of this dynamic went on display when, in April 2018, Roskomnadzor tried to shut down the popular social network and messaging platform Telegram when its founder, Pavel Durov, refused to share encryption codes with the FSB. Once it had received the required court order, the oversight agency spent three days essentially missing the digital mark, blocking upward of eighteen million IP addresses—many belonging to innocent, law-abiding citizens, businesses, and research labs—while still leaving Telegram itself widely available to Runet users, either through normal avenues of access or through virtual private networks (VPNs) or proxy servers. The scope of misdirected outages was large enough to prompt outcries not just from the usual internet-freedom advocates but from average citizens, businesses, and even members of the ruling elite who themselves suddenly had to hunt for ways around government censorship. Some of the more prominent users among the elite spoke out quite actively and publicly, in fact. Master of Instagram,

Ramzan Kadyrov, defended Telegram as a convenient service that should be let alone. Dmitry Medvedev's press secretary Natal'ia Timakova recommended that users download a VPN to get around the blockage ("Press-sekretar'" 2018). Even the Kremlin press secretary and the deputy prime minister signaled their support more implicitly by continuing to use Telegram, despite it being officially banned. And major television networks showed uncharacteristic independence in their coverage of the story, suggesting they had no specific marching orders from the presidential administration on the topic.[21]

Popular reaction to the shutdown was mixed: state-sponsored public opinion polling suggested the Telegram blockage was a concern for only 24 percent of the general population, but the importance jumped to 45 percent for respondents eighteen to twenty-four years old and became still more of an issue given the platform's popularity among professional and political elites—whose opinion mattered more ("VTsIOM vyiasnil" 2018). The fact that twelve thousand protesters turned out for a pro-Telegram rally in Moscow two weeks after the shutdown suggested the issue was more volatile than expected for municipal authorities who sanctioned the surprisingly popular event.[22]

The bungled ban of Telegram was but one of several notable failures that illustrated the considerable gap between the metaphors and mechanics of internet sovereignty. The state-sponsored Sputnik search engine launched with great fanfare in 2014 languished barely used for six years before being banished to the trash heap of aborted digital projects (Braterskii 2020). Ten years of attempts at offering a Russian-made mobile operating system (Yandex-kit, Sailfish, and Aurora) have produced little to show, particularly in comparison with international competitors (Shatilin 2023). And despite its nearly two decades of existence, the domestic video-hosting platform RuTube (launched in 2006) has yet to offer services adequate enough for authorities to follow through with their threats of an all-out ban of YouTube (although the Russian full-scale invasion of Ukraine accelerated efforts, as will be discussed in the epilogue) (Rudnitsky 2024).

As we have seen, the causes for the gap are varied, cutting at least across technological, economic, and political lines. The shortcomings may be best epitomized

---

21. Wijermars (2021b) argues that, while state media coverage of the ban generally supported the Roskomnadzor position, the "policy narratives" they used to rationalize it did not always coincide.

22. Since then, the state has taken a more nuanced approach to Telegram—a development discussed in detail in the epilogue.

by the very language used to implement the law, bureaucratic gibberish along the lines of "technical means for combatting threats." Executive director of the "Society for the protection of the internet," Mikhail Klimarev (2019), argues that the "monstrous chancery language" that riddled both the law and the directives issued to guide its implementation made it nearly impossible to act on and were indicative of the primarily political (and partly greed-based) intentions behind it—as he put it (echoing earlier comments about the busywork of the Institute for the Development of the Internet), a desperate "'longshot' [*vbros*] by Mr. Zharov to somehow justify the imitation of tumultuous activity in realizing the knowingly unrealizable law passed by incompetent deputies." By way of example, he pointed to the inauspicious title of one of the many official documents generated by the law—a "Directive by the Federal Oversight Service in the area of communications, information technologies, and mass communication from 31 July 2019 No. 228 'On the confirmation of the technical conditions for the installment of technical devices for combatting threats, and also the requirements for the networks of communications in the use of technical devices for combatting threats.'"[23]

At the same time, the very vagueness of the language permeating nearly all policies relating to internet sovereignty carried its own benefits for those in positions of authority seeking legal cover to carry out their protection of that power. As the Roskomsvoboda representative Sarkis Darbinian argued, the ambiguity may have been exactly the point, as unspecified key phrases such as "external threats" (*vneshnie ugrozy*) allowed authorities to execute the law however they saw fit (Sedukhina 2019). Whatever the case (and the two aren't necessarily mutually exclusive), the rhetorical shifts, gaps, and abstractions relating to internet sovereignty that I have outlined here are emblematic of internet policy and practice throughout the second half of Putin's presidency: largely ad hoc planning, imperfectly executed, but nevertheless ultimately leading to a digital sphere that has become more "sovereign" than when Putin first came to power. The question is, to what extent does this bricolage of patchwork architecture, authoritarian legalese and the enforcement mechanisms attached to it secure Russian national sovereignty and strengthen the authority of the ruling elite, and to what extent does this more insulated, authoritarian digital communication sphere risk realizing inside Russia the very outcome that Putin warned about in his 2007 address to the global community—namely, the "destruction of the sovereign from within"?

---

23. "Приказ Федеральной службы по надзору в сфере связи, информационных технологий и массовых коммуникаций от 31.07.2019 г. № 228 'Об утверждении технических условий установки технических средств противодействия угрозам, а также требований к сетям связи при использовании технических средств противодействия угрозам.'"

RUNET AT WAR

In this study of over two decades of networking Putinism, we've seen a variety of strategies for dealing with newly emergent digital media, ranging from the opportunistic harnessing of their potential to a more antagonistic impulse to contain and control. To a certain extent, these impulses were more complementary than in tension with one another. Just as Pavlovsky's Foundation for Effective Politics was pumping the "nuo-sphere" with positive content about the younger, more vibrant, but largely unknown President Putin, the FSB was busy ensuring it had updated surveillance equipment built into the swiftly expanding Runet architecture. At the same time the Russian parliament was churning out laws designed to limit negative web-based speech toward those in positions of power, the Institute for the Development of the Internet was funneling increasingly generous funds into financing video games, websites, and other online content that, however vaguely, promoted values and themes dear to the Putin regime.

The study has also shown a gradual shift in the balance between these two impulses, from a relatively laissez-faire approach to a more aggressive effort to regulate political discourse online, punctuated by a four-year flirtation during the Medvedev presidency with visions of electronic government and direct internet democracy. The growing political authority of Navalny, most dramatically illustrated by the massive public protests in 2011–12 and his surprisingly successful mayoral campaign in 2013, proved a critical turning point—a rhetorical watershed, where it became clear to many in power that new media had the capacity to translate political language into action, thereby upending authority's traditional "refusal to acknowledge that utterance may be a form of political participation" and its monopoly over "the right to 'act'" (Kalugin 54). It is in the wake of these significant threats to the Putin regime that we witness an intensification of reactionary measures against digitally mediated oppositional discourse, fueled by a cynical tandem of disruptive trolls and alarmist voices of purity and patriotism from the systemic public sphere, all accompanied by a pliant parliament churning out vaguely worded laws allowing sources of perceived web-borne threats to authority to be labeled, fined, and imprisoned as anything from "pedophiles" and "foreign agents" to "terrorists" and "extremists."

That said, the book also shows that efforts at containing networked public political speech were by no means perfect, in part due to their ad hoc reactionary nature, in part due to incompetency and corruption in state agencies responsible for regulating digitally mediated communication, and in part due to the stubbornly distributed nature of new media technologies themselves. It was one thing to declare the Runet "sovereign" territory; making it so has proven a more complicated task.[1]

Putin's February 2022 decision to launch a full-scale invasion of Ukraine greatly accelerated the push toward Runet sovereignization. Though by necessity selective in its targeting, crackdown on antiwar expression online emerged almost immediately and was accompanied by punitive sentences and broad publicity designed to discourage further subversion ("Zhitelia Kuzbasa" 2022). On 4 March 2022, just eight days after the invasion's onset, the State Duma passed and President Putin signed Federal Law no. 32-FZ, criminalizing "actions that could be interpreted as discrediting the Armed Forces of the Russian Federation" and the "public distribution . . . of knowingly false information containing details about the Armed Forces of the Russian Federation" (Federal'nyi zakon no. 32-FZ 2022). The law criminalized both criticism of and the publication or sharing of information about Putin's so-called Special Military Operation (including referring to it as a "war") that did not correspond to official reporting coming out of the Ministry of Defense ("Il'ia Iashin" 2022). This not only led to the prosecution of individuals—over eighty in the first five months of the war alone (Golubeva 2022) and 278 through April 2024 ("Data" 2023)—but also radically reduced the number of independent news and information outlets reporting on the war inside of Russia.[2]

---

1. Which is not to say there haven't been signs of at least incremental success. For example, by 2024 an estimated 6000 TPSU devices had been installed across Russian networks in accordance with the 2019 sovereign internet law, better enabling Roskomnadzor to censor and block content, including on a targeted local or regional basis ("Freedom" 2024).

2. As of August 2024, authorities had launched over ten thousand cases under the law ("Russia Opens" 2024).

On the same day the law was signed, Roskomnadzor blocked Facebook and Twitter on the Runet, largely in response to the American platforms' ban of the state-run news and propaganda outlets RT and Sputnik (Meaker 2022). Ten days later, Russia declared Meta an "extremist organization" for its statements on the war and blocked Instagram as well. Though the platforms were still accessible through VPNs, their marginalization proved a welcome turn for advocates of a sovereign internet and gave further impetus for those in the cybersecurity sector to advocate for more robust protection (and enhanced budgets to facilitate it). Attempts to purge YouTube from the Runet proved more complicated, largely due to the absence of a viable native-born substitute, but efforts by Roskomnadzor to severely throttle download speeds over the second half of 2024 made the platform all but unusable without VPN by users inside Russia—workarounds that themselves had come under increasing regulatory pressure since the summer of 2021.[3] With a growing portion of antiwar and anti-Putin voices having relocated beyond Russa's physical borders, VPN and YouTube throttling suddenly became even more critical lines of defense of national digital sovereignty. The explosion of *relokanty*—Russian citizens temporarily residing outside Russian territory—also underscored the fragile, if not ephemeral, nature of a digital sovereignty based on physical boundaries.

The war manifested itself likewise in the reorientation of those engaged in the production of more proactive and creative web content. For Kadyrov it offered new opportunities to showcase the military bona fides of his Kadyrovites, though whether they saw serious action at the front or were there merely for show—as "TikTok warriors," as some critics put it—was less clear ("'Narrow misses'" 2024). Egor Kholmogorov embraced the exceptionalist, empire-restoring rhetoric of Putin's initiative and increased his output of "lessons in history," even publishing an 882-page page-turner called *I am Russian: The Boundaries of National Self-Consciousness* ("Russians created their majestic nation-state, one of the world's greatest empires and one of the few universal cultures of humanity" [Kholmogorov 2025]).[4] For its part, the Institute for the Development of the Internet

---

3. At the time of this writing, YouTube remains accessible to Runet users within the Russian Federation but at slower download speeds as a result of intentional throttling back on the part of Roskomnadzor. For details on the Russian government's ongoing—and imperfect—battle against YouTube, see "Russian Authorities" 2024. For an overview of laws regulating the use of and posting information about VPNs, see "Freedom" (2024).

4. Writer Sergei Minaev presents a more ambiguous case of wartime Runet "before" and "after." In addition to his YouTube forays into popular Russian history (taking a page from Kholmogorov's book), he has largely retreated behind the relatively safe halls of the entertainment industry, producing television series satirizing Moscow elite, publishing sequels to his earlier best-sellers, and editing online glossy magazines.

used its enhanced budget to sponsor more content-creation contests and double down on its promotion of patriotic video games ["Otbor prototipov" 2025]). And the Gosuslugi state services platform, which had grown considerably both in usage and trust during the Covid-19 pandemic (Guzik 2023), became a legally binding method for delivering mobilization orders to young Russian men being called into service—which some observers saw as a death knell for the good will the services had built over the years of its implementation (Pertsev 2023).

Yet even these more extreme conditions, prime as they were for capitalization (and manipulation) by authorities keen on putting the country on "wartime footing," provided ample opportunity for disruption and subversion.[5] For two quite different examples, I return to the cases of Navalny and Prigozhin used to frame this study at the outset. For in their own tragic and dramatic ways, the death of Navalny in February 2024 and the dramatic culmination of Prigozhin's career in the spring and summer of 2023 illustrate both the strengths and the limitations of Putin's authority over web-based communication.

There's little question that Navalny's death at the hands of Putin and his punishing incarceration system marked a staggering blow for the Russian opposition movement, dissolving the dreams of the corruption fighter's "wonderful Russia of the future" into a fog of uncertainty, both rhetorical and political (what one commentator called *neiasnaia Rossiia budushchego*, or the "opaque Russia of the future").[6] But as Navalny (2024) himself poignantly reflected in his posthumously published memoirs, this sort of politically motivated punishment was a sign of Putin's fundamental weakness: "Do I have any regrets, do I worry? Absolutely not. The belief that I am in the right, and the sense of being part of a great cause, outweighs all the worries by a million percent. And then, this was all entirely predictable. I thought it over many times and recognized that the increasing effectiveness of our team would lead to Putin's giving the order to imprison me. He would have no other way to resolve his problem."

His murder itself essentially amounted to an admission that, even behind bars, while alive Navalny's voice could not be silenced nor his impact stifled. Even under the punitive conditions of solitary confinement in one of Russia's most remote penal colonies, he continued to put out statements on unfolding political events. He staunchly opposed Putin's invasion of Ukraine, working with his team at FBK to post regular content persuading citizens that the campaign was a desperate and reckless attempt to maintain power and distract the

---

5. For a detailed discussion of the war's mixed impact on Russia's digital infrastructure and its push toward digital sovereignization, see Burkhardt and Wijermars 2022.

6. The periodic intergroup battles that flare up among oppositional groups further dampens optimism in this regard (Vladimirov 2024).

nation from more critical domestic problems ("15 punktov" 2023). As the 2024 presidential elections approached, Navalny's team posted his strategy for agitating against Putin and persuading voters to vote for anyone but Putin, creating a separate website for agitational logistics, advice, and content.[7] Ultimately, after decades of attacks involving hooligans, bots, trolls, green dye, nerve agents, legal proceedings, and a tangled web of laws designed to limit access to the public sphere, the state system apparently saw no other recourse but to remove him from the equation altogether. In the end, at loss for words, they resorted to mute, lethal force.[8]

The case of Prigozhin presented a still more troubling cautionary tale about the persistent web-based threats to the authority of Putin and Putinism. For in Prigozhin, Putin had a veritable jack-of-all-digital-trades, willing and eager to do the dirty work of the state when it came to web-based special operations. It was Prigozhin who thought up, bankrolled, and oversaw the Internet Research Agency back when the notorious "troll factory" was launched in 2013 (Larina 2023a). It was Prigozhin who, after the 2014 annexation of Crimea, expanded that project into the more ambitious Patriot Media Group—a digital network of multimedia outlets whose main goal was to continue the trolling and disinformation work of the IRA and amplify Kremlin-friendly news and information (Kovalev 2017; Zvereva 2020a). And it was Prigozhin who headed up the Wagner Private Military Company (PMC) that gave Putin a formidable military and political presence in Syria and on the African continent in a way that advanced Russia's interests (often quite brutally) while still providing the Kremlin with plausible deniability.[9] So what happens when your communications fixer and master of digital dark arts amasses enough independent power to stage a march on the authorities who made his wealth and success possible? My final case study, by way of parting consideration of the unpredictable powers of digital authority, examines the remarkable rise of Evgeny Prigozhin and the role that the social networking platform Telegram played in enabling his emergence as a wartime celebrity and state-created threat—if not alternative—to Putin's power. My primary interest lies in the rhetorical rather than technical mechanisms underlying this dramatic episode of late Putinism, but the story does require a brief detour

---

7. The strategy is outlined in "Prezidentskie vybory-2024," while the website can be found at www.neputin.org.

8. It is noteworthy that Navalny continued producing creative oppositional content even after his death, in the form of a smartphone app he inspired, Proton-2024, designed to help voters randomize their anti-Putin vote using "the uncertainty principle" of quantum physics ("Reshaem problem" 2024).

9. Financially, Wagner was "private" only in name, receiving a large portion of its budget and equipment from the Russian government and Ministry of Defense (Barabanov and Korotkov 2024; Larina 2023b).

through the remarkable revival of Telegram as the chosen platform for those among the ruling elite inclined to establish a public-facing presence.

Telegram's history with regulators has been rocky at best. Six years prior to the founder and CEO Pavel Durov's 2024 indictment in Paris, he and the platform found themselves in the crosshairs of Roskomnadzor for failing to share with the FSB the digital encryption keys to its notoriously secure messaging service. Despite the platform's ill-fated 2018 regulatory run-in, Telegram proved useful to the political elite for a variety of reasons. First, the platform's reputation for privacy, security, and ease of anonymous posting made it a perceived hotbed for insider information and sorting out power struggles within the elite (Rubin 2018; Loshak 2019).[10] Second, the monetizing aspirations of high-profile influencers eased the state's ability to get its message out without the hassle of enlisting the resources of a troll farm or blogging corp. As one analysis put it, "The secret of the state's success on Telegram lay in the unbelievable willingness [on the part of influential bloggers] to sell out . . . If you have a budget, you can get onto any channel" (Rubin 2018). A third likely reason for the platform's popularity was the minimization of features that made other social media conducive for establishing the sort of networked public spheres that had often served as a nuisance for those in positions of power. Telegram's limited capacity for followers to engage, misdirect, or troll a channel, as one analyst put it, "streamline[d] the often chaotic nature of social media by removing the possibility of discussion" (Farbman 2023, 110). With the comment function disabled and feedback reduced to a finite option of emojis controlled by the channel's owner, the medium functioned more like a centralized network akin to "a megaphone blasting information to a captive audience of millions of followers" (Bergengruen 2022).

When Putin's full-scale invasion led to the closure of Facebook and Instagram, Telegram became the platform of choice among the ruling elite and general population almost by necessity. As Russians grew thirsty for information from the front, the number of Telegram users in Russia doubled from 20 to 40 million between 24 February and 24 June 2022, and pro-Kremlin bloggers and increasingly popular war correspondents (*voenkory*) dominated the list of top twenty channels (by growth) that spring, all but one of them supporters of Putin's war (Pankratova 2022). Though not among the top twenty, former President Dmitry Medvedev stood out for the coarse belligerence of his Telegram posts. The once advocate of direct internet democracy, who had posted with star-struck admiration on Twitter about burgers with Angela and Barak, now launched angry

---

10. For two in-depth investigations into the Russian state's ability to access Telegram-based communication and the platform's purported collaboration with security agencies, see Loucaides 2023 and "Kak Kreml'" 2024.

screeds directed against the "anti-Russian hysteria," the "bald-faced Russophobia of the West," and its "disgusting, criminal, and immoral stance with regard to Russia" (@medvedev_telegram [17 March 2022]).

A closer analysis of eight months and 5,987 posts from one of the Prigozhin-related channels ("Evgenii Prigozhin v Telegram" [@chvk_wagnerr]) between its September 2022 launch and Prigozhin's aborted march on Moscow in June 2023 shows how, even after a concerted clamp down on public political speech, digital media still proved a potent tool for promoting a figure who enlisted personal charisma and professional web-savvy akin to those of Navalny and Kadyrov, but did so in a manner that echoed many of the rhetorical codes and values of Putinism in a communicative space that remained beyond the regulatory eye of the sovereign.[11]

Straight-Talking Authority

For most of his career as a Petersburg entrepreneur, Prigozhin kept a low profile, preferring behind-the-scenes action to public self-promotion (Zvereva 2020a). In fact, those who tried linking him to troll factories, media empires, or mercenary groups risked finding themselves on the receiving end of a lawsuit. This changed notably in the autumn of 2022, when two factors converged to make him among the more prominent state-affiliated voices in Russia's full-scale war against Ukraine: Several Telegram accounts were created in his name, and

---

11. Though Prigozhin officially distanced himself from this and another popular Telegram channel bearing his name shortly after their appearance (@concordgroup_official [5 November 2022, https://t.me/concordgroup_official/3]), he in the same breath welcomed their activity. Given the well-established existence of a substantial network of Prigozhin-related Telegram channels and Prigozhin's history of unfounded denials, it is possible he was being less than forthright here, as well. In fact, based on the nature of the content, it is highly likely the channel was maintained by Prigozhin's media team. Numerous posts featured video footage showing either events conducted in the Wagner Center in St. Petersburg (e.g., 3 March 2023, https://t.me/chvk_wagnerr/3550) or Prigozhin himself, often in relatively intimate surroundings (e.g. on board cargo planes with injured Wagner soldiers returning from battle [13 January 2023, https://t.me/chvk_wagnerr/2046]). Other posts presented Prigozhin's comments in the first-person, as if he himself were authoring (e.g., 11 January 2023, https://t.me/chvk_wagnerr/1960). One clear difference: Compared to the "official" channel, "Evgeny Prigozhin in Telegram" posted far more frequently and devoted considerable attention to promoting Prigozhin and the Wagner brand. Whether this was done by his press team or some closely affiliated and approved group, rather than Prigozhin himself, is of little significance for the study of the social-media framing of a pro-Putin authoritarian alternative I offer here. But given Wagner's well-established record of having nimble media specialists embedded with them in battle (dating at least back to their campaigns in Syria [Kovalev 2017]), it is highly likely the channel was an inside job. For more details on the extent of Prigozhin's vast media empire and online presence, see "Kibervoiska Prigozhina" 2023 and Pankratova 2023.

Prigozhin's Wagner fighters were being touted as one of the only bright spots in an otherwise faltering military campaign. It may well have been coincidental, but the fact that the Prigozhin channels were launched on the heels of Putin's unpopular (and mishandled) "partial mobilization" of additional troops for an operation that was supposed to be "special" (i.e., small and surgical) allowed the Wagner head to cut a stark and immediate contrast between the competency of his battle-tested warriors and the confusion of the Ministry of Defense's war campaign. While Kremlin administrators dissembled about the restricted nature of the campaign, the Prigozhin channel engaged in a multimedia effort to broadcast the heroic feats of Wagner troops deep in battle.

Prigozhin didn't mince his words: This was a real battle with real consequences that inevitably included the ultimate sacrifice of his "brave lads'" lives. Rather than alluding to abstract and confusing notions of "denazification" and "demilitarization," which Putin and state propaganda had been using to articulate the goal of the mission, Prigozhin framed the war in far more basic terms—the "side of good" fighting in the name of "justice" (*spravedlivost'*).[12] And rather than dismissing the opposition as poorly armed NATO puppets led by a Nazi comic with a drug addiction (Russian propagandists' common characterization of Ukrainian troops and Ukraine president Volodymyr Zelensky), Prigozhin operated according to the military adage that warned never to underestimate the enemy, characterizing Zelensky as a "firm, self-confident, pragmatic, attractive guy" (31 October 2022, https://t.me/chvk_wagnerr/332).[13] More importantly, he acknowledged the bravery and prowess of the Ukrainian soldiers, who were, he reminded readers, fellow Slavs: "guys with iron balls just like us," as he put it, channeling a Putinesque machismo that would appear regularly over the nine months of posts (17 October 2022/71).

His straight-talking style even breached the taboo topic of war casualties and deaths. If official Defense Ministry tallies remained unbelievably low through the first ten months of fighting, Prigozhin's portraits of limbless soldiers and gravesites of fallen Wagnerites confirmed graphically that the stakes of the war were real but that Wagner fighters could rest assured their valor and their loved ones would not be forgotten in the event of injury or death (fig. E.1). The channel on a number of occasions featured the Wagner CEO himself accompanying the wounded to hospitals back in Russia allegedly "at his own expense"

---

12. In his monograph on Putin's ideology, Suslov (2024, 27, 275) identifies "justice" as one of the key aspects of Putinism, as well.

13. All subsequent references to the channel come from the same source, "Evgenii Prigozhin v Telegram" (@chvk_wagnerr), with the date of the post and message number noted parenthetically (e.g., 31 October 2022/332). Russia's dismissive attitude toward the Ukrainian military and leadership also raised questions about why Russian troops failed to overwhelm them in a few weeks' time, as was the common expectation.

Евгений Пригожин в Telegram

Сегодня сотни неравнодушных петербуржцев пришли на Белоостровское кладбище проводить в последний путь Дмитрия Меньшикова.

FIGURE E.1.   Montage of video clips of Prigozhin's visit to a Petersburg cemetery to pay his respects to a fallen Wagner soldier (24 December 2022/ 1543).

(2 January 2023/1712; 13 January 2023/2046) and went into detail about how they treated the body of a fallen Wagner fighter as a "shrine" that must be rescued and preserved at all costs ("This is the foundation, the ideology, the culture, [and] the honor code of PMC 'Wagner'" [14 October 2022/34]). (That shrine was particularly sacred due to the ruthless military calculus of Wagner's "last grenade" rule, he explained in the same post, which dictated that a Wagnerite always carry an extra grenade to use on himself to avoid being captured alive by the enemy.)

Branding National Heroes

Prigozhin made few personal appearances in the channel initially; instead it highlighted the feats of his fighters at the front. At a time when the nation lacked models of competency and patriotic self-sacrifice, Wagnerites stood out as a glaring exception, and it was for their sake, he explained, Prigozhin was going public: "These brave lads, who were capable of doing just one thing—fighting, defending the disadvantaged, standing to death on the side of good and justice—have always been in a precarious situation. . . . [They] are heroes . . . and have become one of the pillars of our Motherland. Not blinking or doubting for a second, it's either live or die. Live according to the rules and do what you must, come what may [*bud', chto budet*]" (30 September 2022/27).[14]

The channel used a variety of strategies to valorize Wagner. It embedded war correspondents to document their military successes, most often independently of conventional forces. (As Prigozhin put it, "PMC 'Wagner' almost always works alone—it's more reliable that way" [15 October 2022/37].) It supplemented these with soldier interviews and slickly produced photo and video montages that highlighted their warrior natures and the powerful (male) bonds formed in the heat of battle (fig. E.2).

> INTERVIEWER: "What's the most horrific thing for you?"
> WAGNER FIGHTER: "Somehow getting scared and letting down a comrade. . . ."
> I: "More than dying or getting injured?"
> W: "Yes."
> I: "Why?"
> W: "Well, we were born men, we do men's work. That's why breaking when you are being counted on is a horrific thought." (17 October 2022/89)

More extreme cases of valor became the stuff of social media legend, such as the story of the bomber pilot Aleksandr (a.k.a. "Papa") Antonov's final mission. After losing control of his plane due to antiaircraft fire, Antonov reportedly turned the careening vessel into a fiery projectile aimed at the enemy armed tank division he had been targeting. Even better, Antonov had the wits to announce his kamikaze plans by radio from his burning plane, calling out as he descended, "Here comes Papa, you bastards!" (*Vstrechaite, suki, Papu*)—words immortalized in Wagner lore, thanks to Prigozhin's Telegram (11 December 2022/1274).

---

14. Prigozhin echoes the biblical allusion in a later post explaining his new public-facing profile, noting that "the time [had] come to gather stones" (15 October 2022/53). While this discussion focusses on strategies for lionizing Wagner fighters, readers would do well to recall the group has been accused of committing dozens of atrocities and war crimes over the nearly ten years of its existence, including during the war in Ukraine. For a thorough accounting of these, see Margolin 2024.

Евгений Пригожин в Telegram🇷🇺

Короткое интервью с бойцом ЧВК "Вагнер".

FIGURE E.2.   "A short interview with a PMC 'Wagner' fighter."

Echoing Putinist visions of a multiethnic union, or "Russian World," united under a common flag, the theme of unity and brotherhood extended through dozens of portraits of Wagner fighters. One of Prigozhin's correspondents described how the phenomenon panned out in battle: "You meet very different people among the fighters of 'PMC Wagner.' In the same trench, you might encounter a fighter with a religious symbol on his chevron, and another with a patch of the USSR flag. Their battle experience may also be completely different—one who's been through more than one war, another who hasn't yet acquired such solid battle experience [*bagazh boevogo proshlogo*]. Yet once they sign a contract [with Wagner], they become a unified whole where one of the important rules is 'don't abandon your own'" (25 November 2022/940).

The thematic framing played on religiously infused notions of redemption and rehabilitation when profiling the convicts whom Prigozhin had notoriously recruited to serve in exchange for their freedom (should they survive).[15] In a

15. Prigozhin's first widely broadcasted public citing, in fact, came in the form of a leaked video of his appearance at a regional prison camp that featured him speaking to gathered inmates about the terms of voluntary enlistment in Wagner (Video shows" 2022).

video clip posted to the channel, one former inmate talked about how "serving in 'Wagner' changed his values": "Life is so thin a line when you're sitting in a trench and all that separates you between heaven and earth is the flightpath of a single missile [*odin prilet*]. Many of us here have lost much, and many of us have gained. Look at us all. We've all acquired one big family. . . . Many here who were non-believers have adopted Christianity, been baptized, and many of us have really come to believe. Because when you're sitting there, you don't have anything else left but to believe in God. He alone will help you" (5 January 2023/1774).

These literally entrenched voices of religious, patriotic, and communal ideals evoked core Putinist values in a far more compelling code than the anodyne fodder of photo ops with the patriarch or mandatory courses on the "Foundations of Russian Statehood."[16] The convict recruitment program became the topic of a fifty-minute RT documentary, *Zone of Atonement* (*Zona iskupleniia*), pitched in Prigozhin's Telegram as a story about those who "decided to atone for their guilt with blood" (24 March 2023/4134). The Wagner experience for these men was nothing short of transformative—so transformative, if we are to believe the channel, that most of all who served out the six-month term of duty elected to return to their divisions on the frontlines:

> According to the fighters, they want to catch their wind and return to the front to finish what they started. (1 January 2023/1700)

> In two weeks I'm going back already. It's great work. I found myself, a family, comrades, friends (13 January 2023/2070)

> My values and principles have been reconceived [*pereosmysleny*]. Much has become clear. Many things have become unacceptable (6 January 2023/1799).[17]

The channel made a concerted effort to convert these overarching themes of valor, virility, unity, brotherhood, and sacrifice for the motherland into compelling multimedia recruitment tools. One poster implored potential recruits to "join PMC Wagner and show the whole world what you're worth" (1 December 2022/1051). A brief video invited them to "get the best military training, join the

---

16. Putin signed a directive in January 2023 requiring the creation and obligatory instruction of the course ("*Osnovy rossiiskoi gosudarstvennosti*") at the university level throughout the Russian Federation.

17. Independent reporting suggests these portraits are idealized projections of a far more complicated picture of ex-cons' demobilization that includes the former criminals, newly valorized for their mastery of violence in combat, bringing that violence back to their hometowns and cities (e.g. "Ukral, vypil" 2023).

Евгений Пригожин в Telegram

Друзья! Поздравляем победителей конкурса изобразительного творчества с применением нейросетевых технологий!

FIGURE E.3. Collage of winning submissions to the "Neural network technology" competition, with congratulatory caption below (1 March 2023/3499).

team of victors, [and] join Wagner!" (25 December 2022/1559). Taking a page from the early Rykov playbook, they placed ads on the Russian-language version of Pornhub, beseeching viewers to "Stop jerking off—go and fight!" (*Kvatit drochit' – idi voevat'*) (15 March 2023/3959). In a nod to Prigozhin's expertise at trolling, they produced an English-language video targeting disillusioned (pro-Trump) American veterans who had "dreamed of doing much to make America great again" (tagline: "If you're a true patriot of the future of great America, join the ranks of the warriors of Russia; help defeat evil, or it will be too late for everyone") (30 January 2023/2676).

A March 2023 post announcing the "winners of the competition of creative works produced using neural network technology" carried echoes of both

Navalny, who had a knack for making politics fun through popular contests, and the Institute for the Development of the Internet, for the list of categories for which submissions were invited—all reminiscent of late-Putin efforts to promote patriotism and traditional values in a popular way (fig. E.3). Winning themes included "the family and Russia of the future," "the mysterious Russian soul," and "image of the Russian soldier," with the top three contestants winning "company merch from the Wagner Center" (1 March 2023/3499).

As the buzz surrounding Wagner and its brand grew, so, too, did the amount and variety of user-generated content devoted to the group—much dutifully captured and reposted on the channel. Everything from Wagner flags, banners, comics, and posters to songs, music videos, documentary films, and even poetry graced the pages of the account over the winter and spring of 2023 (fig. E.4; also 6 April 2023/4375, 9 May 2023/5265, 25 May 2023/5762).

By early November, the channel had enough musical content to post a montage of music video "hits" devoted to Wagner, ranging from the rough-cut, violence-dominated rap-accompanied "PMC Wagner" ("The 'musicians' ordered the downpour of 'Grad' [missiles], / It's Wagner – the sky filled with smoke. / We perform to the symphony of the Valkyries, / Covering the enemy with a blanket of lead") (29 December 2024/1643),[18] to the religious, folk-hero infused chanson hit "Wagner" by the aging pop diva Vika Tsyganova ("Orchestrators, soldiers of Russia, / May grace be with you, / Our fallen ones, our saints / And the heavenly hand of God") (21 November 2022/827).[19] Playing more to the digital native generation, a track by the indie rock group Blueberry Hut (Chernikovskaia khata) used a B-52's beat and mix of humor, violence, and low-tech 1990s nostalgia to create a compelling image of the Wagner brand:

> Я не был рождён для любви,
> Я не смогу стать миллионером
> Борьба с верховным властелином тьмы
> Мне не поможет сделать твиттер карьеру.
> Жизнью я награждён
> Лишь один особым талантом
> Я в этот мир пришёл
> Для того, чтобы быть музыкантом

---

18. "'Музыкантам' заказали 'Град' и ливень, / Это Вагнер - небо затянуло дымом. / Выступаем под симфонию Валькирий, / Одеялом из свинца врага накрыло."

19. "Оркестранты, воины России / Пусть пребудет с Вами благодать / Наши павшие, наши Святые / И небесная Божья рать." The Tsyganova tune was billed by Prigozhin's team as the "Wagner Anthem" and is available in its entirety at Sila v pravde (2022). By 4 March 2023, the channel had enough Wagner-oriented songs to create a "playlist" of ten numbers.

Неизвестный художник, подаривший нам в декабре 2020 года комикс про мифического "Вагнера", вернулся к творчеству.

FIGURE E.4. "The unknown artist who gave us the comix about the mythical 'Wagner Group' in December 2020 have returned to their artistic work" (13 December 2022/1333).

["I wasn't born for love, / I can't become a millionaire / The struggle with the supreme lord of darkness / Won't help me make a Twitter career. / I've been awarded with just one talent in life. / I came into this world / in order to be a musician"] (24 November 2022/889).[20]

In a rare moment of reading the stage directions out loud, Prigozhin introduced it as "the Wagner Group engaging in soft power, with youth in particular," praising the video-lyric combination as being "full of memes and references to the internet culture of the young generation, which is critical no matter how you look at it."

For a brief period, Wagner coverage appeared in official state propaganda as well. In an attempt to liven up state television coverage of the war that suffered from flagging viewer interest, prime-time host and Putin favorite Vladimir Solov'ev traveled to the front lines himself during these winter months, on several occasions paying visits to Wagner divisions and then reporting on it in great depth upon his return to the studio (12–13 December 2022/1286, 1329; 16 January 2023/2213; 23 January 2023/2424; 13 February 2023/3027; 16 February 2023/3123).[21] Moscow politicians jumped on the Wagner bandwagon, with longtime "Just Russia" leader Sergei Mironov posing with the iconic Wagner sledgehammer and the lower house voting to extend the law prohibiting the "discrediting" of the Russian army to "volunteer" divisions (20 January 2023/2339; 24 January 2023/2461). Prigozhin's Telegram channel became a powerful promotional and branding tool for the Wagner name and idea—largely at the expense of the Russian military and Ministry of Defense. At a time when Russians were weary of the platitudes fed to them by officialdom and its mouthpieces in the mainstream media, Prigozhin and Wagner offered an authentic-sounding story of bravery and heroism in times the channel openly acknowledged as difficult, all filtered through a robust media operation headed by a master of persuasion and propaganda.

Branding a National Leader

As Wagner's public profile soared, Prigozhin assumed greater visibility on the channel, touting his image as a hands-on boss and informal commander in chief. In a bit of geopolitical trolling, he twice posted videos of himself from the streets of Bakhmut, addressing Zelensky directly, inviting the Ukrainian president to meet with him in the embattled warzone to "sort things out" (20 December 2022/1469; 3 March 2023/3552). The channel hyped Prigozhin's trip to "the hottest Bakhmut

---

20. The complete music video is available at greyswandir_m (2022).
21. For an in-depth analysis of Solov'ev's rhetorical strategies for engaging viewers in the war effort, see Gorham 2025.

front" on New Year's Eve to underscore his support for Wagner fighters and his own bravery and self-sacrifice. "When you have a collective that believes you, that you can support, you have to come to it," one post quoted him as saying. "Every one of them is wondering how their loved ones are celebrating New Years. And I'm supposed to sit there luxuriating in front of the T.V. while they're here toiling away [*batrachat*]? My job is to be here together with them" (31 December 2022/1693). A later post documented Prigozhin on board a military cargo plane, eating cold burgers and sleeping on mattresses with the rest of the injured troops he was escorting back to the Wagner rehab center in the Russian city of Anapa to be fitted for prostheses. The message to the coddled oligarch elite was clear: "The masks are off: some are in a private jet in the Maldives, while others are in a cargo plane from the front. . . . You're either with us. Or against us" (13 January 2023/2046).

Prigozhin's growing dismissiveness of politicians and bureaucrats drinking champagne in their cozy offices back in Moscow, enamored with parades and adorned with honorary military medals, intensified over the course of these winter months in conjunction with his conflicts with the Ministry of Defense. "Heroes of the Fatherland should be on the frontlines, not in warm offices," he declared in a post following the national Day of Heroes of the Fatherland, commemorating general acts of bravery and valor (10 December 2022/1252). By late winter, early spring, he was calling out members of the military high command by name, accusing them of a "shell famine" (*snariadnyi golod*) intentionally designed to destroy Wagner.[22] As if to capitalize on his image as a charismatic, straight-talking man of action, the Prigozhin feed increased the number of recorded audio clips of the Wagner head, many of which featured him berating the treachery of the command authority in increasingly salty language that far exceeded any mat-based standard set by Putin. In an extended recording expressing his frustration with the lack of shells and missiles on the front lines, Prigozhin drew a stark contrast between indecisive bureaucrats in Moscow and soldiers at the front whose lives depended on those decisions getting made—invoking a colorful folk aphorism and creative vulgarism to frame his remarks:

> Like they say, shit boils, blood roils [*govno kipit, krov' burlit*], but my questions about the munitions, unfortunately, remain absolutely unresolved. . . . Someone is sitting, twiddling his thumbs and, based on his mood, deciding on whether or not to give us shells. At that very moment a concrete individual is dying. . . . A concrete wife, daughter, son, or mother is being deprived of their loved one. We lay him in a zinc coffin

---

22. The "shell famine" became a dominant theme in the months leading up to the mutiny, invoked twenty-nine times between March and the fateful "March of justice" in late June 2023.

Евгений Пригожин в Telegram

Жди родная, скоро инаугурация

FIGURE E.5.1.   "Wait my dear, the inauguration will soon be here" (13 March 2023/3860).

and take him to the cemetery to be buried. Is there really no conscience to stop fucking around like a fly on glass? (20 February 2023/3221)

Over the course of the spring, the feed reflected heightened public speculation about Prigozhin's own political ambitions (28 February 2023/3467; 29 April 2023/4987; 6 May 2023; 24–28 May 2024/5736, 5809, 5812, 5842, 5850). The credibility of his denials suffered with every repost of a pseudo-campaign poster presenting Prigozhin in the role of candidate (figs. E.5.1–3).

By March and April 2023, Prigozhin began taking greater liberties presenting his army as more than just an army and himself as more than just a CEO at its head. Wagner suddenly became an "army of a new type," an "idea-driven army" centered around the ideology of "justice" (*spravedlivost'*) (17 March 2024/4000). And Prigozhin, with the help of his own media team, comported himself more

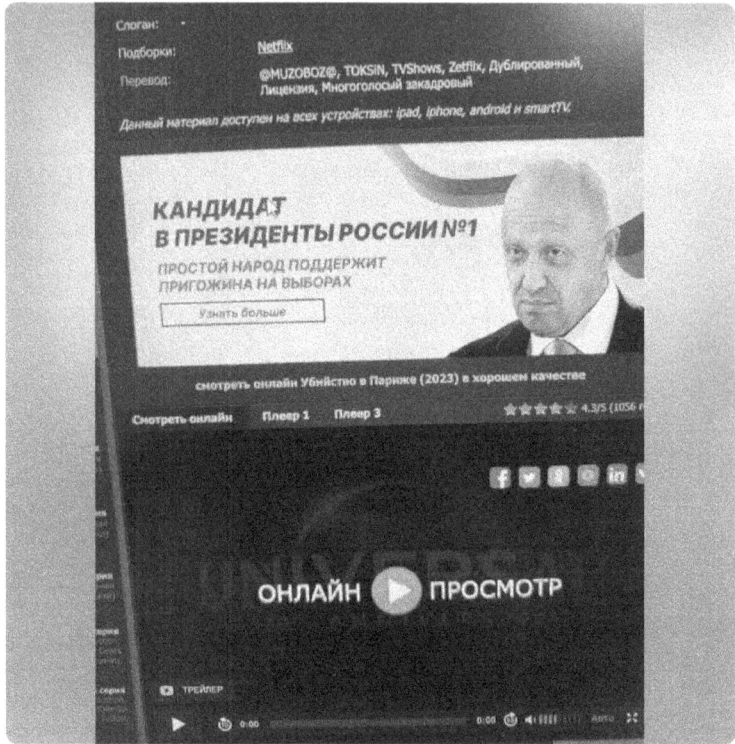

Евгений Пригожин в Telegram

Вот такую рекламу на сайтах стали видеть пользователи...

FIGURE E.5.2. "Here's an ad that users have begun to see on sites" (29 April 2023/4987).

and more like a public political figure, hosting "press conferences" for the first time (15 February 2023/3120) and making himself available for extended interviews—not just with journalists from his own FAN media empire (14 March 2023/3926; 23 June 2023/6457), but with some of the leading war correspondents covering the conflict, including Simon Pegov, author of one of the more influential Telegram channels ("WarGonzo") of the so-called Z-bloggers (10 February 2023/2959; 5 June 2023/6062). His press team even orchestrated televised trips to regional Russian cities to meet with Wagner supporters (1 June 2023/5923).[23]

---

23. In early June, Prigozhin launched a Wagner-sponsored television channel (PMC "Wagner": The Second Front) to counter the blackout supposedly initiated by state media with regards to reporting on the group (2 June 2023/5959).

В Сети развивается «рекламная кампания кандидата в президенты РФ Евгения Пригожина»

FIGURE E.5.3. "An 'ad campaign for presidential candidate Evgeny Prigozhin' is developing online" (12 May 2023/5383; the image's embedded text reads, "You need to shoot straight").

Although he never openly criticized Putin directly, Prigozhin came close enough on occasion to give the more suspicious cause for conjecture. He chastised the Kremlin's hard line on the popular singer Alla Pugacheva and her renegade antiwar husband, noting that she was "much bigger than Vladimir Putin" (2 May 2023/5049). A week later, on Victory Day, in a video-recorded complaint about the ongoing "shell famine," Prigozhin wondered aloud what would happen if the "happy grandad" in power turned out to be a "terminal asshole" (*zakonchennyi mudak*) (9 May 2023/5281).[24] And a post from the very day of the mutiny proudly declared that "the head of 'Wagner' [had] for the first time occupied the

---

24. Prigozhin denied the remarks had been directed at Putin (10 May 2023/5307), but his deflections were coy enough that the association and questions about it lingered for days.

Всюду знаки.

FIGURE E.6.   "Signs everywhere" (2 June 2023/5955).

first position in public opinion polls identifying him as 'a figure engendering trust'" (23 June 2023/6470).[25]

While we may never fully know the calculus that triggered Prigozhin's decision to launch his "March for justice" on Moscow, there were ample signs from the Telegram channels associated with him—the sheer number of subscribers and their level of engagement—that gave cause to believe he had substantial popular backing that translated into both symbolic and political authority, as well. While true that posted expressions of support, however creative, may have been relatively cheap in terms of the risk required to produce them, the fact that Prigozhin was met by crowds of supporters in the streets of the border town of Rostov and a Southern Military Command leadership willing to entertain his ambitions suggests there may have been good reason for him to think he had amassed significant enough authority to shake things up in the upper echelons of power (fig. E.6).[26]

So in the figure of Prigozhin we find not only confirmation of the degree to which authoritarian regimes have become adept at occupying digital space, gen-

---

25. That the poll appears to have come from the US-based *Newsweek* seems, if anything, to be a source of greater pride for the Prigozhin team, who opened the post with a direct quote from the American weekly.

26. That Putin ultimately, in the spring of 2024, replaced Shoigu and had his deputy, Timur Ivanov, arrested on bribery charges, serves as tacit admission that Prigozhin's claims were well founded.

erating viral pro-state memes, and fashioning persuasive profiles of authority. We also see how well-placed state operators can use these resources to ultimately undermine state authority to advance competing power interests. It is true, of course, that Prigozhin was no ordinary blogger. It's not every war correspondent that has his own media empire, a private military, and millions of rubles at his disposal to finance both. But in a political system made up of competing wealth and power interests spread across a variety of state and near-state institutions and a new media environment reliant on the outsourcing of influence and promotion, the potential of future rogue but well-funded and digitally networked patriots cannot be entirely dismissed—particularly if extenuating circumstances make for a more tenuous, volatile political environment, as they did in the fall of 2022.[27]

Prigozhin's dramatic rise to near-legendary status—even more so than Navalny's stubbornly persistent fight to bring an end to what he saw to be a hopelessly corrupt regime—serves as a cautionary tale for those in positions of power in Putin's Russia. As much as they try to constrain, control, and sovereignize new media technologies, those technologies have proven stubbornly resistant to rhetorical monopolization and persistently vulnerable to public political persuasion—whatever the political orientation—through the formation of alternative networked spheres. The history of public language in Russia suggests that windows of open and transformative civic discourse such as those carved out by Navalny and Prigozhin appear but tend to be fleeting. At the time of this writing, in the twilight of late Putinism, we still see signs of rhetorical volatility, however muted. In addition to the democratically inclined Navalny and the foul-mouthed nationalist Prigozhin, we see public posts of the mothers and wives of mobilized soldiers petitioning authorities to bring their sons and husbands back from the front, the disgruntled posts of turbo-patriotic war correspondents lambasting the military (in violation of the law, it should be added) for its gross mismanagement of the war and warning against a Russian capitulation, and a chorus of exiled oppositional voices and initiatives, however cacophonous they may at times sound. All the while, representatives of vlast' continue to fortify the foundation for the networked authoritarianism they have fostered, however imperfectly, since at least 2012: They continue to pass laws that criminalize most forms of public protest, enforce those laws in a selective but increasingly public and punitive manner, and lay the groundwork for wiring a sovereign internet.[28]

---

27. By the accounting of one independent source, there are at least thirty-seven private military companies currently operating in Russia, not all of which answer directly to the Ministry of Defense ("Catalog" n.d.).

28. Even the continued presence of oppositional discourse online, as Wijermars (2021, 16–17) observes, could serve as a useful resource for an authoritarian regime to "gauge public opinion."

Perhaps to greater effect, they incentivize and promote regime-friendly political speech, be it in the aggressive voice of the Z-blogger, or the kinder countenance of the producer of positive content. And they also continue to take advantage of the imperfect realities of new technologies themselves as communication tools—the fact that, regardless of the political orientation of the country in which they reside, virtual public spheres have proven all too susceptible to trolling, disinformation, hate speech, walled gardens, information bubbles, and algorithms driven by corporate interests. How this battle over the networked public sphere evolves remains difficult to predict due to overlapping factors of time, technology, competency, the willingness of the regime to ratchet up repression, and the willingness of the population to live with the disconnect between state rhetoric and reality. But the Navalny and Prigozhin legacies show that, even in the most authoritarian regimes, language still matters for legitimating power and, while digital media most certainly offer new tools for division, repression and surveillance, they continue to pose a threat to any attempted monopoly over public speech.

Acknowledgments

This book is the result of over ten years of research made possible by a variety of colleagues, foundations, and institutions. The earliest germination of the project occurred thanks largely to the Norwegian Research Council, the University of Bergen, Professor Ingunn Lunde, and the international working group of scholars participating in her four-year research project, The Future of Russian: Language Culture in the Era of New Technology. Significant parts of the manuscript emerged from extended visiting scholar appointments and invitations made possible by a handful of generous and perspicacious European colleagues and institutions: Dirk Uffelmann and the University of Passau; Stefan Hedlund and the Centre for Russian and Eurasian Studies, Uppsala University; Lara Ryzanova-Clark, the Princess Dashkova Centre and the Department of European Languages and Cultures, University of Edinburgh; Ekaterina Chown and the Department of Russian and Slavonic Studies, University of Nottingham; Derek Offord and the School of Modern Languages, University of Bristol; Riccardo Nicolosi and Ludwig-Maximilians University, Munich. I'd like to express particular thanks to individuals who have devoted time and thought to this book at various stages, including Eliot Borenstein, Helena Goscilo, Stephen Hutchings, and particularly Vera Zvereva, who has been an inspiring fellow traveler in language and internet studies throughout the project's fruition. And I am grateful to Cornell University Press editor, Mahinder Kingra, and his marketing and production team—Karen Laun, Kristen Gregg, India Miraglia, and Allison Gudenau—for the time, attention, and professionalism they devoted to the book's vetting and final production. Of course, any shortcomings with regard to conceptualization and execution rest with me alone.

The book would be far less cohesive and timely had it not been for the generous funding and support of several granting agencies: the American Council of Learned Societies, the National Endowment for the Humanities, and, for the final push, the National Humanities Center (and the Archie K. Brown Fellowship), its brilliant and welcoming staff, and the inspiring and spirited collegiality of my fellow study-, lunch-, and hiking-mates from the NHC Class of 2023–24. I am likewise grateful to University of Florida librarians (Hélène Huet) and administrators (Mary Watt, Tunde Akinyemi, and Alioune Sow; Paul D'Aneri and Dave Richardson; Joe Glover) who provided critical support in the form of services, time, and funding, and recognized the value of research in the humanities.

Finally, I am eternally grateful to Veronika for her unfailing love and companionship, and to Anna and Jakob for the love, grounding, and welcome distraction they provided during the evolution of this book over such a wonderful decade of our family's life.

Portions of this manuscript include significantly revised and expanded versions of previously published articles and book chapters. Earlier versions of parts of the introduction appeared in "Russian Political Discourse" (in *Encyclopedia of Slavic Languages and Literatures*, ed. Marc L. Greenberg and Lenore A. Grenoble) and "Putin's Language" (in *Putin as Celebrity and Cultural Icon*, ed. Helena Goscilo, chap. 4 [Routledge, 2012]). Earlier versions of the first two sections of chapter 3 appeared in "Politicians Online: Prospects and Perils of 'Direct Internet Democracy'" (in *Digital Russia: The Language, Culture, and Politics of New Media Communication*, ed. Michael S. Gorham, Ingunn Lunde, and Martin Paulsen, chap. 13 [Routledge 2014]) and "Medvedev's New Media Gambit: The Language of Power in 140 Characters or Less" (in *Power and Legitimacy: Challenges from Russia*, ed. Per-Arne Bodin, Stefan Hedlund, and Elena Namli, chap. 12 [Routledge, 2012]). Chapter 5 represents a revised and expanded version of material published in "Троллинг, власть и политическая коммуникация в путинской России (Trolling, power, and political communication in Putin's Russia)," *Neprikosnovennyi Zapas* 123, no. 4 (2020); and "Humpty Dumpty and the Troll Factory: Varieties of Verbal Subversion on the Russian-Language Internet," *Zeitschrift für Slavische Philologie* 73, no. 1 (2017): 79–103. Parts of chapters 5 and 6 contain revised and expanded excerpts from "О 'падонках' и 'кибердружинниках': Виртуальные источники порчи языка (On 'scumbags' and 'cyber patrols': The virtual sources of language spoiling)" in *Nastroika iazyka: Upravlenie kommunikatsiiami na postsovetskom prostranstve*, ed. E. G. Lapina-Kratasyuk, O. V. Moroz, and E. G. Nim, 240–258 (NLO Press, 2016); and chapter 8 represents a substantially revised and updated version of "Beyond a World with One Master: The Rhetorical Dimensions of Putin's 'Sovereign Internet,'" in *Transnational Russian Studies*, ed. Andy Byford, Connor Doak, and Stephen Hutchings, chap. 16 (Liverpool University Press, 2020).

Works Cited

"3 mlrd rublei 2021 uidet iz biudzheta na sozdanie molodezhnogo kontenta." 2021. *Novye izvestiia*, 20 July. Persistent East View URL: https://dlib.eastview.com /browse/doc/69027611.

"15 punktov grazhdanina Rossii, zheliaiushchego blaga svoei strane." 2023. *Navalnyi*, 20 February. https://navalny.com/p/6634/.

"26 marta v tsifrakh i sloganakh." 2017. *New Times*, 27 March. https://newtimes.ru /articles/detail/115992.

Agamov, Aleksandr. 2000. "IV Vserossiiskii internet-forum." 16 March. Persistent Integrum URL, https://aafnet.integrum.ru/artefact3/ia/ia5.aspx/fymyUn2R/3766 /utrmos_D20000316_N50_G121_L2005052704030661_A013.txt.

"Agitatsionnyi videorolik 'NAROD za legalizatsiiu grazhdanskogo oruzhiia'." 2007. *navalny*, 27 September. https://navalny.livejournal.com/163552.html.

Akhmadieva, Anna. 2013. "Rospechat' otkazala kanalu 'Dozhd'' v subsidiiakh." *Izvestiia*, 1 March. https://iz.ru/news/545878.

Akhmirova R. 2012. "Oppozitsiia zavisla." *Sobesednik*, 24 October.

Alekseevskikh, Anastasiia. 2016. "Za oskorblenie v sotsetiakh mozhno budet poluchit' kompensatsiiu." *Izvestiia*, 2 June. https://iz.ru/news/616327.

Alexanyan, Karina, Vladimir Barash, Bruce Etling, Bruce Faris, Urs Gasser, John Kelly, John Palfrey, and Hal Roberts. 2012. "Exploring Russian Cyberspace: Digitally-Mediated Collective Action and the Networked Public Sphere." Berkman Center Research Publication No. 2012-2. https://papers.ssrn.com/sol3/papers.cfm ?abstract_id=2014998.

Al'ians Media. 2003. "Istoriia interneta v Rossiii pishetsia uzhe segodnia." *Novosti Rossii*, 30 March.

Annenkov, Andrei. 2014. "Igor' Shchegolev: 'Ucheniia podtverdili nedostatochnuiu ustoichivost' Runeta pri nedruzhestvennykh "tselenapravelennykh deistviiakh."'" *Ekspertnyi tsentr elektronnogo gosudarstva*, 17 October. http://d-russia .ru/ucheniya-podtverdili-nedostatochnuyu-ustojchivost-runeta-pri-nedruz hestvennyx-celenapravlennyx-dejstviyax.html.

Antonova, Alena. 2000. "Effektivnyi politik otkryl novuiu stranu." *Kommersant''-Daily*, 29 September.

Antonova, Elizaveta. 2019. "Chinovnikov obuchat vesti Instagram i anonimnye Telegram-kanaly." *RBK*, 30 January, https://www.rbc.ru/politics/30/01/2019/5c4f232 a9a7947378ebbadf7.

Arendt, Hannah. 1969. "On Violence." In *Crises of the Republic*. Harcourt Brace Jovanovich.

Arenina, Katia. 2021. "Imperiia kiberstukachestva." *Vazhnye istorii*, 5 May. https://istories .media/reportages/2021/05/05/imperiya-kiberstukachestva/.

"Arkhangel'sk -- zdes' nachnaetsia Arktika." 2021. *ByForeigners*. https://www.youtube.com /watch?v=57HDt_jriDU&t=1413s.

"Arkhiv." 2004. *Zavtra*, 10 March.

"Arkhiv konkursov." n.d. *IRI: Institut razvitiia interneta*. https://xn--h1aax.xn--p1ai/contests/.

Asmolov, Gregory. 2010a. "Aleksei Naval'nyi: 'Ia pytaius' dokazat', chto borot'sia s rezhimom—eto veselo." *Global Voices*, 28 October. https://ru.globalvoices.org /2010/10/29/2703/.

Asmolov, Gregory. 2010b. "Bloggers React to President Medvedev's Silicon Valley Tour." *Global Voices Online*, 26 June. http://globalvoicesonline.org/2010/06/26 /russia-bloggers-react-to-president-medvedevs-silicon-valley-tour/.

Asmolov, Gregory. 2020. "'Sovereign Virus': Fake News as the Kremlin's Crisis Management Tool." *Institute of Modern Russia*, 16 July. https://imrussia.org/en/analysis/3139 -%E2%80%9Csovereign-virus%E2%80%9D-fake-news-as-a-crisis-management -tool.

Atnashev, Timur and Mikhail Velizhev, eds. 2020. "(Pozdne)sovetskie publichnye sfery: Imitatsiia, osvoenie, tvorchestvo." *Novoe literaturnoe obozrenie* 164 (4). https://www.nlobooks.ru/magazines/novoe_literaturnoe_obozrenie/164 _nlo_4_2020/article/22678/.

Avdeev, S. 2011. "Laskovye seti." *Rossiiskaia gazeta*, 11 May.

Badanin, Roman and Mikhail Maglov. 2024. "Vertikal' Kadyrova. Fil'm o tainakh chechenskoi vlasti." *proekt.*, 17 June. https://www.proekt.media/guide/vertical -ramzan-kadyrov/.

Bagirov, Eduard. 2013. "'Naval'nyi dolzhen sidet'.'" *Izvestiia*, 16 May.

Baigarova, Polina. 2010. "'Electronic Russia': Reality or (Empty) Promises?" *Digitial Icons: Studies in Russian, Eurasian and Central European New Media* 3:103–106. https://digitalicons.org/issue03/electronic-russia-reality-or-empty-promises -interview-with-ivan-ninenko/.

Baimukhametov, Sergei. 2017. "'Rebiata, on ne nash, ne s okeana'." *Moskovskaia pravda*, 27 March. East View persistent URL, https://dlib.eastview.com/browse /doc/48506067.

Barabanov, Il'ia. 2011. "Esli by ia ostalsia spikerom Soveta Federatsii, partii ne bylo by v Gosdume." *New Times*, 19 December.

Barabanov, Il'ia, and Denis Korotkov. 2024. *"Nashe delo—smert'": Pol'naia istoriia ChVK "Vagner" i ego osnovatelia Evgeniia Prigozhina*. Meduza.

Bardin, Pavel. 2000. "Marina Litvinovich: 'My—gosudarevo oko. V onlaine.'" *Izvestiia*, 23 November.

Baron, Naomi S. 2008. *Always On: Language in an Online and Mobile World*. Oxford University Press.

Bavil'skii, Dmitrii. 2005. "Vladimirskii tsentral." *Vzgliad*, 23 June.

Baym, Nancy. 2010. *Personal Connections in the Digital Age*. Polity.

Bekbulatova. Taisiia. 2018. "Dissident, kotoryi stal ideologom Putina: Polnaia istoriia Gleba Pavlovskogo—cheloveka, pridumavshego sovremennuiu rossiiskuiu vlast'." *Meduza*, 9 July. https://meduza.io/feature/2018/07/09/dissident-kotoryy -stal-ideologom-putina.

Belokopytova, Vasilisa. 2017. "Bez versii dlia Sailfish – ne otechestvennoe." *Izvestiia*, 26 April. http://izvestia.ru/news/691793.

Beluza, Aleksandra. 2009a. "'Elektronnoe pravilte'stvo poka prebyvaet 'v izgnanii'." *Izvestiia*, 27 April.

Beluza, Aleksandra. 2009b. "Pishite pis'ma v '.rf'." *Izvestiia*, 10 November.

Benkler, Yochai. 2006. *The Wealth of Networks: How Social Production Transforms Markets and Freedom*. Yale University Press.

Bentivegna, Sara. 2002. "Politics and New Media." In *Handbook of New Media: Social Shaping and Consequences of ICTs*, edited by Leah A.Lievrouw and Sonia Livingstone. Sage.

Bergengruen, Vera. 2022. "How Telegram Became the Digital Battlefield of the Russia-Ukraine War." *Time*, 21 March. https://time.com/6158437/telegram-russia-ukraine-information-war/.

Besedin, Platon. 2019. "Evoliutsiia khamstva: Kak vygliadit novyi fashizm." *Moskovskii komsomolets*, 16 April. East View persistent URL, https://dlib.eastview.com/browse/doc/53238177.

Beshlei, Ol'ga. 2013. "Deklaratsiia nezavisimosti." *New Times*, 14 August. https://newtimes.ru/articles/detail/69812/.

Beshlei, Ol'ga, and Igor' Mostovshchikov. 2011. "Sledite za litsom." *New Times*, 8 September. https://newtimes.ru/articles/detail/43075.

"'Bezopasnost' 2.0. OP RF otkroetsia tsentr monitoringa sotssetei." 2017. *Obshchestvennaia palata Rossiiskoi Federatsii*, 1 November. https://old.oprf.ru/press/news/2017/newsitem/42692.

Biagioli, Mario, and Vincent Antonin Lépinay, eds. 2019. *From Russia with Code: Programming Migrations in Post-Soviet Times*. Duke University Press.

Bilevskaia, Elina. 2009. "Elektronnye spory Kremlia s Belym domom." *Nezavisimaia gazeta*, 19 November.

Bilevskaia, Elina. 2010. "On-line politika." *Nezavisimaia gazeta*, 21 January. https://www.ng.ru/politics/2010-01-21/1_online.html.

blondycandy. 2010. "Pochemu v russkoi blogosfere tak mnogo nenavisti?" blondycandy.com, 25 May. http://blondycandy.livejournal.com/214091.html.

Bobrova. Ekaterina. 2006. "Glavnoe—nenavidet' drug druga." *Re:Aktsiia* 21 (15–25 June). http://www.reakcia.ru/article/?1163.

Bodrunova, Svetlana S., Anna Litvinenko, Ivan Blekhanov, and Dmitry Nepiyushchikh. 2021. "Constructive Aggression? Multiple Roles of Aggressive Content in Political Discourse on Russian YouTube." *Media and Communication* 9:181–94. http://dx.doi.org/10.17645/mac.v9i1.3469.

Bogdanov, Iurii. 2015. "Institut razvitiia interneta ukrepit tsifrovoi suverenitet strany." Vzgliad, 12 March. https://vz.ru/society/2015/3/12/734014.html.

Boiarinov, Denis. 2001. "Vlast' tsifr." *Novoe vremia*, 29 April.

Bondarev, Denis. 2017. "Minkomsviazi predlozhilo uzhestochit' trebovaniia k operatoram sviazi." *RBK*, 12 January. http://www.rbc.ru/technology_and_media/12/01/2017/587652c89a794745a5b74256.

Borenstein, Eliot. 2022. *Meanwhile, in Russia . . .: Russian Internet Memes and Viral Video*. Bloomsbury Academic.

Borisov, Andrei. 2002. "Porno voiny Runeta. Epizod 4." Kompromat.ru, 15 March. https://www.compromat.ru/page_11625.htm.

Borodina, Tat'iana and Anastasiia Kashevarova. 2015. "Kreativnyi klass poshel vo vlast'." Izvestiia, 23 December. Persistent East View URL: https://dlib.eastview.com/browse/doc/45914143.

Borodulin, Igor'. 2009. "Provaider dlia 'elektronnogo pravitel'stva.'" *Nezavisimaia gazeta*, 22 October.

Bourdieu, Pierre. 1991. *Language and Symbolic Power*. Edited by John B. Thompson, translated by Gino Raymond and Mathew Adamson. Harvard University Press.

Braterskii, Aleksandr. 2020. "Poiskovik 'Sputnik' soshel s orbity. Kak obespechit' tekhnologicheskii suverenitet." *Finam*, 8 September. https://www.finam.ru/publications/item/poiskovik-sputnik-soshel-s-orbity-kak-obespechit-texnologicheskiiy-suverenitet-20200908-19500/.

Bratton, Benjamin H. 2015. *The Stack: On Software and Sovereignty*. MIT Press.

Budnitsky, Stanislav. 2024. "State Pranking: Deceit and Humor in Russia-West Relations." *Post-Soviet Affairs* 40 (6). https://doi/full/10.1080/1060586X.2024.2374191.

Burgess, Jean, and Joshua Green. 2018. *YouTube: Online Video and Participatory Culture*. Polity. ProQuest Ebook Central, https://ebookcentral.proquest.com/lib
/ufl/detail.action?docID=5502950.

Burkhardt, Fabian, and Mariëlle Wijermars. 2022. "Digital Authoritarianism and Rus-
sia's War against Ukraine: How Sanctions-Induced Infrastructural Disruptions
Are Reshaping Russia's Repressive Capacities." *SAIS Review of International
Affairs* 42 (2): 21–43.

Bykov, Dmitrii. 2007. "MEAN-EYE'v." *Polit.ru*, 26 February. http://www.polit.ru
/author/2007/02/26/bykov_print.html.

Carr, Nicholas. 2007. "Twitter Dot Dash." *Rough Type*, 18 March (reissued 14 April
2009). http://www.roughtype.com/archives/2009/04/dot_dash_dot_da.php.

Cassiday, Julie A. 2023. *Russian Style: Performing Gender, Power, and Putinism*. University of Wisconsin Press.

"Catalog of Russian PMCs; 37 private military companies of the Russian Federation."
n.d. Molfar Intelligence Institute. https://www.molfar.institute/en/catalog-of
-russian-pmcs/.

Chadwick, Andrew. 2013. *The Hybrid Media System: Politics and Power*. Oxford University Press.

Chander, Anupam, and Haochen Sun. 2022. "Sovereignty 2.0." *Vanderbilt Journal of
Transnational Law* 55 (2): 283–324.

Chebankova, Elena. 2013. *Civil Society in Putin's Russia*. Routledge.

Chilton, Paul. 2004. *Analysing Political Discourse: Theory and Practice*. Routledge.

"Chinovniki potratiat 10 mlrd rublei na 'gosudarstvennuiu nravstvennost' v Seti."
2021. *Novye izvestiia*, 17 August.

"Chto mozhet pomeshat' prevrashcheniiu Rossii v elektronnuiu stranu?" 2001. *Kommersant*, 13 July.

Chuprinina, Iunna. 2007. "LESS da LESS krugom." *Itogi* 9 (26 February): 86.

Cohen, C. 1972/2002. *Folk Devils and Moral Panics: The Creation of the Mods and
Rockers*. 3rd ed. Routledge Classics.

Coleman, E. Gabriella. 2012. "Phreaks, Hackers, and Trolls: The Politics of Transgression and Spectacle." In *The Social Media Reader*, edited by Michael Mandiberg.
New York University Press.

Coleman, Stephen. 2004. "Blogs as Listening Posts Rather Than Soapboxes." In *Political Blogs: Craze or Convention?*, edited by Rose Ferguson and Milica Howell.
Hansard Society.

Couture, Stephane, and Sophie Toupin. 2019. "What Does the Notion of 'Sovereignty'
Mean When Referring to the Digital?" *new media & society* 21 (10): 2305–322.

Danilov, Viacheslav. 2016. "Trolli publichnogo litsemeriia." Life.ru, 30 June. https://
life.ru/p/426304.

"Data on Politically Motivated Criminal Prosecutions in Russia." 2023. *OVD-Info* (16
November), https://ovd.info/politpressing.

Daucé, Françoise. 2017. "The Civility of Oppression." *Politika*. https://www.politika.io
/en/notice/the-civility-of-oppression.

Daucé, Françoise. 2020. "Disguising the Internet? Website Design and Control in
Russia." *Digital Icons: Studies in Russian, Eurasian, and Central European New
Media* 20: 1–15.

Davydov, Ivan. 2000a. "Interpol, vypusk tretii, postpredprazdnichnyi." *Russkii zhurnal*,
5 May. http://old.russ.ru/politics/interpol/20000505.html.

Davydov, Ivan. 2000b. "Gleb Pavlovskii o literature, Internete i budushchem."
    Ezhednevnyi zhurnal, 12 December. https://ezhe.ru/data/eks/14.html.
"Debosh debaty." 2007. *Tvoi den'*. Reprinted at http://dadebatam.ru/pressa-o-debatah.
Deibert, Ronald, John Palfrey, Rafal Rohozinski, and Jonathan Zittrain. 2010. *Access
    Controlled: The Shaping of Power, Rights, and Rule in Cyberspace.* MIT Press.
Dik, Sergei. 2019. "Varlamov: Otkliuchenie ot global'noi seti privedet k degradatsii
    Rossii." *DW.com*, 22 March. https://www.dw.com/ru/%D0%B8%D0%BB
    %D1%8C%D1%8F-%D0%B2%D0%B0%D1%80%D0%BB%D0%B0%D0
    %BC%D0%BE%D0%B2-%D0%BE%D1%82%D0%BA%D0%BB%D1%8E%D1
    %87%D0%B5%D0%BD%D0%B8%D0%B5-%D0%BE%D1%82-%D0%B3
    %D0%BB%D0%BE%D0%B1%D0%B0%D0%BB%D1%8C%D0%BD%D0%BE
    %D0%B9-%D1%81%D0%B5%D1%82%D0%B8-%D0%BF%D1%80%D0%B8
    %D0%B2%D0%B5%D0%B4%D0%B5%D1%82-%D0%BA-%D0%B4%D0%B5
    %D0%B3%D1%80%D0%B0%D0%B4%D0%B0%D1%86%D0%B8%D0%B8
    -%D1%80%D0%BE%D1%81%D1%81%D0%B8%D0%B8/a-47996570.
Dobrokhotov, Roman, Nikita Lashuk, and Margarita Belodedova. 2012. "Elena Mizulina:
    'Vikipediia—prikrytie pedofil'skogo lobbi'." *Slon*, 10 July. http://slon.ru/russia
    /elena_mizulina_vikipediya_prikrytie_pedofilskogo_lobbi-809860.xhtml.
Dobrynin, Sergei. 2019. "Suverennyi Russkii Internet: boiat'sia ili smeiatsia." *Radio
    Svoboda*, 16 February. https://www.svoboda.org/a/29772298.html.
"Doktrina informatsionnoi bezopasnosti Rossiiskoi Federatsii." 2000. *Nezavisimaia
    gazeta*, 15 September. http://www.ng.ru/politics/2000-09-15/0_infodoctrine
    .html.
"Doktrina informatsionnoi bezopasnosti Rossiiskoi Federatsii." 2016. *Rossiiskaia gazeta*,
    6 December. https://rg.ru/documents/2016/12/06/doktrina-infobezobasnost
    -site-dok.html.
Dolbaum, Jan Matti, Andrey Semenov, and Elena Sirotkina. 2018. "A Top-Down
    Movement with Grass-Roots Effects? Alexei Navalny's Electoral Campaign."
    Social Movement Studies 17 (5): 618–25.
Dorokhov, Roman. 2012. "Saity v zakone." *Vedomosti*, 19 December. East View persis-
    tent URL, https://dlib.eastview.com/browse/doc/28279966.
Drake, William J., Vinton G. Cerf, and Wolfgang Kleinwächter. 2016. "Internet Frag-
    mentation: An Overview." Future of the Internet Initiative White Paper. World
    Economic Forum.
Dugaev, Daniil, and Daniel' Lur'e. 2000. "Marina Litvinovich: 'Putin prikhodit, i s etim
    uzhe nichego ne podelat''." Internet.ru, 23 March. Reposted at FKML, http://
    litvinovich.narod.ru/iru.html.
Dzekholovskii, Zigmund. 1999. "Bezzastenchivyi duet." *InoPressa*, 27 December.
Earle, Jonathan. 2013. "Smut-Free Web Evokes Censorship Fears." *Moscow Times*, 5
    February.
Edgar, Andrew, and Peter Sedgwick. 2002. *Cultural Theory: The Key Thinkers*. Rout-
    ledge.
"Eks-glava Nokia v Rossii zaimetsia vnedreniem sistem 'suverennogo Runeta'." 2019.
    RBK, 26 September. https://www.rbc.ru/technology_and_media/26/09/2019
    /5d8b4c1c9a7947d3c58f9a48.
Elder, Miriam. 2013. "Chechen Leader Ramzan Kadyrov Bemoans the Burden of
    Instagram." *The Guardian*, 4 March. http://www.theguardian.com/world/2013
    /mar/04/ramzan-kadyrov-struggles-instagram.
Epifanova, Mariia. 2014. "Blokada im. Lugovogo." *Novaia gazeta*, 17 March. East View
    persistent URL, https://dlib.eastview.com/browse/doc/39122611.

Epshtein, Mikhail. 2012. "Russian Spirituality and the Theology of Negation." Center for Democratic Culture at Digital Scholarship@UNLV, https://digitalscholarship .unlv.edu/cgi/viewcontent.cgi?article=1012&context=russian_culture.

Ermolin, Anatolii. 2011. "Instruktsiia ot Vasiliia Iakemenko." *New Times*, 29 August. https://newtimes.ru/articles/detail/42858/.

Erpyleva, Svetlana, and Oleg Zhuravlev. 2021. "What's New about Russia's New Protests?" *openDemocracy*, 3 June. https://www.opendemocracy.net/en/odr/whats-new-in -russia-protests-2021-navalny/.

Ershova, Tat'iana, and Iurii Khokhlov. 2003. "Portaly v korobke dlia organov vlasti." *Nezavisimaia gazeta*, 6 June.

Fairclough, Norman. 1995. *Critical Discourse Analysis: The Critical Study of Language.* Longman.

Fak, Alex. 2003. "E-Russia Faces Uphill Information Battle." *Moscow Times*, 21 August.

Falaleev, M. 2011. "FIO-FIO-SAM." *Rossiiskaia gazeta*, 8 December.

Farbman, Sam. 2023. "Telegram, 'Milbloggers' and the Russian State." *Survival* 65 (3): 107–128.

Federal'nyi zakon No. 30-FZ. 2019. "Federal'nyi zakon ot 18 marta 2019 g. N 30-FZ 'O vnesenii izmeneniia v Federal'nyi zakon "Ob informatsii, informatsionnykh tekhnologiiakh i o zashchite informatsii".'" *Rossiiskaia gazeta*, 18 March. https:// rg.ru/documents/2019/03/20/a1667334-internet-gossimvoly-dok.html.

Federal'nyi zakon No. 31-FZ. 2019. "Federal'nyi zakon ot 18 marta 2019 g. N 31-FZ 'O vnesenii izmenenii v stat'iu 15.3 Federal'nogo zakona "Ob informatsii, infor-matsionnykh tekhnologiiakh i o zashchite informatsii".'" *Garant*, 18 March. https://base.garant.ru/72198118.

Federal'nyi zakon No. 32-FZ. 2022. "Federal'nyi zakon ot 4 marta 2022 g. N 32-FZ 'O vnesenii izmenenii v Ugolovnyi kodeks Rossiiskoi Federatsii i stat'i 31 i 151 Ugolovno-protsessual'nogo kodeksa Rossiiskoi Federatsii." *Rossiiskaia gazeta*, 9 March. https://rg.ru/documents/2022/03/09/armiya-dok.html.

Federal'nyi zakon No. 65-FZ. 2012. "Federal'nyi zakon 'O vnesenii izmenenii v Kodeks Rossiiskoi Federatsii ob administrativnykh pravonarusheniiakh i Federal'nyi zakon "O sobraniiakh, mitingakh, demonstratsiiakh, shestviiakh i piketirovani-iakh"' ot 08.06.2012 N 65-FZ." *Konsul'tantPlius*, 8 June. https://www.consultant .ru/document/cons_doc_LAW_130936/.

Federal'nyi zakon No. 90-FZ. 2019. "Federal'nyi zakon ot 1 maia 2019 g. N 90-FZ 'O vnesenii izmenenii v Federal'nyi zakon "O sviazi" i Federal'nyi zakon "Ob infor-matsii, informatsionnykh tekhnologiiakh i o zashchite informatsii".'" *Rossiiskaia gazeta*, 7 May. https://rg.ru/documents/2019/05/07/fz90-dok.html.

Federal'nyi zakon No. 97-FZ. 2014. "Federal'nyi zakon ot 5 maia 2014 g. N 97-FZ 'O vnesenii izmenii v Federal'nyi zakon "Ob informatsii, informatsionnykh tekh-nologiiakh i o zashchite informatsii" i otdel'nye zakonodatel'nye akty Rossiiskoi Federatsii po voprosam uporiadocheniia obmena informatsiei s ispol'zovaniem informatsionno-telekommunikatsionnykh setei.'" *Rossiiskaia gazeta*, 7 May. https://rg.ru/2014/05/07/informtech-dok.html.

Federal'nyi zakon No. 121-FZ. 2012. "Federal'nyi zakon ot 20.07.2012 No. 121-FZ 'O vnesenii izmenenii v otdelnye zakonodatel'nye akty Rossiiskoi Federatsii v chasti regulirovanii deiatel'nosti nekommercheskikh organizatsii, vypolniaiush-chikh funktsii inostrannogo agenta.'" *Ofitsial'noe opublikovanie pravovykh aktov*, 23 July. http://publication.pravo.gov.ru/Document/View/0001201207230003.

Federal'nyi zakon No. 136-FZ. 2013. "Federal'nyi zakon 'O vnesenii izmenenii v stat'iu 148 Ugolovnogo kodeksa Rossiiskoi Federatsii i otdel'nye zakonodatel'nye akty Rossiiskoi Federatsii v tseliakh protivodeistviia oskorbleniiu religioznykh ubezhdenii i chuvstv grazhdan' ot 29.06.2013 N 136-FZ (posledniaia redakt-siia)." *Konsul'tantPlius*, 29 June. https://www.consultant.ru/document/cons _doc_LAW_148270/.

Federal'nyi zakon No. 242-FZ. 2014. "Federal'nyi zakon ot 21.7.2014 No. 242-FZ 'O vnesenii izmenenii v otdel'nye zakonodatel'nye akty Rossiiskoi Federatsii v chasti utochneniia poriadka obrabotki personal'nykh dannykh v informatsionno-tele-komunikatsionnykh setiakh'." *Ofitsial'noe opublikovanie pravovykh aktov*, 22 July. http://publication.pravo.gov.ru/Document/View/0001201407220042.

Federal'nyi zakon No. 398-FZ. 2013. "Federal'nyi zakon ot 28 dekabria 2013 g. N 398-FZ 'O vnesenii izmenenii v Federal'nyi zakon "Ob informatsii, informat-sionnykh tekhnologiiakh i o zashchite informatsii"'." *Garant.ru*, 28 December. https://base.garant.ru/70552568/.

Federal'nyi zakon No. 436-FZ. 2010. "Federal'nyi zakon 'O zashchite detei ot informat-sii, prichiniaiushchei vred ikh zdorov'iu i razvitiiu' ot 29.12.2010 N 436-FZ." *Konsul'tantPlius*, 29 December. https://www.consultant.ru/document/cons _doc_LAW_108808/.

Fedotov, Viktor. 2002. "Berezovskii nameren ochernit' Putina?" *Dni.ru*, 13 August. https://web.archive.org/web/20021225220817/http:/www.dni.ru/news/analitika /2002/8/13/12992.html.

Filatova, Viktoriia. 2013. "Prichiny detskogo suitsida ishchite vnutri sem'i." *Vecherni-aia Moskva*, 20 March. East View persistent URL, https://dlib.eastview.com /browse/doc/28939939.

"Finalistov premii za luchshie sotsial'no znachimye internet-proekty ob''iaviat 3 marta." 2022. *Novye izvestiia*, 15 February. https://newizv.ru/news/2022-02-15 /finalistov-premii-za-luchshie-sotsialno-znachimye-internet-proekty-ob -yavyat-3-marta-347046.

Fishman, Mikhail. 2012. "Obshchestvennyi interes: Reformy po-khlestakovski." *Vedo-mosti*, 13 July. East View persistent URL, https://dlib.eastview.com/browse /doc/27396176.

Fishman M. 2017. "Usmanov vs. Navalny: How an Oligarch Reignited Political Debate in Russia." *Moscow Times*, 24 May. https://themoscowtimes.com/articles/usmanov -vs-navalny-how-an-oligarch-reignited-politic-debate-in-russia-58077.

Floria, Aleksandr. 2010. "O kontsepte 'khamstvo'." *Svobodnaia mysl'*, no. 1, 185–96.

"Fond 'tainoi imperii' Medvedeva opublikovali otchety o raskhody." 2017. *Nastoiash-chee vremia*, 25 April. https://www.currenttime.tv/a/28451145.html.

Foucault, Michel. 1972. *The Archaeology of Knowledge and the Discourse on Language*. Translated by A. M. Sheridan Smith. Pantheon Books.

"Freedom on the Net 2024: Russia." 2024. *Freedom House*. https://freedomhouse.org /country/russia/freedom-net/2024.

Fuller, Liz and Aslan Doukaev. 2007. "Chechnya: Kadyrov Uses 'Folk Islam' For Politi-cal Gain." *Radio Free Europe/Radio Liberty*, 6 December. https://www.rferl.org /a/1079237.html.

Gabdulhakov, Rashid. 2020. "(Con)trolling the Web: Social Media User Arrests, State-Supported Vigilantism and Citizen Counter-Forces in Russia." *Global Crime* 21 (3–4): 283–305.

Galimova, Natal'ia. 2017. "'Zadacha Putina—pobedit' s khoroshim rezul'tatom." *RBK*, 23 January. https://www.rbc.ru/interview/politics/23/01/2017/5880ae389a7947 3751d5a09e.

Galimova, Natal'ia. 2019. "Rosmolodezh' opredelilas' s kuratorom molodezhnogo kon-tenta dlia Seti Tri voprosa o finansirovanii proizvodstva sotsial'no znachimoi informatsii dlia molodezhi." *RBK*, 15 November.

Gamzaeva, Svetlana. 2007. "Strateg Shantseva i plan Putina." *NG-regiony*, 1 October. https://www.ng.ru/ngregions/2007-10-01/16_shancev.html.

Garmazhapova, Aleksandra. 2013. "Gde zhivut trolli. I kto ikh kormit." *Novaia gazeta*, 9 September. http://www.novayagazeta.ru/politics/59889.html.

Gavrichenkov, Artem. 2021. "Razdelit' internet: kak strany pytaiutsia naiti natsional'nye granitsy Seti." *RBK*, 7 June. https://trends.rbc.ru/trends/industry/5f7de8499a7947adf5412c4a.

"Gazetchiki: Bez politiki." 2005. *Vebplaneta*, 15 December.

Gel'man, Marat. 1997. "Kompromat kak literaturnyi zhanr." *Russkii Zhurnal*, 21 November.

"German Klimenko: anonimnost' iavliaetsia samoi ser'eznoi problemoi interneta." 2016. *TASS*, 30 March. https://tass.ru/obschestvo/3165044.

"'Giprosviaz' ne imeet narekanii k oborudovaniiu, ustanovlennomu v ramkakh zakona o 'suverennom internete'." 2020. *Interfaks*, 18 September. https://www.interfax.ru/russia/727563.

Gladarev, Boris. 2011. "Istoriko-kul'turnoe nasledie Peterburga: Rozhdenie obshchest-vennosti iz dukha goroda." In *Ot obshchestvennogo k publichnomu: Kollektivnaia monografiia*, edited by O. V. Kharkhordin. Izdatel'stvo Evropeiskogo univer-siteta v Sankt-Peterburge.

"Glava Chechni Ramzan Kadyrov raskritikoval deistviia sotrudnikov MVD iz sosednego Stavropolia." 2015. *1TV.ru*, 24 April. https://www.1tv.ru/news/2015-04-24/23963-glava_chechni_ramzan_kadyrov_raskritikoval_deystviya_sotrudnikov_mvd_iz_sosednego_stavropolya.

"Glava komiteta Gosdumy schitaet, chto zakonoproektom o t.n. 'chernykh spiskakh' nedovol'no 'pedofil'skoe lobbi'." 2012. Pravo.ru, 10 July. http://pravo.ru/news/view/74847/.

"Glava Minkomsviazi Rossii zaiavil o neobkhodimosti priniatiia mezhdunarodnoi konventsii po upravleniiu infrastrukturoi interneta." 2014. *Minkomsviaz' Rossii*, 20 October. http://minsvyaz.ru/ru/events/31863/.

Glazunova, Sofya. 2020. "Digital Media as a Tool for Non-Systemic Opposition in Rus-sia: A Case Study of Alexey Navalny's Populist Communications on YouTube." PhD diss., Queensland University of Technology.

Glukhova, Aleksandra. 2020. "Tri karty Vladimira Putina." *Nezavisimaia gazeta*, 26 May. https://www.ng.ru/scenario/2020-05-25/9_7869_authoritarianism.html.

Golubeva, Anastasiia. 2022. "'Imenem Rossiiskoi Federatsii: etogo ne bylo'. Kak vozbu-zhdaiut i rassleduiut ugolovnye dela o 'feikakh' pro armiiu." *BBC News: Russkaia sluzhba*, 3 August. https://www.bbc.com/russian/features-62395221.

Gorbachev, Aleksandr. 2017. "Pochemu na aktsii protesta vyshlo stol'ko podroskov?" *Meduza*, 27 March. https://meduza.io/feature/2017/03/27/pochemu-na-aktsii-protesta-vyshlo-stolko-podrostkov-i-chego-oni-hotyat.

Gorham, Michael S. 2004. *Speaking in Soviet Tongues: Language Culture and the Poli-tics of Voice in Revolutionary Russia*. Northern Illinois University Press.

Gorham, Michael S. 2013. "Putin's Language." In *Putin as Celebrity and Cultural Icon*, edited by Helena Goscilo. Routledge.

Gorham, Michael S. 2014. *After Newspeak: Language Culture and Politics in Russia from Gorbachev to Putin*. Cornell University Press.

Gorham, Michael S. 2024. "Prime-Time Solov'ev: Rhetorical Strategies of a Wartime Propagandist." *Canadian Slavonic Papers*. https://doi.org/10.1080/00085006.2024.2423475.

Gorham, Michael S., Ingunn Lunde, and Martin Paulsen, eds. 2014. *Digital Russia: The Language, Culture, and Politics of New Media Communication*. Routledge.

Goriunova, Ol'ga. 2006. "'Male Literature' of Udaff.com and Other Networked Artistic Practices of the Cultural Resistance." In *Control + Shift: Public and Private Usages of the Russian Internet*, edited by Henrike Schmidt, Katy Teubener, and Natalja Konradova. Books on Demand.

Gorny, Evgeny. 2000. "Internet i filologiia." *Russkii zhurnal*, 1 December. http://old .russ.ru/netcult/20001201_gorny.html.

Gorny, Eugene. 2006. "Russian LiveJournal: The Impact of Cultural Identity on the Development of a Virtual Community." In *Control + Shift: Public and Private Usages of the Russian Internet*, edited by Henrike Schmidt, Katy Teubener, and Natalja Konradova, 73–90.

Gorny, Eugene. 2009. *A Creative History of the Russian Internet: Studies in Internet Creativity*. VDM Verlag Dr. Müller.

"Government Sets e-Russia Plan." 2001. *Moscow Times*, 25 April.

Govorukhin, Stanislav. 2013. "Pora razvernut' obshcherossiiskii front v podderzhku otechestvennoi kul'tury." *Obshcherossiiskii narodnyi front*, 30 September. http://onf.ru/2013/09/30/stanislav-govoruhin-pora-razvernut-obshherossijskij -front-v-podderzhku-otechestvennoj-kul-tury/.

"Govorukhin nazval internet 'pomoikoi v rukhakh Gosdepa'." 2012. Newsru.com, 20 February. http://www.newsru.com/russia/20feb2012/govorukhin.html.

"Gr. Chernikovskaia khata—Ia v etot mir prishel dlia togo, chtoby byt' 'muzykantom'." 2022. *greyswandir_m*, 24 November. https://greyswandir-m.livejournal.com /312397.html.

Granik, Irina. 2009. "Dmitrii Medvedev prikazal regionam stat' elektronnym." *Kommersant''*, 24 December.

Granik, Irina. 2010. "'Kto ne ispolniaet—pust' na ulitsu idet'." *Kommersant''*, 17 March.

Greene, Samuel A. 2014. *Moscow in Movement: Power and Opposition in Putin's Russia*. Stanford University Press.

Grigor'eva, Inna, and Pavel Chuviliaev. 2012. "Dolina trollei. V nee postepenno pre-vrashchaetsia rossiiskii internet." *Novaia gazeta*, 9 April. http://www.novayagazeta .ru/society/52045.html.

Gritsenko, Daria, Annette Markham, Holger Pötzsch, and Mariëlle Wijermars, eds. *Special Issue: Algorithmic Governance in Context*. In *New Media & Society* 24 (4).

Gritsenko, Daria, Mariëlle Wijermars, and Mikhail Kopotev. 2021. *Palgrave Handbook of Digital Russian Studies*. Palgrave Macmillan.

Gritsenko, Daria, and Mikhail Zherebtsov. 2021. "E-Government in Russia: Plans, Reality, and Future Outlook." In *Palgrave Handbook of Digital Russian Studies*, edited by Daria Gritsenko, Mariëlle Wijermars, and Mikhail Kopotev, 33–51. Palgrave Macmillan.

Grove, Thomas, Alan Cullison, and Bojan Pancevski. 2023. "How Putin's Right-Hand Man Took Out Prigozhin." *Wall St. Journal*, 22 December. https://www.wsj.com /world/russia/putin-patrushev-plan-prigozhin-assassination-428d5ed8?mod=e2tw.

Gudkov, Lev. 2004. "K probleme negativnoi identifikatsii." In Lev Gudkov, *Negativnaia iden-tichnost': Stat'i 1997–2002 godov*, 262–99. Novoe literaturnoe obozrenie—'VTsIOM-A'.

Gunitsky, Seva 2015. "Corrupting the Cyber-Commons: Social Media as a Tool of Autocratic Stability." *Perspectives on Politics* 13 (1): 42–54.

Gureev, Maksim. 2005. "Chisto real'no." *Kul'tura* 39 (6 October).

Guriev, Sergei, and Daniel Treisman. 2022. *Spin Dictators: The Changing Face of Tyranny in the 21st Century*. Princeton University Press.

Gurov, Aleksei. 2020. "Google i Facebook meshaiut rossiiskomu internetu." *Life*, 28 August. https://life.ru/p/1342337.

Gurova, Tat'iana, and Dan Medovnikov. 1998. "Zhestkii tsenz na rynke demokratii." *Ekspert* 48 (21 December).

Guseinov, Gasan, ed. 2014. *Russkii iazyk i novye tekhnologii.* Novoe literaturnoe obozrenie.

Gusev, Pavel. 2012. "Deputaty gotoviatsia rasmotret' zakon ob internete." *Izvestiia,* 23 October. https://iz.ru/news/538158.

Guzik, Keith. 2023. "'*Vse* (Everyone) Online?': An Exploration of the Evolution of the Russian Federation's Digital Government Portal During the COVID-19 Pandemic." *Frontiers in Sociology* 8. https://doi.org/10.3389/fsoc.2023.1223957.

Haidt, Jonathan. 2024. *The Anxious Generation: How the Great Rewiring of Childhood Is Causing an Epidemic of Mental Illness.* Penguin.

Hall, John. 2013. *The Importance of Being Civil: The Struggle for Political Decency.* Princeton University Press.

Herrman, John. 2017. "The Return of the Techno-Moral Panic." *New York Times Magazine,* 5 December. https://www.nytimes.com/2017/12/05/magazine/the-return-of-the-techno-moral-panic.html.

Hess, Aaron. 2018. "Theorizing Digital Rhetoric." In *Theorizing Digital Rhetoric,* edited by Aaron Hess and Amber Davisson, 1–15. Routledge.

Hutchings, Stephen. 2022. *Projecting Russia in a Mediatized World: Recursive Nationhood.* Routledge.

Hutchings, Stephen, Vera Tolz, Precious Chatterje-Doody, Rhys Crilley, and Marie Gillespie. 2024. *Russia, Disinformation, and the Liberal Order: RT as Populist Pariah.* Northern Illinois University Press.

Iakimets, Kirill. 2001. "V iavochnom poriadke. Beseda o metamorfozakh grazhdanskogo obshchestva." *Russkii zhurnal,* 9 August.

Iakushev, Vladimir Vladimirovich. 2011. "Kvartira dlia budzhetnika—2." *Blog Vladimira Iakusheva,* 21 April. http://gubernator.admtyumen.ru/governor_to/ru/blog.htm?postId=57@cmsVBVideoPost&mode=1.

"'Iandeks' predupredil investorov o politicheskikh riskakh." 2014. *Runet,* 7 April. http://therunet.com/news/2694-yandeks-predupredil-investorov-o-politicheskih-riskah.

Iashin, Il'ia. 2016. "Ugroza natsional'noi bezopasnosti." http://www.putin-itogi.ru/f/Ugroza-Doklad-IlyaYashin.pdf.

Iastrebova, Svetlana. 2018. "Minekonomrazvitiia razgromilo pravila khraniia internet-dannykh po zakonu Iarovoi." *Vedomosti,* 8 August. https://www.vedomosti.ru/technology/articles/2018/08/07/777556-razgromilo.

"Il'ia Iashin prigovorili k 8,5 godam po delu o 'voennykh feikakh'." 2022. *BBC News: Russkaia sluzhba,* 9 December. https://www.bbc.com/russian/news-63864402.

Il'nitskii, Andrei. 2012. "Politicheskii rebrending i 'levyi perekos'." *Izvestiia,* 14 February.

"Internet-ombudsmen Marinichev: 'Suverennyi Internet' vygoden vlasti segodnia, no on zakonchitsia katastrofoi." 2019. *fontanka.ru,* 12 February. https://www.fontanka.ru/2019/02/12/137/.

"Interv'iu ital'ianskim informatsionnomu agentstvu ANSA, gazete *Kor'ere della sera* i telekomanii RAI." 2003. Kremlin.ru, 3 November. http://archive.kremlin.ru/appears/2003/11/03/2200_type63379_54926.shtml.

Ioffe, Julia. 2011. "Meet the President." *Foreign Policy,* Jan.–Feb. http://www.foreignpolicy.com/articles/2011/01/02/meet_the_president.

"Itogi vyborov mera Moskvy: Sergei Sobianin—51.37%, Aleksei Naval'nyi—27.24%." 2013. *Kommersant'',* 9 September. https://www.kommersant.ru/doc/2274765.

Ivanov, Dmitrii. 2002. "Rossiiskii internet kak sredstvo politicheskoi kommunikatsii. Pervaia glava istorii politruneta." *Russkii zhurnal,* 13 March.

Ivanov, Dmitrii. 2003. "Mikhail Rogozhnikov: 'Strana.Ru sovershenno naprasno maskirovalas' pod SMI,'" *Russkii zhurnal*, 1 April. http://old.russ.ru/netcult/history /20030410.html.

Ivanov, Maksim, and Elena Mukhometshina. 2021. "Gradus ne pomekha." *Vedomosti*, 25 January. East View persistent URL, https://dlib.eastview.com/browse /doc/64407525.

Ivanov, Maksim, Sof'ia Samokhina, and Vladislav Novyi. 2018. "Vlast' sovetuiush-chikh." *Kommersant*. 4 May. https://www.kommersant.ru/doc/3619881.

Ivanova, Ol'ga. 2000. "Kroshka RU." *Kar'era*, 1 December.

"IRI." n.d. *Institut razvitiia interneta*. https://xn--h1aax.xn--p1ai/.

Istomin, Sergei. 2023. "Kadyrov pokazal video izbieniia podzhigatelia Korana svoim synom." *Lenta.ru*, 25 September. https://lenta.ru/news/2023/09/25/izbienie _gordost/.

jack_patterson. 2006. "Samaia pravil'naia istoriia padonkaff." *jack_patterson*, 16 March. https://padonki-history.livejournal.com/1836.html.

Joseph, John E. 2006. *Language and Politics*. Edinburgh University Press.

Kagaltynov, Erdni. 2023. "Putin zaiavil ob oskolkakh granat v telakh pogibshikh pri krush-enii samoleta Prigozhina." *Kommersant''*, 5 October. https://www.kommersant.ru /doc/6254149.

"Kakie biznesy mogut postradat' ot zapreta na khranenie lichnykh dannykh rossiian za rubezhom." 2014. *Telecom Daily*, 9 July. https://telecomdaily.ru/news /2014/07/09/kakie-biznesy-mogut-postradat-ot-zapreta-na-hranenie-lichnyh -dannyh-rossiyan-za-rubezhom.

"Kak Kadyrova iz instagrama izgoniali." 2017. *Kavkaz.Realiia*, 25 December. https:// www.kavkazr.com/a/kak-kadyrova-iz-instagrama-izgonyali/28936335.html.

"Kak Kreml' perestal boiat'sia i poliubil Telegram." 2024. Tsentr-'Dos'e', 12 September. https://dossier.center/tg/.

"Kak ne poteriat' molodezh' v opasnykh setiakh Interneta." 2016. *Obshchestvennaia palata Rossiiskoi Federatsii*, 25 March. https://old.oprf.ru/press/news/2016 /newsitem/33290.

Kalugin, Dmitry. 2016. "A Society that Speaks Concordantly, or Mechanisms of Com-munication of Government and Society in Old and New Russia." In *Public Debate in Russia: Matters of (Dis)order*, edited by Nikolai Vakhtin and Boris Firsov, 52–84. Edinburgh University Press.

Kamyshev, Dmitrii. 2013. "Inostrannyi agent: Za i protiv," *New Times*, 13 May.

Kantyshev, Pavel, and Anastasiia Golitsyna. 2016. "Runet budet polnost'iu obosoblen k 2020 godu." *Vedomosti*, 13 May. https://www.vedomosti.ru/technology /articles/2016/05/13/640856-runet-obosoblen.

Kantyshev, Pavel, and Elizaveta Ser'gina. 2017. "Minekonomrazvitiia snimet rezervnuiu kopiiu runeta." *Vedomosti*, 13 January. https://www.vedomosti.ru /technology/articles/2017/01/13/672826-minekonomrazvitiya-rezervnuyu -kopiyu.

Kanygin, Pavel. 2010. "Beregis'! Dorogu! Gubernatory vykhodiat v Internet." *Novaia gazeta*, 19 March.

Kashin, Oleg. 2007. "Soldaty partii." *Nezavisimaia gazeta,* 16 October. East View per-sistent URL, https://dlib.eastview.com/browse/doc/12750674.

Kashin, Oleg. 2011. "Grazhdanskoe obshchestvo postroilos'." *Kommersant''*, 27 December.

Katz, Jon. 2000. "Flaming Freud: Analyzing Homo Incinerans." Slashdot.org, 9 October. https://slashdot.org/story/00/09/25/180228/flaming-freud-analyzing -homo-incinerans.

Kazakov, I. 2015. "Internet-trollei khotiat kontrolirovat'." *Izvestiia*, 26 August.

KermlinRussia. 2013. "KermlinRussia: budushchee bez opasnogo interneta." *Forbes*, 6 February. http://www.forbes.ru/mneniya-column/protesty/233792-kermlinrussia -budushchee-bez-opasnogo-interneta.

Khamraev, Viktor. 2017. "V Kremle prochtut zhaloby grazhdan." *Kommersant''*, 18 April.

Kharitonov, Vladimir. 2019. "Vrednonositeli. Ob opyte regulirovaniia interneta." *Novaia gazeta*, 20 February. https://novayagazeta.ru/articles/2019/03/18/79906-vredonositeli.

Kharkhordin, O. V., ed. 2011. *Ot obshchestvennogo k publichnomu: Kollektivnaia monografiia*. Izdatel'stvo Evropeiskogo universiteta v Sankt-Peterburge.

Kharkhordin, Oleg. 2018. *Republicanism in Russia: Community before and after Communism*. Harvard University Press.

Khazagerov, Georgii, Vitalii Naishul', and Svetlana Khazagerova. 2005. "Problemy stanovleniia russkogo obshchestvenno-politicheskogo iazyka." *Russkii zhurnal*, 28 February. http://old.russ.ru/culture/20050228_naish.html.

Khimshiashvili, Polina, and Evgenii Kaliukov. 2017. "Peskov ob''iasnil nezhelanie Putina proiznosit' familiiu Naval'nogo." RBC.ru, 15 December. https://www.rbc .ru/politics/15/12/2017/5a33b1719a79476ab7f3426c.

"Kholmogorov." 2005. *Holmogor*, 5 January. https://holmogor.livejournal.com/1064262.

Kholmogorov, Egor. 2004. "100 faktov (62)." *Holmogor*, 8 December. https://holmogor .livejournal.com/1035998.html.

Kholmogorov, Egor. 2017. "Podrostki, zaderzhannye na mitinge Naval'nogo: Diadia Lesha, vashi 'seti' nas vtashchili v avtozak!" *Komsomol'skaia Pravda*, 28 March. East View persistent URL, https://dlib.eastview.com/browse/doc/48509242.

Kholmogorov, Egor. 2025. *Ia—russkii. Grani natsional'nogo samoznaniia*. Knizhnyi mir. https://kmbook.ru/shop/ya-russkij-grani-naczionalnogo -samoznaniya/?ysclid=mb3a3mf0ce644669756.

Khrennikov, Ilya, and Stepan Kravchenko. 2019. "Putin Wants His Own Internet." *Bloomberg*, 4 March. https://www.bloomberg.com/news/articles/2019-03-05 /vladimir-putin-wants-his-own-internet.

"Kiberdruzhina." n.d. *Liga bezopasnogo interneta*. http://ligainternet.ru/liga/activity -cyber.php.

"Kiberstukachestvo klassa liuks: skol'ko stoit garderob Mizulinoi." 2022. *Navalny LIVE*, 24 January. https://www.youtube.com/watch?v=4P5erw8xG2E.

"Kibervoiska Prigozhina: Kak ustroena IT-infrastruktura 'Vagnera', 'Fabriki trollei' i Konkorda'." 2023. Tsentr "Dos'e", 18 March. https://dossier.center/prig-it/.

Kiselev, Sergei. 2014. "Khranit' chest'—sebe v ubytok." *Nezavisimaia gazeta*, 5 August. https://www.ng.ru/economics/2014-08-05/4_honor.html.

Klimarev, Mikhail. 2019. "Dorogo, opasno i nevozmozhno. Pochemu 'suverennyi Runet' nikogda ne zarabotaet." *The Insider*, 13 November. https://theins.ru /opinions/the-insider/187400.

Klimburg, Alexander. 2017. *The Darkening Web: The War for Cyberspace*. Penguin.

Kolesnikov, Andrei. 2012a. "Sistema 'Putin—3.0' k rabote gotova." *Novaia gazeta*, 13 July. https://novayagazeta.ru/articles/2012/07/13/50572-sistema-171-putin-3 -0-187-k-rabote-gotova.

Kolesnikov, Andrei. 2012b. "Vladimir Putin ne privyk razbrasyvat'sia frontami." *Kommersant''*, 4 April.

Kolomychenko, Mariia. 2019a. "Okhrannik suverennogo interneta. Kak vykhodets iz FSO Sergei Khutortsev vozglavil Tsentr upravleniia setiami, kotoryi smozhet otrezat' Rossiiu ot interneta." *Meduza*, 27 November. https://meduza.io/feature /2019/11/27/ohrannik-suverennogo-runeta.

Kolomychenko, Mariia. 2019b. "Putin podpisal zakon o predustanovke rossiiskikh prilozhenii na telefony i gadzhety. Komu eto nuzhno? Chto budet ustanavlivat'?

Apple uidet iz Rossii?" *Meduza*, 2 December. https://meduza.io/feature/2019/12/02/putin-podpisal-zakon-o-predustanovke-rossiyskih-prilozheniy-na-telefony-i-gadzhety-komu-eto-nuzhno-chto-budut-ustanavlivat-apple-uydet-iz-rossii.

Koltsova, Olessia, and Svetlana Bodrunova, eds. 2019. *Public Discussion in Russian Social Media*. In *Media and Communication* (special issue) 7 (3).

Komin, Mikhail. 2016. "Gibridnyi sovetnik." *Novaia gazeta*, 11 January. https://dlib.eastview.com/browse/doc/45975454.

Kononenko, Maksim (Mr. Parker). 2003. "Kogda khvost zaviliaet sobakoi." *Gazeta*, 9 December.

Kononenko, Maksim (Mr. Parker). 2005a. *Vladimir Vladimirovich™*. Kolibri.

Kononenko, Maksim. 2005b. "Zazhech' na noch." *Gazeta*, 7 June.

"Konstantin Rykov (Dzheison Foris)." 2001. Kompromat.ru, 18 July. https://www.compromat.ru/page_11848.htm.

"Konstantin Rykov: Russia.ru stanet russkim Huffingtonpost." 2012. *Vzgliad*, 10 September. https://vz.ru/news/2012/9/10/597463.html.

Kopylova, Vera. 2007. "Lovis', fashist, bol'shoi i malen'kii." *Moskovskii komsomolets* February. https://www.mk.ru/editions/daily/article/2007/02/22/158064-lovis-fashist-bolshoy-i-malenkiy.html.

Kornev, Maksim. 2014. "Kak protivodeistvovat' trolling i agressivnomu povedeniiu v seti." *Media Toolbox*, 31 October. http://mediatoolbox.ru/blog/kak-protivodeystvovat-trollingu-i-agressivnomu-povedeniyu-v-seti/.

Korolev, Igor'. 2019. "Mail.ru podderzhala zakonoproekt o 'suverennom internete'." *C-news*, 18 January. https://safe.cnews.ru/news/top/2019-01-18_mailru_podderzhala_zakonoproekt_o_suverennom.

Korolev, Igor'. 2020. "Vlasti poluchili domennuiu zonu SSSR cherez ugolovnoe delo protiv osnovatelia Runeta." *C-news*, 26 October. https://www.cnews.ru/news/top/2020-10-26_vlasti_poluchili_domen_sssr.

Korolev, Nikita. 2022. "Videoigry patriotov." *Kommersant''*, 16 February, https://www.kommersant.ru/doc/5217413.

Korotkov, Denis. 2014. "Iskrennie trolli Ol'gino." Fontanka.ru, 4 June. http://www.fontanka.ru/2014/06/03/182/.

Korotkov, Denis. 2018. "Povar so svoimi tarelkami." *Novaia gazeta*, 8 November. https://novayagazeta.ru/articles/2018/11/08/78496-provokatsii-prigozhina.

Kotliar, Mikhail, and Mikhail Iushkov. 2021. "Putin zaiavil prevrashchenie Ukrainy v 'kakuiu-to anti-Rossiiu'." *RBK*, 14 May. https://www.rbc.ru/politics/14/05/2021/609e5e829a7947eb211fca8e.

Kotov, Maksim. 2019. "Zakon o nadezhnom internete priniat Gosdumoi." *Ridus*, 16 April. https://www.ridus.ru/zakon-o-nadezhnom-runete-prinyat-gosdumoj-297218.html.

Kovalenko, Anna. 2019. "Prigozhin vozglavit sovet mediagruppy dlia bor'by s 'anti-rossiiskimi' SMI." *The Bell*, 4 October. https://thebell.io/prigozhin-vozglavit-sovet-mediagruppy-dlya-borby-s-antirossijskimi-smi?utm_source=telegram.me&utm_medium=social&utm_campaign=evgeniy-prigozhin-vozglavit-popechitelski.

Kovalev, Alexey. 2017. "Russia's Infamous 'Troll Factory' Is Now Posing as a Media Empire." *The Moscow Times*, 24 March. https://www.themoscowtimes.com/2017/03/24/russias-infamous-troll-factory-is-now-posing-as-a-media-empire-a57534.

Kozlova, A. 2012. "Ne popadaites' trolliu na kriuchok." *Rossiiskaia gazeta*, 10 May.

Krashennikov, Fedor. 2019. "Senator Klishas – novyi simvol rosskiiskoi vlasti." *DW.com*, 8 February. https://www.dw.com/ru/%D0%BA%D0%BE%D0%BC%D0%BC%D0%B5%D0%BD%D1%82%D0%B0%D1%80%D0%B8%D0%B9-%D1%81%D0

%B5%D0%BD%D0%B0%D1%82%D0%BE%D1%80-%D0%BA%D0%BB%D0
%B8%D1%88%D0%B0%D1%81-%D0%BD%D0%BE%D0%B2%D1%8B
%D0%B9-%D1%81%D0%B8%D0%BC%D0%B2%D0%BE%D0%BB-%D1%80
%D0%BE%D1%81%D1%81%D0%B8%D0%B9%D1%81%D0%BA%D0%BE%D0
%B9-%D0%B2%D0%BB%D0%B0%D1%81%D1%82%D0%B8/a-47424718.

Krebs, Brian. 2014. *Spam Nation: The Inside Story of Organized Cybercrime—From Global Epidemic to Your Front Door*. Sourcebooks.

Krivoshapko, Iuliia, Mikhail Pinkus, Anna Iurkova, and Ekaterina Iasakova. 2019. "V zone dostupa," *Rossiiskaia gazeta*, 12 August. Persistent East View URL: https://dlib.eastview.com/browse/doc/54208124.

Krongauz, Maksim. 2013. *Samouchitel' Olbanskogo*. Izdatel'stvo.

Kryshtanovskaia, Ol'ga. 2011. "Belyi dom 'za steklom'." *Nezavisimaia gazeta*, 18 October. https://www.ng.ru/politics/2011-10-18/3_kartblansh.html.

"Kto kupil Vladimir Vladimirovich™?" 2005. *Novaia gazeta*, 1 March.

Kukulin, Il'ia. 2016. "Iz 'padonkov'—v 'patrioty': Voskhod i zakat odnoi internet-subkul'tury v 'silovom pole' sovremennogo rossiiskogo politicheskogo rezhima." *Ab Imperio* 1: 223–76.

Kukulin, Il'ia. 2017. "Cultural Shifts in Russia since 2010: Messianic Cynicism and Paradigms of Artistic Resistance." *Russian Literature* 96–98:221–54.

Kulikov, V. 2017. "Notarius@sud." *Rossiiskaia gazeta*, 22 August.

Kulikov, V. 2018. "Poimaiut na slove." *Rossiiskaia gazeta*, 3 May.

Kurowska, Xymena, and Anatoly Reshetnikov. 2018. "Neutrollization: Industrialized Trolling as a Pro-Kremlin Strategy of Desecuritization." *Security Dialogue* 49 (5): 345–63.

Kuz'mina, Aleksandra. 2007. "Gleb Pavlovskii: SMI—mashina proizvodstva bezal'ternativnogo meinstrima." *Russkii zhurnal*, 17 May. http://russ.ru/Mirovaya-povestka/Gleb-Pavlovskij-SMI-mashina-proizvodstva-bezal-ternativnogo-mejnstrima.

Kuznetsov, Sergei. 2004. *Oshchupyvaia slona. Zametki po istorii russkogo Interneta*. Novoe literaturnoe obozrenie.

Kuznetsova, Alena. 2013. "Chto delat' Naval'nomu v mirnoe vremia bez vyborov, nikto ne ponimaet." *Kommersant''*, 16 September. https://www.kommersant.ru/doc/2280439.

Kvasha, Semen. 2005. "Slysh', bratello, rasslab'sia." Gazeta.ru, 27 May. https://www.gazeta.ru/2005/05/27/oa_158876.shtml.

Laboratoriia Kryshtanovskaia. 2013. "Mental'nost' rossiiskoi molodezhi: politicheskie orientiry i kumiry." *Gefter*, 18 April. http://webcache.googleusercontent.com/search?q=cache:http://gefter.ru/archive/8369.

Langdon, Kate C., and Vladimir Tismaneanu. 2020. *Putin's Totalitarian Democracy: Ideology, Myth, and Violence in the Twenty-First Century*. Palgrave Macmillan.

Larina, Anastasiia. 2023a. "Evgenii Prigozhin priznal sozdaniia 'fabriki trollei.'" *Kommersant''*, 14 February. https://www.kommersant.ru/doc/5826246.

Larina, Anastasiia. 2023b. "Putin: ChVK 'Vagner' pol'nostiu finansirovalas' gosudarstvom—86 mlrd rub. za god." *Kommersant''*, 27 June. https://www.kommersant.ru/doc/6069287.

Latkin, Aleksandr. 2004. "'Elektronnaia Rossiia' ishchet khoziaina." *Izvestiia*, 1 March.

Latynina, Iuliia. 2019. "Razreshite bombit' Voronezh. Kak perevoditsia zakon ob avtonomnom internete." *Novaia gazeta*, 15 February. https://www.novayagazeta.ru/articles/2019/02/13/79539-razreshili-bombit-voronezh.

Latyshev, Aleksandr. 2008. "'Ili uchis', ili do svidaniia!'" *Izvestiia*, 18 July.

Leibov, Roman. 2000. "Duratskii muzei." *Russkii zhurnal*, 3 July. http://old.russ.ru/netcult/20000703_leybov.html.

Leibov, Roman. 2001. "Proba pera." *R_L*, 1 February. https://r-l.livejournal.com
/2001/02/01/.

Lekukh, Dmitrii 2013. "Tango na grabliakh. Posleslovie k moskovskim vyboram."
Odnako2, 12 September. https://politikus.info/articles/politics/6428-tango-na
-grablyah-posleslovie-k-moskovskim-vyboram.html.

Lemutkina, Marina. 2023. "Eksperty rasskazali, kak zashchitit'sia ot kiberprestupnosti
i fekovykh novostei." *Moskovskii Komsomolets*, 14 February. https://www.mk.ru
/social/2019/02/14/eksperty-rasskazali-kak-zashhititsya-ot-kiberprestupnosti-i
-feykovykh-novostey.html.

Leskov, Sergei, and Aleksandr Sadchikov. 2010. "Vladislav Surkov: Genii vsegda v
men'shinstve." *Izvestiia*, 16 December. http://www.izvestia.ru/politic/article3149592/.

Levental', Vadim. 2013. "Fraia zatrollili." *Izvestiia*, 9 August. https://iz.ru/news/555100.

Lévy, Pierre. 2001. *Cyberculture*. Translated by Robert Bononno. Electronic Media-
tions, vol. 4. University of Minnesota Press.

Lialenkova, Tamara. 2017. "Deti i smert'." *Radio Svoboda*, 26 March. https://www.svoboda
.org/a/28388439.html.

"Liga bezopasnogo Interneta budet tsenzuirovat' set' v Kostromskoi oblasti." 2013. *Forbes*,
30 January. https://www.forbes.ru/news/233683-liga-bezopasnogo-interneta-budet
-tsenzurirovat-set-v-kostromskoi-oblasti.

Lipovetsky, Mark. 2011. *Charms of the Cynical Reason: The Trickster's Transformation
in Soviet and Post-Soviet Culture*. Academic Studies.

Litvinovich, Marina. 2001. [Media "presentation" by FEP.] Strana.ru, 15 June.

Litvinovich, Marina. 2002. "Chernorabochie politiki." *InterNet*, no. 14. https://web
.archive.org/web/20020322054102/http://gagin.ru/internet/14/31.html.

Litvinovich, Marina, and Mikhail Rogozhnikov. 2000. "Manifest novogo Media—
Strana.ru." Strana.ru, 28 September. Archived copy available at http://web
.archive.org/web/20020220172301/www.strana.ru/about/01.html.

Lonkila, Markku, Larisa Shpakovskaya, and Philip Torchinsky. 2020. "The Occupation
of Runet? The Tightening State Regulation of the Russian-Language Section of
the Internet." In *Freedom of Expression in Russia's New Media Sphere*, edited by
Mariëlle Wijermars and Katja Lehtisaari, 17–38. Routledge.

Loshak, Andrei. 2019. "'Vlast' kak obsirali v internete, tak i obsiraiut'. Bol'shoe
interv'iu s Kristinoi Potupchik." *Nastoiashee vremia*, 31 October. https://www
.currenttime.tv/a/potupchik-interview/30232662.html.

Loucaides, Darren. 2023. "Intercepted: How Telegram Became a Favorite Tool of the
Kremlin." *Wired* 31 (3): 48. *Gale General OneFile*, link.gale.com/apps/doc
/A747905801/ITOF?u=gain40375&sid=bookmark-ITOF&xid=f12c211d.

Lovell, Stephen. 2015. "Stenography and the Public Sphere in Modern Russia." *Cahiers
du Monde russe* 56 (2–3): 291–325.

Lunde, Ingunn. 2016. "Hashtag Poetics: Political Humor on Russian Twitter."
Zeitschrift für Slawistik 61 (1): 102–18.

Lysenko, Irina. 2019. "Zakon o 'suverennom internete' v Rossii budet rabotat'
po neskol'kim osnovopologaiushchim printsipam." *1RRE^*, 8 May. https://
www.1rre.ru/267025-zakon-o-suverennom-internete-v-rossii-budet-rabotat
-po-neskolkim-osnovopolagayushhim-principam.html.

MacGregor, Caroline. 2004. "Mir Vladimira Vladimirovicha." *Inopressa*, 25 August.

MacKinnon, Rebecca. 2011. "Liberation Technology: China's 'Networked Authoritarianism.'" *Journal of Democracy* 22 (2): 32–46.

Madison, Andrei. 2000. "Monday—Monday: Obzor rossiiskoi pressy (14.02—21.02.2000)."
Russkii zhurnal, 21 February. http://old.russ.ru/politics/articles/20000221_mad
.html.

Magai, Marina. 2015. "Minkomsviazi predlozhit usilit' goskontrol' nad Runetom." *RBK*, 26 March. http://www.rbc.ru/technology_and_media/26/03/2015/551419 309a7947aa840a5742.

Makarov, Maksim. 2013. "Dva kapitana i politruk." *Literaturnaia gazeta*, 24 July. http://lgz.ru/article/-30-6424-24-07-2013/dva-kapitana-i-politruk/.

Makarov, Ruben. 2001. "Kak poluchit' pribyl' ot setevogo SMI." *Nezavisimaia gazeta*, 14 February.

"Maksim Kononenko otkazalsia ot psevdonima 'mister Parker'." 2011. *RIA Novosti*, 14 March. https://ria.ru/20110314/353801813.html.

Makutina, Mariia. 2011. "'Idite ko mne, banderlogi'." *Kommersant''*, 15 December. https://www.kommersant.ru/doc/1838421.

Malcomson, Scott. 2016. *Splinternet: How Geopolitics and Commerce Are Fragmenting the World Wide Web*. OR Books.

Mal'gin, Andrei. 2007. "Prokhindei i prokhindeika." Dni.ru, 4 July. Archived copy available at https://web.archive.org/web/20030202184051/http://www.dni.ru /news/analitika/2002/7/4/11402.html.

Malinova, Olga. 2020. "'Nation' and 'Civilization' as Templates for Russian Identity Construction: A Historical Overview." In *Russia as Civilization: Ideological Discourses in Politics, Media, and Academia,* edited by Kåre Mjør and Sanna Turoma, 27–46. Routledge.

Mal'kevich, Aleksandr. 2020. "Mal'kevich: Tsenzory s YouTube sistematicheski narushaiut Konstitutsiiu." *Tsentr prikladnykh issledovanii i program*, 21 May. http://www.prisp .ru/opinion/5125-malkevich-cenzory-s-youtube-narushayut-konstituciyu-2105.

Malover'ian, Iurii. 2011. "Na miting protiv dotatsii Kavkazu sobralis' 200 chelovek." *BBC News-russkaia sluzhba*, 22 October. https://www.bbc.com/russian/russia /2011/10/111022_caucasus_rally.

"Mama umiraet!" 2012. Vopros, 26 April. http://www.vopros.vologda-oblast.ru /requests/4800.html.

Margolin, Jack. 2024. *The Wagner Group: Inside Russia's Mercenary Army*. Reaktion Books.

Markov, Sergei. 2015. "'Territoriia smyslov': Zametki na poliakh." *Izvestiia*, 22 August. https://iz.ru/news/590304.

"Mashina-mama, mashina-papa: eksperty obsudili glavnye problem tsifrovogo vospi-taniia." 2021. *Obshchestvennaia palata Rossiiskoi Federatsii*, 11 June. https://oprf .ru/news/mashinamama-mashinapapa-eksperty-obsudili-glavnye-problemy -tsifrovogo-vospitaniya.

McAuley, Mary. 2010. "'Govorit' i deistvovat': politicheskii diskurs v Rossii (1989– 1992)." In *Raznomyslie v SSSR i Rossii (1945–2008): Sbornik materialov nauch-noi konferentsii 15–16 maia 2009 goda*, edited by B. M. Firsov, 260–96. Evro-peiskii Universitet v Sankt-Peterburge.

Meaker, Morgan. 2022. "Russia Blocks Facebook and Twitter in a Propaganda Stand-off." *Wired*, 4 March. https://www.wired.com/story/russia-ukraine-social -media/.

Medvedev, Dmitry. 2009. "Dmitrii Medvedev: 'God nazad poiavilsia moi videoblog'." *Blog Dmitriia Medvedeva*, 7 October. http://blog.da-medvedev.ru/post/33/tran-script.

Medvedev, D. A. 2010. "Griadet epokha vozvrashcheniia neposredstvennoi demokratii." *Videoblog Dmitriia Medvedeva*, 31 May. http://blog.kremlin.ru /post/81.

Medvedev, Dmitry. 2011a. "Dmitrii Medvedev: About Myself." Kremlin.ru. http:// archive.kremlin.ru/eng/articles/article200253.shtml.

Medvedev, D. A. 2011b. "Prostranstvo priamoi demokratii budet rasshiriat'sia." *Video-blog Dmitriia Medvedeva*, 16 September. http://blog.kremlin.ru/post/106.

Medvedev, D. A. 2011c. "Dmitrii Medvedev vstretilsia so svoimi storonnikami—pred-stviteliami setevykh soobshchestv." Kremlin.ru, 9 November. http://kremlin.ru/transcripts/13443.

"Medvedev: Internet—veshch' perspektivnaia." 2009. BaltInfo.ru, 15 June. http://www.baltinfo.ru/2009/06/15/Medvedev-Internet--vesch'-perspektivnaya.

"Medvedev—pensioneram v Krymu: Deneg net." 2016. Korrespondent.net, 24 May. https://korrespondent.net/ukraine/3686751-medvedev-pensyoneram-v-krymu-deneh-net.

"Medvedev potreboval ot Shantseva lichno 'kovyriat'sia' v internete." 2010. *Klub regionov*, 17 March. http://club-rf.ru/news/nijegorodskaya-oblast/medvedev_potreboval_ot_shantseva_lichno_koviryatsya_internete/.

"Medvedev Renames Twitter Account to Make It More Informal." 2010. *RIA Novosti*, 19 November. http://en.rian.ru/russia/20101119/161413322.html.

"Medvedev v internete: pervyi vitse-prem'er otvetil za natsproekty." 2007. NEWSRu.com, 5 March. http://www.newsru.com/russia/05mar2007/medved_online.html.

Mel'nik, Aleksandr. 2019. "Internet ot Ilona Maska zapushchen. Suverennyi Internet umer ne rodivshis'? Pochti." *RusMonitor*, 24 May. https://rusmonitor.com/internet-ot-ilona-maska-zapushhen-suverennyjj-runet-umer-ne-rodivshis-pochti.html.

Merezhkovskii, Dmitrii. 1906. "Griadushchii kham." Reprinted at http://az.lib.ru/m/merezhkowskij_d_s/text_0080.shtml.

Merkacheva, Eva. 2013. "Ne zabudem, ne prostim, v Internete otomstim." *Moskovskii komsomolets*, 18 November. https://www.mk.ru/social/article/2013/11/17/946452-ne-zabudem-ne-prostim-v-internete-otomstim.

Miazina, Elena. 2010. "Chinovniki i blogosfera." *Vedomosti*, 13 December. http://www.vedomosti.ru/politics/news/1161162/chinovniki_i_blogosfera_ot_vylazok_k_masshtabnomu_osvoeniyu.

Mikhailova, Antonina. 2010. "Chto besit v Rossii? Khamstvo, oligarkhi i bednye pen-sionery." *Argumenty i fakty*, 4 May. http://www.aif.ru/health/article/34481.

"Mikroblog goda." 2011. *Soiuz Ezhe*. http://ezhe.ru/POTOP/results.html?do=res;2010.

"Mikroblog Medvedeva razdvoilsia." 2010. *Moskovskii komsomolets*, 20 November.

"Milliardy na pokolenie Z: sozdateliam molodezhnogo internet-kontenta dadut granty." 2019. *Novye izvestiia*, 23 December. https://newizv.ru/news/2019-12-23/milliardy-na-pokolenie-z-sozdatelyam-molodezhnogo-internet-kontenta-dadut-granty-297268.

"Minkomsviaz', FSB i Minoborony proveli ucheniia po zashchite rossiiskogo segmenta internet." 2014. *Minkomsviaz' Rossii*, 28 July. http://minsvyaz.ru/ru/events/31441.

Mironov, Sergei. 2007. "Pervaia zapis' bloga." *Vesti ot Sergeia Mironova*, 29 November. http://sergey-mironov.livejournal.com/662.html.

Mironov, Sergei. 2011. "'Edinaia Rossiia' – partiia oligarkhov i chinovnikov." Vesti ot Sergeia Mironova, 13 September. http://sergey-mironov.livejournal.com/333425.html.

Mironov, Sergei. 2016. "Nuzhna li gosudarstvennaia ideologiia? Nuzhna!" *Rossiiskaia gazeta*, 13 December. https://mironov.ru/53960410.

Mirumian, Karine. 2021. "'Politicheskaia pedophiliia'. Kak rossiiskie telekanaly osvesh-chali protesty v podderzhku Naval'nogo." *BBC News: Russkaia sluzhba*, 25 January. https://www.bbc.com/russian/news-55792820.

Mjør, Kåre and Sanna Turoma, eds. 2020. *Russia as Civilization: Ideological Discourses in Politics, Media, and Academia*. Routledge.

"Moivy ne budet." 2008. Lenta.ru, 25 February. https://lenta.ru/articles/2008/02/25/blogs/.

Morley, David. 2007. *Media, Modernity and Technology: The Geography of the New.* Routledge.

Morochenko, Dmitrii. 2000. "Ia drugoi takoi strany ne znaiu." *Vremia MN*, 19 September.

Morozov, Aleksandr. 2013. "Trolli v sumerkakh." *New Times*, 13 December. https://newtimes.ru/articles/detail/72552/.

Morozov, Aleksandr, Gleb Pavlovskii, Kirill Rogov, and Maksim Trudoliubov. 2012. "Chto budet, esli posadiat Naval'nogo?" *Colta*, 17 July. https://www.colta.ru/articles/society/1178-chto-budet-esli-posadyat-navalnogo.

Morozov, Evgeny. 2011. *The Net Delusion: The Dark Side of Internet Freedom.* Public Affairs.

Mostovshchikov, E. 2011. "Soznanie 2.0." *New Times*, 21 November.

Mueller, M. L., and Badiei, F. 2017. "Governing Internet Territory: Icann, Sovereignty Claims, Property Rights and Country Code Top-Level Domains." *Columbia Science and Technology Law Review* 18 (2): 435–91.

Mursaleva, Galina. 2016. "Gruppy smerti." *Novaia gazeta*, 16 May. https://www.novayagazeta.ru/articles/2016/05/16/68604-gruppy-smerti-18.

Musorgskii, Il'ia. 1999. "Pavlovskii i millenium." Kompromat.Ru. https://web.archive.org/web/20240414181217/https://www.compromat.ru/page_26356.htm.

Muzipova, Rimma. 2017. "MVD ne nashlo faktov korruptsii v rassledovanii Naval'nogo 'On vam ne Dimon'." *Novye izvestiia*, 24 May. East View persistent URL, https://dlib.eastview.com/browse/doc/49739142.

Nabatov, Aleksandr. 2013. "Elena Mizulina: 'Nyneshniaia molodezh' putaet svobodu i vsedozvolennost'." *Argumenty i fakty Omsk*, 9 September. http://www.omsk.aif.ru/society/society_details/114945.

Nagornykh, Irina and Roman Rozhkov. 2015. "Vladimir Putin ugovoril IT-Biznes voiti v kreml'." *Kommersant''*, 23 December. https://dlib.eastview.com/browse/doc/45914219.

"'Narrow Misses' with the Enemy and Battles with Bushes: A Closer Look at Kadyrov's Troops as Putin Hands Their Leader Yet Another Award." 2024. *The Insider*, 17 December. https://theins.ru/en/news/277290.

"'Nasha zadacha—vyrabotat' pravila informatsionnoi gigieny'." 2017. *Obshchestvennaia palata Rossiiskoi Federatsii*, 7 July. https://old.oprf.ru/press/news/2617/newsitem/54135.

Navalny, Alexei. 2024. *Patriot: A Memoir.* Translated by Arch Tait with Stephen Dalziel. Alfred A. Knopf.

Navalnyi, Aleksei. 2023. "Moi strakh i nenavist': Pervoe pis'mo Alekseia Naval'nogo posle prigovora.' *Novaia Gazeta*, 11 August. https://novayagazeta.ru/articles/2023/08/11/moi-strakh-i-nenavist.

"Naval'nyi zapodozril v gubernatore Astrakhanshchiny 'trolla:'—zakazal tri nemetskikh avto za 16 mln rublei." 2012. Newsru.com, 12 November. https://auto.newsru.com/article/12nov2012/naval.

"Navalny Again Placed in Punitive Solitary Confinement by Russian Prison." 2024. *RFE/RL*, 14 February. https://www.rferl.org/a/navalny-solitary-confinement-russia-prison/32819584.html.

"Ne tak strashen post dlia gubernatora, kak perepost." 2010. *Obshchestvennaia palata Rossiiskoi Federatsii*, 18 October. http://www.old.oprf.ru/press/news/2010/newsitem/3257.

"Nevod i t.d." 2002. *Russkii zhurnal*, 15 September.

Nikiforenko, Mikhail. 2013. "Shagrenovaia kozha svobody: Tsenzura v Rossii vvoditsia pod razlichnymi blagovidnymi predlogami." *Novye izvestiia*, 16 October. http://www.newizv.ru/politics/2013-10-16/190780-shagrenevaja-kozha-svobody.html.

Nikulin, Pavel. 2014. "Khakery protiv 'fabriki trollei': o platnykh kommentatorakh i agentakh v SMI." *Bumaga*, 2 June. http://paperpaper.ru/aii-media/.

"Nobelevskie laureaty Rossii i SSSR." 2021. *Chitalkin*. https://www.youtube.com /playlist?list=PL6ZF-9jmXX4Oxp_uiHPczQQvOs2CsFsWQ.

Nocetti, Julien. 2015. "Contest and Conquest: Russia and Global Internet Governance." *International Affairs* 91 (1): 111–30.

Nossik, Anton. 1997a. "Zametka shestidesiataia: Skandaly i poklonniki." *Vechernii internet*, 21 February. https://web.archive.org/web/20190913065147/http://www .gagin.ru/vi/21feb1997.htm.

Nossik, Anton. 1997b. "Zametka sto desiataia: Poka zharilsia CRON." *Vechernii internet*, 13 April. https://web.archive.org/web/20170715061837/http://www.gagin .ru/vi/13apr1997.htm.

"Novaia ekspertnaia initsiativa. Soobshchenie o proekte." 2000. *VVP: ekspertyi setevoi kanal*, 31 October. https://web.archive.org/web/20001031162947/http://vvp.ru /info/info.html.

"Novoe obshchestvo." 2022. *Kinopoisk*, https://www.kinopoisk.ru/series/5265111.

Novyi, Vladislav, Anna Balashova, Denis Skorobogat'ko, and Roman Rozhkov. 2014. "Domen - i tochka." *Kommersant''*, 29 April. http://www.kommersant.ru/doc /2462760.

oberkovich. 2001. "Razgovor bez pravil s Sergeem Minaevym." *RBP_ru*, 7 February. https://rbp-ru.livejournal.com/8300.html.

Ofitsial'nyi portal Vologodskoi oblasti. http://www.vologda-oblast.ru/ru/.

"O lige." 2025. *Liga bezopasnogo interneta*. https://ligainternet.ru/o-nas/ (accessed 8 July 2025).

"Onlain priemnaia Gubernatora Vologodskoi oblasti Olega Kuvshinnikova." 2013. https://web.archive.org/web/20130425194006/http://www.vopros.vologda -oblast.ru/.

"O Palate." n.d. Obshchestvennaia palata Rossiiskoi Federatsii. https://old.oprf.ru /about/.

"O podpisanii Soglasheniia mezhdu Pravitel'stvom Rossiiskoi Federatsii i Pravitel'stvom Kitaiskoi Narodnoi Respubliki o sotrudnichestve v oblasti obe-specheniia mezhdunarodnoi informatsionnoi bezopasnosti." 2015. *Pravitel'stvo Rossii*, 30 April. http://government.ru/media/files/5AMAccs7mSlXgbff1Ua785 WwMWcABDJw.pdf.

Osobennaia stat' Rossii. 2021. https://rutube.ru/channel/23678844.

"Otbor kontenta: priem zaiavok s 17 avgusta po 15 noiabria 2021 g." 2021. IRI: Institut razvitiia interneta. https://xn--h1aax.xn--p1ai/contests/sozdanie-i-razmeshchenie -kontenta-priyem-zayavok-s-17-avgusta-po-20-oktyabrya-2021-g/.

"Otbor prototipov igr." 2025. Institut razvitiia interneta. https://xn--h1aax.xn--p1ai /contests/otbor-prototipov-igr/.

Pankratova, Irina. 2022. "Voina i mir v Telegram. Kak patrioticheskie kanaly zakh-vatyvaiut sotsset' Pavla Durova." *The Bell*, 24 June.

Pankratova, Irina. 2023. "Fabrike trollei i mediaimperii Evgeniia Prigozhina ishchut novogo vladel'tsa." *The Bell*, 29 June. https://thebell.global.ssl.fastly.net/fabrike -trolley-i-media-imperii-evgeniya-prigozhina-ishchut-novogo-vladeltsa.

Papacharissi Z. 2013. *A Private Sphere: Democracy in a Digital Age*. Polity.

Parfeneva, Tat'iana. 2009. "Vkus Slova." *Uchitel'skaia gazeta* (50), 15 December. https:// dlib.eastview.com/browse/doc/21060094.

Parfent'eva, Irina and Kristina Astafurova. 2019. "Kirienko nazval ob"em finantsirova-niia dlia molodezhnogo kontenta v internete." *RBK*, 23 December. https://www .rbc.ru/society/23/12/2019/5e00c11c9a79476cb09593e6.

"Patriotizm na eksport. Kak Kreml' trollit inostrantsev." 2014. *The Insider*, 30 May. http://theins.ru/politika/872.

Paulsen, Martin. 2009. "Hegemonic Language and Literature: Russian Metadiscourse on Language in the 1990s." PhD diss., University of Bergen.

Pavliutenkova, M. Iu. 2013. "Elektronnoe pravitel'stvo v Rossii: Sostoianie i perspektivy." *POLIS. Politicheskie issledovaniia* 1:86–99.

Pavlovskii, Gleb. 1999. "Neskol'ko tezisov o rynke informatsionnykh voin." *So-obshchenie.* https://web.archive.org/web/20050117081752/http://soob .ru/n/1999/2/0/0.

Pavlovskii, G. 2000. "Zhurnalistika instsenirovok: po lichnym oshchushcheniam." *Russkii zhurnal*, 2 April. http://old.russ.ru/politics/articles/20000401_gpavl .html.

Pavlovskii, Gleb. 2011. "'Medvedev prevrashchaetsia vnutri praviashchego klassa v osnovnogo kandidata na vyborakh 2012 goda'." Kreml'.org, 2 March.

Pavlovskii, Gleb, Ivan Zasurskii, and Vitalii Kurennyi. 2003. "Agitprop ili samizdat: Beseda Gleba Pavlovskogo, Ivan Zasurskogo i Vitaliia Kurennogo." *Otechestvennye zapiski*, no. 4. http://www.strana-oz.ru/2003/4/agitprop-ili-samizdat.

Penskaia, Elena. 2007. "Modeli i stsenarii liberalizatsii rossiiskikh SMI." *Russkii zhurnal*, 16 May. http://www.russ.ru/pole/Modeli-i-scenarii-liberalizacii -rossijskih-SMI.

Penskaia, Elena. 2011. "Istoriia 'Russkogo zhurnala'. Chast' 1." *Russkii zhurnal* (2 August).

Pertsev, Andrey. 2023. "From Digital Paradise to Digital GULAG." *Riddle*, 14 April. http://ridl.io/from-digital-paradise-to-digital-gulag/.

Peskov, D. N. 2002. "Internet v rossiiskoi politike: utopiia ili real'nost'." *POLIS. Politicheskie issledovaniia* 1:31–45.

Peters, Benjamin. 2009. "And Lead Us Not into Thinking the New Is New: A Bibliographic Case for New Media History." *New Media & Society* 11 (1–2): 13–30.

Phillips, Whitney. 2013. "A Brief History of Trolls." *Daily Dot*, 20 May. http://www.dailydot .com/via/phillips-brief-history-of-trolls/.

Phillips Whitney. 2015. *This Is Why We Can't Have Nice Things: Mapping the Relationship between Online Trolling and Mainstream Culture.* MIT Press.

Philpott, Daniel. 2003. "Sovereignty." *Stanford Encyclopedia of Philosophy Archive*, 31 May. https://plato.stanford.edu/archives/sum2016/entries/sovereignty/.

Pichugina, Ekaterina. 2019. "V Rossii legaliziuiut torgovliu lekarstvami po Internetu." *Moskovskii komsomolets*, 11 October. https://www.mk.ru/social/health/2019 /10/10/v-rossii-legalizuyut-torgovlyu-lekarstvami-po-internetu.html.

Plakuchev, Grigorii. 2023. "'Mochit' v sortire'. V Kremle nazvali aktual'noi frazu Putina 1999 goda." Gazeta.ru, 23 May. https://www.gazeta.ru/politics/2023 /05/23/16748780.shtml.

Plamenev, Il'ia. 2022. "Peskov otvetil na informatsiiu o prisvoenii 'Geroia Rossii' Prigozhinu." *RBK*, 25 June. https://www.rbc.ru/politics/25/06/2022/62b6f21b9a 7947fd6741fe1f.

"PM Signs E-Russia into Action." 2002. *Moscow Times*, 30 January.

"Podkast 'Podvigi obychnykh liudei'." 2021. *Vremia geroev. Podvigi.* https://www.youtube .com/@podvigi.

Poliak, Rimma. 2006a. "Debatam—da?" *Russkie nochi.* Archived copy available at https:// web.archive.org/web/20071130033925/http://nights.russ.ru/events/115959746.

Poliak, Rimma. 2006b. "*ZheZhe zavoevyvaet prostranstvo.*" *Russkie nochi.* Archived copy available at https://web.archive.org/web/20061117201201/http://nights .russ.ru/events/111722334.

"Politicheskie debaty." 2006. DaDebatam.ru. Archived copy available at https://web.archive.org/web/20060613083902/http://dadebatam.ru/.

"Politika smotret' onlain Internet: svoboda ili vsedozvolennost'?" 2013. *Politika*, 30 May. http://vipzal.tv/tv-peredacha/politika-smotret-onlajn-internet-svoboda-ili-vsedozvolennost-30-05-2013-pervyj-kanal.html.

Politkovskaia, Anna. 2004. "Tsentrovoi iz Tsentoroia: Interv'iu s Ramzanom Kadyrovym. *Novaia gazeta*, 21 June. http://politkovskaya.novayagazeta.ru/pub/2004/2004-051.shtml.

"Politekhnologicheskii obman." 2006. Dni.ru, 23 February.

"Polnaia istoriia regulirovanii interneta v Rossii: ot 80-kh i do nashikh dnei." 2024. *iFreedomLab*. https://ifreedomlab.net/campaignes/istoriya-regulirovaniya-svyazi/.

Polovinko, Viacheslav. 2019. "Kak nam ne otkliuchat internet." *Novaia gazeta*, 2 October. https://novayagazeta.ru/articles/2019/10/01/82182-kak-nam-ne-otklyuchat-internet.

Pomerantsev, Peter, and Michael Weiss. 2014. "The Menace of Unreality: How the Kremlin Weaponizes Information, Culture and Money." A special report for the Institute for Modern Russia. https://imrussia.org/media/pdf/Research/Michael_Weiss_and_Peter_Pomerantsev__The_Menace_of_Unreality.pdf.

Ponamareva, Liliia. 2013. "Ramzan Kadyrov na ringe 'pobesedoval' s ministrom sporta." *Kommersant''*, 23 April. https://www.kommersant.ru/doc/2177170.

Popov, Dmitrii. 2021. "Virtual'nyi patriotizm," *Moskovskii komsomolets*, 18 August. Persistent East View URL: https://dlib.eastview.com/browse/doc/69320829.

Poshataev, Vladimir. 2004. "Luchshe men'she, da luchshe." *Parlamentskaia gazeta*, 12 February.

Potsar, Anna. 2013. "Strana pobedivshego khamstva: pochemu v Rossii ne mogut sporit' bez oskorblenii." *Forbes*, 29 March. http://www.forbes.ru/mneniya-column/tsennosti/236228-strana-pobedivshego-hamstva-pochemu-v-rossii-ne-mogut-sporit-bez-osk.

Pravdina, Mariia. 2001. "Vlast' na korotkom provodke." *Kommersant''*, 30 March.

Pravdina, Mariia. 2002. "Informatsionnyi feodalizm." *Kommersant''*, 17 May.

Pravitel'stvo Rossiiskoi Federatsii. 2020. "Postanovlenie ot 18 noiabria 2020 g. No. 1867." *Ofitsial'noe opublikovanie pravovykh aktov*, 23 November. http://publication.pravo.gov.ru/Document/View/0001202011230051.

"Press-sekretar' Medvedeva Natal'ia Timakova posovetovala deputatu ustanovit' VPN. A potom nazvala eto trollingom." 2018. *Meduza*, 2 May. https://meduza.io/shapito/2018/05/02/press-sekretar-medvedeva-natalya-timakova-posovetovala-deputatu-ustanovit-vpn-a-potom-nazvala-eto-trollingom.

"Prezident podpisal zakon o nakazanii za oskorblenie chuvstv veruiushchikh." 2013. RG.ru, 30 June. http://www.rg.ru/2013/06/30/chuvstva-anons.html.

"Prezidentskie vybory-2024. Agitirovat' i golosovat' protiv Putina." 2023. *Naval'nyi*, 7 December. https://navalny.com/p/6672/.

Proskurin, Oleg. 2001. "O iazyke politiki i kontse literatury." *Russkii zhurnal*, 24 December. http://old.russ.ru/krug/20011224-gp.html.

Prosvirova, Ol'ga, and Sergei Sokolov. 2014. "Trolli. Mest' dlia diskussii." *Novaia gazeta*, 12 February. East View persistent URL, https://novayagazeta.ru/articles/2014/02/11/58311-trolli-mest-dlya-diskussiy.

Putin, Vladimir. 2001. "Stenograficheskii otchet o rasshirennoi press-konferentsii dlia rossiiskikh i inostrannykh zhurnalistov." 18 July. http://archive.kremlin.ru/appears/2001/07/18/0000_type63380type82634_28591.shtml.

Putin, Vladimir. 2007. "Vystuplenie i diskussiia na miunkhenskoi konferentsii po voprosam politiki besopasnosti." *Prezident Rossii,* 10 February. http://www .kremlin.ru/events/president/transcripts/24034.

Putin, Vladimir. 2012a. "Demokratiia i kachestvo gosudarstva." *Kommersant'',* 6 February.

Putin, Vladimir. 2012b. "Poslanie Prezidenta Federal'nomu Sobraniiu." *Prezident Rossii,* 12 December. http://kremlin.ru/news/17118.

Putin, Vladimir. 2014. "Vstrecha s molodymi uchenymi i prepodavateliami istorii." *Prezident Rossii*, 5 November. http://www.kremlin.ru/events/president /news/46951.

"Putin ob''iasnil podpisanie pakta Mototova-Ribbentropa i razdel Pol'shi." 2019. *Interfax,* 19 December. https://www.interfax.ru/russia/688612.

"Putin otreksia ot svoego ottsa: Strana ne nuzhna Rossii." 2002. Agentstvo *politicheskikh novostei*, 9 July. Integrum persistent URL: https://aafnet.integrum.ru/artefact3/ia /ia5.aspx/PyMENk2R/1273/apn_D20020709_L2005062005392697_A026.htm.

"Putin otvetil, budet li registrirovat' nashu partiiu." 2018. *Aleksei Naval'nyi*, 27 August. https://www.youtube.com/watch?v=Nyq10d5BPxs.

"Putin pristrunit oligarkhov?" 2002. *Dni.ru*, 4 July. https://web.archive.org/web /20030202184051/http://www.dni.ru/news/analitika/2002/7/4/11402.html.

"Putin: Rossiia ne dvizhets'ia v storonu zakrytiia interneta." 2019. *Kommersant'',* 19 December. https://www.kommersant.ru/doc/4199109.

Pyrma, Roman. 2012. [Personal e-mail to Artem Lazarev (20 January)]. Reposted at kremlingate, 24 February. http://lj.rossia.org/users/kremlingate/.

Radzikhovskii, Leonid. 2013. "'mer' barrikad." *Russiiskaia gazeta*, 6 August.

Raevskaia, M. 2013. "Sotsseti i detskie proryvy vzroslykh." *Vecherniaia Moskva*, 18 April.

Rain Sounds. 2015. "Bezumie kremlevskikh trollei." YouTube, 23 March. https://www .youtube.com/watch?v=mA1HKzWrFx4.

"Ramzan Kadyrov stal liderom chechenskogo odeleniia 'Nochnyikh volkov'." 2015. *TASS*, 23 May. http://tass.ru/politika/1990917.

"Ramzan Kadyrov sygral glavnuiu rol' v gollivudskom boivike." 2015. *Starhit*, 26 May. https://www.starhit.ru/novosti/ramzan-kadyirov-syigral-glavnuyu-rol-v -gollivudskom-boevike-116470/.

Rara, Avis. 2015. "Rossiia. Piter. Tsentr 'internet-trollei' Putina." YouTube, 14 March. https://www.youtube.com/watch?v=fL-59b8OBxM.

Ratilainen, Saara. 2020. "The Networked Architecture of Media Freedom in Contemporary Russia: The Case of Urban Online Magazines." In *Freedom of Expression in Russia's New Media Sphere*, edited by Mariëlle Wijermars and Katja Lehti-saari, 77–95. Routledge.

"Rebenok v sotssetiakh: obezopasit' ot propagandy nezakonnoi deiatel'nosti." 2021. *Obshchestvennaia palata Rossiiskoi Federatsii*, 3 February. https://oprf.ru/news /rebenok-v-socsetyax-obezopasit-ot-propagandy-nezakonnoi-deyatelnosti.

Reiter, Svetlana, Mariia Zholobova, and Anastasiia Korotkova. 2023. "'Chistymi rukami vziat' patrioticheskikh deneg i ne zashkvarit'sia.' Rossiiskii Institut razvistiia interneta shchedro finansiruet voennuiu propaganda. No den'gi u nego berut dazhe te, kto vystupaiut protiv vtorzheniia. Rassledovanie *Meduzy* i *Vazhnykh istorii*." *Meduza*, 6 June. https://meduza.io/feature/2023/06/06/chistymi -rukami-vzyat-patrioticheskih-deneg-i-ne-zashkvaritsya.

"Reiting blogov Twitter." 2011. Yandex.ru, 14 June. http://blogs.yandex.ru/top/twitter/.

"Rekomendatsii Obshchestvennoi palaty Rossiiskoi Federatsii po itogam obshchest-vennykh slushanii na temu: 'Profilaktika vovlecheniia nesovershennoletnykh i protivopravil'nuiu deiatel'nost' v sotsial'nykh setiakh'." 2021. *Obshchestvennaia*

palata Rossiiskoi Federatsii, 3 February. https://files.oprf.ru/storage/documents
/rekomen-deti-socseti03022021.pdf.

"Reshaem problem, za kogo golosovat'. Nam pomozhet Bog. I kvantovaia fizika." 2024.
Navalnyi, 14 March. https://navalny.com/p/6674/.

Revich, Iurii. 2009. "Korruptsiia onlain." *Novaia gazeta*, 18 December.

Revich, Iurii, and Valerii Shiriaev. 2010. "Mezhdu pravitel'stvom i Ru eshche ne post-
avlena tochka." *Novaia gazeta*, 15 March.

Rezchikov, Andrei. 2009. "Liudi vernutsia k vechnym tsennostiam." *Vzgliad*, 7 October. https://vz.ru/politics/2009/10/7/335229.html.

Richter, James. 2009. "Putin and the Public Chamber." *Post-Soviet Affairs* 25 (1):
39–65.

Rodin, Ivan. 2012. "Internet-'bomzhi' v belom dome." *Nezavisimaia gazeta*, 26 July.

Rodina, E., and D. Dligach. 2019. "Dictator's Instagram: Personal and Political Narratives in a Chechen Leader's Social Network." *Caucasus Survey* 7 (2): 95–109.

Rogovskii, A. M. 2006. "Formy i nasilie v kul'ture: temporal'no-psikhologicheskii
aspect." *Chelovek* 1: 62–68.

Rohozinski, Rafal. 1999. "Mapping Russian Cyberspace: Perspectives on Democracy
and the Net." United Nations Research Institute for Social Development, Discussion Paper No. 115 (October). https://www.files.ethz.ch/isn/29036/dp
115.pdf.

Rosen, Tine, and Vera Zvereva. 2014. "Social Network Sites on the Runet: Exploring
Social Communication." In *Digital Russia: The Language, Culture, and Politics of
New Media Communication*, edited by Michael S. Gorham, Ingunn Lunde, and
Martin Paulsen, 72–87. Routledge.

"Roskomnadzor ob''iasnil blokirovku prilozheniia 'Naval'nyi' v Runete." 2021. *RBK*. 24
August. https://www.rbc.ru/rbcfreenews/6124c8489a7947c0b1929627.

"Roskomnadzor trebuet ot nebol'shikh provaiderov ustanovku oborudovaniia v ramkakh 'suverennogo interneta'." 2020. *SecurityLab.ru*, 19 September. https://www
.securitylab.ru/news/512276.php.

"Roskomnadzor: Zamedlenie Twitter ne sviazano s popytkami ogranichit' diskussiiu v
Internete." 2021. *Fontanka.ru*, 11 March. https://www.fontanka.ru/2021/03
/11/69805865/.

"RosPil predlozhil mery po bor'be s ispol'zovaniem latinitsy pri razmeshchenii gosza-
kaza." 2013. *RosBalt*, 23 January. https://www.rosbalt.ru/news/2013-01-23
/rospil-predlozhil-mery-po-borbe-s-ispolzovaniem-latinitsy-pri-razmeschenii
-goszakaza-4083453.

"Rossiia v lirike bloga." 2005. *Novaia gazeta*, 8 April.

Rothrock, Kevin. 2014. "Russia's Parliament Prepares New 'Anti-Terrorist' Laws for
Internet." *Global Voices*, 16 January. https://advox.globalvoices.org/2014/01/16
/russias-parliament-prepares-new-anti-terrorist-laws-for-internet-censorship
-putin/.

Rovinskaia, T. 2014. "Russkaia model' elektronnoi demokratii v mezhdunarodnom
kontekste." *Mirovaia ekonomika mezhdunarodnye otnosheniia* 8: 76–90.

Rozhkova, Natal'ia, Mikhail Zubov, and Dmitrii Katorzhnov. 2014. "Eto 'ZheZhe' nepro-
sta. V Gosdume gotoviat novye ogranicheniia dlia interneta." *Moskovskii komsomolets*, 15 March. https://www.mk.ru/politics/article/2014/03/14/998654-eto
-zhzh-nesprosta-v-gosdume-gotovyat-novyie-ogranicheniya-dlya-interneta
.html.

Rubin, Mikhail. 2018. "Telega iz Kremlia. Rasskaz o tom, kak vlasti prevratili Telegram
v televizor." *Proekt*, 18 November. https://www.proekt.media/narrative
/telegram-kanaly/.

Rubin, Mikhail, and Dar'ia Luganskaia. 2014. "Sovbez Rossii obsudit ugrozu otkliuche-
    niia interneta 1 oktiabria." *RBK*, 22 September. https://www.rbc.ru/technology
    _and_media/22/09/2014/5423e453cbb20f6924319365.
Rubtsov, Denis. 2010. "Svideteli E-government." *Novaia gazeta*, 7 July.
Rudnitsky, Jake. 2024. "YouTube Throttled in Russia in Latest Attack on Social Media."
    Bloomberg, 25 July. https://www.bloomberg.com/news/articles/2024-07-25
    /youtube-throttled-in-russia-in-latest-attack-on-social-media?embedded
    -checkout=true.
Rusiaeva, Polina, Mikhail Rubin, and Elizaveta Surganova. 2015. "Sovet po internetu."
    Ezhednevnaia delovaia gazeta RBK, 23 December. Persistent East View URL:
    https://dlib.eastview.com/browse/doc/45940785.
"Russian Authorities Slowed YouTube Speeds to Near Unusable Levels—So Why Are
    Kremlin Critics Getting More Views?" 2024. *Meduza*, 12 September. https://
    meduza.io/en/feature/2024/09/12/the-russian-authorities-slowed-youtube
    -speeds-to-near-unusable-levels-so-why-are-kremlin-critics-getting-more-views.
"Russian Internet-Isolation Bill Advances, Despite Doubts in Duma." 2019. *Radio Free
    Europe/Radio Liberty*, 12 February. https://www.rferl.org/a/russian-bill-on
    -autonomous-operation-of-internet-advances-in-duma/29765882.html.
"Russia Opens 10K Cases for 'Discrediting' Army Since Invasion – Mediazona." 2024.
    The Moscow Times, 14 August. https://www.themoscowtimes.com/2024/08/14
    /russia-opens-10k-cases-for-discrediting-army-since-invasion-medizona
    -a86022.
Rykov, Konstantin. 2010a. "Reaktivnyi psikhos." *Vzgliad*, 3 March. https://vz.ru/columns
    /2010/3/3/380888.html.
Rykov, Konstantin. 2010b. "Sindrom iutiubatsiia soznaniia." *Vzgliad*, 14 April. https://
    vz.ru/columns/2010/4/14/392844.html.
Safonova, Kristina. 2018. "Putin opiat' ne nazval Naval'nogo po imeni. Eto
    normal'no?" *afishaDaily*, 12 January. https://daily.afisha.ru/relationship/7882
    -putin-opyat-ne-nazval-navalnogo-po-imeni-eto-normalno/.
Sal'manov, Oleg. 2010. "Pochem blog dlia gubernatora." *Vedomosti*, 1 February. http://
    www.vedomosti.ru/politics/news/2010/02/01/937123.
Samokhin, Andrei. 2016. "German Klimenko: 'Internet-tekhnologii pridetsia vnedriat'
    v ruchnom rezhime." *Kul'tura*, 12 January. https://portal-kultura.ru/articles
    /person/126813-german-klimenko-internet-tekhnologii-pridetsya-vnedryat-v
    -ruchnom-rezhime/.
Sanger, David E. 2018. *The Perfect Weapon: War, Sabotage, and Fear in the Cyber Age*.
    Crown Publishing.
"SANKI PETERBURG." 2021. *VTV*. https://www.youtube.com/watch?v=3f3lDGbOuoI
    &t=3s&ab.
Schmidt, Henrike, and Katy Teubener. 2006. "(Counter)Public Sphere(s) on the Rus-
    sian Internet." In *Control + Shift: Public and Private Usages of the Russian Inter-
    net*, edited by Henrike Schmidt, Katy Teubener, and Natalja Konradova, 51–72.
    Books on Demand.
Schmidt, Henrike, Katy Teubener and Natalja Konradova, eds. 2006. *Control + Shift:
    Public and Private Uses of the Russian Internet*. Books on Demand.
Schmitt, Carl. 1932/1996. *Concept of the Political*. University of Chicago Press.
Sedov, Kirill and Kseniia Boletskaia. 2016. "Messendzhery dolzhny indentifitsirovat'
    pol'zovatelei i presekat' obmen nezakonnoi informatsiei." *Vedomosti*, 12 August.
    https://www.vedomosti.ru/technology/articles/2016/08/12/652742-messendzheri
    -dolzhni-identifitsirovat-polzovatelei-presekat-obmen-nezakonnoi-informatsiei.

Sedukhina, Anastasiia. 2019. "'V razvitoi demokratii avtora etogo zakonoproekta dolzhny byli by vyzvat' na dopros'." *Republic*, 13 November. https://republic.ru /posts/95187.

"Sekretar' Sovbez RF ob"iasnil, zachem Rossii nuzhen suverennyi internet." 2019. *Regnum*, 25 March. https://regnum.ru/news/2597907.

Sergeev, Mikhail. 2011. "Bol'shinstvo grazhdan ne zainteresovalis' 'bol'shoe pravitel'stvo'." *Nezavisimaia gazeta*, 22 December.

Shadrina, T. 2014. "Bez vzroslykh ne klikat'." *Rossiiskaia gazeta*, 22 April.

Shatilin, Il'ia. 2023. "Rossiiskaia mobil'naia OS dlia planshetov: chego zhdem." *Telecom Daily*, 7 April. https://telecomdaily.ru/news/2023/04/10/rossiyskaya-mobilnaya -os-dlya-planshetov-chego-zhdem.

Shaw, Saxon, R. 2017. "There Is No Silver Bullet: Solutions to Internet Jurisdiction." *International Journal of Law and Information Technology* (25): 283–308.

Shein, Oleg. 2011a. "Pro Naval'nogo: v pomoshch' konspirologam." *Oleg Shein*, 11 March. http://oleg-shein.livejournal.com/289794.html.

Shein, Oleg. 2011b. "Astrakhanskii Sotsial'nyi Forum." *Oleg Shein*, 2 July. http://oleg -shein.livejournal.com/350851.html.

Shirmanova, Tat'iana. 2012. "Nashe 'elektronnoe pravitel'stvo' rabotaet khuzhe, chem v Afrike." *Izvestiia*, 10 August.

Shishkunova, Elena. 2009. "Dmitrii Medvedev—o virtual'nykh gosuslugakh: 'Chto my prodvinuli? Ni figa my ne prodvinuli poka.'" *Izvestiia*, 1 September. https://iz.ru /news/352501.

Shishkunova, Elena. 2011. "'Bol'shoe pravitel'stvo—eto "ukho", chustvitel'noe k khoro-shim ideiam'." *Izvestiia*, 2 November.

Shubin, Aleksandr. 2010. "Modernizatsiia i postindustrial'nyi bar'er, ili pochemu u Medvedeva nichego ne poluchaetsia." *Neprikosnovennyi zapas* 6: 321–37.

Sidibe, P'er. 2011a. "Nervno-izbiratel'naia sistema." *Rossiiskaia gazeta*, 24 March 2011.

Sidibe, P'er. 2011b. "Kreml' nashel sposob vovlech' grazhdan v uprvlenie stranoi." *Izvestiia*, 28 October.

Sila v pravde Zov. 2022. "Vika Tsyganova—'Vagner'. Prim'er pesni." *Rutube*. https:// rutube.ru/video/9d29c472a36e16fa59c56ddc2e9f1ef9/.

Sivetc, Liudmila. 2020. "The Blacklisting Mechanism: New-School Regulation of Online Expression and Its Technological Challenges." In *Freedom of Expression in Russia's New Media Sphere*, edited by Mariëlle Wijermars and Katja Lehti-saari, 39–56. Routledge.

Sivkova, Alena. 2014. "Personal'nye dannye grazhdan obiazhut khranit' v Rossii s 1 ianvaria 2015 g." *Izvestiia*, 1 September. http://izvestia.ru/news/575983.

"Skol'ko liudei vyshli na ulitsy 26 marta i skol'ko zaderzhali? Karta protesta." 2017. *Meduza*, 27 March. https://meduza.io/feature/2017/03/27/skolko-lyudey-vyshli -na-ulitsy-26-marta-i-skolko-zaderzhali-karta-protesta.

Skripnik, Denis, and Igor' Pichugin. 2003. "Saity rossiiskoi vlasti." *Kommersant*, 22 April.

Smetanin, Mikhail. 2002. "Virtual'noe partstroitel'stvo." *Russkii zhurnal*, 28 March. http://old.russ.ru/netcult/history/20020328.html.

Smirnov, Sergei. 2001. "Chinovnikov otpravliaiut na 'mylo'." *Novaia gazeta*, 2 July.

Snegovaya, Maria, Michael Kimmage, and Jade McGlynn. 2023. "The Ideology of Putinism: Is It Sustainable?" *Center for Strategic and International Studies*, September 2023.

Sobchak, Kseniia. 2017. "Kseniia Sobchak—kandidat 'protiv vsekh'." *Ostorozhno: Sobchak*, 18 October. https://www.youtube.com/watch?v=he68RC4f24k.

Sochnev, Aleksei, and Daniil Kolomiichuk. 2013. "'Chistyi internet' okazalsia belym i pushistym," *PublicPost* (*Radio Ekho Moskvy*), 1 February. http://echo.msk.ru /blog/publicpost/1002660-echo/.

"'Sokhraniaite spokoistvie i ne ver'te feikam'—Aleksandr Mal'kevich." 2020. *Obshchestvennaia palata Rossiiskoi Federatsii*, 20 March. https://old.oprf.ru/press/news /2617/newsitem/52842.

Sokolov, Vladimir. 2016. "Khamstvu boi?" *Argumenty i fakty*, 14 December. East View persistent URL, https://dlib.eastview.com/browse/doc/47987010.

Soldatov, Andrei. 2019. "Po stopam kitaiskikh tovarishchei." *New Times*, 17 April. https://newtimes.ru/articles/detail/179590.

Soldatov, Andrei, and Irina Borogan. 2015. *The Red Web: The Struggle between Russia's Digital Dictators and the New Online Revolutionaries*. Public Affairs.

Solov'ev. A. I. 2004. "Politicheskii diskurs mediakratii: problem informatsionnoi epokhi." *POLIS. Politicheskie issledovaniia* 2:124–32.

Soshnikov, Andrei. 2015. "Stolitsa politicheskogo trollinga." *Moi Raion*, 11 March. http://www.mr7.ru/articles/112478/.

"Sotsseti proveriat na opasnyi dlia detei kontent." 2018. *Obshchestvennaia palata Rossiiskoi Federatsii*, 26 February. https://old.oprf.ru/press/news/2018/newsitem/44227.

"Sozertsatel'noe grazhdanskoe obshchestvo." 2010. *Obshchestvennaia palata Rossiiskoi Federatsii*, 25 November. http://www.old.oprf.ru/press/news/2010/newsitem/3389.

Sperling, Valerie. 2015. *Sex, Politics, and Putin: Political Legitimacy in Russia*. Oxford University Press.

Starikova, Mariia. 2021. "Podschet zaderzhannykh prodolzhaetsia." *Kommersant''*, 25 January. East View persistent URL, https://dlib.eastview.com/browse/doc /64408374.

Starr, Paul. 2004. *The Creation of the Media: Political Origins of Modern Communications*. Basic Books.

"State Mulls E-Russia's $2.6Bln Fate." 2001. *Moscow Times*, 27 June.

"Stat' obshchestvom umnykh, svobodnykh i otvetstvennykh liudei." 2009. *Izvestiia*, 13 November.

"Stenograficheskii otchet o zasedanii Gosudarstvennogo soveta po voprosam razvitiia politicheskoi sistemy Rossii." 2010. *Prezident Rossii*, 22 January. http://kremlin .ru/events/president/transcripts/6693.

Stepanova, Nadezhda. 2005. "Kremlevskii mifotvorets stanet sotrudnikom NTV." *Izvestiia.ru*, 19 August. https://iz.ru/news/305314.

"Sto nedrugov vlasti: kogo i kak nakazyvaiut za neuvazhenie v Seti." 2020. *Roskomsvoboda*, 31 March. https://roskomsvoboda.org/en/post/sto-nedrugov-vlasti-kogo -i-kak-nakazyiv/.

Strukov, Vlad. 2012. "Networked Putinism: The Fading Days of the (Broadcast) Era." *Digital Icons: Studies in Russian, Eurasian and Central European New Media* 7:111–23.

Strukov, Vlad. 2016. "Digital Conservatism: Framing Patriotism in the Era of Global Journalism." In *Eurasia 2.0: Russian Geopolitics in the Age of New Media*, 185–208. Lexington Books.

Strukov, V., and V. Zvereva, eds. 2014. *Ot tsentral'nogo k tsifrovomu: Televidenie v Rossii*. Voronezhskii gusudarstvennyi pedagogicheskii universitet.

Suslov, Mikhail. 2024. *Putinism: Post-Soviet Russian Regime Ideology*. Routledge.

"'Suverenizatsiia Runeta'. Chto s nei ne tak?" 2021. Roskomsvoboda, 8 October. https:// roskomsvoboda.org/en/cards/card/o-suverennom-runete/.

"'Suverennyi internet' negativno otrazitsia na rynke telekoma. Mnenie eksperta." 2019. *Roskomsvoboda*, 27 May. https://roskomsvoboda.org/en/post/suverennyij-internet -negativno-otraz/.

Svantesson, Dan Jerker B. 2017. *Solving the Internet Jurisdiction Puzzle.* Oxford Scholarship Online. https://academic.oup.com/oxford-scholarship-online/search-results?page=1&q=Svantesson%2C%20Dan%20Jerker%20B.%202017.%20Solving%20the%20Internet%20Jurisdiction%20Puzzle&fl_SiteID=6556&SearchSourceType=1&allJournals=1.

Tagaeva, Lola. 2013. "Kudrin o neliubvi vlasti k NKO: 'Ona deistvuet v ramkakh massogo obshchestvennogo mneniia'." *Slon* (26 September), http://slon.ru/russia/kudrin_o_nelyubvi_vlasti_k_nko_ona_deystvuet_v_ramkakh_massovogo_obshchestvennogo_mneniya-996792.xhtml.

Taranov, Sergei, and Gleb Cherkasov. 2017. "Chto budet s Dmitriem Medvedevym posle otcheta v Gosdume." *Novye izvestiia*, 8 April. East View persistent URL, https://dlib.eastview.com/browse/doc/49854069.

Taroshchina, Slava. 2009. "Rodina ili tkemali? Tresh-patriotizm na tresh-TV kak sposob bor'by s nedovol'nymi." *Novaia gazeta,* 3 February. https://novayagazeta.ru/articles/2009/02/04/44039-rodina-ili-tkemali.

Taylor, Brian D. 2018. *The Code of Putinism.* Oxford University Press.

"Tetradka po istorii." 2022. *365 dnei TV.* https://www.youtube.com/playlist?list=PLTRx8hZCl1K6CG4Prwp2JJ-lFWSgsUGQB.

Timurovtsy XXI veka. 2021. https://rutube.ru/channel/23678857/.

Tirmaste, Maria-Luiza. 2011. "'Edinaia Rossiia' vpletaetsia v sotsial'nye seti." Kommersant.ru, 6 May. http://www.kommersant.ru/doc-y/163554.

Tishina, Iuliia. 2019. "Operatory zadumalis' o veshchnom." *Kommersant'',* 21 March. https://www.kommersant.ru/doc/3917500.

Tishina, Iuliia, and Valeriia Lebedeva. 2019. "Rossiiskii soft predostanovilsia." *Kommersant'',* 31 July. https://www.kommersant.ru/doc/4047571.

Titorenko, D. 2006. "Gleb Pavlovskii i durakoemkost'." Sobesednik 11, 21 March. Persistent Integrum URL: https://aafnet.integrum.ru/artefact3/ia/ia5.aspx?lv=6&si=FvYKPE2R&qu=182&st=0&bi=5284&xi=&nd=23&tn,d=0&srt=0&f=0.

Toepfl, Florian. 2012. "Blogging for the Sake of the President: The Online Diaries of Russian Governors." *Europe-Asia Studies* 64 (8): 1435–59.

Toporov, Viktor. 2013. "God total'nogo trollinga." *Izvestiia*, 9 January. East View persistent URL, https://dlib.eastview.com/browse/doc/28358071.

Torop, Anastasiia. 2019. "Sozdat', chtoby otkliuchit'." *Novaia gazeta*, 17 December. https://novayagazeta.ru/articles/2019/12/17/83195-sozdat-chtoby-otklyuchit.

"Tot samyi personazh: kak ne nazvat' oppozitsionera oppozitsionerom." 2017. *Delovoi Peterburg*, 5 April. https://www.dp.ru/a/2017/04/05/Tot_samij_personazh_kak_n.

Travin, Andrei. 2001. "Maksim Kononenko: 'U publiki liubov' k nekrofil'skim proektam'." *Netoskop*, 28 August. http://netoscope.narod.ru/profile/2001/08/28/3268.html.

Tropkina, Ol'ga. 2011. "Pri pravitel'stve mozhet poiavitsia novaia struktura." *Izvestiia*, 17 December. East View persistent URL, https://dlib.eastview.com/browse/doc/26114728.

Tropkina, Ol'ga, and Anastasiia Novikova. 2011. "'Nashi' osvoili trolling i sms-spam." *Izvestiia*, 28 August. https://iz.ru/news/498757.

Tselykh, Aleksei. [2000]. "Marina Litvinovich." *Intern* 26. http://gagin.ru/internet/26/20.html.

"Tsenzor—dokhodnoe mesto." 2013. *Novaia gazeta*, 26 February. https://novayagazeta.ru/articles/2013/02/27/53718-tsenzor-151-dohodnoe-mesto.

Tsukanov, Igor'. 2014. "Igor' Tsukanov: Ot kakikh vragov nado zashchishchat' internet?" *Vedomosti*, 3 October. https://www.vedomosti.ru/opinion/articles/2014/10/03/internet-kabel.

Tsvei, Irina. 2004. "Osoboe mnenie." *Ekho Moskvy*, 18 August.

Tufekci, Zeynep. 2017. *Twitter and Tear Gas: The Power and Fragility of Networked Protest*. Yale University Press.

Tumanova, Ol'ga. 2010. "Chinovniki ne khotiat byt' elektronnym." *Izvestiia*, 11 August.

Turovskii, Daniil. 2018. "Izoliatsiia interneta i zapret anonimnosti. Chto delal German Klimenko na postu sovetnika prezidenta po internetu." *Meduza*, 13 June. https://meduza.io/slides/izolyatsiya-interneta-i-zapret-anonimnosti-chto-delal -german-klimenko-na-postu-sovetnika-prezidenta-po-internetu.

"Uchenik shkoly v Ivanteevke napal na uchitelia i otkryl strel'bu." 2017. *Obshchestvennaia palata Rossiiskoi Federatsii*, 5 September. https://old.oprf.ru/press/832 /newsitem/41942 [full transcript of comments no longer available].

"Ukaz Prezidenta Rossiiskoi Federatsii ot 02.07.2021 No. 400 'O Strategii natsional'noi bezopasnosti Rossiiskoi Federatsii'." 2021. *Ofitsial'nyi internet-portal pravovoi informatsii*, 2 July. http://actual.pravo.gov.ru/content/content.html#pnum =0001202107030001.

Ukhov, Il'ia. 2017. "Naval'nyi dolzhen sidet', potomu chto sam etogo khochet." Life.ru, 2 February. https://life.ru/p/968383.

"Ukral, vypil—na svobodu. Kak pomilovannye vagnerovtsy snova sovershaiut prestupleniia, no ne vsegda vozvrashchaiutsia v tiur'mu." *Verstka*, 25 December. https://verstka.media/kak-pomilovannye-vagnerovcy-snova-sovershayut -prestupleniya-no-ne-vsegda-vozvraschayutsia-v-tyurmu.

"Ushakhidi po ukhabam." 2010. *navalny*, 7 September. https://navalny.livejournal.com /500765.html.

Usmanov, Alisher. 2017a. "Alisher Usmanov protiv Alekseia Naval'nogo." YouTube, 17 May. https://youtu.be/8Mx9yYZd2f0.

Usmanov, Alisher. 2017b. "Alisher Usmanov protiv Alekseia Naval'nogo 2." *VKontakte*, 24 May. https://vk.com/videos429340904?z=video429340904_456239018%2 Fpl_429340904_-2.

Ustinova, Anna. 2020. "Poleznaia zagruzka: v gadzhetakh poiavitsia aggregator s besplatnymi saitami." *Izvestiia*, 18 December. https://iz.ru/1101321/anna-ustinova /poleznaia-zagruzka-v-gadzhetakh-poiavitsia-agregator-s-besplatnymi-saitami.

Vainer, Evsei. 1999. "Akula piara v setiakh interneta." *Soobshchenie*. http://soob.ru/n /1999/2/i/0.

Vakhtin N. 2016. "The Discourse of Argumentation in Totalitarian Language and Post-Soviet Communication Failures." In *Public Debate in Russia: Matters of (Dis)order*, edited by Nikolai Vakhtin and Boris Firsov, 10–30. Edinburgh University Press.

Vakhtin, Nikolai, and Boris Firsov, eds. 2016. *Public Debate in Russia: Matters of (Dis)order*. Edinburgh University Press.

Van der Vet, Freek. 2020. "Imprisoned for a 'Like': The Criminal Prosecution of Social Media Users Under Authoritarianism." In *Freedom of Expression in Russia's New Media Sphere*, edited by Mariëlle Wijermars and Katja Lehtisaari, 209–24. Routledge Press.

van Dijk, Teun. 1997. "What Is Political Discourse Analysis?" *Belgian Journal of Linguistics* 11: 11–52.

Vdokhnoviteli. n.d. https://xn--b1aaffobumib0c5a.xn--p1ai/.

Vedenskaia, Alisa. 2010. "Glavnyi tekhnolog Rossiiskoi Federatsii." *Nezavisimaia gazeta*, 30 August.

Veletminskii, Igor'. 2005. "Sviaz'invest poidet na torg." *Rossiiskaia gazeta*, 29 September.

"Versiia o perevorote ne podtverdilos'." 1994. *Kommersant''*, 30 March. https://www .kommersant.ru/doc/74794.

"Video Shows Prigozhin Recruiting Russian Prisoners for Ukraine Fight." 2022. *Moscow Times*, 15 September. https://www.themoscowtimes.com/2022/09/15/video -shows-prigozhin-recruiting-russian-prisoners-for-ukraine-fight-a78801.

Vinogradova, Ilona, and Bogdan Stepovoi. 2004. "Slysh', bratello, baiku nado pro pravitel'stvo napisat'." *Izvestiia*, 25 May.

Vishnepol'skii, Kirill. 2002. "Internet. Internet." *Kommersant''*, 23 September. https://dlib.eastview.com/browse/doc/4365329.

"V Kremle ob''iasnili, dlia chego nuzhen suverennyi internet." 2019. *Ekspert*, 3 June. https://expert.ru/2019/06/3/v-kremle-ob_yasnili-dlya-chego-rossii-nuzhen -suverennyij-internet/.

"Vladimir Putin otvetil na voprosy uchastnikov mediaforuma ONF v Sankt-Peterburge." 2017. *Pervyi kanal*, 3 April. https://www.1tv.ru/ news/2017-04-03/322765-vladimir_putin_otvetil_na_voprosy_uchastnikov _mediaforuma_onf_v_sankt_peterburge.

"Vladimir Putin pozdravil Sergeia Sobianina s ofitsial'nym vstupleniem v dolzhnost' mera Moskvy." 2013. *Prezident Rossii*, 12 September. http://kremlin.ru/news/19211.

"'Vladimir Vladimirovich.ru' zakryl dustup k saitu, obidevshis' na liberalov." 2006. *Novyi region (Tsentr)*, 24 March.

Vladimirov, Viktor. 2024. "Konsolidatsiia rossiiskoi oppozitsii: vyzovy i perspektivy." *Golos Ameriki*, 4 November. https://www.golosameriki.com/a/russian-opposition -consolidation/7850705.html.

"Vladimiru Putinu zadali vopros o 'suverennom internete'." 2019. *1TV*, 20 June. https://www.1tv.ru/news/2019-06-20/367253-vladimiru_putinu_zadali _vopros_o_zakone_o_suverennom_internete.

"Vlast', Internet i my." 2000. Strana.ru, 28 September.

Volkov, Leonid. 2011. "Kak ia porabotal agitatorom." *O vsiakoi vsiachine*, 9 March. http://leonwolf.livejournal.com/238492.html.

Volkova, Alisa. 2021. "'Khvatit kormit' Kavkaz: Kak menialsia natsionalizm Naval'nogo." *Kavkaz.Realiia*, 1 February. https://www.kavkazr.com/a/31075519.html.

"'Volna feikov na fone epidemii koronavirusa vyiavila probely v zakonodatel'stve'— Aleksandr Mal'kevich." 2020. *Obshchestvennaia palata Rossiiskoi Federatsii*, 3 February. https://old.oprf.ru/press/news/2617/newsitem/52295.

Voronin, Anatolii. 2009. "Na puti k 'Informatsionnomu obshchestvu'." *Izvestiia*, 29 October.

"Vostretsov: Rossiia dolzhna sozdat' svoi analog YouTube." 2020. *DumaTV*, 24 April. https://dumatv.ru/news/vostretsov--rossiya-dolzhna-sozdat-svoi-analog -youtube.

"Vozbuzhdeno ugolovnoe delo o vovlechenii detei v protest 23 ianvaria." 2021. *Interfaks*, 22 January. https://www.interfax.ru/russia/746442.

"Vozvrashchenie 'molodogo Ramzana'." 2025. *Novaia gazeta Evropa*, 5 May. https://novayagazeta.eu/articles/2025/05/05/vozvrashchenie-molodogo-ramzana.

"Vremia pokazhet. Vypusk ot 03.10.2014." 2014. *Pervyi kanal*, 3 October. http://www.1tv.ru/shows/vremya-pokazhet/vypuski/vremya-pokazhet-vypusk -ot-03-10-2014.

"V Rossii poiaviatsia elektronnye grazhdane." 2006. *Obshchestvennaia palata Rossiiskoi Federatsii*, 19 December. https://old.oprf.ru/press/news/2006/newsitem/772.

"V Rossii za god bylo vozbuzhdeno 100 del o neuvazhenii k vlasti." 2020. *Radio Svoboda*, 31 March. https://www.svoboda.org/a/30519801.html.

"Vskrytaia novaia 'fabrika trollei' – s deputatom Shlegelem vo glave." 2014. *The Insider*, 1 August. https://theins.ru/politika/1308.

"V Sovete Federatsii predlagaiut sozdat' rossiiskii internet 'Cheburashka'." 2014. *RBK*, 28 April. https://www.rbc.ru/society/28/04/2014/57041be89a794761c0ce963e.

"Vstrecha Dmitriia Medvedeva s rukovodstvom 'Edinoi Rossii' (stenogramma)." 2009. Vzgliad.ru, 9 April. https://vz.ru/information/2009/4/9/274681.html.

"VTsIOM vyiasnil, skol'ko rossiian vystupaiut za sokhranenie dostupa k Telegram."
    2018. *RIA Novosti*, 24 April. https://ria.ru/20180424/1519263318.html.
"Vybory dlia Putina uzhe nachalis'." 2002. Dni.ru, 10 October. https://web.archive.org
    /web/20030213024757/http:/dni.ru/news/analitika/2001/10/23/980.html.
"Vyderzhki iz stenograficheskogo otcheta o press-konferentsii po itogam vstrechi na vysshem
    urovne Rossiia—Evropeiskii soiuz." 11 November 2002. http://archive.kremlin.ru
    /appears/2002/11/11/0001_type63377type63380type82634_29553.shtml.
"Vystuplenie mitropolita Klimenta na zasedanii 'Internet-obshchenie: kul'turnaia
    revoliutsiia ili kul'turnaia degradatsiia' v Obshchestvennoi palate RF." 2009.
    Russkaia Pravoslavnaia Tserkov', 25 March. http://www.patriarchia.ru/db
    /text/597095.html.
Watts, Clint. 2018. *Messing with the Enemy: Surviving in a Social Media World of Hack-
    ers, Terrorists, Russians, and Fake News*. Harper-Collins.
Weber, M. (1921) 1978. *Economy and Society: An Outline of Interpretive Sociology*.
    Edited by G. Roth and C. Wittich. University of California Press.
Wijermars, Mariëlle. 2021a. "The Digitalization of Russian Politics and Political Partici-
    pation." In *Palgrave Handbook of Digital Russian Studies*, edited by Daria Grit-
    senko, Mariëlle Wijermars, and Mikhail Kopotev, 15–32. Palgrave Macmillan.
Wijermars, Mariëlle. 2021b. "Selling Internet Control: The Framing of the Russian
    Ban of Messaging App Telegram." *Information, Communication & Society*, DOI:
    10.1080/1369118X.2021.1933562.
Wijermars, Mariëlle, and Katja Lehtisaari, eds. 2020. *Freedom of Expression in Russia's
    New Media Sphere*. Routledge.
Yurchak, Alexei. 2006. *Everything Was Forever, Until It Was No More: The Last Soviet
    Generation*. Princeton University Press.
"Zachem podnimali 'Kursk'? Epilog." 2001. Dni.ru, 23 October. https://web.archive
    .org/web/20030213024757/http:/dni.ru/news/analitika/2001/10/23/980.html.
"Zachem v Rossii byl priniat 'zakon o neuvazhenii k vlasti' i kak on rabotaet." 2021.
    Fond tsentr zashchity prav SMI, 20 July. https://mmdc.ru/blog/2021/07/20
    /zachem-v-rossii-byl-prinyat-zakon-o-neuvazhenii-k-vlasti-i-kak-on-rabotaet/.
Zagoruyko, Oleg. 2009. "Russia's Putin Raps Tycoons in Crisis-Hit Town." Reuters, 4
    June. https://www.reuters.com/article/legal/government/russias-putin-raps
    -tycoons-in-crisis-hit-town-idUSL4450983/.
Zaitseva, Svetlana. 2000. "Golubaia mechta Pavlovskogo." Stringer (September).
Zakharchenko, Viktor. 2003. "Vladimir Vladimirovich i Alla Borisovna iz-pod pera Par-
    kera." *Russkii zhurnal*, 3 November. http://old.russ.ru/netcult/20031103.html.
Zakharova, Mariia. 2020. "SMI: Gossekretar' Maik Pompeo . . ." *Maria Zakharova*, 21 Janu-
    ary. https://www.facebook.com/maria.zakharova.167/posts/10221850776568272.
"Zakonodatel'noe regulirovanie internet-prostranstva, nravstvenno-eticheskie aspe-
    kty." 2008. *Obshchestvennaia Palata*, 16 April. Transcript available at https://
    uchebana5.ru/cont/3581552.html.
"Zakon o klevete budet dopolnen: privlekat' budut i za kommentarii v internete." 2012.
    Delovoi Peterburg, 29 August. https://www.dp.ru/a/2012/08/29/Zakon_o_klevete
    _budet_dop.
"Zakon o 'Suverennom internete' stal primeniat'sia dlia politicheskogo davleniia i sokrytiia
    nachala blokirovok." 2021. *Roskomsvoboda*, 29 July. https://roskomsvoboda.org/en
    /post/suvenir-runet-obrastaet-cenzuroy/.
"Zapadnye tekhnogiganty kak ugroza tsifrovomu suverenitetu gosudarstva." 2020.
    Obshchestvennaia palata Rossiiskoi Federatsii, 27 August. https://oprf.ru/press
    /conference/4862.

"Zasedanie mezhdunarodnogo diskussionnogo kluba 'Valdai'." 2013. *Prezident Rossii*, 19 September. http://kremlin.ru/news/19243.

"Zasedanie Soveta Bezopasnosti." 2014. *Prezident Rossii*, 1 October. http://kremlin.ru/transcripts/46709.

"Zashchita detei ot vredonosnogo internet-kontenta." 2021. *Mul'tiblog protoiereia Dmitriia Smirnova*, 11 June. https://www.youtube.com/watch?v=GlsNaOZdLE0.

"Zavinchivanie." 2012. *Rossiiskaia gazeta*, 17 July.

Zherebtsov, Mikhail. 2019. "Taking Stock of Russian eGovernment." *Europe-Asia Studies* 71 (4): 579–607.

Zhilkin, Aleksandr. 2011a. "Platnaia ili besplatnaia rybalka, chto tselesoobraznee?" *Blog gubernatora Astrakhanskoi oblasti Aleksandra Zhilkina*, 24 March. http://alexandr-jilkin.livejournal.com/43643.html.

Zhilkin, Aleksandr. 2011b. "Nevtianaia i gazovaia promyshlennost' regiona i ne tol'ko" (comments). *Blog gubernatora Astrakhanskoi oblasti Aleksandra Zhilkina*, 4 September. http://alexandr-jilkin.livejournal.com/54912.html#comments.

"Zhitelia Kuzbasa oshtravovali po novoi stat'e KoAP o diskreditatsii armii." 2022. *RIA Novosti*, 6 March. https://ria.ru/20220306/shtraf-1776928938.html.

Zinov'eva, Elena Sergeevna. 2013. "Tsifrovoi Vestfal'?" MGIMO universitet, 26 March. https://mgimo.ru/about/news/experts/236588/.

Zittrain, Jonathan, and John Palfrey. 2008. "Internet Filtering: The Politics and Mechanisms of Control." In *Access Denied: The Practice and Policy of Global Internet Filtering*, edited by Ronald Deibert, John Palfrey, Rafal Rohozinski, and Jonathan Zittrain, 30–56. MIT Press.

Ziuganov, G. A. 2017. "Vlast', a ne 'oranzhevyi revoliutsioner' vyvodit liudei na ulitsu." *Pravda*, 4 April. East View persistent URL, https://dlib.eastview.com/browse/doc/48557802.

Zolotov, Viktor. 2018. "Obrashchenie direktora Rosgvardii." 11 September. https://www.youtube.com/watch?v=lZd1yUZD30g (video no longer available). For a copy of full transcript of the video address, see "Glava" 2018.

Zotova, Nataliia. 2021. "Mnogo novichkov, ne vsegda za Naval'nogo: uchenye izuchili protesty v Rossii v nachale goda." *BBC News: Russkaia sluzhba*, 10 August. https://www.bbc.com/russian/news-58143585.

Zubov, Mikhail. 2017. "Naval'nyi i renovatsiia: Vozhdi oppozitsii vziali kredit nedoveriia." *Moskovskii komsomolets*, 16 May. https://www.mk.ru/politics/2017/05/15/chem-otlichaetsya-navalnyy-ot-lenina-vozhdi-oppozicii-vzyali-kredit-nedoveriya.html.

Zvereva, Vera. 2012. *Setevye razgovory: Kul'turnye kommunikatsii v Runete*. Slavica Bergensia 10. University of Bergen.

Zvereva, Vera. 2020a. "New on the Media Menu: How the Establishment of the Patriot Media Group Reflects a New Approach to Controlling Information on the Runet." Guest blog post to *"Reframing Russia for the Global Mediasphere: From Cold War to 'Information War'?"* University of Manchester and the Open University. https://reframingrussia.wordpress.com/2020/04/27/new-on-the-media-menu-how-the-establishment-of-the-patriot-media-group-reflects-a-new-approach-to-controlling-information-on-the-runet/.

Zvereva, Vera. 2020b. "State Propaganda and Popular Culture in the Russian-Speaking Internet." In *Freedom of Expression in Russia's New Media Sphere*, edited by Mariëlle Wijermars and Katja Lehtisaari, 225–47. Routledge.

Zvereva, Vera. 2020c. "Trolling as a Digital Literary Practice in the Russian Language Internet." *Russian Literature* 118 (November–December): 107–140.

Zvereva, Vera, and Aleksandrs Berdicevskis. 2014. "Slangs Go Online, or The Rise and Fall of the Olbanian Language." In *Digital Russia: Language, Culture, and Politics in the Age of New Media Communication*, edited by Michael S. Gorham, Ingunn Lunde, and Martin Paulsen, 123–40. Routledge.

Zykov, Vladimir. 2013a. "Aleksei Volin: 'Zachastuiu u vedomstv net ponimaniia, chto blokirovat'.'" *Izvestiia*, 29 March. http://izvestia.ru/news/547587.

Zykov, Vladimir. 2013b. "Bortsy s pornografiei sozdaiut sotsial'nuiu set'." *Izvestiia*, 28 January. https://iz.ru/news/543625.

Zykov, Vladimir. 2013c. "U krupneishikh saitov Runeta proverili reaktsiiu na zhaloby." *Izvestiia*, 29 August. http://izvestia.ru/news/556231.

Zykov, Vladimir. 2013d. "Volodin predlozhil Runetu vyrabotat' dlia sebia pravila." *Izvestiia*, 9 September. http://izvestia.ru/news/556703.

Zykov, Vladimir. 2016. "German Klimenko: 'Samaia ser'eznaia problema s internetom - anonimnost'.'" *Izvestiia*, 31 March. http://izvestia.ru/news/608118.

Zykov, Vladimir. 2017. "V zakrytom gosinternete poiavitsia messendzher." *Izvestiia*. 5 April. http://izvestia.ru/news/675914.

LiveJournal Posts Cited from Egor Kholmogorov

(holmogor, https://holmogor.livejournal.com/)
Individual post references listed in chronological order by date.

19 April 2001. https://holmogor.livejournal.com/12486.html
1 April 2001 (a). https://holmogor.livejournal.com/8100.html
1 April 2001 (b). https://holmogor.livejournal.com/8461.html
10 May 2001. https://holmogor.livejournal.com/14140.html
24 May 2001. https://holmogor.livejournal.com/19950.html
18 July 2001. https://holmogor.livejournal.com/36377.html
1 August 2001 (a). https://holmogor.livejournal.com/47508.html
1 August 2001 (b). https://holmogor.livejournal.com/47960.html
4 August 2001. https://holmogor.livejournal.com/51543.html
10 October 2001. https://holmogor.livejournal.com/83805.html
4 October 2004. https://holmogor.livejournal.com/883659.html
8 October 2004. https://holmogor.livejournal.com/891289.html
14 October 2004. https://holmogor.livejournal.com/900376.html
20 October 2004. https://holmogor.livejournal.com/908973.html
9 November 2004. https://holmogor.livejournal.com/1072468.html
23 November 2004. https://holmogor.livejournal.com/963993.html
25 September 2004. https://holmogor.livejournal.com/874994.html
13 November 2004. https://holmogor.livejournal.com/942107.html
14 November 2004. https://holmogor.livejournal.com/943156.html
13 December 2004. https://holmogor.livejournal.com/1044860.html
15 December 2004. https://holmogor.livejournal.com/1046814.html
23 December 2004. https://holmogor.livejournal.com/1055865.html
26 December 2004. https://holmogor.livejournal.com/1058345.html
6 January 2005. https://holmogor.livejournal.com/1064683.html
8 January 2005. https://holmogor.livejournal.com/1066036.html
11 January 2005. https://holmogor.livejournal.com/1067084.html
19 January 2005. https://holmogor.livejournal.com/1072468.html
21 January 2005. https://holmogor.livejournal.com/1074422.html
25 January 2005. https://holmogor.livejournal.com/1078580.html

28 January 2005. https://holmogor.livejournal.com/1091136.html

8 February 2005. https://holmogor.livejournal.com/1104614.html

13 February 2005 (a). https://holmogor.livejournal.com/1110035.html

13 February 2005 (b). https://holmogor.livejournal.com/1108455.html

15 February 2005. https://holmogor.livejournal.com/1114285.html

25 February 2005 (a). https://holmogor.livejournal.com/1127447.html

25 February 2005 (b). https://holmogor.livejournal.com/1126606.html

3 March 2005. https://holmogor.livejournal.com/1138038.html

5 March 2005. https://holmogor.livejournal.com/1144183.html

10 March 2005. https://holmogor.livejournal.com/1149251.html

11 March 2005. https://holmogor.livejournal.com/1151328.html

19 March 2005. https://holmogor.livejournal.com/1158146.html

13 April 2005. https://holmogor.livejournal.com/1178319.html

23 April 2005. https://holmogor.livejournal.com/1186144.html

1 May 2005 (a). https://holmogor.livejournal.com/1194519.html

1 May 2005 (b). https://holmogor.livejournal.com/1194887.html

6 May 2005. https://holmogor.livejournal.com/1200007.html

8 May 2005. https://holmogor.livejournal.com/1204981.html

3 June 2005. https://holmogor.livejournal.com/1235359.html

11 June 2005. https://holmogor.livejournal.com/1247709.html

14 June 2005. https://holmogor.livejournal.com/1252491.html

12 July 2005. https://holmogor.livejournal.com/1262844.html

26 July 2005. https://holmogor.livejournal.com/1264060.html

20 September 2005. https://holmogor.livejournal.com/1318952.html

5 October 2005. https://holmogor.livejournal.com/1335607.html

18 October 2005. https://holmogor.livejournal.com/1359460.html

21 October 2005. https://holmogor.livejournal.com/1368428.html

30 October 2005. https://holmogor.livejournal.com/1389719.html

7 November 2005. https://holmogor.livejournal.com/1413422.html

8 November 2005. https://holmogor.livejournal.com/1414783.html

10 November 2005 (a). https://holmogor.livejournal.com/1420967.html

10 November 2005 (b). https://holmogor.livejournal.com/1419715.html

15 November 2005 (a). https://holmogor.livejournal.com/1428541.html

15 November 2005 (b). https://holmogor.livejournal.com/1429721.html

2 December 2005. https://holmogor.livejournal.com/1448136.html

8 December 2005. https://holmogor.livejournal.com/1464605.html

Posts Cited from Navalny's LiveJournal blog (navalny.livejournal.com)

24 April 2006. "O neotvratimosti nakazanii." *navalny,* https://navalny
.livejournal.com/53739.html

11 May 2006. "Chtvertye." *navalny,* http://navalny.livejournal.com/5617.html

12 May 2006. "K nam priedet." *navalny,* http://navalny.livejournal.com/5668
.html

13 May 2006. "GKh." *navalny,* http://navalny.livejournal.com/5908.html

25 May 2006. "Esli." *navalny,* http://navalny.livejournal.com/10269.html

9 June 2006. "My rytsari-dzheda, my bortsy so zlom," *navalny,* https://
navalny.livejournal.com/15529.html

16 October 2006. "Debaty – 8." *navalny,* http://navalny.livejournal.com
/47455.html

31 October 2006. (no title). *navalny,* https://navalny.livejournal.com/53739
.html

20 November 2006. "debaty." *navalny,* http://navalny.livejournal.com/57989
.html

5 February 2007. "Druz'ia moi." *navalny,* http://navalny.livejournal.com
/93712.html

19 February 2007. "Stomatologiia." *navalny,* navalny.livejournal.com/99468
.html.

14 March 2007. "Voprosy postupaiut, poetomu, nado otvechat'." *navalny,*
https://navalny.livejournal.com/109670.html

9 April 2007. "Frendy! Tem, komu interesno, soobshchaiu," *navalny,* https://
navalny.livejournal.com/118367.html

11 May 2007. "Vo frendlente – Evrovidenie." *navalny,* navalny.livejournal
.com/123161.html.

12 May 2007. "Politicheskii botoks im ne pomozhet." *navalny,* https://
navalny.livejournal.com/656017.html

7 June 2007. "Stavropol'." *navalny,* https://navalny.livejournal.com/134273.html

25 June 2007. "Manifest." *navalny,* https://navalny.livejournal.com/139478.
html

29 June 2007. "NAROD protiv Berezovskogo." *navalny,* http://navalny
.livejournal.com/141126.html

10 September 2007. "A my poshly na YouTube." *navalny,* http://navalny
.livejournal.com/155437.html

27 September 2007. "Agitatsionnyi videorolik 'NAROD za legalizatsiiu
grazhdanskogo oruzhiia'." *navalny,* https://navalny.livejournal.com
/163552.html

1 November 2007. "Pro vse," *navalny,* https://navalny.livejournal.com/170744
  .html

26 November 2007. "Marshi." *navalny,* https://navalny.livejournal.com/2007
  /11/26/.

27 November 2007. *navalny,* "Den'gi, deti i Iosef Khobson." *navalny,* https://
  navalny.livejournal.com/59623.html

6 December 2007. "Doklad dvizheniia NAROD. Interesny vashi mneniia."
  navalny, https://navalny.livejournal.com/185724.html

12 May 2008. "Paniushkin—novoe liberal'noe oruzhie." *navalny,* https://
  navalny.livejournal.com/239037.html

19 May 2009. "Anons." *navalny,* https://navalny.livejournal.com/374317.html

10 May 2011. "'Skolkovo'—oi." *navalny,* http://navalny.livejournal.com/583100
  .html

6 July 2011. "Sagra." *navalny,* https://navalny.livejournal.com/602782.html

19 September 2011. "Mastrid." *navalny,* https://navalny.livejournal.com/622427
  .html

8 October 2013. "Nebol'shaia gruppa liudei, bezuslovno, predannykh svoei
  strane." *navalny,* http://navalny.livejournal.com/866661.html

27 November 2017. "Ot dachnogo kooperativa 'Ozera' k dachnomu koopera-
  tivu 'Sosny'." *navalny,* https://navalny.livejournal.com/883305.html

Posts Cited from Navalny's YouTube Accounts (in chronological order)

"Narod za legalizatsiiu oruzhiia." 19 September 2007. *Alexey Navalny,*
  https://www.youtube.com/watch?v=oVNJiO10SWw.

"Stan' natsionalistom." 17 October 2007. *Aleksey Navalny,* https://www.youtube
  .com/watch?v=ICoc2VmGdfw.

"Kub. Instruktsiia po primeneniiu." 24 July 2013. *Aleksei Naval'nyi,* https://
  www.youtube.com/watch?v=z9q94aKBefI.

"Krugi Naval'nogo. Migratsiia i natsional'nyi vopros (polnaia versiia)." 27
  August 2013. *Aleksei Naval'nyi,* https://www.youtube.com/watch
  ?v=WxB7PDyI4YE&ab.

"Vstrecha s izbiratel'iami v Sokol'nikakh." 2 September 2013. *Aleksei
  Naval'nyi,* https://www.youtube.com/watch?v=ZVrNJv8LzVM&ab.

"Izmeni Rossiiu, nachni s Moskvy!" 4 September 2013. *Aleksei Naval'nyi,*
  https://www.youtube.com/watch?v=ebMtVkXZhls&ab.

"Moskvichi o Naval'nom (chast' 1)." 5 September 2013. *Aleksei Naval'nyi,*
  https://www.youtube.com/watch?v=WOWksq7zE3w&ab.

"Viktor Shenderovich – PREROLL." 11 October 2013. *Aleksei Naval'nyi,* https://www.youtube.com/watch?v=7q6C8CETh_k&ab.

"Kak Vladimir Putin svoemu vziatiu 1,75 mlrd dollarov perevel." 11 February 2016. *Aleksei Naval'nyi,* https://www.youtube.com/watch?v=FQ984-2 -Wak&ab.

"Georgii Alburov pro kvartiru Rogozina." 30 March 2016. *Aleksei Naval'nyi,* https://www.youtube.com/watch?v=tx8ZqZtjyT4.

"Sobaki vitse-prem'era Shuvalova letaiut na chastnom samolete." 14 July 2016. *Aleksei Naval'nyi,* https://www.youtube.com/watch?v=tx8ZqZtjyT4&ab.

"Sekretnaia dacha Dmitriia Medvedeva." 15 September 2016. *Aleksei Naval'nyi,* https://www.youtube.com/watch?v=nMVJxTcU8 Kg&t=35s&ab.

"Povar Putina, korol' dizlaikov: istoriia uspekha." 4 October 2016. *Aleksei Naval'nyi,* https://www.youtube.com/watch?v=ZjY3IMXMmVE&ab.

"Kto finansiruet mladshuiu doch' Putina?" 18 October 2016. *Aleksei Naval'nyi,* https://www.youtube.com/watch?v=SH2bbxp46CQ&t=9s&ab.

"Oligarkh Usmanov otkazyvaetsia platit' nalogi v Rossii." 20 October 2016. *Aleksei Naval'nyi,* https://www.youtube.com/watch?v=Qq4RNwfJDSY&ab.

"Tim Kuk protiv Sechina i Millera." 12 January 2017. *Aleksei Naval'nyi,* https://www.youtube.com/watch?v=AYHnay-Z_DA&ab.

"Putinskii chinovnik v ital'ianskoi klinike krasoty."10 March 2017. *Aleksei Naval'nyi,* https://www.youtube.com/watch?v=IEbEN9SbRdM&ab.

"Don't call him Dimon." 2 March 2017. *Aleksei Naval'nyi,* https://www .youtube.com/watch?v=qrwlk7_GF9g.

"Debaty Live. Naval'nyi vs. Strelkov." 20 July 2017. *Naval'nyi LIVE,* https:// www.youtube.com/watch?v=cjbQdbJUibc&ab.

"Debaty Naval'nogo i Sobchak. Polnaia versiia." 18 March 2018. *Naval'nyi LIVE,* https://www.youtube.com/watch?v=gQeAy2ytMnU&ab.

"Kak nam pobedit' 'Edinuiu Rossiiu'." 28 November 2018. *Aleksei Naval'nyi,* https://www.youtube.com/watch?v=Mu-vW9TM-jI&ab.

"Roskomnadzor zablokiroval 'Umnoe golosovanie'." 7 December 2018. *Aleksei Naval'nyi,* https://www.youtube.com/watch?v=FePrO2AtUno&ab.

Episodes Cited from Minaev's Minaev LIVE

26 May 2011. "Minaev LIVE – efir 26.5.2011 chast' 1." *MINAEVLIVE,* https://www.youtube.com/watch?v=b-JiW8UqQP8&ab_channel =MINAEVLIVE.

25 August 2011. "Minaev LIVE – efir 25-8-2011 Chast' 1." *MINAEVLIVE*, https://www.youtube.com/watch?v=hePz-wel1UY&ab_channel =MINAEVLIVE.

1 November 2011. "MinaevLive – 01.11.2011 Kseniia Sobchak." *MINAEV-LIVE*, https://www.youtube.com/watch?v=_ytArasMrNE&ab_channel =MINAEVLIVE.

15 December 2011. "Egor Kholmogorov v gostiakh 'Minaev LIVE.'" *MINAEV-LIVE*, https://www.youtube.com/watch?v=9_QPI3NBjts&ab_channel =MINAEVLIVE.

26 January 2012. "Rossiia bez Putina?" *MINAEVLIVE*, https://www.youtube .com/watch?v=nUdKT_dRZYI&ab_channel=MINAEVLIVE.

2 February 2012. "Oleg Kashin v 'Minaev LIVE.'" *MINAEVLIVE*, https:// www.youtube.com/watch?v=f8xMuMiVOEc&ab_channel =MINAEVLIVE.

4 February 2012. "Minaev Live 4 fevralia." *MINAEVLIVE*, https://www .youtube.com/watch?v=z6mrua5ibZg&ab_channel=MINAEVLIVE.

14 February 2012. "Rykov vs Nosik v 'Minaev LIVE.'" *MINAEVLIVE*, https:// www.youtube.com/watch?v=Sp_4ptn-O68&ab_channel=MINAEVLIVE.

23 February 2012. "Miting v podderzhku Putina v MINAEVLIVE." *MINAEV-LIVE*, https://www.youtube.com/watch?v=bSVLgNm0C4Q&ab_channel =MINAEVLIVE.

Index

www.ingramcontent.com/pod-product-compliance
Lightning Source LLC
Chambersburg PA
CBHW020512270326
41926CB00008B/836